CW00868215

DISCOVERY
AND
INVENTION

DISCOVERY
AND
INVENTION

A COMPARATIVE STUDY ON CIVILIZATION

CHARLES T. STEWART, JR.

Rev. date: 06/10/2019

To order additional copies of this book, contact:
Xlibris
1-888-795-4274
www.Xlibris.com
Orders@Xlibris.com
798089

CONTENTS

PREFACE

The origins of this book go back a long time. In 1963–65, I directed a study for the National Science Foundation of the locational requirements for scientists and engineers conducting research. After a final report, I felt dissatisfied; the question I had tried to answer struck me as superficial. A location near a university strong in science and engineering was obvious. The needs of a highly educated, well-paid, and mobile professional labor force for an environment offering a wealth of cultural and educational opportunities were also obvious. It was no mystery that Silicon Valley was near Stanford University and San Francisco. This was the time of the Cold War, the race to the moon, growing federal expenditures on research and development. The universities were still graduating many majors in science, math, and engineering, and their numbers were supplemented by a huge brain drain from Europe.

Today I ask a different question—what are the conditions under which more of our best minds choose careers in science, math, and engineering? I have tried to answer it in part in my book *The Decline of Learning in America*, but the concern over their supply raises a more fundamental question: what are the characteristics of a society that produces scientists and engineers and promotes research, discovery, and invention—a creative society?

The simple tools made and used by early humans bear little comparison with the advanced technology on which we rely for survival and sustenance. The development of science and technology has been made possible by an evolution of mind capable of conceiving, constructing, and employing them. Many of us are as different from our early ancestors as our tools and knowledge are from theirs. I have focused on the characteristics of diverse civilizations that have promoted or have deterred discovery and invention. My purpose is not to describe but to explain why discovery did not happen and why invention has lagged in most civilizations in order to understand the exceptionalism of Greece and the dominance of the West in scientific discovery and invention.

The question addressed at the end of this book is whether the revolution in science and technology of the past two centuries opens a new stage of civilization, no longer subject to decline and fall or open to external threats, now a world civilization driven by science and technology, incorporating the seeds of its own evolution. Is it the servant of culture or its master?

I have benefited from discussions with and writings of more people than I can remember, including students in a seminar on the economics of science and technical change at the George Washington University. In particular, I appreciate the support of Jacob Perlman, Zola Bronson, and Theodore Suranyi-Unger of the National Science Foundation in my initial research. In writing this book, I have benefited from discussions with many more, in particular Bryan Boulier, Martha Rashid, Richard Schlagel, David Schalk, David Stewart, and members of the informal seniors' discussion group at Sangamore Road, Bethesda, MD. In dealing with such a complex subject, I keep in mind the advice of Walter Buckingham, who told me that he agreed with himself only 90 percent of the time.

I

Introduction

The story of evolution and the history of civilization can be written in terms of discoveries and inventions, from shrugs and grunts to language, writing, and the Internet; from rafts and beasts of burden to the wheeled vehicle, steam locomotive, motor vehicle, and jet plane; from open fire to the blast furnace and microwave oven; from windmill and waterpower to steam engine to nuclear power; from wooden club to steel sword to nuclear bomb; from hunting and gathering to farming to the supermarket; from bone flutes to symphony orchestras. One could go on. How we live, what we do, and how we think are largely by-products of discovery and invention. Some inventions have changed our way of life; others have changed our way of thinking. The human mind is a cultural product as well as the agent of change. Our future depends on what we have yet to understand and learn to do.

In reviewing the history of discovery and invention, our purpose is to identify the conditions favoring and hindering their progress. These include the influence of discovery and invention on the conditions for their own acceleration, in particular their effects on human minds. In the short historical period since the invention of writing, we examine the differences between leading and lagging cultures and civilizations, seeking explanations for Greek protoscientific achievement and its absence in China, for the failure in Rome and Islam, and in recent centuries for the dominance of Europe and North America. Looking toward the future, what can we learn from the experience of the last millennium to maintain momentum for the next, and what limits or barriers do we face in promoting discovery, invention, and innovation in the century ahead?

We must distinguish between discovering and inventing, which are quite different in their cognitive requirements. Invention is the creation of something for the first time. Discovery is not creation but understanding. Invention and innovation are often used interchangeably, but they are distinct processes. Innovation is the spread, the adoption of an invention or discovery.

DISCOVERY

Numerous animals invent. Their inventions may be simple objects and techniques, but they solve problems that animals face. But animals do not discover. *Discovery*, as the term is used in this book, refers to an achievement that is beyond the reach of animals and rare in early human cultures. *Discovery* can have different meanings. It is important to clarify the sense in which this term will be used. One meaning of the word is "to find." Animals find food, water, shelter, and so on. They do so by observation.

The ability to detect the superficial characteristics of material objects and living things is observation of fact. But discovery can also refer to concepts and ideas. The process of discovery, in this case, is not observation; it is search, detection, or creation of order in what appears to be a chaotic world. The purpose of discovery is understanding; its product is knowledge and explanation. "This star moves in the sky" is an observation; "this star follows an orbit around the sun" is a discovery.

The Age of Discovery is associated with Prince Henry the Navigator and Christopher Columbus. I refer to a different age, the Scientific Revolution, associated with Galileo and Newton. The first is geographic, a response to questions such as where and when? The second is cosmological, a response to questions such as why? It is explanation. The patterns we conceive, the orbits, are abstractions.

Discovery is learning for the first time. Every human being discovers many things as he advances in years, but these are discoveries only for the individuals, not for the society or the species. Often the first discovery is ignored or forgotten, and only a later rediscovery is propagated and remembered.

The subject of discovery in recent centuries has focused on scientific discovery and specifically on the decipherment of the laws of nature, on generalities rather than on specificities. It has become abstract, theoretical, mathematical. The Scientific Revolution and the Industrial Revolution that it empowered now dominates our lives.

In many cases, discovery is progress toward understanding reality but not yet there, just an approximation of the real world. The atom was first conceptualized by Democritus, demonstrated to exist more than two millennia later. The concept itself has changed considerably since Democritus. The Niels Bohr model is quite different and the current model still more different. One might say that Newton did not discover the laws of gravity, aided by millennia of observation. Einstein showed that Newton's theory is not an exact replica of reality, just a close approximation. These discoveries are more like a stepladder than a pole vault.

These are discoveries in the natural world. There is another domain of discovery, the mind. On a mundane level, there is a vast warehouse to run. I do not know its contents or where or what is shelved, which is overstock that needs ordering. I must classify each item for storage and retrieval. It is a messy process full of detours, dead ends, and occasional flashes of insight that may have no end. There is no best system. There is no order to be discovered; it must be created. How to increase the mental resources for creativity? What knowledge should be accumulated? How to acquire the ability to identify and retrieve knowledge relevant to particular needs? The Dewey decimal system of the mind is always changing; there is no best classification.

INVENTION

Invention, as the term is used in this book, is a solution to a problem as perceived or conceived by the inventor. The product of invention is an object or process. (There are many inventions or solutions in search for suitable problems as well.) The object need not be concrete, in the conventional sense of visual, palpable objects. Just as there are discoveries in the domain of the mind, not nature, there are inventions as well that are ideas, not objects. Language is the greatest invention; writing is another. So is a symphony orchestra. Its music may be written or may be heard. Instruments are needed to write, to play, but they do not embody the idea; they merely communicate it. The invention is the concept, the idea; the object or procedure is its implementation, its embodiment. Inventions, like discoveries, are a continuing process as better solutions, or a better understanding of the problem, are conceived.

The word *invent* has many meanings. People are inventing all the time—how to explain a faux pas, to improve a stew, to remember appointments. How to distinguish a daily activity from inventions? First, the invention has to be new to the community, if not the species. A particular invention can be made multiple times, in different communities. Simultaneous inventions have become common as global communication promotes knowledge sharing and common goals. Second, an invention must be generic in some sense; it is not just a response to a specific event by a specific person. Inventions must be shared. Some of the drawings in Leonardo da Vinci's notebooks do not qualify as inventions since they were not implemented, no one knew about them, and they had no consequences. They are biography, not history.

What of the alternative use of the term to signify a fiction or falsehood? This meaning of *inventing* as fabrication, falsehood, or fiction was first noted in literature five hundred years ago according to the *Oxford Dictionary of the English Language*. It reflects something of a negative reaction to change and novelty widespread in the past and not uncommon even today.

The greatest inventions, language and writing, are social, the product of countless inventors. They cannot be monopolized but must be shared. Mathematics, like language, consists of a large number of inventions. Both are disembodied processes. Some of the most important inventions are social—organizations and processes for collective decision-making or for cooperative effort, legal systems, and elections.

One must distinguish between *invention*, the noun and the result, and *invent*, the verb and the process. The inventor has a goal in mind, and inventing is the process of achieving that goal. But many inventions are accidental—a new use is discovered for an existing object, such as a sharp stone or a piece of charcoal. Such inventions may be accidental rather than intentional. I suspect that most inventions by animals, hominids, and even early humans were of this nature—serendipitous discoveries. What distinguishes them from discoveries is that the invention was discovered rather than invented. The function of the invention is inferred ex post, a solution in search of a problem.

Invention may be classified along a continuum between two polar extremes, discovery and invention proper. The discovery is often fortuitous, accidental. The finding that the cinchona bark is effective against malaria is just a discovery; quinine is the resulting invention. Another characteristic of discoveries is that, even today, they do not always require a scientific base or dedicated effort—they could be made at any time. The curative powers of bread mold could have been discovered two thousand years ago; in fact, it was discovered who knows how many times well before Fleming.

The invention is the outcome of a goal-directed process. What is possible, even what is likely, depends on the current state of science and technology. The timing of some inventions, and some discoveries, is important in terms of their consequences.

Invention is problem-solving behavior. Discovery, by contrast, is a search for order in a chaotic world. These are quite different cognitive processes. It should not be expected that relevant behavior fits precisely into one or the other category. Some inventions—an increasing share—may require discovery, or the process of invention may result in discovery as a by-product. And discovery relies increasingly on invention and opens up new possibilities for it. The fundamental difference between the two is that there may be multiple solutions to a problem, but there are no alternative realities. The Pythagorean theorem is a discovery; there is no alternative relation between the hypotenuse and other sides of a right triangle. The decimal system is an invention. Other systems have been invented and are in use.

INNOVATION

Innovation is the dissemination of something new, potentially an invention. In recent times, the gap between invention and its utilization has widened. Edison did not manufacture electric light bulbs; he only invented them and made prototypes. Ford did not invent the automobile, but he did put it on the road. Many inventions are never put to use; knowledge about them is not disseminated, or they are too costly, dangerous, or not of interest to the society in which they are made. Innovation often involves some invention not just of processes for production but also of uses that have not been conceived of by the inventor. There may be modifications in the original invention to facilitate production or to adapt it to new uses. Without innovation, inventions are stillborn.

The transfer and adoption of technologies is also essential for progress. In historical times, the dissemination of knowledge has often been the consequence of marauding armies or of traveling traders. Around the middle of the first millennium BC, the establishment of a Persian empire opened the way between Mediterranean Europe and distant Asia, India in particular. Alexander spread Greek arms and learning to the Indus. Later, the Roman and Islamic civilizations gathered the knowledge of many peoples and built on it—a combination of discovery, invention, and transfer. More recently, writing and new technologies of communication have greatly facilitated the spread of knowledge as well as its generation.

Discovery and invention have been predominantly the achievement of individuals. They may not be revealed to others or may never be implemented. Cumulative discovery and invention is a social rather than an individual process. Discoveries and inventions must be announced, they must be accepted, and there must be innovation if there is to be scientific or technological progress. Wide knowledge of a new discovery leads to further discovery, replacement by a superior technology. Thus, knowledge, acceptance, adoption, and implementation become part of the process of discovery and invention. Columbus was not the first European to discover America, just the first with a public information and relations officer (himself) aboard.

The progress of discovery and invention depends on a supply of inventors and discoverers and a demand for the knowledge and products of their work. Historically, there have been large differences in the pace of discovery and invention and also in social and cultural attitudes toward novelty and change. In the following chapters, we explore the large differences between cultures and seek explanations. We also consider the gains in human cognitive abilities resulting from the great inventions of language and writing, among others, and how they may influence the continuing supply of discoveries and inventions.

SUMMARY

Chapters 2 and 3 are historical, from animal toolmakers and tool users to the invention of agriculture. What are the characteristics of animals most prone to make and to use tools? What are the conditions under which such activities are most likely to occur? How did hominids and early humans advance on animals?

Chapter 4 is comparative, starting with the invention of writing. We examine the two earliest civilizations on which there is abundant information, Sumer and Egypt, seeking to understand intercultural differences in the level and in the kind of achievement and considering the circumstances that may have contributed to the difference.

Chapter 5 focuses on Greek advances in abstract thinking and their contributions to the Scientific Revolution much later. There are numerous hypotheses proposing to explain their achievements by contrast with the founder civilizations, Egypt in particular. They are not mutually exclusive. I attempt to evaluate their relevance and significance. The foreshortened civilizations of the Western Hemisphere will be mentioned only in the context of parallel evolution of discovery and invention.

China (chapter 6) is by far the longest uninterrupted civilization in history. Hence, it must be compared both with the founder civilizations and Greece and with the Europe that retrieved the Greek achievements, corrected and advanced on them, and created the Scientific and Industrial Revolutions. During its long history, China has accounted for many inventions; but in discovery, it has lagged both classical Greece and modern Europe. Seeking to understand China's lag is the inverse of explaining Greek and European achievements.

In the light of what has been learned in the contrast between Greece and China, Chapter 7 considers briefly the two civilizations with full access to the Greek achievement—Rome, which did not advance it, and Islam, which did briefly but changed its mind and turned against it. Why was the opportunity neglected by Rome and rejected by Islam?

It was backwoods Europe, not one of the older and more advanced civilizations, that picked up where Greece had led and advanced much further. Chapter 8 asks what is new and different in the Western culture, how the process of discovery and invention has revolutionized society and perhaps the species itself. What started as the Scientific Revolution and became the Industrial Revolution was without precedent, traveling in unexplored territory. Finally, we take a look at the more distant future: what are the alternative scenarios in a world dominated by a culture of science and technology but a population still mired in traditional cultures, at odds on its uses and ends? The Industrial Revolution is over; what comes next?

II

Origins of Discovery and Invention among Animals

Creativity did not originate with humans. Some discovery and invention long preceded the rise of hominids in evolutionary and in universal time. But why consider invention and discovery by other animals?

Homo sapiens too is an animal who evolved from other primates, who in turn had evolved. The behavior of tool-using animals tells us something about that of our immediate ancestors since most of their tools, until quite recently, were not much different from those used by apes. Animal inventions and their adoption inform us on the conditions for change and progress.

Changes in animal behavior and accomplishments that are not exclusively attributable to genetic evolution are exceedingly slow, with some isolated exceptions. Their results are modest to the modern mind but important for survival. Long time spans would be required to trace such progress. Most of the evidence is fragile and perishable, much of it intangible, such as evolution of communication. Occasionally, one can observe an animal discovery or invention and witness its transmission to the next generation, but most of the evidence must be comparisons of members of the same species in different locations and observation of differences in behavior, in culture.

The numerous hominids, from one or more of which we are descended, are all extinct. We cannot observe their behavior and can only infer uncertainly from old bones and stones that remain. The apes who share our distant ancestors survive, providing perhaps our best information on the ways of life and behavior of early hominids. But other animals also offer evidence of invention and innovation and of the qualities that promote them. To explore the roots of creativity, one must consider both the abilities required and the conditions under which they are expressed. Apes, dolphins, and other animals in captivity solve problems and demonstrate abilities not observed in their native habitats. One must also consider the conditions for dissemination and preservation of new knowledge.

There is another reason for discussing man's animal ancestors, our prehuman roots, and that is the nature of aggression. Fighting for dominance, for food, for sex is common; but intercommunity warfare is also found among our nearest relatives. Weapons were among the original tools. When institutionalized in war with weapons of mass destruction at its disposal, aggression is the greatest threat to the future of progress and of civilization itself. But this is a subject for consideration toward the end of this book.

LEARNING: COGNITIVE VERSUS GENETIC

Until recently, the prevailing view—following Descartes—has been that animals are automata. Now almost opposite views are gaining support—that many animals have consciousness, some even self-consciousness, reasoning ability, occasionally even a moral sense. What is clear is that animals learn; learning is the foundation of discovery and invention. Even some low forms of life adapt and use tools. But do they discover, with its implication of conscious awareness? Do they invent, with its implication of intent? Learning can be the product of serendipity and natural selection or of cognitive processes. It is only the latter that concerns us. Discoveries by animals are not explanations, just particular findings.

Bacteria and viruses quickly develop resistance to antibiotics, but that learning is solely genetic change. Some ants "invented" agriculture, growing fungi fifty million years before *Homo sapiens* but without a cognitive component. When generations are measured in days instead of decades, offspring are in the thousands instead of one or two at a time, and infant mortality is very high, genetic "learning" can be sure and swift. Some economists have found that even ants and bees have mastered Economics 101 and Physics 101; they are better at cost/benefit analysis than humans. This is all very interesting but no indication of creativity or cognitive ability. One might as well argue that meteors have mastered Newton's laws of motion.

The difference between genetic change and cognitive change is, first, that genetic change may come at a very high cost through chance variation and a brutal system of natural selection; cognitive change can be self-selected, independent of chance variation. Second, cognitive change can come much more quickly since it can spread horizontally, almost simultaneously, via innovation, communication, and imitation. Genetic change spreads only vertically, down the chain of generations. Third, genetic change is indefinitely replicated, until displaced by further change. Cognitive change can undergo modification at every transfer, and it can be forgotten; it is not passed on automatically but must be learned, taught, and relearned.

How to distinguish between learned behavior and genetic determinism? Learned behavior in the wild can be observed. In the case of orphaned young animals, do they know what to eat, what to avoid, how to use sticks to seek food or stones to break nuts? Do they build shelters, or must they be taught? Do they learn through observation, imitation, or homeschooling by the parents? Many ducks learn to fly in a V formation. How this has come about we do not know. No avian Galileo has ever figured out that this formation is aerodynamically efficient. A Darwinian explanation is more plausible, that by prolonged unintentional trial and error, those flying formations that took advantage of aerodynamics and rotation of the lead bird had higher survival rates. But orphaned ducks and geese have to learn to fly this way.

An indirect indication is the number of young that the female of the species produces, the time it takes them to reach maturity, and life expectancy. If the female produces hundreds or thousands of young, they cannot rely on instruction for survival. Species bearing infrequently and in small litters, especially if one at a time, are likely to depend on years of learning by the young for their survival and that of the species. If training or practice is important, it is likely that the knowledge will be passed on to the younger generation. Chimp mothers have been observed providing detailed technical information to their young on the use of stones to crack nuts. The genetic component of behavior declines relative to the learning component as we move up the tree of evolution, but it is always important.

Apes and primates are overstressed if the purpose is to learn about conditions for discovery and invention. They are our first cousins. But other animals, quite different from us and only remotely related, also occasionally discover and invent; they provide additional observations of ability to invent and on conditions favorable to invention.

Discovery is learning for the first time; nearly all learning is but rediscovery. Animals discover new feeding grounds and new foods and pass this knowledge to their offspring. Birds locate new nesting places and establish new migratory patterns, which their offspring must be taught. This is discovery as defined in the Age of Exploration. Whether any animals have discovered, in the scientific sense of the term, is highly doubtful. Birds ride on wind flow and rise on thermals, but how do they learn, and what do they understand? We cannot enter the mind of an ape as it uses levers and projectiles, much less the mind of a dolphin or an intelligent clam, the octopus, and observe whether repeated experience of cause and effect has ever led to any general principle, but it is doubtful—to empirical rules, perhaps; to general principles, no. Many animals ask "what?" Do apes, dolphins, elephants ever ask "why?" Not to our knowledge.

TOOL-USING AND TOOLMAKING BEHAVIOR

Man has been described as the toolmaking animal. Apes and some monkeys are the principal tool users in the animal world. They have learned to use sticks and stones as tools, as means of access to food, as defensive or aggressive weapons. Chimps use sticks not only to fish for termites and other insects but also as toothpicks and for extraction of loose teeth (Wade 1999, 2070). Bigger sticks are used for extended reach, as clubs, as projectiles, as flyswatters, as levers. They are shaped into spears and used for hunting, perhaps for warfare (Beck 1980, 45–105; Gibbons 2007, 1063). They use stones to pound nuts open, as anvils, as projectiles and use leaves as sponges, cleaners, protective covering. Other apes use a variety of tools but less often than chimps (Moura and Lee 2004, 1909). Capuchins and other monkeys also are frequent tool users.

Tool using, even toolmaking, is not limited to primates or even to animals we consider advanced. Among nonprimates, elephants are the most adept users and makers of tools. Wild elephants lay grass on their backs for protection from insects and sun, wave branches to drive off biting flies, use grass to wipe their ear cavities, plaster grass and mud on cuts and injuries, and use twigs to reach food and to dislodge leeches. They throw objects with trunk and foot and brandish branches at people, vehicles, and other animals. Some have used branches to block traffic, uprooted trees and used them to knock down a fence. They dig water holes and plug them with bark and grass (Chevalier-Skolnikoff and Liska 1993). Their burial behavior will be mentioned later. In captivity, they take up paint and brush and musical instruments (Kaplan 2000, A1, A29). But even in the wild, they draw lines in the sand with sticks. They kick and play ball with their front feet (Alexander 2000, 53).

Vultures use small stones to break ostrich eggs. Various bird species have learned to drop stones as a defensive tactic or at shellfish and nuts to break them open. Some herons use bits of bait to attract fish. Some of Darwin's finches, the nuthatch, the black-breasted buzzard, the Egyptian vulture, the black cockatoo, and the blue jay use tools.

Wild New Caledonian crows fashion forked twigs to reach food, and a captive one recently consistently bends straight wires into hooks to lift a food bucket embedded in a tube (Weir, Chappell, and Kucinich 2001; Hunt 1996). There are instances of crows and parrots solving multistep problems such as using a stick to reach a tool to recover food (Taylor et al. 2007).

An octopus in Puget Sound has been observed patiently waiting until a clam has opened its shell, then inserting a pebble so the bivalve could not close it, and proceeding to eat it at its leisure—tool use for sure, but foresight and planning? There are tool-using animals not noted for IQ—wasps, ant lions, worm lions, as well as the brainier species (Griffin 1984, 118–32; Vauclair 1996, 53–83).

Use of objects as tools is largely limited to species with the physical ability to manipulate them—the tentacles of an octopus, the trunk of an elephant, the agile hands of apes and monkeys. But there are partial exceptions to most rules. The dolphin is very poorly equipped with prehensile organs; its flippers are useless, and only its beak can grasp and manipulate objects. Nevertheless, some dolphins use tools. A dolphin has been observed to kill scorpion fish and use the poisonous spine to drive an eel from its lair; others have used bits of fish as bait to attract other fish and covered their beaks with sponges for protection. Captive dolphins have used feathers and broken tiles to wipe or scrape their surroundings in imitation of their keepers (Cannon and Micklethwaite Peterson 1994, 182, 184). Given their physical limitations, most of their inventions must take other forms—communication approximating language, in complexity, and observed organized behavior, whether to herd the fish they eat or to attack the sharks with whom they compete and by which they are threatened.

The most extraordinary behavior of dolphins is their apparent empathy for humans, which has been known for thousands of years—saving them from drowning, protecting them from shark attacks. And in the Mediterranean, Asia, and South America, they herd fish for local fishermen to catch. They are not trained, just volunteers. On the coast of Brazil, fishermen and dolphins have cooperated for centuries; the dolphins herd the fish and signal to the fishermen when to cast their nets. Such teamwork is found also in other parts of the world. How it came about initially we do not know, but the practice has been handed down for many generations (National Geographic program March 29,2003).

Many animals that can use tools have the physical capacity to make them. But only apes, monkeys, and elephants have been confirmed to do this frequently. Toolmaking is a near monopoly of primates but so primitive by our standards that it can scarcely be differentiated from tool using—monkeys stripping leaves from a twig before using it to fish for termites, orangutans tearing off a leafy branch to use as a sort of raincoat, elephants gathering sheaves of long grasses to cover their backs to protect themselves from a blazing tropical sun and biting insects. The use of a stick as a lever or as a club by chimps rarely involves much manufacture. Perhaps the most complex tool production is the making of sponges by collecting leaves, macerating them by chewing, and squeezing them into a ball or the shaping of a stick into a spearpoint by gnawing.

Animals with access to man-made objects learn to put them to use; apes build ladders by piling boxes, for instance. Orangutans construct ropes by braiding straw. A number of apes as well as elephants in zoos have been taught to paint, and their products are selling well. Human observation of animal behavior in the wild does not reflect the full range of their performance, much less their capabilities. What animals do is a function of the environment, of perceived needs and opportunities, as well as of abilities. The gorilla rarely uses tools in the wild, but in captivity, it is as adept as the chimp.

Humans have long used various domesticated animals as tools in hunting, fishing, and guarding. But there are instances of cooperative activities between humans and wild animals that amount to reciprocal tool use. Already noted is the practice of dolphins helping fishermen. The Gbaya people of Cameroon rely on a bird, the greater honeyguide, to locate honey nests, for which the birds are rewarded with a cut of the take. The hunters summon the bird by whistling, singing, or rhythmically tapping on tree trunk with machetes (*Smithsonian* 2001, 78–83). Not all such behavior may qualify as tool using, according to the restrictive definition of Beck (1980, 6–10) that the tool must be an external object free of attachment that is manipulated by the user, a functional extension of the body to attain an immediate goal. Call it employment.

ANIMAL INVENTION

Invention may be adaptation to environment or may be a means of altering the environment. The former predominates among animals and early humans; the latter has grown in importance since the invention of agriculture.

Tool-using and even toolmaking behavior need not be the product of invention. We do not regard the beautiful webs of many spiders or even the complex nests of some birds as inventions. Nor is invention limited to tools. What of the procedures involved in hunting, fishing, construction of shelters?

Initially, it is enough to ask which species bear young that survive without support or tutorials by adults of the species, which species experience prolonged dependency and require extensive learning. Apes, dolphins, and elephants take almost as long to reach maturity as humans and can live to a ripe old age. Much of what they learn has been discovered or invented by their ancestors.

Discovery and invention will be limited to cognitive achievements, to the exclusion of progressive change that comes about by chance variation and natural selection. If tools are used in the wild, they have probably been invented and then transmitted. Direct observation of an invention by an animal in its natural habitat is extremely rare. Invention is more frequently observed among captive animals, but there is some question about the role of observation and imitation versus autonomous invention.

The initial invention in nearly all cases must be inferred from its behavioral consequences. Behavior that has to be learned by individual members of the species must have been invented at one time. Another indication that animals invent is based on comparison of behavior of different populations of the same subspecies that have no contact with each other. Behavior that is universal in some groups and absent in others is likely based on invention. In particular, such groups should "speak" somewhat different "languages." There are a vocabulary of sounds and a vocabulary of gestures and postures. We know that, even among current human populations, the meaning of a particular gesture may vary widely; what is a sign of pleasure in one may be an insult in another. Spoken languages are mutually unintelligible; they differ in structure as well as in sound. Why should we expect monkeys everywhere to have identical gestures and vocalizations? As a matter of fact, they do not. Such cultural differences result from local inventions.

There are other differences in behavioral repertoire of members of the same species in distant habitats. Chimps use stones and sticks to crack nuts and hard fruit in some areas, not in others (Kummer and Goodall 1985, 209–12). Meat-eating by baboons and chimpanzees appears to be restricted to limited populations (Strum 1975).

Miyadi (1964) studied the behavior of more than twenty macaque troops scattered in Japan. Nonuniformity proved to be a fundamental characteristic of troops as well as of individuals among Japanese macaques. He found that larger troops tended to have a larger vocabulary than smaller troops, but the sounds made in one troop were not so unique that they could not be understood by members of another. The troops were not completely isolated; solitary monkeys may travel between troops and serve as agents for diffusion of culture. When it came to behavior patterns, however, there were large differences—choice of diet, paternal care of babies, sexual behavior. One macaque learned to wash sweet potatoes in seawater before eating them and to use trays for this purpose. The principle was later applied by the same macaque, Imo, to cleaning wheat by flotation. Imo's discovery or invention was probably accidental. But its application to the flotation of grain was extraordinary. It revealed understanding and qualified as cognitive transfer to a slightly different domain. But only some members of the troop adopted these practices, mainly the younger macaques (Hirata, Watanabe, and Kawai 2002).

Self-medication by animals, especially by primates (but also parrots and elephants)—such as swallowing selected leaves or grass to rid themselves of intestinal parasites, eating clay for diarrhea and detoxification, or using natural insect repellants—can plausibly be explained as discoveries, although Engel (2002) makes no such claim. Their use is problem-solving invention. Some selected medications are bitter and unpleasant to the user, suggesting conscious diagnosis and what we anthropomorphically might call future orientation or gratification deferment. Some animals are addicted to drugs—goats to coffee beans, llamas to coca leaves, some primates to the alcohol in fermented fruit. These are discoveries rather than inventions.

One may question whether the elaborate nests of some birds or the complex burrows made by some mammals are more than instinctive, but the elaborate engineering works of beavers in carefully selected sites and with selected materials seems to be invention, if not toolmaking of a higher order than that exhibited by apes. They may not be tools strictly speaking, but they are functional modifications of the environment, long-term goal-directed activities whose production sometimes relies on tools (Griffin 1992, 80–100). Such inventions have reproductive and survival value.

Tool using is common among chimps, orangutans, and some species of *Cebus* monkeys; it is rare among wild gorillas, who, however, are capable tool users in captivity. Why the difference? In all species, invention is a rare event. Perhaps it is no rarer among gorillas and orangutans than among chimps. But chimps are social animals; their inventors are observed and imitated, their achievement passed on to succeeding generations. Orangutans in Sumatra are much less dispersed than in Borneo and are more frequent tool users. The gorilla lives in small relatively isolated family groups whose invention is unlikely to be observed, imitated, or passed on. Solitude is equivalent to secrecy. Socialization is analogous to communication, a precursor condition for language. Numbers also matter; larger numbers mean more inventions. *Cebus* monkeys greatly outnumber the great apes.

The general conditions propitiating the use of tools, according to Van Schaik et al. (1999), are opportunities, if not dietary needs, for extractive foraging as exemplified by hard nuts that must be cracked open or termite mounds; manipulative skills; the intelligence required for invention and observational learning; and social tolerance in a gregarious setting. Some of these conditions raise the question of need and intent. Most of the inventions observed or implied by animal behavior are not needed; they may be convenient or useful. They may expand sources of food or facilitate its procurement. Many inventions start with a chance discovery, and the inventive process is conceiving the discovery as a solution and identifying a problem it can solve, such as mud and insect bites. It is a primitive cause-and-effect approach. If there is a case for intent, it is the cracking of some very hard nuts, which are an important component of diet when other more easily obtainable foods are not in season (De Waal 2001, 243–45). The process involves hitting a nut many times with a heavy rock with precision, to crack it without crushing it. It is hard work and takes long to master. Could it have been invented by chance in play?

What these quite different evolutionary paths of very diverse species in different environments share is an element of versatility—problem-solving ability, invention if you will, that transcends their environment. Animals in captivity, primates in particular but also dolphins, have demonstrated an ability to invent, to solve problems, much more frequently than in the wild (Yerkes 1929). Observers suggest that a major reason for the greater inventiveness of animals in captivity is that they have a great deal of free time since they need not forage for food or be concerned about security. Some of this free time is devoted to play, chancing on serendipitous results observed and learned. There is also time for random experimentation and for dealing with problems posed by their keepers (Beck 1980, 93–94).

In nearly all cases, we have no idea how long ago brainy animals first used tools, first made tools, or first developed the vocabulary and other traits of culture that they exhibit today. One cannot rule out the possibility that some inventions by animals have been, in fact, copied from observed behavior of humans or hominids as humans have copied animal behavior at times (which foods to eat) and as, no doubt, nonhuman animal species copy each other. Such copying is an innovation, not an invention. But for most animal discoveries and inventions, an interspecies derivative origin is implausible.

The octopus is a special case. Most subspecies are solitary but have a relatively advanced central nervous system and exhibit the ability to learn, adapt, and behave strategically and have been observed to use a variety of tools for different purposes and to make tools (Mathur, Anderson, and Wood 2010, 123–35). The large and complex brain may be the result of the wide range of sensory modalities to be processed and of stimulus responses (including shape and color changes) available to the octopus. It is an outlier in another respect; it does not benefit from maternal tutoring or example. The mother produces many offspring at one time and then dies, leaving them to fend for themselves. And it has a short life span (Hanlon and Messenger 1996, 1, 110, 115, 149). The octopus is an autodidact; it learns without the benefit of homeschooling or imitation. It solves problems not found in its environment or presented by sensory evidence. Lifting a lid on a jar by a counterclockwise, spiral motion or even inserting a pebble in a clam to prevent its closing suggests a level of foresight, of abstract reasoning, incredible in a mollusk. This exception to the common traits of other tool-using and toolmaking animals raises questions about the relation between physiological characteristics and the evolution of cognitive abilities (Wells 1978).

COMMUNICATION

Most inventive achievements, whether by animals or perhaps even by hominids, have been solitary, never adopted by others. The same inventions may have been made repeatedly before they came to be incorporated in the behavioral repertoire of the group, population, and species. This has happened occasionally even in the case of modern man; much has been forgotten or reinvented. The step from invention to innovation or technology transfer requires communication. It also requires a willingness to learn and change one's ways. Communication can substitute for direct observation or magnify its reach. Conditions favoring transmission include group living, increasing the likelihood of observation, and what Van Schaik et al. (1999, 726) calls "social tolerance," which I interpret as tolerance of differences, openness to the new, a natural curiosity.

Discoveries and inventions differ in transferability. Some, such as gnawing a stick to a point, can be transferred by demonstration alone. Observers can understand some of its uses. So can fishing for termites but only in proximity to a termite mound. But if a chimp eats clay, other chimps will be dumbfounded. How can the eater inform them that clay is treatment for intestinal ailments? Appropriate words or gestures must be created and adopted first.

Animals can communicate with sounds, gestures, postures, vibrations. Many animals invent a variety of calls that are symbolic—alarm calls. They distinguish between several kinds of predators. Food calls likewise discriminate between various foods. These calls are all object words serving as subjects, with verbs implicit. They are single words, not sentences. But primates, cetaceans, elephants, and perhaps some birds are capable of communicating complex and varied information, too complex to be mere vocabulary; they possess protolanguage of sorts, even if it does not encompass human rules of grammar. We cannot understand their languages but can infer their complexity from resulting behavior.

Primates have been observed learning new concepts, expressing them in sound or gesture, sometimes transmitting them to other members of their group. Primates in different habitats have different "vocabularies" and "dialects." Probably, so do cetaceans and elephants. Also important is the ability to communicate at a distance. Cetaceans can transmit and receive messages for miles; so can elephants. Apes and humans are more limited in range. Mobility enhances the speed and range of transfer.

The greatest human invention is language. Some animals can be taught many words. But what have they invented on their own? How close has animal communication approached language? Communication beyond the simplest calls implies a society of sorts—family, troop, pride, colony, an association of members of the same species with whom to communicate. The ability to communicate with one's peers is the most important requirement for dissemination of knowledge. That is one reason why tool use is a near monopoly of social animals. Complex communication approaching language can modify behavior without the need to observe. It can provide more information than observation alone about conditions, ends and means. The stock of knowledge is not constant. Experience results in learning of particulars. Memory and anticipation lead to knowledge generalized: wasps sting; this fruit is bitter but will ripen. "Language" is continuously revised and expanded to reflect new knowledge. Animal vocabularies are invented and learned, not natural and fixed. They can evolve too swiftly to be solely the result of genetic inheritance.

Apes and dolphins and some parrots have been taught rudimentary human language, with vocabularies of hundreds of words and some mastery of syntax, complex communications abilities not seen in the wild (Griffin 1992, 211–32). Koko, the gorilla, has mastered sign language for over two thousand words/phrases; Kanzi, the bonobo, can "read" and "type" over five hundred words and use them in sentences employing lexigrams, symbols analogous to writing and reading among the Sumerians and early Egyptians. The apes are closely related to us and similar in their sensory apparatus and perception of the world. We expect that any ape language would have developed along tracks similar to our own, but their communication falls well short of our concept of language. Some birds, unlike apes, are able to pronounce words. The linguistic ability of Alex and other captive African grey parrots seems to be equivalent to that of apes (Pepperberg 1999, 110). How complex is the communication in the wild of these parrots we do not know, but the capability is there. Pepperberg, in her memoir on Alex, tells us that once when he wanted nuts and humans ignored his repeated spoken demand, he spelled it out, letter by letter, using recently taught letters but figuring out the spelling on his own. A literate parrot? Not really, but he has understood the correspondence among the object, the spoken word, and the script. Further evidence is Alex's invention of words, synthesizing words he already knew of visually similar objects— "corknut" for almond and "banerry" for apple, a combination of *banana* and *cherry*.

Dolphins have been trained by the U.S. Navy for a number of complex tasks in which they exercise some independent decision-making. *Training* is not the right word; what has been achieved is complex interspecies communication more than words—sentences. In the ocean, their sensory world is dominated by sound.

Although elephants have been domesticated for millennia, only recently have we learned about most of their vocalizations, which are in the lower registers beyond the range of human hearing, as well as other means of receiving and conveying information (Alexander 2000, 229–43). Like many other animals, they have senses that humans lack—an ability to detect vibrations many miles away and to send signals this way by stomping (O'Connell-Rodwell, Arnason, and Hart 2000). Most of their vocal communication is also at great distance. Originally sea mammals, their sensory inputs are more sound than sight. Their sense of smell is keener than a dog's. The world they perceive must be quite different from that of humans. Except for a few rumbles and trumpeting, no one knows what they say. Perhaps we should consult mahouts. But the behavior associated with their communications suggests diversity and complexity approximating the abstraction of language.

The most impressive instance of cognitive composition I have read is that of elephants in Botswana, which when food runs low in one area protected from poachers gather at night and dash 30 km to another protected area (*Economist* 1999, 92–93). They understand the need for night travel to avoid poachers and appear to have a precise knowledge of the boundaries of the protected areas. It seems incredible that any one elephant would have acquired all this geographic information on its own, in particular because the preserves have only recently been established. More likely, elephants are capable of the complex communication required to piece together bits of information from different sources into a cognitive map accepted by all members of the group. There had also been agreement on the place and time of congregation and its purpose. If this is not a language, it behaves like one.

An earlier instance of complex communication and rational behavior change in the wild was the adjustment of elephants in 1919 to mass killings. Once peaceful, they came to hate humans and became dangerously aggressive, charging vehicles on sight. And they radically altered their way of life—hiding in the bushes in daytime, feeding at night (Alexander 2000, 177). Fifty years later, when none of the original elephants was probably still around, they maintained their hostility and nocturnal habits. Again, this revealed an ability to generalize, to foresee consequences of behavior, and communication between generations sufficiently complex to induce them to persist in lifestyles contrary to their natures.

These two examples incorporate all steps in innovation: cognitive inputs of learning, memory and communication, and the cognitive output, change in behavior. It is not surprising that social animals have a near monopoly on toolmaking and other forms of invention. What we don't know is the structure of the large number of distinct vocalizations by elephants or dolphins,

The languages of all nonhuman species, to the best of our knowledge, are quite limited as the sole means of communicating inventions, which in most cases requires a fairly extensive vocabulary as well as some syntax. There is no evidence of technology transfer by animals in the absence of direct observation; communication may play an auxiliary role. Animal communication may be complex but is not developed for this purpose. It must be done by demonstration, by example, which is one way of communication but a very slow way of spreading knowledge. Even a chimp may find it difficult to teach its offspring how to fish for termites by sound and gesture alone.

The effectiveness of communication as a means of disseminating new information depends on the structure of animal society. Is it organized in small groups, families, solitary individuals, or in larger aggregations? Migration provides opportunities for mutual observation. Do different troops, herds, prides, and so on mingle or always maintain separation? Do individuals shift from one to another group or not? Mingling, adoption, and migration provide opportunities for technology transfer as well as for other kinds of information sharing.

Longevity could be the most important influence on innovation— the bequest and adoption of new knowledge. An animal may be a slow learner, but over a long life, it may acquire much knowledge and have prolonged contact with more than one succeeding generation. The matriarch in societies of elephants plays a critical role in preserving and passing on accumulated knowledge.

COGNITIVE ABILITY

Communication is, on one hand, an invention; on the other hand, the content of communication reflects the cognitive abilities as well as the knowledge of both sender and receiver. Since we cannot decipher most of the communications of animals, information on their cognitive abilities is based on observation of their behavior and of changes in behavior. We infer cognitive abilities from behavior.

The more advanced animals, both wild and domesticated, can anticipate outcomes and take the steps necessary to attain desired results, which among domesticated animals often means learning to communicate one's wishes to humans. They can imagine and develop specific means of communication. This behavior suggests consciousness. What it clearly demonstrates is an understanding of means-end relations, including temporal sequencing. They also have a grasp of spatial relations, without which they would not be able to conceive or construct shelters.

A basic understanding of cause and effect is fundamental for toolmaking. Carrying stones to a distant site for nut cracking or preparing spears long before or far from their target suggests foresight, planning for the future, whereas tool use can be momentary. Discovery, on the other hand, requires the ability to generalize from particulars—wasps sting—and to classify—these creatures are wasps. Classification is an essential step in creating language.

Nevertheless, animal conception of the future is quite limited. The instances just mentioned above may be described as an extended present rather than a future detached from the present. There is little evidence of effort devoted to making tools except for immediate use. It is the construction of shelters and the practice of collecting or secreting seeds and nuts allegedly for future consumption. But it is not clear that these inventions were intentional rather than genetic selections. They are not the work of the most advanced species.

Cooperation, in which each animal is both tool and tool user, implies a shared sense of purpose and individual initiative directed toward the common end.

Cetaceans—in particular *Tursiops*, the bottlenose dolphin—have large and complex brains with a well-developed neocortex. Their intelligence is as great as that of the great apes, if not greater. The puzzling question is, to what purpose is the large and complex brain of dolphins developed? How do they put it to use? It is widely believed that the explanation lies in their intense social interaction. Bottlenose dolphins can recognize many others by voice signal and can recall that signal for decades. Their complex communications permit cooperation in strategies for herding fish, fighting sharks, and training as underwater seamen for naval warfare.

The fact that the brainier species—primates, cetaceans, elephants— are highly social is widely accepted as an explanation for their cognitive abilities. The correlation is there, but the direction of causation troubles me; it might well be the reverse. Some primates, the gorilla and the Bornean orangutan, are not social but just as brainy. Many species not noted for IQ are highly social. What does *social* mean? Scale, differentiation, interdependence? Apes are self-aware and can consider the expected responses of others to their own acts. So are dolphins and elephants. Under these conditions, social interaction becomes a much more complex activity than simple herding behavior (Bonner 1980, 190–99). It is an invention. The cognitive ability that allows complex interaction is the same kind of ability that can make tools—planning ahead, foreseeing outcomes.

According to Herman (1960, 419–21; 1990, 349–63), there is evidence of cognitive convergence between some cetaceans and some advanced primates; they are cognitive cousins. They demonstrate advanced capabilities for classifying, remembering, and discovering relationships among events; for forming response rules of general utility; and for manipulating symbols. Their elaborate social matrix implies extensive and complex communication. Dolphins represent their world through arbitrary auditory symbols. Chimps and bonobos are capable of self-recognition, advance planning, and symbolic play. They are aware of others' intentions and practice deception and manipulation (Jolly 2001, 231, 249). It raises the question of determinism.

The cognitive similarity between birds and mammals is also surprising, given their difference in lifestyles and physiology. Observed performance, in any case, is only a limited, partial indicator of ability. The more intelligent species are all underachievers.

ABSTRACTION

Some species have made limited progress in the use and making of tools and discovery of new sources of food or the means of obtaining them via cultural change. The ability to discover general principles about the environment requires capacity for abstract thinking, which is not entirely absent in some animals. But it is limited in scope and established in very few species. (This remains a matter of controversy and a problem of definition.) Some intentional inventions also require expectations. Stone chipping is hard work, rarely undertaken in a specific case. It has not been developed until hominids have appeared.

There are indications in some animals of the ability for thinking that reflects an understanding going beyond the case specific. Communication is an exercise in abstraction, the use of vocal and visual symbols. It is the origin of abstraction and its primary purpose. An invention is first conceived as an alternative future. And a system of communication is also a transmission belt and storage system for innovation.

Initial tool use and toolmaking, or invention, is often the serendipitous outcome of play or near-random trial, not what we conceive of as an experimental process. But if the finding that a stick may be used as a lever, club, probe, or rake is to be learned and remembered, the finder must have some insight into association or cause and consequence, some ability to generalize from the first instance to other future uses.

Trial-and-error learning implies some objective, not just random experimentation. A successful trial is thus more likely to be remembered and generalized, its use repeated than an accidental success. But still, tool use or toolmaking remains the act of a single individual. Transmission to others requires learning by observation, if not by more complex processes of communication. Learning by observation is more than simple imitation or copycat replication. Awareness of consequences is an important, if not essential, condition for recall and innovation.

We have shown the ability of some species in captivity to master the rudiments of human language, the greatest abstraction of all. What about the subset of language, with its own vocabulary? Many species can count; many can differentiate between more and less, larger and smaller numbers, a minimal foundation for arithmetic. Alex, the grey parrot mastered the concepts of "none" or zero, of equivalence, of greater and smaller, as well as Arabic numerals (Pepperberg, 189–97). Alex also taught himself to add. Tested on numbers from a platter of objects of different shapes and colors (how many green squares, red triangles, etc.), when asked at the last trial, he gave the sum of the previous answers. The question is how much more he could have mastered and shown us given how much time was devoted to repetitive trials for the scientific record, for which he often showed boredom and annoyance? Some apes and elephants also can add. They may understand abstract numbers divorced from any object as Alex apparently does. What else can they do with numbers? We do not know. Many other bird species can add and subtract. Arithmetic obviously has survival value.

OTHER INDICATORS OF COGNITION AND CREATIVITY

Aesthetics. Long before hominids and humans advanced beyond simple tools and toolmaking, they exhibited advanced creative imagination in other areas—art and religion. Art and religion require abstraction, without which there is little invention or innovation and much less discovery. It is reasonable to assume that their origins can be other than found among some animals. I am focusing on the imagination of apes, elephants, and dolphins, the last two the products of evolutionary paths very different from that of apes and humans, which have also resulted in large brains, complex communication, and flexible behavior.

One aspect of creativity is aesthetic. Apes and elephants especially exhibit visual creativity, some birds vocal originality (De Waal 2001, 149–76). Elephants draw in the dirt with sticks and stones; many elephants in captivity, and many apes, paint (Chevalier-Skolnikoff and Liska 1993, 211). Ruby, the artistic elephant in the Phoenix Zoo, became such a distinguished abstract expressionist that she earned an obit in the *Washington Post* and many other newspapers across the land, not to mention half a million dollars. Ruby clearly knew what she wanted to do, to the point of disapproving and correcting the work of a less accomplished elephant (Gilbert 1990, 40–51). Elephant artists know what colors and patterns they prefer. Unemployed elephants in Thailand have been trained at three art schools, developing regional styles in their painting, according to Yale University art historian Mia Fineman (Kaplan 2000, A1, A29). Many years ago, a chimp at the Baltimore Zoo won a painting competition whose sponsors had neglected to limit contestants to humans; the resulting dispute about the prize money reminded me of the days of slavery.

Let us admit that most paintings by elephants or apes are scrawls and smudges and that their music is noise as would be the case had we chosen one hundred humans at random and given them paintbrush or trumpet. But a few—such as Congo, the chimp, or Ruby, the elephant—show promise. And many show interest.

One finds an aesthetic sense apparently also in bowerbirds. The males construct elaborate nests and decorate them with flowers— replaced when wilted—and assorted, bright, and colorful objects to attract the females. They paint them with a mixture of charcoal powder and saliva, using a bark wad as brush, revealing preferences for patterns and colors, which differ in different areas (Hall 1965, 133). Such behavior seems too diverse and complex to be attributable solely to genes. If the objects are rearranged in the absence of the bowerbird, it will replace them exactly as before on its return. Clearly, the arrangement is by design, with ornaments placed to increase the perception of depth. If not aesthetics, at least a sense of order (Kelley and Endler 2012).

The sensitivity of elephants to music has been noted since Greek and Roman days. They do not care for clashing cymbals but are enraptured by flutes, tapping the rhythm with their feet (Delort 1992, 134–35, 145–48). In Thailand, unemployed elephants have been taught or learned to play percussion and wind musical instruments (Alexander 2000, 103). Some observers, including the music critic for the *Bangkok Post*, claim that what the elephants are improvising is music, not distinguishable from some modern music composed by humans (*Economist* February 3,2001, 44). If this is so (and given the character of some modern "music," it is a big if), then elephants are not only composing and performing music but also giving some indication of music appreciation; they know what they are doing, and there are patterns in their performance. They do have a keen sense of rhythm, flapping their ears and swishing their tails to the beat, rocking back and forth. Sometimes they add their own trumpeting accompaniment to the melody. This is what one expects of animals who rely more on sound, which is sequential, than on sight, which is simultaneous. But gorillas in captivity sing, and one listens to Pavarotti sing for hours, tapping in rhythm (Page 1999, 193).

Dolphins love music. Perhaps somewhere in their vocalizations, we can find not communication but expression—composition.

What to make of animal aesthetics? Imagination and creativity for sure, some invention perhaps. But what the listeners prefer, what the artists among them compose, is order, not solution to a problem. Aesthetics is a precursor to discovery rather than invention.

Death. Another aspect of imagination is the attitude of these advanced animals toward death of close kin. All three species respond to death of their fellows with mourning and prolonged depression. Awareness of death and of one's own mortality is one source of religious creativity. One expects an understanding of death, and a deep emotional reaction to death, first among animals whose young are few in number and experience a prolonged period of dependence and training, such as the apes, elephants, and dolphins. The attachment is primarily that of mother and immature offspring. Second, animals that are highly social are most likely to extend the filial-maternal relation to other members of the group.

Both elephants and some dolphins are highly social creatures, whom we might expect to miss and grieve for lost members of their group. As to the apes, it is among the chimps and bonobos that we expect an appreciation for the death of members of their group—sorrow, frustration, anger.

Goodall (1986, 59, 101) notes the prolonged depression of chimpanzees, sometimes leading to death, after the death of a mother. She describes a chimp mother carrying a dead infant for days as though alive. But she thinks it highly unlikely that chimpanzees understand the concept of death (Goodall 1999, 146, 152). A dolphin has been observed circling her deceased offspring for over eight hours, making high-pitched vocalizations (Connor and Smolker 1990, 355, 360). In another case, a male kept circling the body of his female friend constantly, refusing food, whistling constantly, until he too died three days later (Cannon, Richard and Micklethwaite Peterson, 1994, 183). Parrots too exhibit distress; they scream and shriek at the death of conspecifics. They mate for life and can become depressed and die when their mate dies.

But the most extraordinary behavior on the occasion of death is that of elephants. They mourn their dead and try to bury the bodies with dirt and leaves. Why? Who knows for sure? Occasionally, they have done this to animals of other species and humans, including a sleeping woman who dared not move when awakened. This respect, if not mourning, for members of other species is impressive. They have some concept of death, recognizing and fondling bones, especially the skull, years later. They move the bones, sometimes a considerable distance. They smash the tusks, perhaps understanding that they are the occasion of poaching (Moss 1982, 33). There are Shakespearean scenes of an elephant who has lost her offspring and of a son who has lost his mother passing by the place of death years later and fondling the bleached bones while other elephants seem to stop in silent contemplation (Douglas-Hamilton 1976, 189–204). This may be anthropomorphism, but I see nothing wrong with it as long as we remain aware. We are much better at it than we could possibly be at "loxodontomorphism."

Other. Chimpanzees have been observed making threatening gestures against thunderstorms, performing dances, and silently watching spectacular sunsets. Goodall (1990, 241) observes what she described as protoreligious behavior in their reaction on facing an impressive waterfall. "[W]ere the chimps expressing feelings of awe such as those which in early man surely gave rise to primitive religions, worship of the elements?"

Many animals exhibit what one might label as moral behavior as evidenced by altruism or reciprocal altruism, A fishing cormorant in China refused to continue fishing because it has not been given the seventh fish caught as per "contract" with the owner (also suggesting an ability to count to seven at least). Another refused a fish after only six catches. Pryor (1990, 346) reports that a captive dolphin refused a fish reward because it has not performed the required task to its satisfaction—truly a sense of self and of ethics.

One problem with relying on the performance of specific animals as representatives of their species is that, in any advanced species, there is a wide range of abilities of every kind. This is no problem with pigeons or mice since so many have been subjected to the same tests that the results can be dealt with statistically. Besides, they may be bred selectively. As to chimps, the range of genetic variation is far greater than among humans; one might expect a very wide range of abilities. Alex, the African grey parrot who not only mastered a large vocabulary of words but also clearly understood them and used them correctly in speech, may not have been the average parrot. The bottlenose dolphin that has done clever imitations of the behavior of seals, skates, and turtles may be an atypical dolphin. But then Galileo and Einstein are not typical humans. Still, enough primates, cetaceans, elephants, and parrots have been observed to assure us that the star performers are representative of their species even if they may not be average.

BRAINS

Intelligence is a complex, multidimensional concept. We try to estimate the intelligence of lower species by testing how fast and how well they master human tricks and human language. How well would we do if elephants or dolphins, even apes, were testing us? There are other tests—memory, counting, self-awareness (the mirror test), problem-solving. Although animal invention is not limited to what we consider to be the most intelligent animals, it is most common among them.

Howard Gardner has identified multiple dimensions of intelligence, seven originally. We are all specialized, most animals much more so than humans. This diversity makes it very difficult to compare individuals, much less species. What concerns me are those aspects of intelligence that contribute to invention and discovery. Any of them may contribute to a particular invention, although logical-mathematical ability is often critical. Memory, a process rather than intelligence, is important since it is a determinant of the amount of knowledge we accumulate and put to use. Observation and attention is another ability, if we could pin it down in brain structure. These are cognitive inputs. Reasoning, the cognitive process, is the use of inputs to create outputs, including discovery, invention, and imagination. In the mammalian brain, the hippocampus is critical for memory, the neocortex for reasoning.

One approach to estimating the intelligence of different species is a comparison of brain size and composition. Differences in intelligence have been estimated by measuring the relation between brain and body size across species. Jerison (1973) estimated a scale of the ratio of brain to body weight by regressing the ratios of many species of varying size. The relation for mammals had been believed to be a 2:3 log-linear ratio of brain to body weight, reflecting body surface area as determinant of physiological needs. More recently, a ratio of 3:4 has been widely accepted, reflecting the relation of metabolic rate to brain weight (Harvey and Krebs 1990). From this ratio, one can estimate surplus processing capacity, how much of the brain is not required to manage routine bodily functions but available for discretionary cognitive activities. This "surplus" or encephalization index is presumed to be an indicator of relative intelligence. Apes are well behind us; the bottlenose dolphin is closer to humans. But surplus cerebral processing capacity does not tell us much about the ability to discover or invent. It may be devoted to extraordinary memory or to particular sensory modalities.

A further refinement is the functional differentiation in mammals—the ratio of the neocortex to the rest of the brain and of particular components associated with language or other higher cognitive functions. The percentage of the brain surface covered by the cerebral cortex is slightly higher in some cetaceans than in humans, but the cortex layer is thinner; the ratio of cortex volume to total brain volume for the bottlenose dolphin and the chimpanzee are slightly more than half the human. Other animals are considerably lower.

Cognitive potential achievements also depend on the stock of knowledge of the individual. Thus, longevity and memory—for which the hippocampus is critical—are important qualifications. Folktales about elephant memories are confirmed. The elephant's hippocampus is the largest, larger than the human.

Brain size and structure may reflect a potential that is not revealed in studies of behavior. These ratios refer to the macrostructure. There are speculations that the microstructure could matter most—the number of neurons, the number and pattern of interconnections or synapses, the folding of the brain.

One other difference sets humans apart. Their neurons are smaller and more densely packed, twice as many per volume than mammals.

Birds capable of flight are subject to severe weight constraints not found in mammals, bats excepted. Their physiology is designed to save weight. Birds have evolved weight- and volume-economizing central nervous systems. Their brain structures are quite different from those of mammals. They do not have a significant neocortex but manage to perform its functions in their striatal areas. Neuron size and density is twice that of mammals, even higher than in primates, similar to humans. Corvids, the toolmaking and tool-using champions; the parrot family; and songbirds allocate a disproportionate share of their neurons in large clusters to higher cognitive functions (Chodosh 2016).

Volume or ratio approaches for estimating intelligence must be limited to similar species. Even then, brain comparisons are but substitutes for comparisons of minds.

Housekeeping brain size requirements are closely related to body mass, but this is not true of cognition. At the upper levels of cognitive activity, a large number of neurons and a significant weight are needed, regardless of body mass. As far as the neocortex or the cognitive brain is concerned, minimum size matters. For small creatures to be very smart, they must be narrowly specialized. This is particularly true of the ability to learn, to accumulate knowledge.

Consider the octopus. Its brain is hierarchical, a central brain and eight brainlets in its tentacles. The neurons are much larger and different from those other species. It is an intelligence more alien than any conceived by science-fiction writers in the outer reaches of the galaxy. Yet it exhibits cognitive abilities similar to those of crows or macaques, performing much the same task, communication excepted. Perhaps the hierarchical structure has evolved to allow a smaller central brain to squeeze through small apertures, perhaps to economize on energy.

CONCLUSION

All animals are specialized; direct comparisons are possible only along specific cognitive dimensions. Parrots and crows are different. Crows are great problem solvers, whereas parrots learn abstract concepts—different intelligences. It may be specialization that allows some birds, parrots in particular, to master the rudimentary human language. The brain of an African grey parrot (or a crow) is very small compared with that of apes or dolphins. Is it in the same intellectual class? I think not. Many animals might be called idiot savants. Humans are the least specialized animals, the most versatile and adaptable.

Culture change among numerous animal species includes inventions that are occasionally learned and adopted by other individuals and transmitted through the generations. Among these inventions are tool use and, more rarely, toolmaking but also symbolic communication—sounds and gestures. Some species possess, on one hand, the cognitive abilities to invent and, on the other, the communicative abilities to disseminate inventions and discoveries. The common characteristics of the species that use tools most frequently—some of which also make tools, including symbolic communication—are a limited number of offspring, usually born one at a time; a long period of maturation, during which they learn from mothers and other adults; a long life; and a complex social organization. Inventions by social animals are more likely to be observed, imitated, and perpetuated. Longevity is not just about opportunity; learning is cumulative as in the elderly leader of an elephant troop or wolf pack. Cumulative knowledge can become an input to further creativity, such as the parrot Alex's invention of new words.

The inventive octopus is a living proof that none of the traits mentioned above are necessary for creativity; they refer to innovation, not invention. The octopus is short lived, solitary, untutored. Its fantastic brain structure is evidence of dissociation of structure and function. Different paths converge on the same invention. Differences in inventiveness between species are greatly exaggerated. The species that does not invent does not survive.

I omit the consideration of domesticated species since their behavior has been engineered by humans. Among wild species, some have been studied intensively—primates, parrots, elephants, dolphins. Our knowledge is twofold. There are detailed, intensive studies of particular individuals in captivity—Alex, the African grey parrot, and Koko, the gorilla—others have observed on large social groups over several generations. What the individual experiments confirm is that these advanced species have a wide range of cognitive abilities not observed in their natural environment but readily exercised in a different environment. This is not environmental determinism, rather species versatility and inventiveness. The group studies reveal conditions for innovation, if not invention. They show that species very different in their physical capabilities, in their environment, and in their brain structures create analogous inventions and share some cognitive traits, such as foresight and a basic understanding of cause and effect.

Individuals in captivity are more inventive than in the wild because they have the leisure and security, being spared the threat of predators and the need to forage. Thus, the need to invent cannot explain all inventive activity. The attributes of inventive species refer to the propensity to invent as well as to the ability to invent. What to call it? Perhaps curiosity?

There remains one puzzle: how it is that some members of a number of species possess abilities far beyond those used in their natural habitat? In particular, what is the origin of the ability for abstract reasoning? This is the question of spandrels, proposed by Gould and Lewontin (1979)—mutations not selected for current use but finding a role under new circumstances. Perhaps they are the origin of natural selection.

REFERENCES

Alexander, Shana. 2000. *The Astonishing Elephant*. New York: Random House, 53.

Beck, Benjamin B. 1980. *Animal Tool Behavior—The Use and Manufacture of Tools by Animals*. New York: Garland STPM Press. See also Goodall and Berman 1999, 188–89.

Bonner, John Tyler. 1980. *The Evolution of Culture in Animals*. Princeton: Princeton University Press.

Cannon, Richard C., and Dawn M. Micklethwaite Peterson. 1994. *The Lives of Whales and Dolphins*. New York: Henry Holt and Company.

Chevalier-Skolnikoff, Susan, and Jo Liska. 1993. "Tool Use by Wild and Captive Elephants." *Animal Behavior* 46 (2): 209–19.

Chodosh, Sarah. 2016. "Bird Brains Have as Many Neurons as Some Primates." *Scientific American* (June 17, 2016).

Connor, Richard C., and Rachel E. Smolker. 1990. "A Quantitative Description of a Rare Behavior Event: A Bottlenose Dolphin's Behavior toward her Deceased Offspring." In *The Bottlenose*

Dolphin, edited by Stephen Leatherwood and Randall Reeves, 346. San Diego: Academic Press.

Delort, Robert. 1992. *The Life and Lore of the Elephant.* New York: Discoveries - Harry N. Abrams, Inc.

De Waal, Frans. 2001. *The Ape and the Sushi Master—Cultural Reflections by a Primatologist.* New York: Basic Books.

Dicke, U., and G. Roth. 2008. "Intelligence Evolved." *Scientific American* (August/September):

Douglas-Hamilton, Iain, and Oria Douglas-Hamilton. 1976. *Among the Elephants.* NY: Wytham Publications Ltd., Viking Press.

"Not So Dumbo." *Economist* (May 15, 1999)

"Thailand's Elephant Music." *Economist* (February 3, 2001): 44.

Engel, Cindy. 2002. *Wild Health—How Animals Keep Themselves Well and What We Can Learn from Them.* Boston: Houghton Mifflin.

"Gbaya People—Suiting up for the Honey Wars." *Smithsonian* (August 2001): 78–83, photographs by Gilles Nicolet/Saola.

Gibbons, Ann. 2007. "Spear-Wielding Chimps Seen Hunting Bush Babies." *Science* 315 (February): 1063.

Gilbert, Bil. 1990. "Once a Malcontent, Ruby Has Taken up Brush and Palette." *Smithsonian* 21 (9): 40–51.

Goodall, Jane. 1986. *The Chimpanzees of Gombe: Patterns of Behavior.* Cambridge, MA: Belknap Press of Harvard University.

———. 1999. *Through a Window: My Thirty Years with the Chimpanzees of Gombe.* Boston: Houghton Mifflin Company.

Goodall, Jane, with Phillip Berman. 1999. *Reason for Hope—A Spiritual Journey.* New York: Warner Books.

Gould, S. J., and R. C. Lewontin. 1979. "The Spandrels of San Marco and the Panglossian Paradigm: A Critique of the Adaptationist Programme." *Proceedings of the Royal Society of Biological Sciences* 205 (1161): 581–98.

Griffin, Donald R. 1984. *Animal Thinking.* Cambridge: Harvard University Press.

————.1992. *Animal Minds.* Chicago: University of Chicago Press.

Hall, K. R. L. 1968. "Tool-Using Performance as Indicators of Behavioral Adaptability." In *Primates-Studies in Adaptation and Variability,* edited by Jay, Phyllis. NY: Holt, Rinehart & Winston.

Hanlon, Roger T., and John B. Messenger. 1996. *Cephalopod Behavior.* Cambridge: Cambridge University Press.

Hart, B. L., L. A. Hart, M. McCoy, and C. R. Sarath. 2001. "Cognitive Behavior in Asian Elephants: Use and Modification of Branches for Fly Switching." *Animal Behavior* 62 (5): 839–47.

Harvey, Paul H., and John R. Krebs. 1990. "Comparing Brains." *Science* 249 (July): 140–6.

Herman, Louis M., ed. 1980. *Cetacean Behavior: Mechanisms and Functions.* New York: John Wiley & Sons.

Herman, Louis M. 1990. "What the Dolphin Knows or Might Know in Its Natural World." In *The Bottlenose Dolphin,* edited by Stephen Leatherwood and Randall R. Reeves, 349–63. San Diego: Academic Press.

Hirata, S., K. Watanabe, and M. Kawai. 2001. "Sweet-Potato Washing Revisited." In *Primate Origins of Human Cognition and Behavior*, edited by T. Matsuzawa, 487–508. Tokyo: Springer.

Hunt, G. R. 1996. "Manufacture and Use of Hook Tools by New Caledonian Crows." *Nature* 397 (January): 249–51.

Jay, Phyllis, ed. 1968. *Primates—Studies in Adaptation and Variability*. New York: Holt, Rinehart & Winston.

Jerison, Harry J. 1973. *Evolution of the Brain and Intelligence*. New York: Academic Press.

Jolly, Alison. 1991. "Conscious Chimpanzees: A Review of Recent Literature." In *Cognitive Ethology—The Minds of Other Animals*, edited by Carolyn A. Ristau. Hillsdale, NJ: Lawrence Erlbaum Associates Publishers.

Kaplan, Fred. 2000. "Art from the Massives." *Boston Globe*, March 19, A1, A29.

Kelley, Laura, and John Endler. 2012. "Illusions Promote Mating Success in Great Bowerbirds." *Science* 335 (January): 335–38.

Kummer, H., and Jane Goodall (1985). "Conditions of Innovative Behavior in Primates." In *Animal Intelligence*, edited by L. Weiskrantz, 203–14. Oxford: Clarendon Press.

Leatherwood, Stephen, and Randall R. Reeves, eds. 1990. *The Bottlenose Dolphin*. San Diego: Academic Press.

Locklear, Christian. 1990. "Review of Incidents Involving Wild Sociable Dolphins Worldwide." In *The Bottlenose Dolphin*, edited by Stephen Leatherwood and Randall R. Reeves, 125–35. San Diego: Academic Press.

Mathur, Jennifer, Roland C. Anderson, and James B. Wood. 2010. *Octopus: Ocean's Intellectual Invertebrate*. Portland: Timber Press Inc.

Matsuzawa, T. ed. 2001. *Primate Origins of Human Cognition and Behavior*. Tokyo: Springer.

Miyadi, Denzaburo. 1964. "Social Life of Japanese Monkeys." *Science* 143 (February): 83–86.

Moss, Cynthia. 1982. *Portraits in the Wild—Behavior Studies of East African Mammals*, 2nd ed. Chicago: University of Chicago Press.

———. 1988. *Elephant Memories—Thirteen Years in the Life of an Elephant Family*. New York: Fawcett Columbine.

Moura, A. C., P. C. Lee, and Ann Gibbons. 2007. "A Spear-Wielding Chimps Seen Hunting Bush Babies." *Science* 315 (February): 1063.

Moura, A. C., and P. C. Lee. 2004. "A Capuchin Stone Tool Use in Caatinga Dry Forest." *Science* 306 (5703): 1909.

O'Connell-Rodwell, C. E., B. T. Arnason, and L. A. Hart. 2000. "Seismic Properties of Asian Elephant (*Elephas maximus*) Vocalizations and Locomotion." *Journal of the Acoustical Society of America* 108 (6): 3066–72.

Page, George. 1999. *Inside the Animal Mind*. New York: Doubleday.

Pepperberg, Irene. 1999. *The Alex Studies: Cognitive and Communicative Abilities of Grey Parrots*. Cambridge: Harvard University Press.

———. 2008. *Alex & Me*. New York, Harper Collins.

Pryor, Karen. 1990. *The Domestic Dolphin*, 346. San Diego: Academic Press.

Ristau, Carolyn A, ed. 1991. *Cognitive Ethology—The Minds of Other Animals.* Hillsdale, NJ: Lawrence Erlbaum Associates Publishers.

Schusterman, Ronald J., Jeanette A. Thomas, and Forrest G. Wood, eds. 1986. *Dolphin Cognition and Behavior: A Comparative Approach.* Hillsdale, NJ: Lawrence Eilbaum Associates.

Strum, S. C. 1975. "Primate Predation: Interim Report on the Development of a Tradition in a Troop of Olive Baboons." *Science* (February): 755–57.

Taylor, Alex, Gavin Hunt, Jennifer Holzhaider, and Russell Gray. 2007. "Spontaneous Metatool Use by New Caledonian Crows." *Current Biology* 17 (17): 1504–7.

Van Schaik, Carel P., Robert O. Deaner, and Michelle Y. Merrill. 1999. "The Conditions for Tool Use in Primates: Implications for the Evolution of Material Culture." *Journal of Human Evolution* 36 (6): 719–41.

Vauclair, Jacques. 1996. *Animal Cognition—An Introduction to Modern Comparative Psychology.* Cambridge: Harvard University Press.

Vogel, Gretchen. 1999. "Chimps in the Wild Show Stirrings of Culture." *Science* 284 (June): 2070.

Weir, Alex A. S., Jackie Chappell, and Alex Kacelnik. 2002. "A Shaping of Hooks in New Caledonian Crows." *Science* 297 (9): 981.

Weiskrantz. L., ed. 1985. *Animal Intelligence.* Oxford: Clarendon Press.

Wells. M. J. 1978. *Octopus—Physiology and Behavior of an Advanced Invertebrate.* London: Chapman and Hall.

Yerkes, Robert M., and Ada W. 1929. *The Great Apes—A Study of Anthropological Life.* New Haven: Yale University Press.

III

Prehistory: Hominids and Homo

In the previous chapter, we have suggested that the seeds of creativity are found in a wide range of animals. Some species placed in an environment providing possibilities for learning and creativity largely absent in a state of nature have revealed considerable versatility in problem-solving—in the invention and use of tools. The pace of progress, glacial in the animal world, picks up slightly with the rise of hominids. But discoveries and inventions are not all alike. With hominids and early humans, some inventions become sequential; there is progress in technology and in understanding. Inventions grow in complexity, imposing greater requirements on discoverers and inventors, as well as on the environment. Our own species, *Homo sapiens*, is much brainier and less brawny than its ancestor of two million years ago, *Australopithecus erectus*.

The conditions under which discoveries and inventions flourish or falter are not given; they have undergone dramatic change in the course of human history.

CREATIVITY AND SURVIVAL

Creative ability is an essential but far-from-sufficient condition for discovery and invention. If we could observe early *Homo sapiens* two hundred thousand years ago, overlooking their striking similarity to our own appearance, their behavior would seem more like that of apes in the wild in our time than to our own. Only their bipedalism will set them apart.

Yet those early humans, to the best of our knowledge, had all the abilities found in the species living today. There were Cro-Magnon, and probably Neanderthal (both had bigger brains than modern humans), potentially capable of the achievements of a Euclid, a Mozart, or an Edison. We know there were great artists among them. But no symphonies were written. Sophisticated musical instruments were still to be invented as was musical notation, and the socioeconomic conditions to form and maintain an orchestra were far in the future.

Some primitive tribes only recently were said to have no word for a specific number greater than three. That does not mean they were lacking in mathematical ability; they simply had no need for a decimal system, algebra, or calculus and had other priorities in their creative activities. After all, even crows and cormorants can count to seven at least.

How complex abilities arise that appear to have no function at the time remains something of a mystery. Perhaps we conceive them only in terms of their modern uses and fail to understand how they might have contributed to survival under radically different circumstances. Perhaps they were accidental, harmless mutations until conditions arose under which they could be brought to bear. Spatial-visual competence is an asset for subsistence and survival for most animals, but it can be turned to architecture, visual arts, and safe driving. Temporal sequences and sound discrimination have survival value in many contexts and can be turned to music or language. The versatility of number competence is less obvious; perhaps it arises from group living and group sharing. Even primitive construction requires simple geometry. Both spatial and temporal experience is soon abstracted into number. What was once relevant for survival has become useful for culture.

THE STONE AGE

In considering prehistory, all dates are tentative. Every year new discoveries challenge existing consensus or open up new areas of inquiry. Improved techniques result in redating of many events and reconsideration of the meaning of anthropological and archaeological findings. For our purposes, precise dates are not important; what matters is the sequence of events, their interconnections, and the changing pace at which subsequent events follow their predecessors. For historical dates, I have relied largely on George Ochoa and Melinda Corey's *The Timeline Book of Science* (1995).

Hominids and apes have evolved along separate lineages from a common ancestor some six million years ago. We know very little about the hominids or even of the early history of *Homo sapiens*. All we have is old bones, stone implements and weapons, garbage, little else. We infer behavior and achievements from these relics and the environments in which hominids and early humans have lived. Anthropologists have drawn inferences also from observing the behavior of the most primitive peoples in remote areas of the planet, a reservoir of ancient knowledge that has all but disappeared. But the basis of our knowledge of the dim past remains largely speculation based on excavation.

Bipedalism apparently first arose in forests (Gibbons 2002, 214–15) but became essential once our ancestors lost the protection of the trees as forests became savannas. This change of environment involved a shift from a mainly herbivorous diet to a hunter-scavenger-gatherer lifestyle and exposed our early ancestors to dangerous new predators. For a not very large biped, slow in land or water, lacking claws or teeth usable for defense or aggression, numerous social inventions were required for survival—collective protection against large predators, organized hunting, group sharing, and caring. All these social inventions had been practiced by some animal species but perhaps not as systematically as by hominids. Hunting involved division of labor by sex. Education was no longer just by mothers, food gathering, but also by males for hunting, protection, and war.

Many hominid types are known to have lived, but there are no surviving members of any of them. How they have all become extinct we do not know. The big-brained Neanderthal, sharing the same unknown ancestry, who has coexisted with modern humans for many thousands of years, is the biggest mystery of all, though there is something of him in most of us. Another species, Denisovan, with which humans have also interbred, has been recently discovered in Russia.

For all we know, Neanderthal was roughly on a par in cultural and technological development and possessed all the abilities, resources, and tools available to humans at the time. Why did they disappear? Neanderthal had two disadvantages. First, stockier and heavier than *Homo*, they required more nutrition to survive during the Ice Age. Second, Klein (1995, 183) told us that Neanderthal was short lived, aged early, and suffered from fragile bones. My inference is that the ratio of able-bodied adults to population was smaller for Neanderthals than for sapiens; today we would say that Neanderthal had a higher dependency ratio. Hence, there would be very high infant and child, possibly adult, mortality. The human advantage may not have been cognition or culture, just longevity and health.

The tiny recently discovered hominids in the island of Flores raise questions. Their position in the hominid tree of life is under dispute, probably australopithecines. Some question whether their brains are large enough to make and use the tools found in their proximity. More curious is the explanation of their survival long after all other hominids disappeared, perhaps after Neanderthal became extinct.

Five species of apes, with whom we share a common ancestor, are still found in their natural habitats, but the numerous intermediate types of hominids have all disappeared. They failed to develop the tools or social organization or to acquire the knowledge required to survive in the environments in which they lived. Life for our ancestors was precarious.

The human species is slow in reproduction; infants are born at an earlier stage of development than other mammals to allow for a larger brain. The prolonged period of dependency requires strong social bonding. The young need many years of nurturing before they can fend for themselves.

It is a miracle that primitive man survived. Early humans barely did (Ambrose 2001a). The fact that genetic variation among humans is minuscule, much smaller than among their first cousins, the chimpanzees, suggests that they have almost become extinct, perhaps some seventy thousand years ago, during a prolonged period of extreme cold after the eruption of the Toba supervolcano. During most of their existence, humans have been just another animal species, high on the food pyramid due to their social cohesiveness combined with primitive weapons. They have had one great advantage over most of their competitors—a very varied diet that has increased their chances of survival whatever the changes in their environment.

The prolonged period of child dependency also promotes sedentariness. A permanent encampment permits many inventions not feasible for migrants, such as shelter construction, storage of food and other valuables, and artifacts too heavy or bulky to backpack. Sedentariness has also been possible with a diet relying on grains and tubers, seasonal and storable.

What did hominids accomplish in the way of discovery and invention that set them apart from apes? The first inventions that advanced hominids beyond the achievements of other animals living today were the manufacture of stones with sharp edges as cutting tools. The lithic revolution was started some 2.5 million years ago by *Homo habilis* and lasted past the invention of agriculture by *Homo sapiens*, until copper and bronze came into use. Other advances in knowledge, new artifacts of wood and other perishable materials, left no trace.

Hominids, like apes today, used stones as hammers to break nuts and perhaps shellfish. Over millions of years, some stones would have been fractured by the pounding, producing sharp edges and points. After thousands of such accidents, a smart *Homo habilis*—or several—took notice, found the broken stones useful, and thought of fracturing stones rather than just nuts, a cognitive transfer. Statistically speaking, stone technology was inevitable, although breaking nuts with stones was not. One can then predict improvements in techniques and in choice of materials, an invention of new uses for sharp stones.

Apes crack nuts. Many times, they must have split stones in the process. But to our knowledge, they have never deliberately split or shaped stones. Yet they have the manual dexterity and the brute strength, and their achievements in captivity lead one to believe that they have the cognitive ability to do so. But splitting and shaping stone tools is hard and prolonged labor not for immediate consumption like nuts but for unknown uses in some remote future. Hominids did this, while apes have not.

Hominids hunted in groups. They needed weapons to bring down large prey and to defend themselves. Some animals used sticks and stones for weapons, but hominids went a step further—axes, sharp knives hewn from stone, stone-pointed spears. Whenever they brought down large prey, they had to share—divide it among the "hunters" and reserve a share for members of the group not part of the hunting party, women and children. For this, they needed tools with sharp edges to dismember the carcass, to cut up the meat. They also needed scrapers to prepare the hide for clothing. Hominids needed a variety of stone tools; apes did not. And necessity, at this stage, was the mother of invention.

Need was not enough to explain the hard long work of shaping stones and stone fragments into a variety of useful tools. Hominids required the ability to imagine the future beyond the immediacy and specificity of hunters and food-gatherers. They required the cognitive ability to engage in prolonged effort for unknown uses in some indefinite future. Perhaps initially, artifacts were made by the intended user; but in time, some hominids became skilled, leading to specialization and division of labor, which was the foundation of property and trade.

The pace of progress speeded up with the advent of *Homo erectus*, close relative who may have been the intermediate ancestor of our kind. Technology evolved, from crude, fractured stones to sharp flakes chipped or pressed from stone cores to evermore finely worked cores with shapes adapted to various old and new uses. One major advance was the invention of composite tools perhaps three hundred thousand years ago. They included axes and knives made of stone blades attached to wooden shafts, stone-pointed spears. They represented a higher level of complexity. Hominids had long used handheld stones and wooden clubs and poles. Putting them together was a small step in imagination. But technology seemed to remain static for very long periods, including much of the history of our own species (Foley 1988; Ambrose 2001b). However, new uses of technology were conceived.

There must have been shaped wooden implements such as spears earlier than stone—chimps had them. Wooden digging sticks for obtaining edible underground roots, tubers, may also be of ancient origin. They permitted hominids to invade seasonal new habitats or survive climate changes that turned forests into savannas. Much later, they contributed to the invention of agriculture. We cannot be sure which hominid species made which discovery or invention, but they were passed on to other species and ultimately to *Homo sapiens*, or they were reinvented.

Many animals make shelters as do insects. Weaverbirds and bowerbirds create quite advanced nests. But as we move up the scale of living things, we move from genetically determined behavior to clear inventions, learned and passed on by example and communication. No other species has developed the great diversity of shelters appropriate for different habitats.

As early *Homo sapiens* followed hominids out of Africa into Europe and Asia, clothing became an essential tool for survival in some areas during the last Ice Age. In many places, shelter also became important, and humans lacking natural shelters created shelters of varied design, using materials available in the habitat. We are not accustomed to thinking of clothing and shelter as tools. Beck (1980, 1–12) excluded them from his definition of *tool*. Tools or not, they were critical inventions, responses to changes in environment and climate. When or where they were first used we have no idea; it could have been done any time after hominids mastered the technique of stone splitting or flaking to produce sharp edges. Clothing was initially from animal hides cut and scraped with stone tools and stitched together with animal sinew through holes bored by crude awls. Animal skins may have been made into portable shelters. These were intentional responses to needs.

It is less clear why *Homo*, perhaps hominids, developed means of water transport, initially rafts, no doubt. We know that the ancestors of the Australian aborigines had developed means of seagoing transportation because they got to Australia some fifty to sixty thousand years ago. Stone tools were a necessary but not sufficient condition of all these inventions. For strings, ropes, straps, and knots, some method of binding different components together—an underestimated invention—was also essential. The advance from the invention and manufacture of single-component tools (a pointed stick, a hammer stone) to multicomponent weapons (shelter, boat) represented an advance in abstraction as well as in complexity.

FIRE

The second great invention by hominids, *Homo erectus* in particular, was fire perhaps as long as 1.7 million years ago. Fire of natural origins was occasionally available, and human ancestors learned to use it for light and heat. Early on, *Homo erectus* first learned to preserve fire; but only much later, *H. erectus* or our own kind learned to make fire at will. First came the discovery of properties of fire ignited by natural events. Fire had to be transported from its natural origin to hominid habitations. It had to be preserved, glowing embers that could be easily brought to flame. There were numerous small discoveries and inventions—knowledge of combustible materials, fireplace structure, the effects of heat.

The timing of the ability to make fire is subject to dispute. A recent study suggests that hominids, presumably *Homo erectus*, had mastered the ability to make fire (Goren 2008) as long as 790,000 years ago, much earlier than previously thought (Alperson-Afil and Inbar 2004). Even assuming the timing is correct, we do not know whether fire-making knowledge persisted, how often it was invented, or when this knowledge became widespread.

Hominids were not sedentary, leaving little trace. There is circumstantial evidence from hearths long in use, dating back to two or three hundred thousand years, that Neanderthals as well as early humans were able to make fire, probably by striking iron-bearing stone, producing sparks to ignite tinder—a technique that survived into the nineteenth century in flintlock muskets. The flint-and-pyrites method of producing sparks might have resulted from the accidental observation of the phenomenon in the course of shaping stone tools. But learning how to make fire by producing sparks was a considerable cognitive achievement.

It was humans who mastered the ability to create fire by friction, heating wood to ignite tinder. This must have happened many times in different places as suggested by the multiple techniques of making fire— fire drill, bow drill, saw, plow (Rossotti 1993, 23–24). The drill and the bow and arrow were technical inventions, surpassing in complexity and abstraction the techniques of stone chipping that preceded them.

Over two million years ago, meat and other edibles would have been accidentally exposed to the heat of camp or forest fires many times. Inevitably, some hominid took notice, and cooking was invented. Fire also proved useful in splitting stones, in hardening wood tools and weapons, in preserving meat by cooking and smoking. Eventually, it led to ceramics and metallurgy. During the same long period, wet clay exposed to the heat of burning campfires was converted into a hard, rocklike substance many times. To our knowledge, no *Homo erectus* took notice or took advantage. It was more than halfway through the history of our kind that the first fire-hardened clay figurines were made, and not till some 16K BP (16,000 years before the present) that ceramics—pottery—was invented in Japan and soon in a number of other locations. Ceramic containers were used in societies that did not live hand to mouth but stored surplus foods in season for later distribution.

The discovery of the uses of fire in the shaping of metal and in production of metal from ore did not come until well after the agricultural revolution. These achievements also were made independently in several, if not many, places. We know that early metallurgy was reinvented in the Western Hemisphere, not brought by migrants from Asia. Independent invention suggests common needs and opportunities. But why were they made so close together in time?

Deliberate burning of brush and forest converted them to grasslands, feeding increased herds for human hunters and, much later, clearing land for farming. Fires were used to stampede prey toward hunters (Goudsblom 1992, 27–32). In some places, these uses were required for survival; in others, they fostered population growth and opened up new opportunities for invention.

Fire was not needed for survival, but it was needed to expand the range of hominid occupation into colder climates and to increase the quantity and variety of edible foods and was useful for protection. Some human populations, such as the Andaman islanders, never did master fire, limiting their potential for further invention. Of course, once population and migration had adapted to the availability of fire, it became essential.

Ancient myths accorded fire, not stone tools, pride of place (Rossotti 1993, 239–54). The old idea of the eternal flame is a reminder of the first step in the mastery of fire. The keeper of the flame would be the one responsible for preserving fire for the community or would be the one who knew how to make fire. Most likely, he/she became a religious figure, perhaps the first religious leader in the original religions of hominids. Fire worshippers, descendants of the Zoroastrians, the Parsis, persist to this day.

LANGUAGE AND SPEECH

Mental life before language must have been a somewhat chaotic mix of stimuli, sensations, and ideas—a vast buzzing confusion of cognition. Naming an object, a quality, or an idea creates a small oasis of order—focus and exclusion. It represents the lowest level of abstraction. It identifies, represents, and segregates from others, from environment, foreground from background. A plurality of names—a large collection of tiny isolated oases of meaning—is itself without order. But it permits a second level of abstraction—classification, a calculus of relations. From nouns, one advances to adjectives, adverbs, implicit verbs—a system for classifying information that permits its organization, structuring, and communication.

Language was the most important human creation of all time. Unlike stone tools, fire, and many other early inventions, language was a social invention; it was not soliloquy. Language initially meant speech. Concepts must be expressed or converted into symbols that can be perceived by others. There was no moment nor a single inventor but millions of inventors, a gradual, cumulative evolution from the gestural, postural, and auditory communications of animals and early hominids.

The *Oxford English Dictionary* has just passed the million-word milestone. But that is vocabulary. *Language*, speech, means "grammar," converting a series of words into a meaningful pattern, a sentence. This job is never finished.

The causal relation between genetic change and the development of protolanguage among hominids is disputed among experts (Tomasello 1999, 13–55). The need for cooperation more complex than found among wolves or even apes has been a central condition. We do not know when hominids or early humans have had the cognitive ability to develop and use syntax and grammar. Klein believes that there was another genetic change around 50,000 to 60,000 years ago that enabled humans to create language. Its invention is inferred from the major increase in cultural complexity of human society and in group size, rapid population growth, and migration. The migration from Africa all the way to Australia some 50,000 years ago might not have been possible had the migrants not possessed rudimentary language. But causation can run both ways, and growing cultural complexity might have accelerated a process long underway.

One must distinguish between the capacities for language and for speech. The former is cognitive; the latter is physiological. The former may have been widespread long before linguistic communication. There is much dispute on the role of genetics as the cognitive foundation of language. Anthropologists focus on evidence of the physiological ability to speak—the genetic mutations that have provided the capacity for uttering the range of sounds and combinations of sounds found in human languages. This is speech, not language. It is relevant for the evolution of language but not for the capacity for language.

There is some evidence that the capacity for speech developed rather suddenly among early humans as a result of mutations in the gene FOXP2 some 250,000 years ago (Enard 2002). There are disputes whether Neanderthal had a larynx and motor control capable of finely modulated articulation required for a large vocabulary and complex speech. It now appears that Neanderthal also shared the same mutation and had the physiological capability for the large repertoire of vocalizations employed in speech (Krause 2007). The implication is that the genetic change first arose among the common ancestors of *Homo* and Neanderthal.

There is no single origin in time or place. The fact that at least one species of hominids had been thinly scattered across three continents and early man had reached a fourth, Australia, suggests that language evolved independently in many places; there is no single ancestral tongue. Hundreds of languages are still spoken in New Guinea today. The many differences between languages in such characteristics as word order and tenses, never mind the actual words that have been created, are clearly inventions. Much early vocabulary was place specific.

Our language is still riddled with reminders of prelinguistic communication—punctuation marks, articles, and pronouns, which once were gestures and postures. Oral communication in some languages is almost impossible without accompanying gestures. In any case, vocal and visual communication in advanced species is demonstrably inventive.

Language is the prime example of the saying that the whole is greater than the sum of its parts. The parts are words—vocal labels for objects, conditions, activities, ideas that are creations but not inventions as solutions to specific problems. Any word will do as a label for an object or concept as long as its use finds consensus. It is the sum of words and the rules of their combination, the grammar, that constitute the invention. The growth of population has increased the need for communication, and the growth of knowledge has increased its scope.

Language is a social invention. Most hominid and early human inventions were designed to overcome limitations of the body, to extend its powers. They were substitutes for fangs and claws, extensions of reach, and multipliers of strength. They could be solitary inventions. The social inventions, on the other hand, contributed to increased group size and improved coordination, which compensated for the physical limitations of individuals in hunting and gathering, in protection from predators. A shift from gestural to vocal information exchange increased the range as well as the content of communication.

Social inventions influence the pace and direction of technical and scientific discovery, invention, and innovation. Language facilitates innovation by permitting the spread of discoveries and inventions without the need for direct observation. Even without writing, another social invention, language greatly enhances the probability that new knowledge will be preserved for generations. It vastly increases ability to learn and to acquire, transmit, and preserve knowledge. And as language evolves, it becomes the primary thinking resource for those who share it. We do not know what thoughts humans entertained before language; much could not be communicated, therefore not preserved. Language ends this isolation; it pools the cognitive resources of all members of a communication group. It is also a revolution in education. Knowledge, wherever originated, can quickly spread.

There are advantages of scale and scope in the growth of language. The larger the group, the greater the need for a common language and the more extensive its content and range of expression. Migratory groups, such as seafaring peoples, spread their language over extensive areas and, in the process, expand and enrich their own linguistic resources. Bigger is better.

Language is abstract and complex; its mastery, never mind invention, requires a cognitive capacity beyond the reach of any animal as far as we know. The FOXP2 mutation may also contribute to the cognitive ability required; so do other genes. But language capability is independent of the ability to speak and may have preceded it. Deaf-mutes are capable of language.

Our concern is with the impact of language on human behavior and culture, which in turn has contributed to the growth of language. The vocabulary of primitive peoples still living a hunter-gatherer existence in the twentieth century is tiny compared with any modern tongue.

They are constrained by their environment and way of life, by their knowledge and experience, in what they can express and communicate. The difference between the potential of the human brain and mental achievements among primitive peoples is vast.

The ability to communicate with one's peers is the most important condition for progress. This means complex language. Until the development of writing, this meant travel—human migration from place to place. Isolated populations, animal or human, with no contact with others of their kind are inevitably backward. This is one reason chimps are more advanced than gorillas. Little is known about the time dimensions of migration of primitive man, but we suspect they have been much slower than in historical times, such as Alexander. The taming of horses and camels and the development of river and oceangoing boats, themselves inventions, accelerated the means of exchanging information at a distance.

The stress on communication should not overlook language as a great advance in cognitive ability and cognitive resources, the first cognitive revolution of the species. Words lend precision to concepts and ideas and perpetuate their meaning. Grammar accomplished the same task for relations between words. Long before writing, they enhanced memory. Language reorders the mind of its user by categorizing and classifying its subjects—sensation, ideas, cognitive processes.

Thinking is subvocal speech. If we lack a word for a new idea, it is unlikely to be defined, recalled, or transmitted. Most new knowledge is conceptual, not sensory. The realms of the imagination—stories, explanations, theories—could not be transmitted by observation. It is not just knowledge but also mental horizons: what do individuals think about, what questions come to their minds, what are the domains of their curiosity? Language—speech—has embodied and generated an unprecedented cognitive revolution, a revolution not of brain but of mind cognitively different from the prelinguistic mind.

The vocabulary and grammar of language is a cognitive resource. Language is the universal taxonomy, the first level of abstraction of objects, ideas, events, relations. It extends the boundaries of cognition. Naming an object, quality, or idea identifies, represents, and segregates.

It is also a storehouse of cognitive resources available beyond personal experience or personal memory. Words and their interconnections are the principal raw material and structural components for the ability to conceptualize, to think. Communication requires a shared classification of reality that words represent. Words are the building blocks of phrases, sentences, and paragraphs that provide structure and organization to the speaker. They are the basic level of abstraction in the search for order in the world. Speech represents a higher level of abstraction than vocabulary. Language confers a leap in cognitive ability without requiring further genetic change. It is not too much of an exaggeration to say that thinking is subvocal speech.

NEOLITHIC INDUSTRIAL REVOLUTION

Homo erectus, in two million years, took a small step forward from primate and hominid ancestors. *Homo sapiens* has been around for two hundred thousand years. During most of their existence, humans were just another animal species, high on the food pyramid due to their social cohesiveness combined with primitive weapons. They had one great advantage over most of their competitors—a very varied diet that increased their chances of survival whatever the changes in their environment. Then they experienced a burst of creativity—a Stone Age industrial revolution variously dated as starting some forty to sixty thousand years ago (Balter 2002; Gibson and Ingfold 1993, 355–62).

Humans began to make tools and the art of ivory, bone, and antler. There were major improvements in stone-working technology and resulting tools and weapons, beads, carvings, and art. The Neolithic industrial revolution included bone sewing needles and thread, fishhooks and line, bow and arrow, fire-making saws and drills, oil lamps, spear-throwers, and harpoons. What these and other inventions had in common was that they were composite—involving two or more components. Most of the tools and weapons invented by *Homo erectus* and early sapiens, such as the spear and the ax, were simple extensions or enhancements of the human arm and hand. The new inventions were much more diversified in process and purpose.

The growth of language was an essential condition for this acceleration. The accumulation of discoveries and inventions, in turn, promoted increasing complexity of communication.

Among the Neolithic Revolution inventions were the first machines: the bow and arrow and the bow drill for making fire. One converted pull by the archer on the bowstring into propulsion of the arrow by the bow. The other converted linear motion into rotary motion. Both had moving parts. They were among the first technical inventions, far surpassing in complexity and abstraction the techniques of stone chipping that preceded them. The bow and arrow were invented an estimated sixty-four thousand years ago on the basis of arrowheads found in South Africa. The invention spread throughout the world, except to Australia. The implication is that the early emigrants from Africa, who went to Australia some fifty thousand years ago, did not have bows and arrows. It was the most important human invention before agriculture, permitting hunters to kill dangerous game at a distance, including other humans. It was also a great intellectual achievement, the first machine, a very complex pair of devices. The inventors who added fins to the arrow must have had a good sense of the physics of motion. As to the inventor of the bow, was he an adept user of the spear-thrower who conceived of impetus and invented a new way to generate it?

Early inventions were simple observations of natural experiments that yielded the product directly—fractured stone, charred meat. They were little more than chance discoveries. Our ancestors, climbing or descending hills, must often have grasped and bent saplings for support and observed them swing back when released, occasionally propelling fruit or nut. From many such experiences, the idea of a flexible bowstave may have arisen. But combining it with bow strap and pebbles, later with bowstring and arrows or darts, could not be observed; it had to be imagined. The bow and arrow could not have been the by-product of chance discoveries or extensions of existing technology. Their invention required a different process—an abstract goal in mind, a concept of how to reach that goal, and a goal-directed trial and error that, in turn, generated multiple discoveries and inventions. What materials were suitable as bowstrings, woods for bows? How should the bows be shaped? But how they first learned of the relation between friction and heat leading to the fire drill is a mystery to me.

An underestimated discovery/invention was that of the thread, the line, the string, the cord, the belt—a very strong, long, and very flexible object common to many of the inventions of preagricultural *Homo*. Perhaps the first was animal gut or leather strips or vine to attach stone blades to wooden shafts or a string to stitch furs into clothing well before the invention of the bone or ivory needle, which greatly facilitated sewing of all sorts. In the Stone Age revolution, it became crucial—as the bowstring—in the bow drill. It was also essential as the fishing line connecting pole and hook and the harpoon line. Different materials were used for different purposes—animal gut, leather strips, flax, hemp, and other vegetable fibers. Another likely early use was the binding together of bamboo stems or logs to form a raft, the first watercraft, possibly with vines. That was how humans must have reached Australia.

Perhaps some inventions were interconnected. Fishing lines, harpoons, bowstrings, and fire-making bow drills shared a common need for a strong, flexible thread or cord. The knowledge gained might have led to new products and uses. The concept of the rotary drill, whether hand or bow operated, had multiple applications, including the potter's wheel and, later, perhaps the great invention of the wheel in Sumer. But such technological trajectories and transfers (with the exception of string perhaps) required a theoretical understanding of the principles involved, which was lacking until later. We do not know which inventions were independent, which were a transfer of technology from the domain where created to another domain by a very ingenious *Homo sapiens*.

There are several questions about this "industrial revolution." Much of the claim of stagnation until some sixty thousand years ago rests on the apparent fact that stone-chipping technology changed little over hundreds of thousands of years and varied little geographically. But it might have been put for new and more complex uses. Also, how can we know that the advances we have identified did not occur much earlier than those examples we have located and dated? The oldest bone needles found, dated eighteen thousand years ago, are very fine, unlikely to be the first ever made.

Another possibility is the absence of information on inventions that leave no trace. One of these is the development of language; another is the technologies employing perishable materials. At some time, they learned that wood points could be fire hardened, converting sticks into deadly weapons. By 50K BP, if not earlier, they could build boats, which were used to settle Australia. They would have invented oars, perhaps fashioned crude sails. No one knows when they learned to hollow out logs to make dugouts, followed later by lighter boats of reed and bark and animal skins. Nor can we know for sure when hunters first used bows and arrows to extend their range and increase their safety.

Evidence of an important invention long forgotten is the discovery in South Africa of stone tools seventy-five thousand years old shaped by heat treatment and pressure flaking. This technique does not reappear in the archaeological record until some sixty thousand years later (Mourre et al. 2010). Rudgley (1999, 142, 261–63) suggests dates for first achievements much earlier than other writers: Homo erectus developed language 300–350K BP, domesticated fire by 400K BP.

Humans also made extraordinary discoveries in foods and medications that we may not be able to date. But some were made by early humans or even their predecessors. Some foods are poisonous, but they learned how to detoxify them. Poisons were also collected from plants and animals, smeared on darts, and used in hunting. In the case of remedies for the prevention or treatment of various diseases, the discovery was extraordinary because the effectiveness was highly variable and only observable with significant time lag. How did our primitive ancestors come to suspect that willow bark relieved pain and lowered temperature? They had to eat willow bark. Even then, improvements were gradual, prevention not provable. There were no statisticians around, no controlled case studies, no thermometers. Medicine in primitive cultures also included diagnoses that were bizarre and treatments that were useless and often harmful, which nevertheless persisted in use. Such practices did not qualify as solutions to problems or inventions, just as fictions and fabrications.

Another possible explanation for the concentration of discovery and invention in this late period of human existence is population numbers. One reason why so little was accomplished in the first 150K years of *Homo sapiens* was that there were so few of them. The population preceding the supervolcanic explosion of Toba was estimated at three hundred thousand. Toba greatly reduced human population. Previous discoveries and inventions were lost, forgotten.

The bottleneck in human population reduced to a few thousand breeding adults (Ambrose 2001a). It was a close call. There were few potential inventors around for millennia thereafter. Then followed rapid population growth. Humans started their migration from Africa around 60K BP and soon spread all the way to Australia. So much migration suggests population pressure on food supply, but any numbers would be guesswork. Even more recent estimates cover a wide range. Settlement in a wide range of environments and climates created new needs and opportunities. More people meant not only more potential inventors but also more artifacts to be preserved and found. The timing was right; the Neolithic industrial revolution began not too long afterward.

Ultimately, what distinguishes the Stone Age industrial revolution from the earlier period of human existence is not population or even the proliferation of inventions and discoveries. More significant than specific inventions were increases in product diversity, complexity, and rate of change that merit the term "industrial" (Klein 1995). Abstract conceptualization is implicit in the conceiving of multicomponent instruments, some with moving parts. There was also evidence of accelerated technological trajectories such as ceramic beads to pottery There was diversity of solutions to a common problem such as fire making, diversity of uses of a tool, such as string.

The growth of knowledge itself has facilitated progress. The population bottleneck, which has been highly selective, may have resulted in some gain in cognitive ability. Significant discoveries and inventions require rare talent. The blossoming of invention suggests cognitive advance. So does the growth of language. Anthropologists of the future may hypothesize that *Homo* before this time had just been a predecessor, that sapiens is more recent. By this time, the communicative and cognitive revolution—that is, language—had been established. Perhaps we underestimate our remote ancestors. *Homo* had used fire for heating stones to make tools and invented clay baking, bonding, vitrification, and metallurgy by 40K BP. If these dates are correct, then some of these inventions had been forgotten and had to be reinvented.

The increase in complexity of object and tool inventions in the Neolithic Stone Age required a great deal of work, time, effort, and skill in their production. One does not make a bone needle for a single stitch and an arrow for a single hunt. Toolmakers, if not inventors, must think beyond an extended present, into a future. This is not an abstract notion of future time but a task-specific extension of need and use.

When humans, or hominids, first came to conceive of a future we do not know, such conceptions of product- or project-specific future had to be nearly universal by the time humans began to erect massive structures that took years of community effort to build. Without it, there would have been no religion, no agriculture, no civilization, no science.

ART, RELIGION, AND ABSTRACTION

So far, invention was about subsistence and security. But the Neolithic Revolution was more than industrial—tools, weapons, objects of practical use. Invention took other forms as well, art and religion prominent among them. *Homo* created the clay figurines above mentioned, beads, and other body ornaments. Cave drawings were clearly symbolic, and some were of great artistic quality. Flutes were also invented, as well as drums and rattles. These all represented a new direction for creative effort, perhaps new abilities. The arts differed from other early inventions in that they had no motivation in subsistence or survival. They were not a response to need but to novelty.

However they may have originated, they motivate discovery as well as an increasing share of inventions as a society advances beyond pressing needs. There is more to drawing than charcoal and stone walls. Cave art and ornamental objects tell us that there had been leisure at the time.

Another direction of creative effort was the invention of religion. This occurred long before it was reflected in enduring physical objects—temples, idols. We know not when. Like art, it was not a response to subsistence or security needs. The abstract ideas of creation and of causation, the desire for explanation, would arise in individual minds but could not be disseminated without a fairly advanced language.

We do not know when religion was first invented, when art was first created or appreciated. Like language, it is a gradual process. What we do know is their universality. All peoples and cultures, to our knowledge, have created and appreciated art; all have had some religion. This fact suggests that they offer some survival or evolutionary advantage. But if they do, there is no confirmed evidence of any genetic basis. Art and religion are human creations, not biological gifts. They differ from language, also a human creation, in that the ability to develop language (or speech) requires specific genetic mutations. Artistic or religious talents are not specific to their subject, nor is a sense of beauty, or faith, limited to the products of human imagination. Similarities between religions are understandable from the human condition—accident, illness, aging and death, and the mystery of the cosmos. But similarities in aesthetics are more difficult to explain. Can we speak of an aesthetic sense analogous to our physiological senses?

Art and religion—why mention them in connection with discovery and invention, science and technology? What is their relevance? They are inventions but also constitute an advance in the cognitive abilities of the species after the giant leap forward in cognitive resources and abilities, which is language. Art, religion, and science—all three demand the faculty of imagination, creativity, and abstraction in particular, without which there is little invention and less discovery. The presence of any of them implies the existence of this faculty. Hence, we look not just for toolmaking and tool use among animals and hominids but also for evidence of aesthetic imagination and religious belief. The last leaves no physical evidence until late in the rise of *Homo sapiens*; its prior existence remains a matter for speculation.

Mithen (1996, 151) does not believe that religion, art, and scientific thinking can be explained as an evolutionary response to a challenge but as a redesign of the mind. Donald (1991, 95–128) agrees since adaptive genetic changes tend to be very specific, narrow in focus, whereas religion, art, and other abstract thoughts are very general and diverse. They are inventions. The cognitive abilities involved in religion and art do not appear to have resulted from evolutionary adaptations specific to these uses.

Art. Visual arts and music do not need language, and their origin may have preceded language. But this is not true of the art of verbal expression—storytelling, oratory, literature, the products of language. Initially dominated by the ear, it has been translated into visual form—writing. Like much music and painting, it is referential, symbolic, abstract.

Early evidence of art is limited to carvings, drawings, crude musical instruments, and objects made for personal adornment. Other means of aesthetic expression leave no physical evidence. Neanderthal created art—ocher drawings, carved mammoth teeth, ornaments (Appenzeller 1998). Humans in southern Africa engraved ocher one hundred thousand years ago and also drawn with ocher (Balter 2009). The earliest example of art, or symbolic expression, known at this time consists of hatched marks scratched on stone with red ocher some seventy-seven thousand years ago in South Africa.

Crude clay figurines of obese females, if called art, are not so labeled for their aesthetic qualities. We do not know what they meant to their makers or owners. Aesthetics as a criterion for art is a much later development. Representative art (drawing, sculpture), to us, is mere representation of an object (the Statue of Liberty excepted). But to their makers, it may have had quite different meaning; it may have been endowed with power, fortune, or symbolized deity. Some early and not so early art was an integral part of religious belief and practice. The distinction between art and aesthetics should be familiar to us, considering that there are so many art movements in every genre in the twentieth century.

The cave paintings in France and Spain are considered art, even great art, by the standards of our time. The earliest of a number of magnificent cave drawings, Chauvet and Altamira, dated between thirty-two and thirty-six thousand years ago, are masterful in representation, expression, composition, even perspective. No record has been found so far bridging the gap from scratches to paintings. Their cave art already reveals most of the artistic creations known today. Apart from representation, there is exaggeration—simplification such as line outlines, stick figures of animals and humans, dots, abstract designs, and inscrutable signs. And the art is signed by the artist. Or that is a plausible interpretation of the bare hands surrounded by dark paint. Cave art drawn twenty thousand years later seems no more advanced or diverse than the earliest. What they have meant to the artists and their community we do not know.

How old is art? Mithen (1996, 162–63) believes that some of the earliest cave drawings are on a par with Renaissance masterpieces, that there is nothing gradual in evolution. Balter (1994) suggests that the human capacity for artistic expression has been there from the beginning. But it is a mistake to compare the drawings at Chauvet, the earlier red ocher hatchings, as though each were representative of humans at that time. We know nothing about the relevance of the hatchings to an assessment of the artistic or symbolic attainments of humans at the time. They should not be overinterpreted. Others believe that such quality is unlikely to have sprung full blown; there must have been earlier, perhaps much earlier, art less sophisticated than Chauvet.

My opinion is that these paintings are the product of experienced artists, not just reproduction of animals by people with photographic memories. No aurochs posed for them. Many are compositions, not copies. Their skill is the product of personal experience, not learning from previous generations. That experience could be part of the vast collection of drawings, the product of many years of work and who knows how many artists. Recent discovery of similar cave art in Spain dated at sixty thousand years must have been the work of Neanderthals.

Some humans can copy precisely what they can see—a genetic endowment, no experience needed. But it was a latent capability until some change in culture or circumstances gave it an opportunity for expression, a function. It could have been nothing more than the discovery of caves as canvas for prehistoric painters. The concentration of great cave art in a limited geographic area and the similarities among the art in different caves suggest a single common origin.

How could there have been a multimillennial tradition? The only drawing surfaces available were rock, the only drawing material universally available was charcoal, and in some places, there was ocher. Charcoal drawings exposed to the elements would not have survived a single year.

The artistic ability demonstrated in Chauvet and other cave paintings was presumably rare then; it is certainly rare today. There is little evidence of selection for artistic ability in intervening millennia. Appreciation of art—aesthetic sense—is another matter. If people value beauty, those who have beauty or those who can create beauty are valued. Aesthetics may have no evolutionary value in itself, but since it is so widespread, if not universal, among modern humans, it must be selective.

There is no agreement on the origin of art, whether it is a product of natural selection or a cultural product with evolutionary consequences (Dutton 2009, 85–102). What is the evolutionary function or value of aesthetics? A common view is that art originated as a means of attracting the opposite sex. But it assumes that the opposite sex already has had some appreciation for art. Our evidence for hominid artistry is limited to Neanderthal and *Homo sapiens*, but aesthetic sensibility may have existed among their ancestors.

The aesthetic sense can refer to symmetry and balance, to complementariness and contrast, or to coherence, unity, harmony, and dissonance—an ordered universe. Aesthetics is the search for and imposition of order. It is the predisposition for discovery.

From a cognitive perspective, most drawing and painting is representative of a two-dimensional abstraction from a three-dimensional reality; some is a further abstraction, one-dimensional, linear representation of the two-dimensional abstraction. Nonrepresentative art is abstract but not an abstraction. The meaning, the function of cave artworks, is unknown. Its diversity suggests the same range of meanings and function in civilized society.

Art is a prelinguistic method of communication; aesthetics may be an attribute. Painted editorials were not invented by Picasso. Powerful ones were painted by Rembrandt; think of *The Night Watch* and Turner's *The* Fighting Téméraire, *Tugged to Her Last Berth to Be Broken Up*. One does not ask whether they are pretty; they were visual commentary on their times. Music is nonlinguistic speech. Aesthetic art is a superior skill, but to what end? It is a quest for order but could be desire for novelty.

Dissanayake (2000, 129–40) argues that art contributes to communal bonding. The broad range of artistic expression in human cultures is better described as a social bonding experience. Much early, art is a communal project. Storytelling, dancing, and performances involving several modes of aesthetic expression (ornamental display, singing, rhythm, or music) leave no physical trace for anthropologists. We know of their early existence from their universality among the primitive peoples of whom we have historical knowledge. But these aesthetic performances have not been individual; they have been group performances for audiences. Nor could single individuals build architectural structures or accomplish the great cave art unassisted. These artistic expressions often involve close relation of art and religion. Art as social bonding is really reciprocal communication.

Artistic creativity fulfills the need for belonging, meaning, and competence. Art is not just about aesthetics; much of it is an attempt to capture the sublime, the majestic, the tragic, the whole range of human emotions. Such art is not always pretty, but more than aesthetic art, it reflects the origins of artistic expression and its close association with religion throughout history. Religion too is a social bonding invention.

Art that is neither bonding nor aesthetic search for order is best described as a search for novelty or inventiveness. In art, if not in aesthetics, there is an implication of novelty as well as skill. Many "artists" in recent times have sacrificed all pretense of aesthetics for the sake of novelty. But some art serves a cognitive rather than aesthetic function—a search for the constant, lasting, essential, or enduring features of objects, surfaces, faces, or circumstances (Zeki 1998) to acquire a deeper knowledge of them (Dissanayake 2007). The close association of art and religion is a cognitive rather than merely aesthetic relation.

Art subjects, forms, styles, and preferences are inventions, but the aesthetic sense is a cognitive ability. In the visual arts, the dimensions are simultaneous; the subject can be representational. In music, tone, tempo, stress, and patterns take time, much longer than the normal span of retention. The quality of coherence and unity becomes a hierarchy; it can be viewed in the small scene or in the large or for the entire composition. Creative people in technical and scientific fields speak of the beauty of their equations or formulas or designs. But most of us are puzzled. When painters, engineers, physicists, and writers use the same words to describe their work, to what do they refer? In any case, it is an aspect of abstract thinking.

Art is plural, one reason it defies definition. If words are representation, art is composition (poetry, play, story—abstraction at a higher level). Visual arts and music likewise are compositional, whether or not representational in their elements. Craft has purpose; art embodies meaning. When we run into utilitarian objects such as pottery carefully decorated with abstract patterns, it is no longer just a pot.

Art is an indicator of capacity for abstraction; so is the aesthetic sense. Neither is per se selective in a Darwinian sense that we can tell, but they are indicators of cognitive abilities that endow humans with the ability to survive and progress. Many forms and styles of art are inventions. Artistic creation involves inventiveness and reflects imagination. Presumably, there is some transfer of such qualities of mind to and from other kinds of inventive activities. Its purpose reveals a higher level of abstraction than mere crafts—the shaping of tools and utilitarian objects.

Religion. Religion, like language, was a great invention. Why did it become a universal aspect of human cultures, and how did it contribute to cognitive advances and the genesis of science?

Religion is a set of beliefs shared and rituals practiced by groups. Surviving religions all have explanations of the origin and nature of the universe and of the human race, theories of human behavior, and moral codes. Religion is a social invention. Belief has provided a sense of metaphysical security, a sense of order in a chaotic universe, including a sense of destination for the individual believer. Those who have shared religious beliefs and practiced the associated rituals and customs have been a community; they have derived a sense of belonging and personal identity. This is its evolutionary contribution; it provides social cohesion among believers, a sense of place through a common set of beliefs but also a shared code of conduct. There had been no alternative means for the formation of large permanent, cohesive groups; hence, it was important for survival long before the invention of agriculture. There is no way of knowing when religion first came into being and played this role. It might be described as the earliest form of nationalism.

The evolutionary role of religion relies on the assumption of natural selection between groups rather than between individuals. The cohesive group can focus its efforts toward common projects, and in warfare, it can prevail over groups whose members are less dedicated to the common interest or smaller. The existence or possibility of group selection is debated, but there is no other plausible explanation for the universality of religion or for the common elements among all religions (Wade 2009, 67–74).

Group size was an important factor in the preservation of new knowledge before the invention of language and of writing. We do not know what Neanderthal may have thought or believed, but their groups were smaller than those of sapiens.

The social function of religion was twofold: the bonding of believers into a cohesive group and promoting and enforcing a behavioral code or morality that placed the interests of society above individual self-interest, promoting altruism and willingness to sacrifice oneself for the well-being of the group (Norenzayan and Sharif 2008). Early religion was a means of cohesion and control in the hunter-gatherer stage of evolution. It demanded loyalty and generated trust (Wade 2009, 29, 39; Wilson 1997). The ethical component of religion long predated it as a condition of group living. Helping and sharing practices and norms essential for group coherence and survival were formalized into ethics and reward and retribution—if not in this life, then in an afterlife. This involved a primitive causal thinking.

With language, it has become possible to acquire knowledge far beyond the range of experience or capability for verification. But error is human, and deceit was practiced long before the hominid lineage. Whom should one believe? What should one believe? Whom should one trust? It makes sense to trust the dead—the ancestors—in preference to the living. Once a society becomes hierarchical, trust can be directed toward the living—the priest, the medicine man, the sage, the scholar, the scientist—in matters subject to their jurisdiction. These oracles, in turn, have diverse means of obtaining and verifying knowledge. Most of what any one of us thinks he knows is based on trust.

Religion is a system of shared beliefs that is characteristic of human interaction in every field of endeavor. Faith is belief in the unproven or not provable. In an uncertain world, a largely unknown world, it serves as guide to behavior when and where instinct or experience fails. Trust is at the heart of scientific endeavor as much as in religious belief. Without trust and the belief or faith it engenders, each of us is a Robinson Crusoe in the sea of knowledge.

Faith is just another word for *trust*. It is the religious equivalent of the aesthetic sense—the need and ability to believe. Faith simplifies and orders thought by constraining assumptions and conclusions. It does not dictate process; it circumvents it. It is necessary for the growth of knowledge. Faith is a trait of self-expression, self-preservation; beyond evidence or proof, it resists contrary evidence. Revelation is the way to the truth. Belief, on the other hand, can be fragile and vulnerable to every counterindication, ever on trial, subject to revision or refutation. Religion is shared faith; belief may be one's own.

The origin and core of religion is its cosmology. Surviving religions all have explanations of the origin and nature of the universe and of the human race, theories of human behavior, moral codes, reward and retribution, destination, if not concepts of an ideal society; the last is an equivalent of aesthetics.

We do not know what hominid or *Homo* has first wondered about life and death, the world around, and the sky above and imagined origins and destinations, extrahuman will, and causation. Religion may flourish for many millennia without leaving a trace. The earliest structure known so far that is considered a temple is only some eleven thousand years old. But it is so large in area and so advanced in stone sculpture that there must have been much earlier antecedents. Its size and similar but smaller structures in the region suggest a religion shared by many people over an extensive region (Curry 2008). The meaning and function of the earliest structures considered to be temples or icons or objects of veneration is unknown.

Probably the earliest component of cosmology was belief in an afterworld. In dreams, humans entered worlds outside daily experience; occasionally, they encountered people known to be dead. It was only a small step to conceive of life after death in other worlds, in human immortality. Invention of an afterlife had a factual foundation in the mind of primitive humans. Dreams were evidence. Burials with the presence of burial goods for use by the deceased are circumstantial evidence of belief in an afterlife. Ancestor worship involves the belief that the dead had influence in the real world, that it was possible to communicate with them and seek their aid. Human burial, as far back as ninety thousand years ago, suggests the prevalence of a belief in an afterlife, in particular when accompanied by grave goods. Neanderthal also buried their dead, reflecting an early belief in a reality beyond the evidence of the senses. But language seems a prerequisite for other aspects of religious cosmology. That would place the origins of formal religion just before the time frame of the Stone Age industrial revolution.

A second component was an explanation of the origin and governance of the universe—the identification of the natural forces that dominated the environment and endowed them with initiative. Agency was attributed to natural phenomena and objects such as the sun and to imaginary beings, immortals in another world. It was a crude theory of causation.

The invention of religion entails the ability to conceive of a world that could not be observed by the senses, to construct hypotheses about the behavior of natural phenomena, to reason in terms of cause and effect, to imagine and invent means of control, to change outcomes

(Culotta 2009). Their real-world equivalence is irrelevant. Religion, like science, ensures some consistency, if not uniformity, of belief. It provides a sieve to eliminate contradictory or inconsistent beliefs. It orders knowledge and seeks to order behavior.

The cosmological role of religion was the very beginning of scientific discovery. Primitive cosmologies were constructs of the imagination, an agency-ridden cosmos, a work of fiction. But pondering about cosmological issues led to the systematic study of the heavens, which played a key role in the origins of both religion and science. The motions of heavenly bodies and seasonal changes could be observed without instrumentation. Careful observation could lead to precise predictions. Humans early engaged in systematic data collection of the heavens and made discoveries about the regular cycles of the sun, moon, and planets for their religious significance as well as for their practical value. The heavens could not be manipulated; thus, predictions based on the observation of regularities were a predecessor of deductive reasoning. Early astronomy led to physics and mathematics, eventually to Copernicus and the Scientific Revolution.

It was not just astronomy. Much folk medicine had a religious origin; medicine men were also priests. Together with countermedicine—the hex, the curse, the use of poison—they were origins of biology and chemistry. Alchemy was part revelation, part experimentation.

Science and religion share motivation and objectives—understanding the nature of the universe as an end in itself or, through knowledge, a drive to control for the benefit of humanity. They seek order out of chaos, the reduction of uncertainty, the ability to predict, to foreordain.

The first hypotheses started as religious beliefs. The original interpretations of the meaning and nature of the heavenly objects, however, were not hypotheses subject to testing. Astrology was not astronomy.

Science and religion differed radically in their methods—revelation, divination, and sometimes hallucination versus evidence, logic, and the scientific method. Early religions developed techniques—rituals—for influencing or requesting the deities to act in the supplicant's behalf. Singing, music in early religions, was a means of communicating with the supernatural world. But religion was also the beginning of systematic observation, data analysis, and inference. Creatures that do not think in this manner, or about these things, are unlikely ever to generate an advanced civilization. Whether they are believers or not is immaterial.

Science's and religion's origins differed. Religions were invented or claimed to be discovered by a process of imagination, revelation, whereas the scientific process of discovery was evidence and experiment. The panoply of primitive deities and the myths of creation were products of imagination. Religion's concept of reality, of causality, was otherworldly.

Agency is at the heart of religion; process is appeal to agents via prayer or ritual. The evolution of science has been the reverse— increasing stress on process, relegation of agency to the background, and its elimination by Greek thinkers and modern science. Thus, the difference in order is that, for religion, it is a moral order—a search for meaning. Order for science is, or becomes, natural, not moral. For both, it is a concordance of causes and consequences.

Religions are a flight from chaos; so, of course, is science. It is also a quest for security, and faith provides a sense of both. Order, in turn, creates a sense of control. But religion is also a search for meaning. Is it conceivable that science, order without agency, would have come into existence without the preexistence of the agency-ridden cosmology of religion? Could some mind among primitive humans convert them into followers of the cosmos of Copernicus and Newton?

The fear of the unknown, the uncertain, has—as its subjective counterpart—the fear of suffering and death. The evolution of religion is a progressive imposition of order and control. From early animism immanent in nature has evolved a more structured pantheon of gods— of natural phenomena, of place and region, of occupations, of tribes. This pantheism, in turn became a hierarchy with a top god, who gradually eclipsed the other deities and monopolized power and deity. Inevitably, the quest for order and control leads to monotheism, and tribal faith becomes ecumenical religion; and finally, it leads to laws but no lawgiver, science. One could make a case that it is the quest for order, not language, that sets humans apart from animals. Religion is invention; science is discovery.

AGRICULTURE

Humans began to differentiate themselves from animals with construction of their own habitat. From huddling in natural shelters, caves, they advanced to construction of their own shelters, meeting places, and burial sites in places of their choosing. Through food collection and storage, they liberated themselves from daily struggle for subsistence—another advantage for survival. Then came the final separation from the natural environment—the invention of agriculture and animal husbandry. Humans created their own food, liberating themselves from most of the vagaries of the environment. One outcome was lower infant and child mortality; hence, farmers quickly outnumbered hunter-gatherers.

A fixed location also created the conditions for inventions that could not be carried on the backs of hunters and gatherers. The first of these must have been food storage. Many foods could be stored for months. Hunter-gatherers learned how to prolong the life of other foods by cooking, smoking, and perhaps salting. But stored food had to be protected from predators. Pottery served that purpose, among others. Storage promoted a sedentary lifestyle. Perhaps the Stone Age industrial revolution itself added so many tools, weapons, and accessories to group property that portability became a burden. A fixed habitat and agriculture were mutually supportive.

The lifestyle sets limits on what is possible or practical. Like animals that in captivity show capabilities not demonstrated in the wild, the sedentary humans became more versatile and creative. Sedentariness in many places preceded the adoption, if not the invention, of agriculture.

Agriculture involved long-term planning and group collaboration and specialization. Complex language was necessary, including the means of expressing the future, to engage in an activity that would yield no benefits for months and that might have required continuing effort. Agriculture required cooperation communally for territorial protection, food storage, and sharing. Sooner or later, it led to sedentary existence, territoriality, and the concept of communal property. Harvests sometimes exceeded the needs of the group or its storage capacity; sometimes they fell short, leading to barter and markets. Population growth led to the rise of cities, specialization, trade, governments, and wars. The contribution of language had been a huge advance in cognition and communication. That of agriculture was in resources and institutions.

There was acceleration of progress, however defined. The growth of population and its settlement increased the frequency of the rare combination of talent, circumstances, and survival of discoveries and inventions.

Agriculture created many new needs and opportunities. First among them was agriculture itself; many small discoveries and inventions were made—plant selection, planting, weeding, fertilizing, watering, harvesting, and crop storage. Sedentariness opened up opportunities for inventions that were not portable—shelter furniture, ovens, pathways, drainage, and irrigation. The growth of villages and the rise of towns also created new opportunities for invention.

Agriculture was first invented some twelve thousand years ago in the Middle East in Anatolia and spread to Sumer and Egypt and then independently in the Indus River valley, China, New Guinea, and several places in the Western Hemisphere (MacNeish 1991, 34). In Mexico and Central America, agriculture dates to more than nine thousand years ago. It is as old in Peru (Dillehay et al. 2007). There is no evidence of technology transfer between several regions that are believed to have developed agriculture independently. There is no prior contact between hemispheres except for migration of hunter-gatherers. Nor is it reasonable to assume such transfer between regions with different climates and conditions and, in particular, specialized in different cultivars—wheat and rye in the Middle East; diverse grains in China before the introduction of rice, corn, and beans; squash in Central America; and potatoes in the Peruvian Andes and rivers flowing to the Pacific, as well as beans and squashes, some of which may have come from Central America. In New Guinea, it was taro and bananas.

Farming practices also differed—irrigation in some regions, drainage or land building in others. Independent development of irrigation in numerous areas does not strike me as miraculous. It should be obvious to early farmers on riverbanks.

We cannot rule out the possibility that the idea of reliance on planted food crops may have spread from one locus to another in the Eastern Hemisphere—Egypt, Mesopotamia, the Indus valley, and China—through migration of ideas rather than people or practices. It is least plausible to speculate that the Americas or New Guinea owe anything to Asia. In any case, the knowledge necessary to initiate farming was probably available long before it was put to use.

In the Western Hemisphere, the most important crops were unknown elsewhere. Cultivation of some plants began soon after migration from Asia, without the long history of familiarization with local flora characteristic of the Eastern Hemisphere. Corn was developed from teosinte, a very different plant, between ten and seven thousand years ago. Thus, invention of agriculture not long after its invention in the Middle East suggested an abrupt change triggered by factors common to both hemispheres.

If it is true that the Western Hemisphere was settled by primitive hunters from Siberia 13K BP, it is amazing that people developed agriculture from new cultivars in three to four thousand years in both Central America and South America. Inventions of tools and weapons travel well, but discoveries require communication to travel at all. (There are suggestions of earlier migrations from Asia, and then the question becomes, which of them initiated farming?)

There is evidence of starts of cultivation in Syria and the Yangtze River area around thirteen thousand years ago, which were interrupted by the acute cold spell of the Younger Dryas, resumed later (Pringle 1998). Knowledge about edible plants, their annual life cycles, the conditions under which they flourished, and their uses had been accumulated long ago by peoples in many regions. Knowledge of animals improved hunting, and trapping ability eventually led to domestication of some species. Most of this is not reflected in artifacts; it must be inferred as conditions for the nearly simultaneous independent invention of farming in several areas around the globe. Cultivation was followed by plant domestication—the improvement of yields and other desirable qualities through selection. The knowledge of astronomy acquired by numerous prehistoric peoples, perhaps for religious purposes, led to the invention of the calendar, useful for knowing when to plant.

Agriculture, sedentariness, and ceramics were closely related in function and also in time. There was no single sequence; there were examples of every combination, including farming by itself in New Guinea. Many groups had moved well beyond the hand-to-mouth life of gatherers; they collected durable foods for nourishment simply because their supplies were highly seasonal. In some instances, human groups were already sedentary (Balter 1998). Some inventions important for agriculture—such as mortars and pestles, digging sticks, and stone sickles—were made well before farming. Agriculture greatly increased the need for safe storage of seeds and nuts and other edibles from the elements and from animals. Ceramics—pot making—followed no universal order. In most cases, it followed cultivation; but in some places—Japan, for instance—it came well before farming. Thus, the technology complementary with agricultural production and a shift in diet toward agricultural products were already underway in diverse locations.

Hunter-gatherer societies are profoundly conservative. Sedentary farming is a radical change in way of life. It is not surprising that much of the growth of agriculture was growth of population and territory rather than adoption and that hunter-gathering societies have persisted to the present day, even though they are aware of the benefits of other lifestyles.

A nomadic lifestyle is incompatible with accumulation of any kind. So is present orientation. These behaviors have been observed among hunter-gatherers in recent centuries and must have prevailed before agriculture (Sahlins 1972, 30–32). But some groups have stored food, and some have settled down. Their behavior has suggested a concern for the future. Whether storage has reflected or generated a sense of the future, it has been an agricultural requirement.

Hunting permitted a nomadic lifestyle. But food gathering promoted behavior and inventions that predisposed some early humans for sedentary agriculture. Grains, nuts, and tubers were easy to store. Humans must live near storage sites to protect them and to eat. Some food storage took the form of domestication of ruminants: sheep, goats, and cattle, was meat storage on the hoof, which was mobile. They could be moved in season to better pastures. They needed herding and protection from carnivores.

The wolf, perhaps first collaborating with humans in the hunt, evolved into the domesticated dog, shepherd and guardian of the flock. Its role in enabling agriculture is underappreciated. It protected crops from herbivores and other predators and alerted the humans. Cats did not need to be domesticated to do their job; it was the job that domesticated them.

Hunters had learned to share not just with each other but also with members of the group who did not participate in the hunt. The group had a sense of common property; it may have been territorial as well. It was in a position to protect the growing crop, to reap the gains, which were beyond the capacity of individuals. The egalitarianism characteristic of hunter-gatherer groups militated against surplus accumulation. The individual who accumulated a surplus was antisocial unless he/she distributed it to others. It was one thing for a group to share a meal; it was quite another for it to share a harvest.

Adoption of agriculture required an advance in cognition beyond that of Stone Age toolmaking. Like making stone tools, it required much labor in advance of any benefit by creatures who lived mainly in the here and now. But unlike tools, the delay in benefits was known. The future was definite; planning required provision for subsistence till harvest time and, after harvest, storage enough for subsistence until the next harvest. For early farmers, the future was definite; for hunter-gatherers, it was vague or nonexistent. But the early farmer's future was specific about process and product. It was not yet future orientation. The idea of individual property rights over land, or over agricultural products, did not exist. There had to be some notion of property in the ultimate harvest to justify the effort—another social invention.

The complex relation between settlement and agriculture—sometimes preceding, sometimes following—was explainable by mixed economies, gradual shifts. Settled farming was a risky enterprise requiring a much longer period of preparation and performance than hunting or gathering. It was exposed to depredation by herbivores; harvests were vulnerable to weather and disease. On both counts, one would expect humans to hedge their bets, shifting gradually. This was what happened (Balter 1998; Pringle 1998). For long periods, at first, agriculture supplemented hunting and gathering, and then hunting and gathering supplemented agriculture. In many areas, it was a seasonal division of labor. With the slash-and-burn farming in the tropics, the farm itself moved every few years. Mining, including water management structures, was by people who remained migratory. Factors influencing settlement included the nature of the crop itself— root versus seed or leaf.

A shift from hunting and gathering to agriculture requires a high tolerance for risk and uncertainty. Only high population density or a scarcity of game and natural harvests drove many to a final commitment to agriculture. This inadequacy of the old economy could result from population growth or from climate change, reducing the productivity of hunting and gathering. There is no reason to expect the identical set of incentives or compulsions in every case. It is still notable that settled agriculture arose in a number of distant locations independently at roughly the same time, historically speaking.

Why Agriculture?

The origins of agriculture raised three questions: Why was it adopted at all, considering the radical change in way of life involved and the fact that most people remained hunter-gatherers for millennia after the agricultural revolution, some of them to the present day? Why did not farming begin much earlier? Why was it initiated almost simultaneously and independently in numerous locations? Ultimately, it was a response to the inadequacy of a hunter-gatherer way of life, its uncertainty, or its failure or its limits.

There are two common explanations for the rise of agriculture: climate change and population growth. Population pressure, for whatever causes, explains why; climate explains when. But climate change had the same effect in many areas whose inhabitants did not develop agriculture. And farming was adopted in a wide range of climates.

The climate argument is twofold. The extreme variation in climate before the end of the last ice age made agriculture impossible (Burroughs 2005, 18–73). It is true that, in the higher latitudes, one could not expect agriculture earlier on a large enough scale and persisting long enough to leave incontrovertible evidence for anthropologists. But climatic variability was less in the equatorial latitudes, and the extremes were less unsuitable for farming than in temperate zones. But even in the equator, as far as we know, there was no agriculture before 10,000 BP. The climatic amelioration that was favorable to agriculture also increased the productivity of hunting and gathering and expanded the area in which humans could survive by such means. Thus, climate as a cause rather than a condition for agriculture refers to an abrupt change for the worse in the post–Ice Age or Holocene climate system. Less rain, lower temperatures, reduced the productivity of hunting and gathering, generating population pressure. But in fact, the climate change was for the better—warmer.

Agriculture arose independently in areas with quite different climates—the Middle East, New Guinea, Mexico, and Peru in Northern and Southern Hemispheres; in temperate and tropical climates; and in desert and jungle. I doubt that they all share a common explanation. Cohen (1977, 1–17) pointed out that major climatic changes had occurred repeatedly in the past with no such consequences. Why now? During the Ice Age, temperatures were never too low in many tropical areas. The absence of earlier agriculture, to our knowledge, must be attributed to the reluctance to change one's accustomed way of life.

It is not plausible to me to attribute agriculture to any common cause. Neither climate change nor population pressure is a sufficient explanation, and neither is necessary. Agriculture was initiated in many places but led nowhere. In swampy areas of highland New Guinea, it was based on taro and bananas (Denham et al. 2005; Bellwood 2005, 19, 42–45). The farmers could plant them, leave, and then return to harvest. There was no implication of permanent settlement. New Guinea, the Amazon, and many other regions did not experience population pressure. They supplemented their diet with subsistence farming but did not need to rely on it. These regions were never too cold for agriculture. Climate favorable for agriculture also increased the productivity of hunting and gathering.

The traditional response to food shortage was migration. The best-known places of origin of agriculture and the birth of civilizations were fertile river valleys. In fact, the essential geography may have been deserts; there was nowhere else but the river valley oasis for people to go and survive. But other centers of early agriculture retained the option of maintaining the traditional hunter-gatherer lifestyle.

Cohen (1977, 18–70) argues that the near-simultaneous population pressure on the environment was a result of population growth and tendencies toward equalization of population pressure on diverse environments resulting from migration, exogamy, and differential mortality. Cowgill (1970) questions the assumption of population growth. But the implication is that a decline in mortality preceded agriculture. A plausible hypothesis is that, yes, it did because sedentariness or a semisedentary lifestyle, accompanied by food storage, became widespread, especially in regions where the productivity of gathering was highly seasonal.

The key factor was not population growth as such but growth in the size of many population groups. A decline in infant and child mortality at a time of very high fertility seems to me the most plausible efficient cause of growth of population and of group size. Adoption of permanent shelter and food storage would reduce mortality. Then the question would be, why the nearly simultaneous adoption of permanent shelter and food storage? Increased group size was promoted by the growth of language and inventions from the Stone Age industrial revolution. Weapons such as the bow and arrow increased the productivity of hunting. Tools—such as sickle, digging stick, and mortar and pestle—and ceramics increased the ability to collect and store food. Animal husbandry was another form of food storage. Domestication of cattle, sheep, and goats was also a more efficient use of land than hunting for game. The advantages of a sedentary lifestyle and food storage must have been substantial for population growth and leisure. The gain in productivity from agriculture was a bonus.

One may as well ask, why was ceramics invented in numerous locations at almost the same time why in some places before agriculture? There was a demand for storage and sedentary living preceded climate change.

Permanent shelter and food storage reduces infant, child, and maternal mortality, a by-product of better nutrition. As group size in hunter gathering increases, larger territories are needed, productivity declines, and too much time is spent commuting and burden bearing. Or subsistence territory may expand until it impinges on the territory of another group and there is conflict. This sequence of events is independent of climate change.

The fundamental difference between the two methods of subsistence is productivity. Land used for hunting and gathering has very low productivity, limiting population density and group size. The same land in agriculture can produce a multiple of the hunter-gatherer food supply; it can accommodate much larger groups and population densities. It also increases employment opportunities for women and children.

It is the ability of sedentary population groups to grow that must lead to pressure on food supply. Mobile hunter-gatherers were soon greatly outnumbered by those who made the leap to settled lifestyle and food storage. The further step, adoption of agriculture, must have further reduced mortality. Farming spread largely by the growth of farming populations and their migration and settlement of new lands, a kind of agricultural imperialism.

Vast areas in Brazil, Borneo, Africa, and New Guinea are still peopled by hunter-gatherers who practice some agriculture but do not depend on it. Sahlins (1972, 44) considered the explanation that hunter-gatherers had a good life, ample food, and lots of leisure; why should they forsake it for the hard labor of agriculture? Leisure cannot explain the widespread failure to adopt agriculture millennia after it had been introduced elsewhere. The hunter-gatherer stage of social organization had much leisure, but it was unpredictable in timing and duration and limited in the uses that could be made of it. Adamant resistance to change seems a more plausible explanation than love of leisure. Perhaps the very concept of an agricultural lifestyle was too abstract for most minds. The prehistoric farmer had no more leisure, but it was more predictable in timing and duration and a much wider range of uses (Sahlins 1972, 30–32). Leisure is an element in discovery and invention, but so is lifestyle.

Agriculture and Civilization

Farming in many climates is highly seasonal. Crop yields are surpluses at harvest time. They may be larger than needed to feed the farmer till the next harvest or not large enough. Thus, farming generates unintentional food supplies and demands for food. This is the beginning of a new stage in evolution both historically and cognitively. Humans in adopting agriculture domesticated themselves. They opened opportunities and revealed abilities not evident in the wild.

Farmers or some groups learn to produce surpluses not for their own needs but for barter. This change in motivation from subsistence to exchange or sale is a profound change in culture. The individual farmer, the small group, and the village abandon isolation and self-sufficiency and adopt a new lifestyle of interdependence with many others. The farm or the group evolves from a self-contained economy from autonomy to interconnection, gaining access to products it does not produce.

If farmers have crops to barter, artisans and travelers will provide articles that farmers want. There must be a place and a time when transactions can be concluded. A stopping place for travelers becomes a marketplace. In time, craftsmen who traveled to the market with their products move to the town, which becomes a manufacturing center with a permanent market. Eventually, a new occupation develops—the trader who is neither producer nor consumer but manager of demand and supply. If traders, buyers, and sellers are to meet, there must be a common measure of time, a calendar. This was the beginning of astronomy not in the domain of religion but in that of society. The lunar cycle was discovered and probably was the original town clock combined with the daily cycle of the sun.

Another new requirement that would result in numerous discoveries and inventions was measurement—weight, volume, and many other qualities whose common denominator is number. Early humans could count; many animals can. They could add and divide. But some modern hunter-gatherers had words to count to three and, beyond that, "many." The vocabulary of language had to grow. Farmers had to know about ratios to barter. With credit, the ratio was interest; and with government, it was taxation. This is a topic for the next chapter.

There are farmers with surplus they don't want but no current need to barter for other commodities. Others with current need for food or other commodities have no assets to offer in return. They are potential lenders and borrowers. The sense of the future based on the crop cycle is adapted to lending and borrowing, credit and debt. The lender, or banker, joins the trader in town but much later.

Property among hunter-gatherers was limited to items of personal consumption and the tools for hunting and foraging. Trade required an expended concept, including the products of the farmers and artisans' labor, and the means of production, including land.

As a town grew in size and diversity, it faced problems of order and security and needs for infrastructure such as potable water, sewage disposal, road maintenance. The authority structure of hunter-gatherers did not travel; a new structure was needed: government. Its services required taxation. Records of residents and their payments must be kept. Whether in business or in government, writing had to be invented, the next great social invention after language that was also a cognitive advance, to which we shall turn in the next chapter.

Trade stimulated improvements in transport and communication. It led eventually to invention of money, a common medium of exchange. It also required a modicum of safety and trust, provided by shared behavioral, if not moral, codes and by religion or government. But the extent to which these inventions followed sedentary agriculture varied widely. All these were new demands for order. One result was occupational specialization. It was individuals who concentrated their minds on a particular line of work who were most likely to invent.

A city was more than a large number of people living and working at close quarters. It had structure and multiple functions. It was another great social invention. What we have was a sequence of social inventions, one creating the need for another, sometimes leading to civilization. Civilizations were the cultures that delivered on these needs, which were dynamic and evolving. The earliest cultivation, in Syria and Turkey, was not where the first civilizations arose. Early civilizations were located in fertile river valleys surrounded by desert. It was the concentration of population and large-scale organization that promoted technological progress as well as progress in other respects. Inventions were much more likely to be made, observed, imitated, and perpetuated under these circumstances.

HUMAN EVOLUTION: GENES, ENVIRONMENT, OR CULTURE?

How would one explain the evolution of *Homo sapiens* from a hunter-gatherer animal to a farmer and city dweller? Was it genetic change or cultural advancement? In either case, was progress autonomous, or was it dictated by the environment? Today environment and culture are almost synonymous. But before civilization, there was a question of autonomy. In the last sixty thousand years, one cannot attribute progress to environment because humans were living in many different environments through most of the world.

Our interest is in the progress of some civilizations to the Scientific Revolution and the failure of others. No one claims a genetic basis for the difference. The generic change is relevant only to the origin of language and the Neolithic industrial revolution that ensued.

Genes indicative of linguistic ability have been identified in early humans and in Neanderthal. We do not know when they first occurred, whether they may have existed in *Homo erectus*. But these changes arose and spread widely long before language (i.e., before they could have a survival or reproductive advantage).

Language was a social invention, which took a long time to create and is still in progress. It could not proceed until a significant proportion of a group had acquired the genetic capability for language. Perhaps the rapid growth of population after the bottleneck of the Toba volcanic eruption and the need to migrate accelerated the invention of speech.

The only relevance of the debate refers to the cultural-technical explosion variously dated as starting around sixty to thirty thousand years BP. What we are finding out through new brain-imaging techniques is the extent to which diverse human cognitive abilities are modularized in the brain, inheritable. Which are the products of mind, educable? Has there been some genetic mutation that empowered the cultural explosion or not? And if there was, what was it?

Genes and culture operate by different time scales. As far as historical humans are concerned, since the invention of writing, genes are a given; only culture changes. But it is not either/or. Genes influence and constrain culture, but culture, in turn, affects the process of natural selection among genes. For today and tomorrow, how important is the cultural component compared with inherited cognitive ability? Which is likely to limit future advance? It remains a political and ethical more than scientific issue. For the prehistoric evolution of hominids and humans, there is no consensus, different perspectives, sometimes conflicting opinions. I leave a brief discussion of diverse explanations of the progress of early humans to an appendix.

An intriguing finding, whose status as of this writing is no more than speculation, is a genetic change first appearing thirty to fifty thousand years ago in the dopamine receptor DRD4, linked with personality traits of novelty-seeking and attention-deficit hyperactivity disorder (Wang et al. 2004; Olson 2002). One speculates about a possible role in the Neolithic industrial revolution and later in the hyperkinetic curiosity of Phoenicians, Greeks, and much later the Portuguese—does it have a genetic base absent from our remote ancestors? Perhaps the Polynesians and the Vikings roamed the seas driven by curiosity, not by limited local resources and population pressure.

Culture influences genetic evolution in two ways. Genetic traits offering reproductive advantage depend on the prevailing culture; the hunter-gatherer culture differs from sedentary agriculture. But culture may also influence group survival and reproductive success. Groups that are closely bonded work together, protect one another, and succeed in competition with other groups.

The development of complex language is widely considered to be a, if not the, key to the acceleration of invention and discovery. Learning and using a language develops and exercises cognitive ability for which the brain has the potential but would not have been developed to the same extent in the absence of language. This first cognitive revolution is an evolution of mind but not of brain.

The difference between brain and mind is another aspect of distinguishing genetics and environment and culture. Brain function is not given at birth. The brain evolves with experience, becoming as much an environmental and cultural product as a biological given. In terms of creativity, Charles Murray (2003) provides evidence on the near monopoly of discovery and invention in recent centuries by members of the Western civilization. The brains at birth of people of other cultures are in no way inferior with regard to any ability of which we are aware, but the developmental experience is quite different, and so are the results.

In the absence of hard evidence to the contrary, I argue that nearly all the progress of the human species is attributable to culture, not genetic change, and to mind, not brain. The necessary genes, brains, were present at the beginning; everything else is a human achievement, not a chance mutation.

Mithen (1996, 64, 151) rejects explanations in terms of new forms of social organization, specialization, some major invention, or use of language, asserting instead that this explosion was the result of a redesign of the human mind. The progress from hominids to *Homo* and from early *Homo* to modern man was the development of several isolated intelligences or domains, such as technical, natural, linguistic, and finally cognitive interconnection, achieved perhaps around 60K BP. He attributes this evolution to genetic change presumably encoded in the genes of early humans in the Near East, who spread throughout the world (182), but offers no evidence that it was more than simply cultural change, that it was evolution of mind, not brain.

Rudgley (1999, 239) tells a rather different story of our ancestors, stressing continuity and suggesting much earlier dates for signal accomplishments. "To change substantially and rapidly, a culture must already have a great potential, a reserve of ideas and abilities which are known but not put into practice."

Merlin Donald (1991) sees cultural evolution as a reflection of cognitive development. Whereas the earlier stages were associated with genetic evolution, since the creation of language, cultural progress may have proceeded independent of any anatomic change. Prehominid cognition was episodic, event driven. Hominids first advanced to the mimetic cultural stage consisting in concrete, isolated events. With the invention of language, humans advanced to mythic culture involving attempts at causal explanation, prediction, and control, at integration of knowledge. With the invention of writing, humans advanced beyond myth making to theoretic culture with external symbolic storage.

Gibson (1993, 308–9) considers the relation among tools, language, and cognition in human evolution. Language and mathematics multiply new phenomena on which cognition may operate, generating new knowledge. She stresses that tools do not suggest the intellectual level of hominid and early human cognitive levels; it is how tools are used, the context within which they are made and used, the complexity of social-technical networks of which they have been a part that reflect cognitive levels. Nevertheless, as inventions of increasing complexity have been made shortly before and after the agricultural revolution, they have required greater cognitive achievement in conception if not in use, a shift from the perceptual to the conceptual (Gibson 1993, 264).

Tomasello (1999, 201–17) stresses the social intelligence of humans with both genetic and cultural foundations. Tattersall and Schwartz (2000) attribute the cultural explosion to a change in technology, from the Mousterian (stone flakes), long shared by both Neanderthal and *Homo sapiens*, to the Aurignacian (shaped core and a variety of shapes for different uses), giving *Homo sapiens* a distinct edge over Neanderthal. They speculate that language is the key invention behind the cultural explosion, which has been too sudden and spread too fast to be explained by the slow process of genetic change and its dispersion over continents. They see the advance of *Homo* and disappearance of Neanderthal as the result of cultural evolution, not genetic. After all, *Homo* has been around for more than a hundred thousand years, living much like Neanderthal. The coexistence of the two species for up to twenty thousand years in some areas suggests that *Homo* has had no genetic advantage over Neanderthal.

Nicholas Wade (1996) invokes or assumes a specific genetic change on numerous occasions, fortuitously arising whenever there is a change in the environment or other challenge or opportunity. Near the end, he devotes a couple of pages to assure us that we have some autonomy because our genetically conditioned reflexes are largely responses to society, which he has previously assured us is the product of a fortuitous genetic drift. According to Wade, although progress has been genetic change, much of it has been in response to environmental challenges.

Jared Diamond (1987) agrees without invoking genes. The Amerindians did not progress like the Eurasians because of an unpropitious environment—north-south rather than east-west orientation, lack of cattle and horses for domestication, and so on. On the other hand, Mann (2005) tells us that the Amerindians did very well, mastering the environment and changing it to their benefit. According to Diamond, Amerindians lacked autonomy; their culture was the product of their environment. According to Mann, the reverse was true; Amerindians demonstrated great enterprise and ingenuity. Culture was one aspect of environment; nature was another.

When very knowledgeable people disagree so much, what are we to make of it? Genetic change affecting an entire population is a slow process over many generations. Cultural change can take place far more rapidly, and an invention can disseminate throughout a population very quickly. Environment loses its autonomy with the rise of civilization and becomes endogenous as humans create their own environment. Most writers on the Neolithic industrial revolution do not suggest genetic change as a factor. The main exception is Richard Klein (1995).

IS THERE STRUCTURE IN TECHNOLOGICAL PROGRESS?

Early stone technology is within the ability of modern apes. The development of early tools preceded the process of encephalization resulting in big-brained *Homo*. At some point, and perhaps it was the invention of fire, hominids advanced beyond the capabilities of apes.

Early discoveries—the uses of fire and of stone fragments—were accidental. They were findings, such as "fire is hot" and "stone cuts," not explanations or understandings. Discoveries came by chance. But they led to inventions, the techniques for creating and shaping stone, which were intentional.

The early inventions were simple observations of natural experiments that yielded the product directly—sharp stone, charred meat, hardened clay. Initially, they were little more than chance discoveries. Form often was function. Further invention required a different process—a goal in mind and conceptualization of a process to attain that goal.

The earliest sequences of discovery and invention were not logically necessary but statistically predictable. *Homo erectus* used stones as hammers to break nuts and perhaps shellfish. Over millions of years, some stones would have been fractured by the pounding, producing sharp edges and points. After thousands of such accidents, a smart *Homo erectus*—or several—took notice, found the broken stones useful, and thought of fracturing stones rather than just nuts. Statistically speaking, stone technology was inevitable, although breaking nuts with stones was not. The invention of hafted tools seems inevitable. Humans had long used handheld stones and wooden clubs and poles. Putting them together was a small step in imagination.

Fire of natural origins was occasionally available, and human ancestors learned to use it for light and heat. Over two million years, meat and other edibles would have been accidentally exposed to heat of camp or forest fires many times. Inevitably, some *Homo erectus* took notice, and cooking was invented. During the same long period, wet clay exposed to the heat of burning campfires was converted into a hard, rocklike substance many times. It is surprising that, to our knowledge, no *Homo erectus* took notice or took advantage, and it was more than halfway through the history of our kind that the first fire-hardened clay figurines were made and not till some 15K BP that ceramics, pottery, was invented in a number of different locations. Statistically, it is plausible to predict the invention of cooking and ceramics. Hominid inventors had the ability to think in terms of cause and effect.

It is the frequency of identical inventions that suggests a pattern. Intentional inventions are responses to needs and opportunities. Multiple independent inventions, notably ceramics and agriculture but many others as well, raise questions. Why do they occur so often in widely separated places and cultures? What is the relative role of chance or necessity and multiple independent inventions or diffusion from a single source? There has been both. If independent, there must be some logic to the evolution of technology. The fact of rapid diffusion suggests necessity more than chance. The path of progress will be roughly the same whether discovery/invention has been made once and disseminated or made multiple times in many places independently. After the settlement of the Western Hemisphere, the case for independent discoveries and inventions is overwhelming. Earlier, there had been a possibility of diffusion. The mere fact of their near simultaneity in distant and diverse regions is a strong indication of intentionality, understanding of needs. Their frequency testifies to their inevitability.

Much invention is cumulative, each forward step leading to additional advances. There are technological trajectories. Campfires lead to blast furnaces and microwave ovens. But this is a trajectory in retrospect. In prospect, there are only possibilities, not statistical probabilities. They are not predictable. A technological trajectory is a series of inventions and improvements with a common purpose that is structured—a better arrowhead, a better plow.

In Paleolithic times, successive improvements were so far apart in time and place, sometimes by a different hominid species, that they are best regarded as sequential rather than structural. As far as we know, inventions by primates and early hominids were isolated, dead end. When adopted, the new objects or techniques were replicated with little or no modification. It was not until after the invention of language, especially late in the Neolithic industrial revolution, that more and more inventions led to modifications and improvements rather than a series of disjunctive changes. In association with increased complexity, the sequence of invention became more structured into technological trajectories.

Other inventions created a need for complementary inventions. Crops needed storage; ceramic pots protecting them from moisture and from vermin were a solution. Ceramics led to the potter's wheel and fire and promoted fire-making techniques. Wood had to be cut and split. Surpluses sometimes exceeded the needs of a family or community; they led to barter. Trade, in turn, required a medium of exchange, eventually money. It required record keeping, which in turn demanded the invention of writing. And there were cognitive advances—numbers, measures. Chance had little to do with these inventions.

There were cognitive transfers of technology to different uses. Its significance was in the cognitive process involved—abstraction from the specific use to a general function with multiple potential uses. Whatever the original use of sharp stone fragments, they were adapted to multiple uses—slice, chop, scrape, puncture. In some cases, the technology itself was adapted to new uses—heat for cooking, ceramics, eventually metallurgy. This was a series of accidental discoveries, followed by inventions. The practice and tools of burying the dead may have contributed to digging sticks for edible tubers. Think of the diverse uses and products of animals originally domesticated for meat.

Moving forward in time, inventions and discoveries were made of increasing complexity—from stone hammers and anvils for cracking nuts or bones to mortar and pestle for grinding grain, from pursuit of game to fish and animal traps, from spears to bow and arrow. In retrospect, invention followed a logical path. But looking forward would be speculation. Increasing complexity and sophistication required the prehistoric equivalents of Euclids, Archimedeses, Galileos, and Newtons. Such minds are rare and the conditions under which they can be productive rarer still. Only large populations can yield some continuity in the progress of invention and discovery.

Complexity was not just in conceptualizing the invention. Growing complexity of inventions sometimes took the form of multiple components, sometimes of greater knowledge and skills required for their production or employment. These were task-specific cognitive requirements. They must be learned.

In addition to intentionality and complexity, inventions and discoveries became less likely to be solitary achievements. Maintenance and uses of fire were cooperative activities involving division of labor and incipient specialization; sedentary agriculture involved planting, tending, harvesting, processing, storage, bartering, a family or group enterprise. The inventor, the artisan who manufactured a tool or product, and the users were less likely to be the same person. Knowledge was shared and disseminated. Lone inventions lost and forgotten became less common.

Humans began inventing objects and behaviors that were not related to survival, subsistence, or security. Art, musical instruments, and religion—if responsive to needs—referred to inner needs, subjective well-being. Discoveries and in astronomy and in mathematics also began to be made in response to curiosity, to the desire to know, whether or not they may have proved useful in daily living. Stargazing was the origin of basic research. Perhaps someday geneticists would be able to explain human interest in science.

The process of discovery underwent an evolution similar to that of invention—from simple to complex, from concrete to abstract, from particular to general. Most "discoveries" by early human were discovery as observation. But a growing share of discoveries were the result of trial and error. "This type of stone is easily split or shaped. That is not." Binary decisions became gradated. "Some materials burn better than others." Such learning contributed to the stock of knowledge of many animals. But the eureka experience—wood burns, wood floats, furs warm—was a generalization based on numerous concrete observations. These cognitive creations may be a monopoly of hominids. "Fire makes meat tender," hence the invention of cooking. "Animal furs keep one warm in winter," hence the invention of clothing.

The eureka experience is the discovery of a general principle rather than of a particular fact, not through a process of trial and error but by that of cognitive closure. We do not know exactly how cooking or fur clothing or rafting were invented, whether the discoveries on which they were based originated from a flash of insight or from repeated trial and error. The invention may have come first and the discovery later.

The product of discovery is knowledge, which did not take a tangible and durable form until the invention of writing. Earlier, there is no evidence of knowledge, only inference from behavior. How much of human preliterate or prelanguage thinking has been strictly about particulars, empiricism? How much has it extended beyond the borders of the particular to the general, the abstract? We do not know. The existence of religion and art implies that such reasoning ability has been common.

REFERENCES

Alperson-Afil, Nira. 2008. "Continual Fire-Making by Hominin at Gesher Benot Ya'aqov, Israel." *Quaternary Science Review* 27 (September): 1733–39.

Ambrose, Stanley H. 2001a. "Late Pleistocene Human Population Bottlenecks, Volcanic Winter, and Differentiation of Modern Humans." *Journal of Human Evolution* 34 (6): 623–51.

———. 2001b. "Paleolithic Technology and Human Evolution." *Science* 291 (March): 1748–53.

Appenzeller, Tim. 1998. "Art: Evolution or Revolution?" *Science* 282 (November): 1451–54.

Appenzeller, Tim, and Michael Balter. 2002. "What Made Humans Modern?" *Science* 58 (February): 1219–25.

Balter, Michael. 1998. "Why Settle Down? The Mystery of Communities." *Science* 282 (November): 1442–45.

———. 1999. "New Light on the Oldest Art." *Science* 283 (February): 920–22.

———. 2002. "What Made Humans Modern?" *Science* 295 (5558): 1219–25.

———. 2009. "Early Start for Human Art? Ochre May Revise Timeline." *Science* 323 (January): 569.

Beck, Benjamin B. 1980. *Animal Tool Behavior—The Use and Manufacture of Tools by Animals*. NY: Garland STPM Press.

Bellwood, Peter. 2005. *First Farmers—The Origins of Agricultural Societies*. Malden, MA: Blackwell Publishing Ltd.

Bickerton, Derek. 2014. *Language, Mind and Evolution*. Cambridge: Harvard University Press.

Burroughs, William J. 2005. *Climate Change in Prehistory—The End of the Reign of Chaos*, 18–73. Cambridge: Cambridge University Press.

Cohen, Mark Nathan. 1977. *The Food Crisis in Prehistory— Overpopulation and the Origins of Agriculture*, 1–17. New Haven and London: Yale University Press 1977.

Cowgill, George L. 1970. "Population Pressure as a Non-Explanation." In *Population Studies in Archaeology and Biological Anthropology: A Symposium*, edited by Alan C. Swedland, 1278–83. *American Antiquity* 40 (2).

Culotta, Elizabeth. 2009. "On the Origin of Religion." *Science* 326 (November): 734–87.

Curry, Andrew. 2008. "Seeking the Roots of Ritual." *Science* 319 (January): 278–80.

Denham, T. P., et al. 2005. "Origins of Agriculture at Kuk Swamp in the Highlands of New Guinea." *Science* 301 (5630): 189–93.

Diamond, Jared. 2005. *Collapse: How Societies Choose to Fail or Succeed.* New York: Viking.

Dillehay, Tom D., Jack Rossen, Thomas C. Andres, and David E. Williams. 2007. "Preceramic Adoption of Peanut, Squash, and Cotton in Northern Peru." *Science* 316 (June): 1890–93.

Dissanayake, Ellen. 2000. *Art and Intimacy—How the Arts Began*, 129–40. Seattle: University of Washington Press.

Donald, Merlin. 1991. *Origins of the Modern Mind—Three Stages in the Evolution of Culture and Cognition.* Cambridge: Harvard University Press.

Dutton, Denis. 2009. *The Art Instinct: Beauty, Pleasure and Human Evolution*, 85–102. New York: Bloomsbury Press.

Enard, Wolfgang, Przeworski M, Fisher SE, Lai CS, Wiebe V, Kitano T, Monaco AP, Pääbo S. 2002 "Molecular Evolution of FOXP2, a Gene Involved in Speech and Language." *Nature* 418 (6900): 868–72.

Foley, Robert. 1988. "Hominid Species and Stone Tool Assemblages." *Antiquity* 61 (233): 380–92.

Gibbons, Ann. 2002. "In Search of the First Hominids." *Science* 295 (February): 1214–19.

Gibson, Kathleen R., and Tim Ingold, eds. 1993. *Tools, Language and Cognition in Human Evolution*, 355–62. New York; Cambridge UK: Cambridge University Press.

Goren-Inbar, N., N. Alperson, M. E. Kislev, O. Simchoni, Y. Melamed, A. Ben-Nun, and E. Werker. 2004. "Evidence of Hominin Control of Fire at Gesher Benot Ya'aqov, Israel." *Science* 304: 725–27.

Goudsblom, Johan. 1992. *Fire and* Civilization, 12–41. London; New York: Allen Lane—The Penguin Press.

Harpending, H. C., S. T. Sherry, A. R. Rogers, and M. Stoneking. 1993. "Structure of Ancient Human Populations." *Current Anthropology* 34: 483–96.

Klein, Richard G. 1995. "Anatomy, Behavior, and Modern Human Origins." *Journal of World Prehistory* 9 (2): 167–98.

Krause, Johannes, Carles Lalueza-Fox, Ludovic Orlando, Wolfgang Enard, Richard E. Green, Hernán A. Burbano, Jean-Jacques Hublin, Catherine Hänni, Javier Fortea, Marco de la Rasilla, Jaume Bertranpetit, Antonio Rosas, Svante Pääbo. 2007. "The Derived FOXP2 Variant of Modern Humans Was Shared with Neanderthals." *Current Biology* 17 (21): 1908–12.

MacNeish, Richard S. 1991. *The Origins of Agriculture and Settled Life.* Norman, OK: University of Oklahoma Press.

Mann, Charles C. 2005. *1491*. New York: Alfred A. Knopf.

McEvedy, Colin, and Richard Jones. 1978. *Atlas of World Population History*, 342–51. New York: Facts on File.

Mithen, Stephen. 1996. *The Prehistory of Mind—The Cognitive Origins of Art, Religion and Science*, 355–62. London: Thames and Hudson Ltd.

Mourre, Vincent, Paola Villa, and Christopher S. Henshilwood. 2010. "Early Use of Pressure Flaking on Lithic Artifacts at Blombos Cave, South Africa." *Science* 330 (October): 659–62.

Murray, Charles. 2003. *Human Accomplishment—The Pursuit of Excellence in the Arts and Sciences, 800 BC to 1950*. New York: HarperCollins Publishers.

Norenzayan, Ara, and Azim F. Shariff. 2008. "The Origin and Evolution of Religious Prosociality." *Science* 326 (October): 58–62.

Ochoa, George, and Melinda Corey. 1995. *The Timeline Book of Science*. New York: Ballantine Books.

Olson, Steve. 2002. "Seeking the Designs of Selection." *Science* 298 (November): 1324–25.

Pringle, Heather. 1998. "The Slow Growth of Agriculture." *Science* 282 (November): 1447–50.

Rossotti, Hazel. 1993. *Fire*. Oxford, New York: Oxford University Press.

Rudgley, Richard. 1999. *The Lost Civilizations of the Stone Age*, 942, 949. New York: The Free Press.

Sahlins, Marshall. 1972. *Stone Age Economics*, 30–32. Chicago and New York: Aldine-Atherton Inc.

Seki, Semir. 1998. "Art and the Brain." *Daedalus* 127 (2): 71–103.

Tattersall, Ian, and Jeffrey H. Schwartz. 2000. *Extinct Humans*, 230–40. Boulder, Colorado: Westview Press.

Thomlinson, Ralph. 1975. *Demographic Problems, Controversy over Population Control*, 2nd ed., table I. Belmont, CA: Dickenson Publishing Co.

Tomasello, Michael, 1999. *The Cultural Origins of Human Cognition*. Cambridge: Harvard Univ. Press.

———. 2014. *A Natural History of Human Thinking*. Cambridge: Harvard University Press.

Wade, Nicholas. 1996. *Before the Dawn—Recovering the Lost History of Our Ancestors*. New York: The Penguin Press.

Wang, E., Y. C. Ding, P. Flodman, J. R. Kidd, K. K. Kidd, D. L. Grady, O. A. Ryder, M. A. Spence, J. M. Swanson, and R. K. Moyzis. 2004. "The Genetic Architecture of Selection at the Human Dopamine Receptor D4 (DRD4) Gene Locus." *American Journal of Human Genetics* 74 (5): 931–44.

Wilson, David Sloan. 1997. "Human Groups as Units of Selection." *Science* 276 (June): 816–17.

IV

The Beginning of History

FROM AGRICULTURE TO WRITING

The previous chapter dealt with more than nine-tenths of human existence on the earth, from the origins of *Homo sapiens* to the invention of agriculture. Most invention and discovery is yet to come, but the foundations are in place. It is not true that prehistoric peoples had no history. We know little about it. What we know of the earliest civilizations is incomplete and no doubt distorted by the accidental discovery of this or that archaeological remain, an accidental preservation of a particular document but not others. Much is lost because no single source survives. Recorded history may be said to begin with the invention of writing some five thousand years ago, although it was a slow, not yet completed process of converting thought and speech into visual symbols. This great social invention will broadcast achievements through space and time.

Humans lived nearly 150,000 years before the invention of language, probably by 60K BP. The Stone Age industrial revolution soon followed, lasting past the birth of agriculture 10,000 years BP. But it took only another 5,000 years from agriculture to the invention of writing and just another 5,000 to the nuclear age. There was acceleration.

Much progress in agriculture, in its early years, improved cultivars, tools, and irrigation and in ceramics textiles and civil engineering. But the truly memorable inventions were the wheel and bronze, which were the beginning of a technological revolution. Each opened up innumerable opportunities for use and further invention. The idea of rotary motion may have come from the fire drill already in use. So was the potter's wheel. The first wheel was used in 3500 BC in Sumer, although they may have been invented earlier in the Indus valley.

The metallurgical revolution started with copper. The earliest copper tools known, knives and sickles, were made shortly after the beginning of agriculture. They were easier to shape and lasted longer than stone but were no better in performance and did not replace stone. The Stone Age may be said to have ended with the invention of bronze shortly after the invention of writing. Bronze was expensive and used mainly for weapons. Metals did not begin to permeate the economy until the smelting of iron in around 1500 BC. Steel quickly followed, and a new technological revolution began.

What was extraordinary in the early development of metallurgy was the large number of chance discoveries, followed by inventions in just a few millennia. Copper ores were discovered and the process of extracting the metal from ore by heating; facilities were invented for extracting metal and molds for shaping the molten metal. Natural alloys of copper were discovered and found to be much harder, the alloying agent identified as ore of tin, and bronze was invented. Iron was obtained by chance from heating stone, the ferrous ore was identified, and the Iron Age opened up potentials for technology not available earlier. Some of these discoveries were not by chance but the likely result of deliberate search and experiment by informed people. How did they learn that particular kinds of rocks yielded particular metals if heated? Many ore deposits were then identified in many locations.

The speed with which discoveries and inventions, mainly made originally in the Middle East, spread throughout and all the way to China and India was also unprecedented. Some of this took place before the invention of writing. There may have been some multiple discoveries and inventions, but innovation and transfer of technology was the main process. What contributed to so much discovery and invention and to rapid innovation?

Perhaps the growth of population played a part. Estimated world population at the beginning of agriculture was five million, which grew to seven million in 4000 BC, doubling each of the next three millennia to fifty million (McEvedy and Jones 1978). No doubt the areas that first evolved large-scale agriculture, Sumer and Egypt, grew even faster.

But more important was a third great social invention—the city. What started as a marketplace for buyers and sellers grew into a permanent location for traders. Then it became the workplace for artisans, who made objects for sale. It was the city, surviving on trade and linked with its hinterland, that required the invention of writing.

Hunter-gatherer groups were largely self-sufficient. Farmers who advanced from subsistence agriculture to producing for barter became customers. The artisans skilled in their occupation were the inventors. The increased scale of production provided the market's need for metals and other materials. The clustering of the new occupations in cities and trade between cities improved the flow of new knowledge even before the invention of writing. Cities were places to go. A growing share of the population lived in cities, exposed to diverse experiences. Trade, as well as urban living, was a cognitive stimulus. Many more minds appear to have been prepared in this period to discover and then invent.

An achievement not usually regarded as invention was the employment of animals domesticated for other uses as draft animals. Chariots needed horses. Large amounts of fuel, clay, stone, and ore had to be brought together. Cities had to be supplied. Draft animals were not essential but contributed to the speed and scale of development.

By 3000 BCE, the vast majority of human inventions were still ahead, but the most important ones—language and writing—had been already made. They were necessary precursors of the flood that was to follow. Discoveries in the sense of learning about the structure and functioning of the material world were still predominantly in the future. Invention and discovery were unrelated for the time being (with the possible exception of metallurgy). The conditions propitious for or required for invention were already in place to a limited extent. But the conditions for discovering the secrets of nature were yet to arise.

A note about dating: Up to this point, dates have been expressed as "before the present." But during historical times, dates are usually identified as BCE and CE. The closer we come to the present, the more important the difference is between the two. To avoid confusion, I use BCE and CE in some cases.

AMNESIA

Many of the claims of ancient accomplishments of cultures and civilizations other than those that now receive credit are probably true. Probably, most discoveries and many, if not most, inventions in the distant past were forgotten and lost, then had to be rediscovered and reinvented again and again before they became part of the standard repertoire of human societies. But what matters is the discovery, the invention that is not stillborn, like Leonardo's, but that survives and has progeny.

The conditions for innovation—the spread of new knowledge and its preservation—are just as important as that for discovery and invention. Egyptian hieroglyphic and demotic scripts had been known by many over thousands of years, but no one in the world could read them in recent centuries; they had to be deciphered through the fortunate discovery of the Rosetta stone, which has the same writing in those scripts and also in Greek. A similar fate has befallen the cuneiform script of Sumer. More recently, the writings of the Mesoamerican civilizations and the strings and knots of the Incas have been forgotten. Much has been lost, and what remains is only partially deciphered.

Perhaps most astounding is the Indus civilization, whose writing has not been deciphered. Recent archaeological findings reveal it to be more extensive in area and larger in population than Mesopotamia and more advanced in some technologies, certainly in urban organization, than its contemporary. It is incredible that such a major invention as writing should be lost. The Indus valley people traded with the Ubaidians, who founded the Sumerian civilization in Mesopotamia. Perhaps they were related. But we know little about it, compared with our knowledge of the Middle East and Egypt (Lawler 2008).

Even where decipherment is not a problem, much has been lost. Writing impressed on clay tablets as in Sumer can last indefinitely if protected from erosion by wind and water. But the Phoenicians, who invented the alphabet later improved by the Greeks, wrote on perishable papyrus, and most of what they wrote is lost. Parchment is more durable, but much of what the Greeks wrote is also lost. Much writing carved in stone as in Egypt is commemorative, not representative, of the people and their culture.

We know a great deal about Chinese culture and civilization because it has persisted for millennia to the present day; so much of the past has been preserved. They wrote on wood before the invention of paper. We know a great deal about ancient Egypt, although its civilization ended at the hands of invaders more than two thousand years ago, because it lasted thousands of years because so many artifacts are in stone and others preserved by virtue of the dryness of the climate. Still, there is much ignorance, much guesswork passing as theory. We speculate on how the Egyptians built their pyramids and hollowed out granite blocks into sarcophagi and how the Incas have moved huge stones and cut them precisely.

WRITING

Language and writing were more than inventions; they were cognitive revolutions. A hundred thousand years ago, humans lived much like apes who had learned to fracture stone into useful tools and how to preserve fire. The growth of language propelled the Neolithic industrial revolution, followed by agriculture. A human centenarian today, not so rare anymore, would have lived 1 percent of the period since the rise of agriculture, 2 percent of the time since the invention of writing, over 40 percent since the start of the Industrial Revolution. What were the conditions that permitted or promoted such an incredible acceleration?

We have no reason to believe that human brains are any better than they were sixty thousand years ago. Minds are another matter.

Speech provided a sound specific to each object, feeling, and experience. In so doing, it provided identity to each word and erected boundaries between the phenomena for which words had been invented. It ordered the external world of objects, activities, and relations as well as the internal world of ideas. The linguistic mind was very different from the nonlinguistic mind, more complex as well as organized.

MEMORY

Before writing, there was memory. Spoken language is limited to the moment and the place, the only record being in the memory of speaker and listeners. Communication at a distance depended on the survival of messengers and was restricted in scope and in reliability by the limits of human memory and the tendency to color recollection with imagination. The same risks and limits hamper the verbal preservation of information over time, a process that may involve repeated retelling with some modification at each stage. Noah's flood was the Mediterranean pouring into what had been a freshwater lake some seven thousand years ago, raising its level some two hundred feet. He may have had his dog and sheep aboard his fishing boat.

With accumulation of knowledge, prehistoric peoples initially were generalists, with some division of labor between sexes. But some showed greater aptitude for this or that task and became specialists in stonework, wood carving, or preparing hides for clothing or shelter, tracking animals, or capturing prey. With the growth of knowledge, many groups developed memory specialists to preserve and pass on knowledge. The bard was the memory specialist in group history, recalling, retelling, and embellishing the past. The medicine man was the botanist, who specialized in remembering what was known about plants and their uses, to some extent also the chemist. The astronomer remembered the phases of the moon and knew the circumnavigation of the stars, the solar year, and the procession of the seasons.

Memory is fallible, and the untimely death of a repository of knowledge before training a successor could erase much of a group's cumulative knowledge. Different groups knew different things. Even with language, or rather many mutually incomprehensible languages, much knowledge was not shared widely; much false knowledge persisted. New knowledge sometimes required new words, which had to be shared and incorporated in language for preservation.

Writing converted speech into visual symbols. It did not add to order; it simply extended speech in space and time. Until little more than a century ago, speech was limited to the range of human hearing and could not be preserved at all, except through conversion into visual symbols.

Unlike speech, writing separates narrator from listener in time and space. And it endlessly multiplies the potential audience for any discovery or invention. It also reduces error resulting from transmission and repeated retelling and subjects its content to permanent scrutiny.

Writing initially had a private function, to extend and perpetuate the memory of individuals and organizations. It was invented for record keeping, unleashing the individual mind from rote memorization. Writing as visual speech became necessary as society grew in complexity and expanded in area. Initially an aide-mémoire, a private script soon became a social invention. As word symbols multiplied and came to be known by many, writing become a means of general communication, a social function. This critical social invention was made in most early cultures independently.

SCRIPTS

The original words in early writing were pictographs, which evolved into logographs—simplified and abstracted but still representative. Most words in speech are not names of physical objects; they are concepts and ideas. Symbols for such words are ideographs, imaginary references rather than abstractions that can be represented pictorially. They are adjectives, adverbs, verbs, relational terms, pronouns.

They were slow and late in entering the vocabulary of speech. Creating visual designs for such words was hard, and learning and using them was an increasing burden on memory. So writing in symbols was not a full equivalent of speech. Speech was accompanied by gestures; writing was not. The Sumerian script had some one thousand symbols, tiny by our standards, even though any of them might have had multiple meanings.

The earliest writing, logograph, had the great disadvantage; as the number of symbols increased, learning them required years of study. Few spent the time required to become literate; fewer achieved full literacy. Readers could only decipher the symbols they had learned.

Full literacy is the ability to read words one has never seen before and words that one does not know. Only phonetic scripts economize on memory and offer full literacy. The burden on individual memory may explain why it is these scripts that were forgotten and had to be rediscovered.

Most logographic scripts evolved into or were replaced by phonetic symbols—a much smaller number, quickly learned. The first were syllables, and syllabaries remain the scripts used by many languages to this day. They divorce the script from the meaning or the appearance of the word of which they are a part. Some of these, in turn evolved into alphabets. Phonetic scripts were based on the discovery that the sounds of spoken language could be replicated by a very limited number of symbols. A phonetic script is quickly learned, and reading ability is not limited by a person's vocabulary.

Phonetic writing and the alphabet in particular further advanced the organization of knowledge and, to some extent, of minds. A phonetic alphabet is a simple means of classifying knowledge for the purpose of easy storage and retrieval. There is no single simple alternative way of doing this. Without it, some knowledge is lost or difficult to retrieve from archives, libraries, books, or dictionaries. The vast majority of human knowledge is external to any one individual, some external to all. Writing and other means of preservation of knowledge are the universal memory of the species. It stores anything that can be expressed in language. The scribe replaced the specialized mnemonist. Phonetics removed limits on the vocabulary of language, the raw material for most intellectual activity.

The Greeks added vowels to the Phoenician alphabet, improving the correspondence between writing and speech and further simplifying writing and reading. Phonetic scripts reduced the need for memory. All this took place in a very short time, historically speaking, and in most of the early civilizations, underscoring the need for writing. The evolution from pictographs to a phonetic alphabet took over two millennia. Phonetic writing was invented wholesale, not piecemeal.

A critical difference between scripts is the ease with which a new word can be added to the standard vocabulary. With a phonetic script, there is no problem. But with nonphonetics devising a new word-symbol, popularizing it and learning it are all difficult. The evolution of such languages is slowed. Scripts also differ in their level of abstraction. Writing has evolved from pictographs, directly representational of objects, to the alphabet that is abstractions from speech.

COGNITION

A second cognitive revolution was the result of the invention of writing. Unlike language, writing—for most of its history—was mastered by a small minority. Even today, billions cannot write or read. Phonetic writing systems represent a second level of abstraction—visual, superimposed on the original abstraction, that is, spoken language. Writing and reading are cognitively different from speaking and listening. Writing (and speaking) is cognitively more demanding than reading (and listening) since it requires composition—choice of words, their order, and indicators of their interrelations. We can compare the cognitive processes and abilities of literate and illiterate people, even though we cannot compare language-endowed with language-deprived persons.

Literacy is more than the open door to the cumulated knowledge of mankind. It also enhances our ability to learn and to use what we know. Reading and writing represent an evolutionary leap in cognitive ability (Fondacaro and Higgins 1985). Literacy is cognitive gain in two ways.

First, it augments cognitive resources. One learns by reading much that one will not learn from personal experience or from conversation with others. Reading also increases one's vocabulary. Literate people have more words at their command—cognitive resources—than the illiterate. But this is phonetic literacy, which includes every word available in speech.

Reading and writing are more objective, precise, analytical, and logical than oral communication (Scribner 1997). Readers display larger vocabularies and greater range and complexity of expressions. There is some dispute over the extent and nature of cognitive gains associated with literacy but little doubt that they are significant (Olson 1991). Among them are the ability to generalize instead of thinking only in particulars, to use analogy, and to classify according to common abstract properties (Scholes and Willis 2001). This is ability to order. Such abilities are found with much greater frequency among literates.

Speaking and listening, as well as reading and writing, help shape the neural circuitry of the brain in childhood, but it is reading that most contributes to enhancing the capacity for abstract thought by increasing vocabulary. To a considerable extent, thinking is subvocal speech. Einstein laughed when he was told this, but try to conceive or explain $E = mc^2$ without a large vocabulary of abstract concepts and their corresponding words. Those who lack the words are cognitively impaired as well as limited in ability to learn and communicate. Writing more than reading is the exercise of abstract thought, forming words and organizing them into coherent thought—phrases, sentences, paragraphs. The punctuation, spacing, sequential organization, syntax, and grammar—which the reader takes for granted—the writer must impose on script to express meaning and to communicate to others and to oneself at some future time.

Some structural devices, such as punctuation, were introduced much later; understanding text in the early days could be detective work, solving a puzzle. When looking at the earliest civilizations, one should not expect immediate gains in cognitive resources or abilities. Very few people learned to read. Written vocabularies were quite small initially. And the knowledge available in writing that is not readily obtained by observation or conversation was limited. It would be nearly three millennia until the founding of the Library of Alexandria, five to Gutenberg (Narasimhan 1985). The ability was there, but the resources for exercising it were limited.

LANGUAGE STRUCTURE AND COGNITION

Languages of civilized societies differ not just in vocabulary but also in structure. Word order—subject, verb, object—is common, but some languages employ different word orders. The modifier-modificand order also varies. In English, it is adjective-noun. In Latin languages, it is the reverse. These differences in sequence do not seem to matter for cognition.

Languages differ markedly in the composition of their vocabulary, with implications for cognitive styles. There are two basic ways of converting a string of words into meaningful patterns: clauses and sentences. Grammarians use terms such as *analytic* and *synthetic* to differentiate between these two approaches to versatile language. The first approach, synthetic, early in the evolution of writing, was to modify the sound and spelling of a noun or verb to suggest its relation to other words in a sentence, for instance, state's rights. Verbs can be modified to state tenses as well as other relations. The Latin cases—possessive, dative, ablative, nominative, and accusative—are the best known example. But there are only five cases; each case is ambiguous, and it encompasses multiple meanings. Think of *Sierra Leone* in early Portuguese. It can mean "mountain lion" or "mountain of, with, for, or full of lions."

The analytic approach is the creation and use of words designed to specify the interrelations of nouns and verbs in a sentence—conjunctions, prepositions, and also adjectives and adverbs, which modify the noun. It is a later evolution of language. There is almost no limit to the number of words expressing relations between or characteristics of other words, whereas the number of modifications of a single word for the same purposes is quite limited. There is a large gain in precision and range of expression.

The abundance of prepositions, conjunctions, pronouns, adjectives, and adverbs facilitates in understanding the relation between a series of words and organizes them into sentences, clauses, and phrases. This is important before the adoption of punctuation to guide the reader.

Another difference between languages is the abundance of abstract nouns, such as height, color, and age in analytic languages, their rarity in synthetic languages. Many languages can convert an adjective into an abstract noun by adding a syllable or two—*hard* to *hardness, acid* to *acidity.*

The result is a difference in the cognitive process of speaking, reading, and thinking. In synthetic languages, these processes are largely word by word; the reader must surmise how successive words relate to one another, and meaning may be uncertain at the level of the clause and sentence. In analytical languages, the unit is the sentence, separate words linked by variants of each word and by prepositions and the like. These elements allow the reader to identify sentences long before punctuation existed or was standardized by Aristarchus of Alexandria two thousand years ago.

These differences have consequences for cognition even among the illiterate since they are part of the language, not just of the writing. But the languages most deficient in abstract words of all sorts are those written in nonphonetic scripts. It is very difficult to create and adopt characters for ideas lacking a visual equivalent.

Not all linguists accept the view that language shapes thinking, that a shortage of abstract words and modifiers is associated with concrete, empirical ways of thinking and with an absence of abstract thought. But language shapes communication, and that is a critical component of discovery and invention. From an evolutionary standpoint, thinking creates vocabulary and structure; from an operational standpoint, it is language that then shapes thinking. Lera Boroditsky (2011) describes cognitive differences among currently spoken languages.

Another difference that seems pertinent to discovery and invention is agency. Some languages tend to avoid agency and prefer the intransitive: "he broke the vase" versus "the vase was broken." These are quite different ways of conceiving events. Since both versions can be said in each language, the difference is not linguistic but cultural in origin.

ORIGINS OF WRITING

Writing originated first in Sumer in around 3300 BC, almost simultaneously in Egypt and the Indus valley, later in China. The scripts appear unrelated, although the idea of a visual symbol representing an important word could have been exported from Sumer through traders; the needs were shared. From the Nile to the Indus, there were contacts and trade. Probably, this was also true of Sumer and China; the Jade Road preceded the Silk Road. There is a difference: Egyptian and Chinese script reflect their origins as pictographs, but it is not so clear that Sumerian cuneiform shares that derivation. Writing by the Olmec and Maya in Mexico and Guatemala was certainly independently invented.

The purpose and role of earliest writing differed—accounting for Sumerian cuneiform invented by traders, ceremonial for Egyptian hieroglyphics, the work of government and priests. Whatever the original purpose, the record-keeping role of writing spread to all sectors of society and promoted the growth of written vocabulary, which evolved from record keeping to preservation of information and knowledge and as a means of communication alternative to speech.

Stone incisions and impressions on clay tablets suffice for record keeping and last indefinitely, but they do not travel well. Early writing surviving to this day is largely monumental—stone inscriptions on palaces, temples, and tombs. Papyrus is lightweight, portable material used for written communication. But papyrus proved highly perishable. Most of the writing of the Egyptians and others has been lost.

The growth of trade required writing as a means of inventory and as a record of transactions. Among the first written words were stylized drawings of common nouns—goods stored, exchanged, bought, and sold. Stacking clay tablets incised with the symbol for sheep or wheat was clumsy. The spoken words for some numbers already existed;

number symbols had to be invented and their scope extended. These were not pictographs but early symbols for abstractions.

The growth of government also required writing as a record of population, of supplies and their apportionment, and of taxes and expenditures. Government, like traders, needed a number system. Institutionalized religion also had need for an extrahuman memory device.

NUMBERS

A number system, like a language script, was another necessary and inevitable invention. Many animals can count. Some can add and subtract, and no doubt, so can hominids, even if they had no words. This was numbers as counting, arithmetic, a genetic endowment. Numbers were invented early in human history, perhaps before the invention of language. There were multiple notches on bones 30K BP, some perhaps much older. The egalitarian society of hunter-gatherers required sharing and partitioning. All humans had an innate sense of number, but many had words only up to three; all higher numbers were simply "many." Without the words, some primitive people today were unable to think about numbers with any precision (Gordon 2004).

With adoption of agriculture, it became necessary to develop an extended, if not open-ended, number system. The need for a generic number system did not exist until human society evolved into large-scale organization with specialization and trade, palaces and temples. A notation was needed for measures of weight, length, and volume for all the different items being traded as well as for the number of items themselves.

Numbers, at first, were object specific rather than abstract concepts as reflected in modern language—brace, pair, team, flock, flight, gaggle, herd, school, crowd. Notches on a stick or stone were unwieldy when large numbers were involved. Stamping a symbol for grain on clay tablets was a cumbersome inventory.

Proper names and symbols for each of a potentially infinite series of numbers of objects and dimensions were out of the question. So an abstract number system employing number symbols and words was needed. Number systems capable of expressing any number were invented in several cultures, perhaps in many locations. The Babylonians invented a number system, but with base 60, it was clumsy to use and difficult to learn. Systems with base 10 were developed in a number of places. Ten was such an obvious base that imitation was not implied. I don't know when Methuselah lived, but in his time, numbers greater than 800 could be counted.

The system of symbols was supplemented by spoken and written words, translated into common language. Some of the first symbols in early writing were numbers. The development of number systems was separate from that of written languages but could not proceed far without it, for a number system required script, whether its own or borrowed from the prevailing script. Eventually, a number system required both—one for speech, another for computation. Later, symbols were invented for mathematical operations and also translated into language.

The barter terms of trade advanced the concept of number, not just counting but relation. This was math; it had to be learned. Money was the critical invention that required conversion of numbers into a number system abstracted from whatever objects were being numbered. It had to be invented to advance beyond a barter economy to buying and selling, to a price system, initially with a standard of value, be it grain or silver. It allowed government to tax and spend instead of drafting labor for public works and collecting part of the harvest for resources. Money was a convenient store of value. In time, metal disks or coins acquitted a nominal value divorced from the commodity value of their material. This was a number system of value abstracted from any specific object. It promoted specialization and trade. Money created credit, saving, borrowing, lending, and investment. The payment of interest was a cognitive advance from simple numbers to ratios—the interest rate. This was a leap forward in abstraction; numbers stood alone—nouns, not adjectives.

A number system is equivalent to language in its area, a leap in cognitive capability. A number script is an advance in communication, in memory, in capacity for calculation.

Numbers, in turn, promoted advances in mathematics. But language developed long before writing, whereas the ability to verbalize any number, a number system, probably did not; system and script were coinventions. The enhanced cognitive and communicative ability was essential for the development of mathematics and nearly all future scientific and technical progress. Its comparative recency may explain why mathematical ability, unlike linguistic ability, is rare. But its domain is limited to select knowledge and communication, whereas language is all-purpose.

Devlin (2000, 10–12) describes mathematical ability as encompassing the following: number sense, numerical ability, algorithmic ability, ability for abstraction, sense of cause and effect, logical reasoning ability, and relational reasoning ability. This is number as math, a later development not of genetic origin. But it is implied in discoveries—such as lunar and solar years, which led to a calendar—and by an elaborate construction of all sorts that required precise numerical computation. Some of this preceded the invention of writing as evidenced by the masterful engineering accomplishments of preliterate peoples in Egypt, Mesopotamia, and the Americas. But such computation could not be generalized, standardized, and preserved without a number system and writing.

Devlin (2000, xv, 43) also claims that math ability and language ability are much the same. But language ability based on genetic change did result in language perhaps two-thirds through human existence on the earth. A sense of relative size, weight, and distance is also old. But the ability had to be learned. Like writing, it involves cognitive change. It is a product of mind, not brain. Recent imaging research has found that mathematicians assemble bundles of neurons to do their math.

Numbers, like writing, involve both discovery and invention. The decimal system is an invention; the Pythagorean theorem is a discovery. But mathematical discovery is about the characteristics of a human invention, the number system. Likewise, phonetic writing is a discovery about a human invention—language (or, more specifically, speech).

The number system, including numerals and signs for mathematical operations, is now universal and divorced from speech, from language, for it has no content, just pure abstraction. But applications are to specific objects or to lower-level abstractions such as weight, density, length, and curvature. The quantities represented themselves are standardized in nonlinguistic symbols—chemical formulas, dollar signs, the metric system. The Scientific and Industrial Revolutions would have been impossible without them.

THE FIRST CIVILIZATIONS

Nearly all the early civilizations—the Indus valley, Mesopotamia, and Egypt—as'well as the early cultures of Mesoamerica and the Peruvian coastal region, were hydraulic societies. Farming was the nearly universal occupation, water the key resource, and its management the principal function of government. (In China, this was a latter development.) Most of them were in river valleys or plains bordered by desert or semidesert. Population growth required intensive agricultural development through irrigation, the construction and maintenance of canals and levees, and other water management works. In parts of Mesoamerica and Mesopotamia, the environmental challenge was drainage. Hydraulic infrastructure increased the productivity of land, permitted population growth, enhanced security, and required large-scale organization. Cause and effect interacted, leading to organized society.

Wittfogel (1957) found much in common among all the early civilizations, including those in the Western Hemisphere with no possible contact across the oceans. They were cultures of tyranny and submission, their population subject to forced labor. He attributed their similarities to the need for large-scale water management. Government had to draft labor to construct and maintain canals, levees, and other structures for irrigation or drainage of agricultural land. The land itself was owned by the state. Whether dominated by palace or temple, the state ruled despotically through punishment, inspiring fear and submission. It controlled production, allocation, and distribution through a huge bureaucracy. Rulers controlled the product of land and labor and used the surpluses in monumental construction. The evidence was written in stone, notably the pyramids and the enormous tombs of the pharaohs, the terra-cotta army of the emperor Qin, and the similar, if less grandiose, tombs, palaces, and temples in the other riverine civilizations.

But Wittfogel himself finds these same characteristics in numerous societies not involved in water management or similar pursuits. They are common among all early urban societies, which require the production and distribution of social goods and services that cannot be well provided by individuals for themselves, such as transportation, defense, urban water supply and sewage disposal, and safety. What is common among the diverse despotisms is not water management but monopoly of power and central allocation of resources, including the very large-scale regular drafting of manpower and its use for public works, including palaces, temples, and royal tombs.

Before the development of private property, the state must own the resources needed or draft them. All power, all property, belongs to the ruler. None of this is surprising. In the absence of markets and private property rights, how else is a society to perform tasks essential for its subsistence or survival? Benevolent despots were rare, rational ones more common. What may seem odd today is that rulers in all these early civilizations seem afflicted with the grandiosity syndrome, exhibited in the spectacular construction unrelated to water management, transportation, or defense—the royal tombs, palaces, temples. Some of the rulers regarded themselves as gods; others claimed descent from gods. Free riding was a problem in hunter-gatherer societies; it has been magnified with civilization.

The first civilizations arose in different continents, largely independently, and some remained largely independent throughout most of their history. How do we date their beginning so that we may compare their development? We really don't have an obvious starting point—the first settlement of a given minimum size or given range of functions. Even if we have, there is no certain knowledge when this threshold has been reached by different civilizations. Perhaps it does not matter.

What I propose to use is the origin of writing—not mere notation for trading house accounting but a visual version of language. All the early civilizations invented writing, a cognitive leap in human evolution, essential for trade, taxes, and tithes. The range of uncertainty in the timing of this indicator is in centuries rather than millennia—perhaps around 3500 BC for Sumer, a few centuries later for Egypt and the Indus valley, 1500 BCE for China, and 1000 BCE for the Olmec. Only Sumer and the Olmec are indisputably original; the others may have been influenced by earlier scripts.

What discoveries and inventions are likely to be made in the early civilizations? Authority monopolizes surplus and channels discovery and invention, if it does not discourage them altogether. The lack of private ownership of land is a hindrance to invention, the lack of markets other than the state a hindrance to investment. Economic surplus flowed to the top, to palaces and kings, to weapons and war. The ruler and bureaucratic elite engaging in monumental construction and conspicuous consumption consist the main available market for invention and discovery (foreign trade aside).

One would expect progress in the arts and architecture, in weaponry, in management, in agriculture, little else. Most of the population lacked knowledge, resources, or incentives for invention or innovation. Skilled craftsmen arose to supply the wants of the wealthy. They were the ones who did most of the inventing in the interests of their work.

All early civilizations developed practical number systems for counting and measuring and the arithmetic and geometry required to deal with lengths, areas, shapes, and volumes. This involved the dissociation of an attribute from an object, an exercise in abstraction. It was a gradual process, whose development we cannot date, that preceded writing. Not surprisingly, they were all engineering cultures, concerned with the concrete, the practical. Speculation or hypothetical thinking was not their cognitive style.

These first civilizations were also characterized by a major cultural change—an extended time horizon, an orientation toward the future. The evidence is in the large construction projects undertaken that required many years to complete, whether water management or monumental, *deferred gratification* in current terminology. To some extent, this characterized the first farmers on an annual scale and some construction projects prefarming, pre-permanent-settlement. But for civilizations, it was a requirement on a grand scale. But this was a project-specific future, not the future as an abstract concept—a vessel of time without content.

Nevertheless, there are differences among the earliest civilizations in conditions, characteristics, and behavior. Focusing on these differences may shed light on differences in achievement, specifically on discovery and invention. Comparisons are possible because some old-world first civilizations appeared at about the same time. Two civilizations arising at almost the same time and in contact with each other on which we have much information are Egypt and Sumer. The third, in the Indus valley, also in contact with Sumer, is much less well known; its script has not been deciphered. Those in China and in the New World lagged not far behind. Perhaps this should not be surprising, given the fact that agriculture also began roughly at the same time in all the areas involved. The procession to the present appears well ordered.

SUMER AND MESOPOTAMIA

Little is known about the original inhabitants of Sumer, the Ubaidians. They were not the first farmers, but they were the first to develop writing and to invent the wheel, bronze, and many other objects and methods. Writing here began with traders, not state bureaucracy or priesthood. What were the characteristics of Sumerian civilization that favored such creativity?

Sumer was centered in the lower reaches of the Tigris and Euphrates Rivers, but Sumer's influence ranged far beyond this region. The delta of the Tigris and Euphrates was a flat and flood-prone plain with numerous watercourses pouring their waters into the sea. This geography may explain that its society was a number of city-states retaining autonomy even when one among them became dominant. These states were often at war with one another. Conflict had been a major spur to invention since the time of hominid hunter-gatherers to the present day.

Another feature of its geography was the lack of key resources, among them wood for construction, metallic minerals, and stone. What it had in abundance was the key resource, water and soil. Canals, dams, and levees were its key infrastructure. Clay was abundant, used as the original writing material. Fuel was tar and other oil products oozing from underground deposits. The wheel was invented in Sumer, first as the potter's wheel, but soon adapted for carriages well suited to the flat terrain—chariots for war, carts for trade, and the waterwheel for drainage and irrigation.

Sumer's resource poverty dictated that it must import and therefore produce goods for export. Cities traded with one another, but more important was their trade with regions to the north and east rich in the resources that Sumer lacked. Draft animals were bred and carts and sailboats built to carry the trade goods to market. What originally was barter trade gradually became purchase and sale with various mediums of exchange, grain and silver in particular. True markets developed.

Numbers

Extensive trade required accounting. Before there was writing, there were symbols for numbers. Thousands of years before writing, Sumer used clay tokens in ceramic containers with a symbol for the commodity inventoried. With development of writing, it became possible to combine symbols for number and for objects to be counted. The hydraulic economy and the monumental structures also required accurate measurement of length, area, volume, and angles.

Although Sumerians started using clay tokens to represent numbers eight thousand years ago, they never developed an abstract number system (Bottero 1992a, 75). Their numbers referred to specific objects. Weights and measures, likewise, were not abstract concepts but object specific. This was true in regard to common usage. However, mathematical achievements preserved in computational tables—squares, cubes, roots—suggested that some Sumerians had moved beyond numbers as adjectives modifying common nouns to numbers as nouns in their own right. It took the Babylonian successors to invent a generic abstract number system. But it used base 60, requiring a large vocabulary of number-words and symbols. The simple and, to us, obvious decimal system was invented later in several places.

Another great Sumerian invention was a medium of exchange, a precursor to money. Trade by barter was clumsy, time consuming, and limited. Buying and selling was a much more efficient process leading to greater volume. But it required a common denominator and numbering or counting. Sumer initially used seashells and barley but then adopted a silver standard. A medium of exchange did more than promote trade; it facilitated borrowing and lending, taxation, and creating a market economy. It was a step toward number as an abstract concept, the ratio of two numbers rather than a modifier of particular objects. This implied not only symbols and words but also widespread knowledge of the system. Thinking in terms of minas and shekels extended the number measurement system into a new realm, that of values and prices (Devlin 2000, 10–12).

Writing

Although the invention of writing is conventionally dated around 3300 BC, in fact, this date represents the culmination of many millennia of invention and innovation. The cuneiform script was logographic, its first language synthetic and largely monosyllabic. Sumerian script lacked verb tenses, prepositions, conjunctions, and some pronouns (Bottero 1992, 83, 96). The absence of abstraction in language carried over into thinking. Sumerian script had only some one thousand symbols. Granting that spoken language had words for which there was no symbol and that some symbols represented more than one word or meaning, it is still a minuscule repertoire compared with languages of later civilizations.

Although cuneiform characters had originated as pictographs, they became so abstracted and simplified that they became almost unrecognizable. The cuneiform script took years to master. As Sumer's realm became populated with Akkadians, some of their words were adopted by Sumerians. Signs were created to represent the sound of letters and syllables and first used for such Akkadian words. Gradually, the signals replaced some of the Sumerian characters, the cuneiform characters. Most characters were retained, although no longer needed. Syllable sounds made reading easier and also allowed reading and writing spoken words for which there was no character. Thus, written vocabulary grew larger, loser to the spoken language. Cuneiform writing, including syllables, was adopted by other languages and survived for nearly three thousand years.

Although the script was developed for business, writing was needed for state and temple administration, as well as for the extensive private trade on which the city-states depended for materials and products not locally available, as well as for revenue. Schools were established primarily to train scribes for the needs of the palace and the temple. These schools, in time, opened up to the citizenry, becoming centers of scholarship (Kramer 1959, 1–5). Textbooks were imprinted on clay tablets, and curricula diversified as did the writing on tablets. Presumably, this was one way in which inventions and discoveries were preserved and passed on.

A large number of Kramer's list of thirty-nine firsts that he attributed to Sumer are what we would call publications—a Sumerian-Akkadian dictionary, a farmer's manual, a pharmacopoeia, a medical manual, legal codes, a library index. The manuals were themselves compendia of discoveries and inventions. They reflect an interest in learning and dissemination of knowledge, for which literacy would be needed.

What we see is the beginning of the institution building required to realize the potential of writing and literacy, institutions for promotion, accumulation, and dissemination of knowledge. The benefits of literacy are limited by the availability of reading material. But the culture failed to adopt a phonetic script or to develop a generic abstract number system. These are social inventions.

Property and Power

The rulers in early civilizations had the power to appropriate the economic surplus of their realm and to use it as they pleased. The development of private property was simply the extension of these powers as rights to others and their prolongation through inheritance. Private property rights allowed extension of incentives to invest, invent, and innovate to many citizens, which were otherwise available only to the rulers. Private property was a late and limited development. Initially, supply was a bigger problem than rights. Land was the dominant resource that could be owned, and nearly all of it was public, that is, it belonged to the palace or the temple. The rulers would grant land to subjects according to their occupation, but these grants were limited in time. Essentially, land was given on long-term rent-free lease. Even when privately owned, property rights were limited. Property was subject to arbitrary confiscation and partition by inheritance (Wittfogel, 257). Even later, under Babylon, there was a limited supply of land available for purchase and sale. Nevertheless, there were large private agricultural landowners.

A monopoly of power and great concentration of productive resources, at best channel invention and limit innovation in the interests of a small elite. Few had the opportunity. Yet Sumer was inventive, the most inventive among the first civilizations. Its superior performance cannot be explained by technology transfer. Others did not have to invent because Sumer had done it for them. There were instances of long lags by others in adoption of inventions that were known, a lack of innovation.

The Sumerian city-states depended on irrigation systems to survive and on their maintenance and expansion to grow. The irrigation systems and wars required a strong central authority; tax revenues were needed to supply the armies, bureaucracies to administer tax collection and state expenditures. Their kings took pride in the material prosperity of their subjects and were constrained somewhat by councils and assemblies and by laws of their own making. This was not bottom-up authority but rather autocracy limited by the aristocracy. The fact that private property was possible; that citizens lived under a rule of law, however corrupted in practice; and that they were often engaged in wars, sometimes defending their cities from attackers, fostered a level of voluntary cooperation not found in some other hydraulic societies. There was a sense of communal identity.

Law was a great social invention. The oldest known legal code was the code of Ur-Nammu, king of the city-state of Ur, circa 2100 BCE. It reduced uncertainty in society by specifying punishment, eliminating authoritarian discretion. More importantly, it required equal treatment regardless of individual wealth, power, or position. It limited the scope of authority.

Invention

From the beginning of recorded history, it is possible to ask three questions: (1) Who were the inventors and innovators, and what was their position and role in society? (2) What were the conditions conducive to invention and innovation? (3) What were the determinants of innovation? More specifically, was the path of invention and innovation determined in the past, or was it a matter of choice or chance? Was it a response to predictable "survival" needs of society, to possibilities of scientific and technical learning, or to preferences of a society secure and free to entertain a wide range of options? Similar, if not the same, questions may be asked of discovery, the difference being that early civilizations were inventive but lacked a talent for discovery.

Who were the inventors? This was a time when the concept of private property for land and durables was still under development. It would be a very long time before conception, never mind acceptance and enforcement of private property in ideas. Only those who could make practical direct use of an invention were likely to conceive of it, and no one else might put it to use. If use of a new invention required resources, it imposed a further limitation on innovation.

Who did the inventing and how were inventions perpetuated we do not know but suspect that much of it was the work of palace and temple staffs. The schools had to be responsible for most of the evolution of writing. The leading inventions were clearly a response to the environment. The realm of Sumer was flat, treeless, and short on stone. Clay was the dominant raw material; hence, the potter's wheel and the brick mold were logical inventions. In the flat terrain, wheeled vehicles—particularly war chariots—were the superweapons of the time. Wheeled plows increased productivity of the dominant industry. Animals domesticated for other use were devoted to transportation, load bearing, and power.

Proximity to the great Tigris-Euphrates river system and to the seas and the importance of trade favored invention of sails to supplement poles and oars for propulsion. Much of the mathematical development was related to trade, taxation, and water management engineering.

At least we can judge for whom inventions were valuable. The chariot was for war, but the cart was for trade; so was the sail. Writing was mainly for the palace and the temple; so was casting of copper and bronze. Several inventions were for agriculture and irrigation. The schools for scribes were initially in the temples, but in time, writing became more versatile than the recording needs of the center, and recording was never a monopoly of palace and temple. But it was in medicine that treatises were written, that empirical reasoning and experimentation was practiced, although doctors still believed in supernatural influences (Bottero 2001, 162–82).

Enterprise

Traders were employees of the palace and temple but also bought and sold on their own account. There were public employees, bureaucrats, and self-employed entrepreneurs. But their right to own property was limited. Traders were given a temporary grant from the ruler rather than permanent ownership acquired by purchase (Wittfogel, 254–57, 263). Nevertheless, traders had some incentive to produce and invest and some access to capital for that purpose. They would have invested in sails and carts and possibly invented them.

As farm surpluses increased, there was a growth of manufacturing— craftsmen working with stone, clay, metals, and textiles. Who were the artisans who produced goods for domestic consumption and for export? The temples owned land and had workshops. Artisans, like traders, worked for the bureaucracy but, to a growing extent, worked and sold their products on their own account to consumers and to traders, a private economy.

Not all farmland was public. There were large private agricultural landowners whose wealth gained them influence. Traders, artisans, and landowners combined were a large private, potential market for new ideas, as well as a potential origin. Sumerians or their rulers seemed to accept novelty, to lack a fear of change.

Culture

The Sumerians were inquisitive. They wanted to know everything, to explain everything. What they produced were lists, descriptions, and classifications of the material world around them. But these lists were based on casual empiricism rather than analysis. They lacked general principles. The closest approximation to analytical thinking was in their medical literature that classified diseases and detailed their diagnosis, typical courses, and available treatments. But even this literature was not free of omens. The cultural climate was favorable for the advance of knowledge, but the intellectual tools were short.

Their metaphysics—explanation of natural events—relied on predicting the behavior of humanoid deities and produced an extensive literature on omens as predictors but lacked logical inference. Omens relied on analogy, empirical coincidence, casual association, and correlation rather than causation. They were intolerant of uncertainty.

Kramer (1959, 123, 262) lists among the values of Sumerian society truth, laws, order, and freedom as well as wisdom and learning. Order and freedom have a difficult relationship; besides, each has multiple meanings. Kramer also stresses rivalry and superiority as a motivation. A quest for mastery is one approach toward reducing uncertainty. Perhaps rulers were influenced by competition with their neighbors, the changing fortunes of particular city-states, or exposure through trade and war with diverse other cultures.

Sumer was the first to have a written legal code, important in reducing uncertainty about the consequences of individual conduct and the caprices of the rulers. This was an advance in freedom as well. There were assemblies of appointed notables; they had little power, but they had a voice (Kramer 1963, 289). This too was a contribution to order and reduction of uncertainty. The sociocultural climate for discovery and invention was favorable.

Sumer was overrun by the Akkadians, who founded Babylonia, and other invaders and cultures followed. But they assimilated the culture of Sumer and preserved its knowledge, including its script, in a way succeeding and improving on rather than replacing Sumer. It was not only the first civilization but also the most important among the early ones in terms of its influence on world history. It had progeny.

So far, we have noted the achievements and characteristics of Sumer that may have contributed to its inventiveness. But it was not Sumer but other cultures that advanced on Sumer's original contributions. It never developed an abstract number system, and it never went beyond its very complex cuneiform writing system to the much simpler phonetic systems, which were the visual equivalent of speech. It failed to evolve from the concrete, empirical, and specific way of thinking, from description to analysis, to develop a habit of abstraction and logical reasoning.

In sum, environment was a given. It required interregional trade. It facilitated multiple city-states but did not bar union. Trade led to the origin of writing and its wide dissemination. It also created a niche for a private economic sector. What was distinctive about Sumer was its quest for knowledge, its acceptance of change and desire for novelty. These attitudes contributed to its numerous inventions and discoveries.

EGYPT

This long-lived civilization, second only to China in duration, was driven by a passion for order, a fear of chaos. Throughout its history, the main source of chaos was the unpredictable Nile River flood, which resulted in years of plenty and years of famine. The major function of the Egyptian government was to control the flow of the Nile, to provide irrigation and prevent flooding, and to stockpile food in government granaries for distribution in times of need. In later years, when Egypt saw itself no longer as the center of the world and as the only civilization, chaos also came from without—invasions by Libyans, Hittites, Persians, and later Greeks and Romans.

This passion for order ruled out adaptation and change of any sort. It was a god-ridden society; stasis required persistence, unchanged, of rituals and their expressions in temple architecture, tombs, hieroglyphic inscriptions, and art styles (O'Rourke 2002, 116). It not only discouraged invention and discovery but it also delayed adoption by Egyptians of major inventions made elsewhere.

In later years when Egypt had lost its isolation, it turned against foreigners. Persians and Jews were particularly hated because their religions were incompatible with that of Egypt. Greeks and Romans were tolerated because they were polytheistic and saw their gods as universal, not tribal, and were inclined to believe that they had Egyptian counterparts, which even may have been imported from Egypt. Greeks first came to Egypt with respect, to learn from its long accumulation of knowledge. Then came Alexander.

The State

The pharaohs were the agents for the gods or were the incarnation of gods, hence to be obeyed without question. This combination of obedience and fear of change was not compatible with progress of invention or innovation. Neither was the monolithic character of the state through much of its history. What is striking about Egypt was the scale of its administration as the first territorial state, all other entities being little more than city-states at the time.

Administration involved statewide collection, storage, and distribution of food. It also involved the management of the immense construction projects that dominated some eras of Egyptian history— the pyramids and other monumental tombs and temples. These, more than water or food management, required a state on a large scale.

Huge workforces were involved in obtaining building materials for the pyramids, in transporting them to the sites, in stone cutting and shaping, and in erecting the pyramids, tombs, and monuments. These were efforts continuing for years, sometimes for entire reigns. The workforces had to be conscripted, transported, fed, and housed. We still don't know how some of the steps in construction were accomplished, but the organizational requirements are impressive. So was a canal dug between the Nile and the Red Sea.

Flood levels varied widely from year to year and with them agricultural production. Neither the territorial state nor the vast bureaucracy was needed for water management. It could be done regionally and locally according to Assman (1996, 73). The same can be said for the chief state function of food storage and distribution to cope with the variability of agricultural output. But low water flow would give upriver regions an advantage over downriver and cause conflict. Thus, unity avoided conflict, preserved order, and more or less equally distributed the consequences of Nilotic variability throughout the land.

The pyramids and other monument building also required more than local organization in the first two millennia of Egyptian civilization. After that, threats from other states required a national capability and response. However, Egypt became a vast territorial state before its orgy of monument building long before it faced external threats.

Egypt was not dependent on imports for basic needs. Trade with other regions was monopolized by the court and, in fact, was conducted on the pretense that it was no more than an exchange of gifts between sovereigns (Wittfogel 1957, 255). Under these conditions, there was no independent trading class. Property grants (land) were temporary, providing no incentive for long-term investment. There was no inheritance of property; grants provided current income only. In the absence of money, a medium of exchange, internal trade was no more than barter. The limitations on private property and the absence of a market were deterrents to invention, and the culture was a deterrent to innovation.

Writing and Invention

Egyptian hieroglyphs were invented shortly after Sumerian script. They retained some resemblance to the pictographs from which they had been derived, unlike cuneiform. Writing was the product of the state and remained a near monopoly of the palace and temple. Unlike Sumer, the spread of literacy was discouraged. For the rest of the population, there were scribes (Assmann 1996, 122). Egypt invented a phonetic system for writing new words for which there was no hieroglyph, mainly foreign words, but did not use it to replace the hieroglyphs. The language, verbs in particular, lacked inflection and was short on abstraction, on concepts and ideas. It was so limited in vocabulary. The number of hieroglyphs was some eight hundred until the arrival of the Greeks and Romans, when they multiplied (Loprieno 1995, 12). This made learning to read and write so difficult that the system was abandoned.

For all its longevity and accumulation of empirical knowledge, Egypt was not the leader in the critical inventions of early civilization. Like all the others, it invented a system of numerical notation, a calendar, various measuring processes, and the beginnings of mathematics (the geometry of irrigation and flood control). It is credited with the invention of paper, from papyrus, and the ox-drawn plow, little else of great significance that was not first invented elsewhere. Egypt had no waterwheel until the Persian invaders came; it was late in entering the Bronze Age and lagged in the Iron Age. Money was introduced by the Roman conquerors (O'Rourke 2002, 109). Egyptian delay in innovation was not for lack of knowledge of its neighbors and their achievements. Plato contrasted Egypt's fear of change (in his time) with the Greek passion for novelty. The prohibition of change brought innovation and development to a halt (Assmann 1996, 343–44, 356).

Over the millennia, Egypt compiled much knowledge about many things—the movements of the sun, planets, and stars; plants and animals; biology and medicine; geology and chemistry or alchemy; geography; and engineering. This empirical knowledge was preserved in temple libraries, the near monopoly of the priesthood, much of it in inaccessible hieroglyphic script. Much of it was involved in temple rituals. The Egyptian elite during the time of the pharaohs were inclined to label their hieroglyphs "top secret" and restrict their learning to a select few. Any cognitive gains from reading and writing were not shared. The Greeks who came as conquerors held the opposite view and built the great Library of Alexandria, whose manuscripts were burned later.

Akhenaton was a pharaoh born out of his time. His monotheism, with the sun as deity, was more radical than that of any of the great religions that survived to this day. It was abstract, depersonalized, and lacking any prospect of redemption—the reason Assmann (1996, 214–28) gave for its short life span and its erasure from Egyptian memory. I suspected that the threat it represented to existing holy occupations and careers was also a factor. Its cosmology was an advance in order that might have presaged modern physics, but little came of it. Egypt was not ready.

When the same myths are found in different cultures and different times, they must contain a kernel of common fact or a clue about the character of the societies where they are told. One myth, which we know as the story of Moses, occurs time and again: a baby is lost or abandoned, rescued, and brought up in a royal household and rises to great power. There is a difference: Sargon of the Euphrates carved out a great empire throughout the Middle East. But Moses was forced to flee Egypt. I suggest that what these myths have in common is the possibility that someone of humble origins can rise to the pinnacle of influence and power. Any society prizing such a tale has the prospect of individualism and meritocracy. But Egypt is different; it turned away the foundling who had risen high and forced him out, leading a rabble of outcasts and misfits, according to Egyptian versions. Egypt had already lost wars to invaders and turned inward in response.

Had Egypt remained a congeries of competing city-states as it was in its early days, there might have been no pyramids, but the prospects for diversity, innovation, and change would have been far better.

Egyptian civilization ended with Alexander's conquest in 332 BC, the Greeks who built Alexandria. Egyptian culture had no heirs. On the contrary, Egypt was Hellenized. The hieroglyphs were abandoned, and pagan religion was displaced by Christianity.

SUMER VERSUS EGYPT

Sumer and Egyptian civilization arose contemporaneously, and they were in contact early on. At its height, Sumer extended to the Mediterranean. Similar though they were, there were differences. In particular, Sumer and its successor, Babylonia, invented earlier and far more and evolved more rapidly in technology. It was the most inventive of the early civilizations. It was first in writing. It may have led others in the development of mathematics. Its successor civilizations were first to use iron and steel.

There were differences that may help account for the leadership of Mesopotamia. A similar comparison cannot be made with the Indus valley civilization, also in contact with Sumer, for lack of adequate knowledge.

A major difference was environmental. Sumer had multiple watercourses with needs for canals, drainage, and irrigation, whereas Egypt was a linear settlement along the Nile Valley. Sumer was resource poor; Egypt was self-sufficient. As a consequence, the first depended on interregional trade; the second engaged in limited barter. Sumer was surrounded by other peoples; Egypt was a nation apart. Trade promoted the use of numbers and the creation of a quasi-monetary system, which was a cognitive advance in Sumer, not in Egypt.

Another major difference was the role of the private sector. In Sumer, much of the trade was in private hands; there was private property, private investment and production, and competition between a multiplicity of states. In Egypt, the bureaucracy held a monopoly of power and allocated resources. There were no independent traders, no private traders, just some informal local barter. Most artisans were employees of the palace or temple. It is the self-employed artisan or trader who is most likely to experiment, to seek and serve different customers and markets, to discover, and to invent new products or processes. Private property in land, in capital, or in the product of one's labor offers incentive and opportunity in Sumer not available in Egypt.

City-states strung along the Nile were consolidated under a single ruler early on. Sumer was in independent city-states. The difference was consistent with topography, but one cannot say that it was inevitable. It just was. Competition and war between these city-states persisted for two millennia. War has been a great stimulant for invention throughout human existence. Local kings needed the support of their citizens; therefore, there was less despotism and more individual freedom. Autocracy was tempered with aristocracy and legal codes.

The most important invention in every one of the first civilizations was writing. In Sumer, writing was initiated by traders and quickly came into widespread use. Schools taught writing, and many publications facilitated the spread of knowledge and its preservation. In Egypt, writing was invented by the temple and palace and remained their monopoly. There were few readers, almost nothing to read.

Their linguistic development was much the same—a limited written vocabulary, a shortage of abstract words to express and communicate abstract reasoning. Hattiangadi (1987, 205–7) asserts that the proliferation of abstract nouns is a very late stage in linguistic evolution. In terms of number of characters, there was little difference. But I suspect that, in terms of meanings, Sumer forged ahead. I doubt that the Sumerian literary classics could have been adequately translated into Egyptian hieroglyphs.

Private property rights and multiple trade centers explained the role of writing, the spread of literacy, and the diversification of the uses of writing in Sumer. In Egypt, in the absence of private property rights, central collection and distribution was more important than trade. Writing remained a monopoly of the palace and temple.

These differences in environment, trade, writing, and political structure encourage or discourage discovery and invention, but neither require nor preclude. If there is a causal factor, it is the attitude toward change and novelty.

The Sumerian city-states were in constant interaction with one another and involved with other cultures. Sumerians were not the meek fellahin of Egypt but competitive individualistic peoples. Pharaonic Egypt was a closed, self-contained civilization. It came to glorify its past. Knowledge did not filter down to the people or travel from other cultures.

A quest for order probably is characteristic of all cultures. But the meaning of *order* is quite different. Order to the Sumerians was reduction of ignorance and uncertainty; it was about knowledge. It was consistent with change and novelty; it sought novelty. The search for order in Egypt had nothing to do with the pursuit of knowledge. It feared novelty and assumed that change was for the worse. Egypt remained the prisoner of its environment; Sumer advanced beyond it. Its achievements were adopted and adapted by Babylonia and other successor cultures.

WESTERN HEMISPHERE

It is safe to say that the civilizations of Central America and of Peru had no contact with the Old World and initially may have had no contact with each other. They came to an abrupt end at the hands of the Spanish but might have suffered a similar fate simply from exposure to European culture and achievements.

If they were to be compared with the old-world civilizations, it should be not the Europe of 1492 but the hydraulic cultures of antiquity. With what date, what stage of development elsewhere, should the Western Hemisphere cultures of 1492 be compared? The development of agriculture would be one possibility. As stated in chapter 3, it was found in Peru not long after it was established in the Middle East and then in Central America not much later. The crops and the methods were different from those of the other hemisphere, and there was no indication that emigrants from Asia were anything other than hunter-gatherers. But these were the dates of adoption of agriculture, not of its invention. As previously discussed, population pressure required adoption of practices already known but not employed. The complementary invention of ceramics used for crop storage was also made independently.

A second invention was the city. At the time of the "discovery," what is now Mexico City was perhaps the largest city in the world. Urbanization on a large scale meant specialization and trade over an extensive region, requiring organization and management, written records that might have told us much about the culture. When cities were first created, we do not know.

I suggest that the invention of writing is the best indicator of comparable dates. It was invented between 3300 and 300 BC in Sumer and Egypt. When was it invented by the Olmec? The earliest record is 1000 BCE or two thousand years later than those of the Middle East. There may have been writing on perishable materials even earlier. Thus, they were roughly equivalent historically to Mesopotamia and Egypt, around 500 BC, when Greece and Rome were already civilized.

The Olmec was the earliest civilization in the hemisphere, which was succeeded by the Maya. The Aztecs whom the Spaniard encountered were an empire rather than a civilization. Since Olmec script has not been deciphered, we know little about the achievements of this founder civilization. But the script tells us that there was a need for record keeping and hence some number system.

The Mayan civilization goes back to the fifth and sixth centuries BCE when its first cities appear. We do not know which achievements were its own and which were inherited. Its script goes back to 100 CE. The civilization declined abruptly in the eighth and ninth centuries. Some claim it had ended. In fact, remnants have survived especially in Yucatan, but its creative days were over. Its decline had many causes; there are disputes over their relative importance. There was climate change, environmental degradation, overpopulation, and political discontent (Pringle 2009).

In Central America, the environment was complex, extensive in area, with water storage a requirement for agricultural output in large semidesert areas, drainage in others. Its distribution of population and resources was also diverse.

The Maya advanced beyond numbers to an object-free number system, including zero. They used base 20, whereas the Incas used base 10. The Mayan concept of number was advanced, beyond counting to the relations reflected in their ability to predict eclipses. But what mathematics they invented or what uses made of it, beyond the geometry implicit in their architecture and infrastructure, we do not know.

What went on in the minds of the sages who explored the heavens and pondered on the nature of the universe, we may never know. But they did learn enough to be able to create calendars and predict eclipses. Were there cosmological discoveries as well as inventions of astronomical instruments? Mann (2003) compares Mayan priests to Greek philosophers, but that is speculation. They were inventive. There were social inventions implicit in the functioning of Mexico City and engineering inventions in large underground water reservoirs and in the complex architecture of their step pyramids and other structures. Technological inventions included rubber, looms, and intricate "paintings" in multicolored stones.

What was the character of the Mayan language that might serve as cognitive resources for discovery and invention? Most of Mayan writing carved on stone has been deciphered recently. It was a combination of hieroglyphs and consonants. It tells us a great deal about gods and kings. But little remains of the more prosaic texts written on processed tree bark, the equivalent of papyrus. Most of it was destroyed by the Spaniards in the sixteenth century.

Millions still speak Mayan languages. Languages evolve in five centuries, but it is possible to assess the spoken vocabulary, much larger than the hieroglyphic symbols, as well as the structure of the language.

In 1492, it was synthetic; nouns and verbs were modified to state characteristics and relations. But it was also endowed with adjectives and adverbs. It possessed the analytical parts of speech, conjunctions, prepositions, pronouns, abstract nouns, and analytical words.

The vocabulary gives us a clue about the linguistic resources for abstract reasoning, for logical thinking, that were available at the time. But so, by implication, do the achievements themselves. Mayan intellectual accomplishments and the sheer size and complexity of Mexico City suggest the availability of abstract nouns and relational words. How can one predict eclipses and communicate that knowledge otherwise or conceive of zero? Most astounding is the unprecedented short time lapse from the beginning of writing to its number system and astronomy and in complexity of language, although none of these achievements can be dated precisely.

The earliest cultures in South America were on the Pacific coast from Ecuador to Chile, centered in Peru. The environments of early cultures were similar to Egypt's, huddled near rivers surrounded by desert. They were small scale; no great rivers flowed to the Pacific coast of South America. The coastal cultures, in time, populated the Andes highlands and extended their influence to the Amazon basin. The elaborate pottery on the island of Marajó at the mouth of the Amazon and its name itself speak of their reach. Coast, Andes, and Amazon were three quite different environments. Later, the Andean culture—the Inca—prevailed and was the one survivor. It was unique in that water management was not a central concern of the state.

The Pacific coast cultures were gradually absorbed in the Inca empire after the twelfth century AD. What was a tribe in the mountains of Peru became a city-state in the twelfth century CE and soon began expanding its territory by military means. The Inca proper were a minority in a vast empire of many cultures, ethnicities, and languages. Some of the achievements attributed to the Incas were those of other cultures before they had been assimilated. Metallurgy was well developed early by other people.

The Inca civilization, unlike all other early civilizations, was centered in high elevations, cool and almost treeless. It was not a hydraulic society but totalitarian. Its massive drafts of labor were for urban buildings and infrastructure. Stone had to be quarried, transported, cut, and shaped. There was no script for communication. Evidence of what they were and what they accomplished is limited to structures, objects, shards, and reports of sixteenth-century Spanish priests and explorers. It was also the shortest civilization in history. One cannot really compare it with other civilizations, only some of its components. The empire lasted little more than one century.

In astronomy, they calculated a calendar combining solar and lunar cycles. In mathematics, they had a number system, base 10, but the evidence of its use is their engineering and architecture. There is implicit mastery of geometry with incredible precision of their stone shaping.

The Incas' were inventive in overcoming the limitations of their environment. Lacking wood in the Andes, they built suspension bridges with rope and, on Lake Titicaca, made boats of bundled reeds and constructed floating island farms. They constructed earthquake-proof buildings whose walls were not rectangular stones piled on one another but interlocking polygons, erected on a foundation of large pebbles acting as roller coasters in a quake.

The Chavin in Peru and other older cultures along the river valleys flowing from the Andes to the Pacific had no writing. The Inca writing system was an anomaly and a mystery.

The quipu writing system was so radically different from other systems in the Western Hemisphere, or elsewhere, that it had to be an independent development (Mann 2003). This unique way of writing was wholly abstract—cords and knots. There is no trace of a pictographic ancestry. The cords varied in length and color. Additional variables were possible by interweaving strands of different colors. The knots—which varied in type, location, and spacing—were symbols for a base 10 positional system of numbers. The system of cords pendant from a rope or stick provided other variables—horizontal and vertical order, variation in spacing, subsidiary pendant and subpendant cords providing hierarchy. Unfortunately, most quipu were destroyed, and the knowledge of the quipu makers and "readers" was lost.

Quipu were reported to record laws, songs, oral history, and religious myths, in addition to their record keeping of goods, tribute, and dates (Ascher and Ascher 1981, 12–35, 74–75, 77–79). Quipu making required prolonged formal training. The ability to record in this manner and to "read" would be the monopoly of a few. This abstract system does not seem possible as an evolution from pictographs.

Writing was a slow and complex construction project and was more appropriate for archives than for communication. Incas communicated by voice mail, runners with memorized messages. Its abstraction denotes an advanced script that, however, lacks the simplicity and utility of other advanced scripts. Its multidimensional character was a greater burden on memory than the two-dimensional cuneiform or hieroglyph. It is incredible that this script had no ancestry or that social memory should precede communication as motivation for inventing a script. It implies a terminally backward- looking, authoritarian culture.

Although the Inca script has not been deciphered, Quechua is still spoken by millions in large cities, evidence of the advanced level of civilization in the culture it once served. We have the vocabulary and structure of Quechua speech. It was highly synthetic, short on the linguistic resources for abstract reasoning and for logical thinking, which Maya had evolved.

Early in the sixteenth century, Spanish explorers reported seeing cities on the Amazon and its tributaries. But they were depopulated and disappeared. Some of those surviving may have become hunter-gatherers. With subsistence agriculture, we do not know whether these "cities" were just settlements or had urban structure and performed urban functions.

The evidence so far, early in the investigation, has found many settlements, some that must have been towns based on agriculture, fisheries, and forest management (Heckenberger et al. 2008). We do not know whether they were self-contained or interrelated. Large circular earth embankments enclosing soil improved with charcoal and broken ceramics suggest agricultural settlements in the jungle, not just on riverbanks. (Watling et al. 2017). They are found in the southwest corner of the Brazilian Amazon, on the borders of Peru and Bolivia. Several hundred have been revealed after deforestation, and satellite imaging is revealing thousands more. They are trenches with and outer earth embankments in geometric shapes (circles, squares, etc.), some with diameters of hundreds of meters, some interconnected to others. The embankments may serve multiple functions—erosion control, deterrence of foraging animals, property lines. The shapes do not follow precisely the contours of the terrain. They appear to enclose agricultural settlements. Plots of black soil had been found. Their improvement by residents long ago by burying charcoal in the soil was an invention probably driving from the discovery that wood ash from burning the forest is good fertilizer.

Near the mouth of the Amazon, the oldest ceramics in the hemisphere so far was found in an ancient site dated seven to eight thousand years ago (Roosevelt et al. 1991). Settlements and ceramics raised the possibility of a culture in the Amazon that was advanced in some respects. Its people had migrated from the cultures near the Pacific coast. But the environment of the Amazon, and its agriculture, had nothing in common with the original cultures.

Another mystery, to the south of these settlements in the Brazilian southwest Amazon, is the survival of the Guarani language. It is dominant in Paraguay, including its cities other than the capital, Asuncion. But the Guarani were hunter-gatherers with some subsistence farming and tribes, not urbanized or dependent on trade, whose vocabulary and language should not suffice for urban living today. There must have been something more to their culture if their language is functional in Paraguay's cities. In the Amazon, it is settlements, structures, and practices that suggest a lost culture; in Paraguay, it is language.

Discovery and Invention in the Americas

Hunter-gatherer immigrants who came from Beringia quickly traveled down the Pacific coast to South America and then spread inland. The environments were new, and so was the flora. They quickly created new cultivars and invented tools and farming practices appropriate for very diverse environments. How do the civilizations of the Western Hemisphere in 1492 compare with those of Eurasia in the first millennium BCE?

Ceramics was developed independently in several locations. It was both discovery and invention, closely allied with sedentary life and farming. It came early. Ceramics throughout the hemisphere, although nearly all utilitarian, assigned a greater role to decoration and ornamental distinction than old-world ceramics, a bias also found in metallurgy.

In metallurgy, the Western Hemisphere lagged the Old World. Gold and copper came first as elsewhere. In most areas, the processing of copper into ornaments and tools was limited to hammering and shaping by melting the metal found in nature. The Incas were more advanced; they smelted ores and developed various alloys, mainly those with gold. There was some bronze, but there was no Bronze Age and no iron. The uses of metals was quite different from that of the Old World. Metals and alloys were used more for ornamental and ritual than for utilitarian purposes as was the case in the early years of metallurgy elsewhere (Quilter 1998). Although there were some metal tools and utilitarian objects, the Stone Age prevailed.

What some claim was missing among the great early inventions was the wheel. This would not be entirely true. They understood circular rotary motion and employed it in a variety of ways. They had wheeled toys, fire drills, and perhaps potter's wheel devices. But they lacked draft animals. The conditions favoring chariots and carts were missing. In Central America, the terrain was a challenge for wheeled traffic. There were swampy areas and waterways but also valleys, steep hillsides, and jungle. Considerable investment and maintenance would have been required for the smooth paths needed. Pedestrian traffic was much more adaptable to the terrain. The main region suitable for wheeled transport was the Altiplano in the Andes, between eleven and thirteen thousand feet of elevation. The people had llamas that served as pack animals but were ill suited as draft animals; they were too small. The hemisphere was short on animals suitable for domestication as sources of power and transport.

In architecture and civil engineering, there were extraordinary accomplishment but little knowledge of how they were achieved or of the underlying state of understanding of physics or mathematics. What is most impressive was their ability to move and locate precisely shaped massive rocks in mountainous terrain. It could not have been done simply by massed manpower as in Egyptian pyramids. Was there an understanding of physics and the use of ropes as levers? One also wondered about the Mayan construction process of the steep step pyramids in Central America. Egyptian pyramids were big; Mayan pyramids were beautiful.

There were numerous mostly accidental discoveries of stimulants, painkillers, herbal medications, and disease diagnoses but nothing suggesting experimental methods.

The contribution of the Western Hemisphere to the global civilization was limited to the past five centuries. It was predominantly agricultural and of great importance as a source of cultivars unknown to the rest of the world and now of dominant importance—maize, potatoes, cassava, and peanuts, not to mention the addictive drugs tobacco, chocolate, and coca and fruits such as avocado, pineapple, and papaya. The very high-yield food crops made possible the dramatic increase in world population, which did not take place until the twentieth century. Its consequences influenced scientific and technological agendas for the twenty-first century.

The significance of the Western Hemisphere for this book is as evidence of the inevitability of major discoveries and inventions—agriculture, ceramics, metallurgy, the city, and other social inventions, in particular the cognitive revolution that was writing, as well as a number system and early mathematics: arithmetic and geometry. One other combination of discovery and invention appears universal—the decipherment of the movements of the heavens and the invention of a calendar. The parallels between these isolated cultures and those on the other side of the globe are striking. Unfortunately, we do not have from the Western Hemisphere civilizations the abundant records in cuneiform script engraved in clay from Sumer and the phonetic writings of successor civilizations. Much of what we have is memorial writing carved in stone.

The animal kingdom has the octopus, the intelligent clam that breaks all the rules. The Western Hemisphere had its octopus, the Inca, who built a civilization without writing. But what I find most striking about this parallel evolution is that, after two hundred millennia on the earth, *Homo sapiens* should compress the great inventions of agriculture, ceramics, metallurgy, and writing in such a brief period.

INDUS AND CHINA

The Indus valley civilization may be as old as Sumer. It was in contact with Sumer and may have been responsible for some of the inventions attributed to Sumer. They could be in contact by sea. The land between them was crisscrossed with trade routes and contained a number of cities, whose history we know little about at this time. Indus was more extensive in area than Sumer proper, probably larger in population. Like Sumer, it appeared to have consisted of multiple city-states rather than a single state and ruler. But its script had not been deciphered so that it was not possible to examine its cognitive character or achievements that did not take material form. Linguists had determined that its language was synthetic (agglutinative) but no more. It left no heirs comparable to Babylonia and Assyria to preserve and advance its achievements.

The Indian contribution to the rise of science in the West is primarily in mathematics via the Islamic civilization. We do not know whether it originated in the Indus valley civilization. India, unlike China, is plural. Much of the writing subsequent to the Indus civilization was on perishable bark. We lack the detailed record of discovery, invention, and their culture and cognitive environment available for China. At this time, it cannot be compared either with the founder civilizations or with Greece.

China was unique as a civilization, which was almost contemporaneous with those of the Middle East but survived and persisted into the twentieth century. Some technologies first appear in China in advanced form, suggesting that they were imported from elsewhere rather than developed indigenously. But China went on for millennia with an impressive record of inventions. However, it never experienced the cognitive revolution that arose in classical Greece and never had its own Scientific and Industrial Revolutions. Thus, it is appropriate to compare it not just with the early civilizations but also with Greece and then with Europe as it advanced beyond Greek achievements to the development of science and the Industrial Revolution that followed.

Why did China, with several millennia to contemplate and with a long record of technological progress, fail to duplicate Greek intellectual achievements and move beyond them to modern science? This is all the more puzzling because it was in contact with Islamic civilization and its Greek heritage and had direct exposure to European achievements since the 1500s. We defer discussion of China to chapter 6 after considering Greek achievements and the conditions that may have promoted them.

REFERENCES

Ascher, Marcia, and Robert Ascher. 1981. *Code of the Quipu—A Study in Media, Mathematics, and Culture.* Ann Arbor: University of Michigan Press.

Assmann, Jan. 1996. *The Mind of Egypt.* New York: Henry Holt and Company.

Boroditsky, Lera. 2011. "How Language Shapes Thought." *Scientific American* (February): 63–65.

Bottero, Jean. 1992. *Writing, Reasoning and the Gods.* Chicago: University of Chicago Press.

———. 2001. *Everyday Life in Ancient Mesopotamia.* Baltimore: Johns Hopkins University Press.

Deehaene, Stanislas, **Felipe Pegado, Lucia W. Braga, Paulo Ventura, Gilberto Nunes Filho, Antoinette Jobert, Ghislaine Dehaene-Lambertz, Régine Kolinsky, José Morais, Laurent Cohen**. 2010. "How Learning to Read Changes the Cortical Networks for Vision and Language." *Science* 330 (December): 1359–64.

Devlin, Keith. 2000. *The Math Gene—How Mathematical Thinking Evolved and Why Numbers Are Like Gossip.* Basic Books.

Fondacaro, R., and E. T. Higgins. 1985. "Cognitive Consequences of Communication Mode: a Social Psychological Perspective." In *Literacy, Language, and Learning—The Nature and Consequences of Reading and Writing,* edited by D. R. Olson, N. Torrance, and A. Hilyard, 75–101. Cambridge: Cambridge University Press.

Gordon, Peter. 2004. "Numerical Cognition without Words: Evidence from Amazonia." *Science* 306 (October): 496–99. See also Pica, Pierre, **Lemer C, Izard V, Dehaene S**. 2004. "Exact and

Approximate Arithmetic in an Amazonian Indigene Group." *Science* 306 (October): 499–503.

Hattiangadi, J. N. 1987. *How Is Language Possible?* La Salle, Indiana: Open Court.

Heckenberger, Micjsel J., **J. Christian Russell, Carlos Fausto, Joshua R. Toney, Morgan J. Schmidt, Edithe Pereira, Bruna Franchetto, Afukaka Kuikuro**. 2008. "Pre-Columbian Urbanism, Anthropogenic Landscapes, and the Future of the Amazon." *Science* 321 (August): 1214–17.

Kramer, Samuel Noah. 1958. *History Begins at Sumer.* Garden City, NY: Doubleday & Company, Inc.

———. 1963. *The Sumerians—Their History, Culture, and Character.* Chicago: University of Chicago Press.

Lawler, Andrew. 2001. "Writing Gets a Rewrite." *Science* 292 (June): 2418–20

Loprieno, Antonio. 1995. *Ancient Egyptian: A Linguistic Introduction.* New York: Cambridge University Press.

Mann, Charles C. 2003. "Cracking the Khipu Code." *Science* 300 (June): 1650–52.

———. 2005. *1491: New Revelations of the Americas before Columbus.* Knopf.

McEvedy, Colin, and Richard Jones. 1978. *Atlas of World Population History*, 342–51. New York: Facts on File.

Narasimhan, R. 1985. "Literacy: Its Characterization and Implications." In *Literacy, Language, and Learning*, edited by D. R. Olson, N. Torrance, and A. Hilyard, 177–97.

O'Rourke, P. J. 2002. "Letter from Egypt." *Atlantic Monthly*, September, 104–16.

Olson, D. R. 1991. "Literacy as Metalinguistic Activity." In *Literacy, Language, and Learning*, edited by D. R Olson, N. Torrance, and A. Hilyard, 251–70.

Pringle, Heather. 2009. "A New Look at the Mayas; End." *Science* 324 (April): 454–56.

Quilter, Jeffrey. 1998. "Metallic Reflections." *Science* 282 (November): 1058–59.

Roosevelt, A. C., Housley, Da Silveira, M. Imaz, Maranca, S. and R. Johnson. 1991. "Eighth Millennium Pottery from a Prehistoric Shell Midden in the Brazilian Amazon." *Science* 254 (5938): L1621–161624.

Scribner, S. D. 1997. "The Cognitive Consequences of Literacy." In *Literacy Mind and Social Practice—Selected Writings of Sylvia Scribner*, edited by E. Tobach, R. J. Falmagne, M. B. Parlee, L. M. W. Martin, and A. S. Kapelman, 165–69, 183. Cambridge, UK: Cambridge University Press. See also Scribner, S. D. 1997. "The Practice of Literacy." In *Literacy Mind and Social Practice*, edited by E. Tobach R. J. Falmagne, M. B. Parlee, L. M. W. Martin, and A. S. Kapelman, 190–205. For a more extensive discussion, see Scribner, S. D., and Michael Cole. 1981. *The Psychology of Literacy*. Cambridge: Harvard University Press.

Toynbee, Arnold J. 1947. *A Study of History*, vol. I. New York: Oxford University Press.

Watling, Jennifer, José Iriarte, Francis E. Mayle, Denise Schaan, Luiz C. R. Pessenda, Neil J. Loader, F. Alayne Street-Perrott, Ruth E. Dickau, Antonia Damasceno, and Alceu Ranzi. 2017.

"Impact of Pre-Columbian 'Geoglyph' Builders on Amazonian Forests." *Proceedings of the National Academy of Sciences* 201614359. doi:10.1073/pnas.1614359114.

Wittfogel, Karl. A. 1957. *Oriental Despotism—A Comparative Study of Total Power.* New Haven: Yale University Press.

V

Greece and the Culture of Reason

INTRODUCTION

A great mystery is the fact that all past civilizations have followed a trajectory of discovery and invention that peaked and then stagnated or declined. In some cases, the stagnation or death of a civilization can be attributed to external factors—think of the Incas. No one knows what would have happened otherwise. But in others, the stagnation cannot be explained in such terms. This mystery is particularly pertinent to China because its civilization has persisted without interruption five thousand years almost to the present day. It is a large area with a large population, sheltered by the Himalayas, the desert, and the tundra. It has an impressive record of invention. Thus, we must ask why it has experienced no intellectual flowering such as Greece's but also why it has not undergone a scientific revolution such as Europe's.

The other great question is the dominance of Europe in discovery twice in 2,500 years and in invention for the past 700. What are the conditions that promote decline? What are the special circumstances that explain European activity (and recently, that of its offshoot, the United States)?

The intellectual revolution in Greece from the sixth century BCE had no counterpart in other cultures and no sequel until more than a thousand years later in Europe. Rome is a mystery—heir to classical Greece, knowing its language, possessing its writings, taught by its scholars, yet making no contribution to its intellectual heritage. It was an engineering culture, and its intellectual elite pursued a different agenda. It left us Roman law, Latin, and a plethora of advances in urban infrastructure, aqueducts, and the Colosseum. Its passion for order was of this world, not of the universe.

Islam also had access to Greek writings and, for a time, was a culture of intellectual ferment and significant achievement, but nothing came of it as it succumbed to a culture of authority and servitude. It is a bigger mystery than Rome, for it chose to reject its legacy from Greece and regress, not advance.

The culture of discovery we call science arose in only one place, Europe, and its intellectual foundations were laid predominantly in one culture, classical Greece. The Industrial Revolution that was based on the Scientific Revolution likewise was a European achievement. It is true that one may identify individuals in other cultures who were great inventors and some who may have pursued knowledge in a scientific manner. But their cultures or civilizations stagnated all the same. There was no Aristotle or Archimedes in other cultures, no Copernicus, Galileo, or Newton. Perhaps in time, others would have replicated the Greek and European performance, but none did.

What needs to be explained is the advance, not the failure to advance, and change, not stasis or regression. Many cultures and civilizations failed to survive or did not advance for diverse reasons. It was Greece and Europe that laid the foundations for the modern world in science and other areas of human endeavor. What distinguished the culture that succeeded Greece, and its eventual successor, Europe? What did they have in common that contributed to their achievements? No one denies that other cultures made many and significant advances, but their contributions to the modern world were leveraged through Europe.

How have conditions for discovery, for scientific thinking, differed from the conditions for invention, which appears to have prevailed elsewhere, particularly in China? Do conditions for discovery and invention still differ between the West and the rest? What can such conditions tell us about the prospects for discovery and invention in the future? Another way of putting it is why discovery and invention finally became conjoined in Europe? Their interdependence has been important since Galileo and now is essential for further advance.

The period with which we are concerned is from the sixth century BCE through the second century CE, basically from Thales (636–546 BC) to Ptolemy (AD 85–165) and Galen (AD 130–210). The area is that of Greek culture, which has changed over the centuries but extended over much of the eastern Mediterranean (and briefly far to the east). The culture persisted under Roman rule and lingered on in the Byzantine Empire after the fall of Rome, but achievements tapered off.

We are not speaking of the Greek people at large; few of whom engaged in logical debate about the nature of reality. On the contrary, they worshipped a miscellany of anthropoid deities representing occupations, natural phenomena, and human traits, in whose behalf they sentenced Socrates to drink hemlock and drove Aristotle into brief exile. But there was a minority found in several Greek cities large enough to establish a subculture, to people schools and academies, and to transmit their traditions generation after generation for nearly a thousand years. What was there in the culture of the common people that produced so many philosophers and protoscientists who contributed to discovery and invention?

We cannot settle for a great man's explanation of history. That is no explanation; it is just a matter of chance. There are no great men without a supporting cast, a receptive audience, a following. It is these that must be explained.

ABSTRACTION

Inventions are typically considered to be objects—tangible, concrete—although many, including the most important, language, are not. But language, writing, and other procedural inventions are empirical, auditory, visual, and sensory. Discoveries, on the other hand—the Pythagorean theorem, the circulation of the blood, the orbit of the earth around the sun, the chemical composition of water—are not things or objects but generalizations, patterns, and concepts. They are abstractions. One does not see; one conceives. The ability to abstract, as well as its practice, is essential for discovery. They are needed for some inventions but not for many.

It is necessary to distinguish between the power of abstraction and other products of imagination. All cultures imagine a past, a future, some explanation for the order they observe in nature. Most of this qualifies as fabrication or fiction. Abstraction is a derivation from reality; imagination need have no such foundation. Thus, abstraction is ultimately testable; imagination is just an invention in the mind, a construct, a composition. By abstraction, I mean a process of derivation, the verb. Abstract is the adjective, the opposite of concrete; it can also mean the product of a process of abstraction, but I will not employ this meaning.

It is the practice of abstraction that distinguishes classical Greek culture from most others, both before and after its time. But Greek theorizing, even if more construction than abstraction, differs in another way from the imagination of other cultures—the absence of agency.

THE NATURAL WORLD

What were the achievements of Greek intellectual minority that constituted a cognitive revolution, a major advance in the progress of discovery and invention? In brief, they were objectivity in their outlook on the world, abstraction in their concept of reality, the logical techniques to search for truth and certify its attainment, and the organization of knowledge to make it accessible and useful for understanding. We know what they did and suspect how they did it but are puzzled about why they did it.

Other cultures have held an organic view of nature—spirits, gods, and agents that have ruled the waves, moved the sun and moon, and created rain, thunder, and lightning. Even today, billions of people still believe in an agency concept of nature, be it religion or Chinese feng shui. For others, the idea of agency has been deleted from the natural world but retained in the ideas of creation and salvation.

The Greek philosophers were the first to conceive of nature objectively, without recourse to agency of any sort. What is amazing and unexplained is that they accomplished this in a single bound, without the intervening steps of religion reform from primitivism to monotheism found in some other cultures.

Thales (636–546 BCE) was the earliest notable Greek philosopher. He sought the fundamental reality behind natural phenomena, abstracting basic principles from the content of experience. But he mentioned souls and gods. Since most of his writing was lost, we are not sure what role religion retained in his cosmos. Anaximander (611–547 BCE) perhaps was the first to assert purely natural explanations of physical processes (Schlagel 1984, 67–78).

Other cultures evolved slowly, from disorderly polytheism to a universal deity and lesser deities with limited jurisdiction—tribal, city, nature deities (rain gods, grain gods)—until only one universal God remained. That was as far as they got until the Scientific Revolution in Europe. To my knowledge, the only effort to move directly from primitive religion to monotheism, a smaller leap, was Akhenaton in Egypt. He failed; he was ahead of his time. Egypt was not ready. There were interests vested in the old worldview.

By contrast, the Greek priesthood of the multiple deities—which much of the population worshipped—did not rise against the philosophers. There were occasional charges of impiety. Yet they were highly respected members of society who came from the upper classes. Most of the time, they were secure. Were the people unaware that the Greek philosophers were rejecting all their beliefs? Perhaps, but the people were tolerant of diversity; Athens was a democracy.

COSMOLOGY

The nature that Greek philosophers and protoscientists conceived was quite different from the nature they perceived. They rejected the evidence of the senses as a reflection of ultimate reality. Nature was abstract. The universe, space, time, matter, and number were conceived apart from any reference to objects or circumstances (Schlagel 1984,

91–103). Not all Greek thinkers were of one mind on abstraction. The skeptics accepted sensory evidence for lack of a demonstrable alternative. Nor did Epicurus accept the Aristotelian causality as a complete explanation of change. He believed that nature was not entirely deterministic; there was an element of chance, of unpredictability. But these were qualifications, admissions of ignorance. The core concept, the absence of agency, was not challenged. What was important was that all views, speculations, and hypotheses were open for discussion and debate.

In cosmology, almost every conceivable alternative known today was propounded by some thinker (Lloyd and Sivin 2002, 128). The universe was bounded or infinite in space and in time; there was one universe or many. The infinite variety of matter was reducible to earth, air, fire, and water; to atoms according to Democritus; to numbers according to Pythagoras. To Plato, matter was an illusion; reality consisted in ideas.

Pythagoras (sixth century BCE) discovered a musical scale whose formula was repeated in successive octaves. His concept of ultimate reality was abstracted from this discovery and generalized to the cosmos. Reality was numbers combined in an endless variety of patterns. He saw all natural phenomena as mathematical structures. He conjectured that the movements of the heavenly bodies and their distances reflected numerical patterns similar to the musical scale (Schlagel 2010, 36–39). The Pythagoreans attempted to convert astronomical observations into a mathematically coherent system.

The atomistic theory abstracted from divisibility to atoms. It was associated with Democritus (460–370 BCE), although there were other contributors, including the originator, Leucippus. The size, shape, accumulation, and organization of atoms accounted for observed diversity. Their movements might create multiple worlds separated by vast empty space (Schlagel 2010, 53–68). It was an effort at abstraction from observable reality, a hypothesis. It would be more than two millennia before discovery would become possible.

Both Pythagoreans and atomists conceived of the cosmos as a complex structure—a mechanism—and sought to deconstruct it into its simplest, most basic components, from which they could reconstruct an orderly pattern of reality. Theirs were bottom-up constructions of the universe, from the simple to the complex. Democritus's was ultimately testable; it was an abstraction. But Pythagoras's number cosmos seemed more a construction built on analogy than an abstraction.

Plato's concept of reality was quite different from the approaches of Pythagoras and Democritus. It was important for its influence in later civilizations. The cosmos had two tiers. Reality was ideas, not things. Later civilizations would call this tier spiritual. These ideas or forms were perfect and eternal; they were categories. Sensory appearance referred to imperfect derivations from these forms. The material world was not real, just the shadows or replicas of ideas. Plato ordered reality from the top down, characterized by relationship rather than cause and effect. It was more organic than mechanic. But Plato's cosmos was a composition, imaginary, abstract but not an abstraction. Plato also added a craftsman or demiurge as creator of reality.

There was another perspective on cosmology whose basic components were neither atoms nor numbers but elements: earth, water, air, and fire. Their endless combinations constituted the diversity of matter. Strictly speaking, they were not elements but states of matter—solid, liquid, gaseous, incandescent. It was first proposed by Empedocles (492–432 BCE). This approach was more a taxonomy than a concept of fundamental reality.

The version of reality that mattered most for posterity was that of Aristotle (384–322 BC), who studied the contributions of his predecessors. Contrary to most Athenian philosophers, he accepted the evidence of the senses. He rejected the atomic theory of Democritus, opted for the "four elements" explanation of the diversity of the material world, and added numerous partitions between opposites beyond hot and cold, dry and wet. He added a fifth "element," the ether, to avoid admitting that there was such a thing as empty space or vacuum. This element did not mix with the other four.

His contribution to cosmology was process, the interaction or relation of events in space and time. Aristotle dissected cause and effect into a four-cause explanation and description of change: final, formal, material, and efficient causes (Schlagel 1984, 229–32). The concept of causality could be viewed as abstraction from agency. He attributed order in the universe to a prime mover, a purely abstract concept he invented to account for the initiation of change. To account for the motions of the heavenly bodies, he proposed a system of many concentric spheres that roughly approximated celestial change as observed from the earth.

SPACE

Space, initially location or filled with matter, was conceived as abstract space, object-free space (Goody and Watt 1963, 324). Some could not conceive of space as a vacuum and imagined that it was filled with a substance not perceptible to human senses.

Aristotle did not believe that space was empty because he breathed it and witnessed evaporation and subsequent clouds, fog, and rain. But proponents of absolute space—free of objects, unbounded—prevailed as evidenced by Euclidean geometry—abstract line, area, and volume.

Abstract space implies that objects are self-defined and self-identifying. An object may change locations, and it may persist over long periods, but it remains the same object. One might call this a mechanistic concept of reality as contrasted to an organic concept. Time was more complicated. It was about events, not objects, about change.

TIME

The concepts of time and time measurement were needed for coordination and group effort. The distinction between time and specific events began early in human history given the day-night cycle and the cycle of the seasons. Well before civilization, it must have been conceived as daytime, travel time, and harvest time, which can refer to a period or to a process. Early cultures calibrated the lunar cycle and, later, the solar year. But this was a fragmentation of time, not its abstraction. The founder civilizations developed instruments for measuring time, such as sundials and water clocks, which the Greeks improved, abstracting time from any particular event (other than the measuring instrument itself). These instruments also further fragmented time, from periods to continuous flow. This was empirical time. Greek historians conceived of time as a separate dimension, which ordered historical events in terms of causes and consequences, rather than simply a sequence of events (Toynbee 1952, 135–38, 147–48). The philosophers went further to the concept of an abstract—event-empty, dimension-lacking direction. This Greek concept of time was analogous to that of one of the dimensions of space, not yet a measure of change as it came to be conceived later.

The Greeks asked, "What is the ultimate reality of time? Is there absolute time, event-free, in the absence of change? Or is time no more than relative, a particular relation of events?" Some conceived of time as eternal duration (Schlagel 1985, 195–96). Plato argued for the existence of empty time—time even in the absence of change or events. It was an absolute time within which events were positioned. This concept of time lacked direction; before and after referred to events, not to time. Aristotle, on the other hand, saw time as relational and dependent on change but distinct from change, apart from events. It was numberlike, a means of measuring change, the relation between events (Annas 1975). This division of opinion continues today.

Adoption of settled agriculture required a sense of the future in terms of subsistence and security. But the future as an abstraction was yet to be invented. Unlike abstract time, it is directional, rooted in the present. To the extent that Greeks thought about the future, they viewed it as cyclical, not directional. But repetitive time had content. Greeks loved novelties. Perhaps novelties were generalized to novelty but not further abstracted to the idea of a future with limitless possibilities subject to our agency, a precursor to the idea of directional change, of progress. There was no difference among past, present, and future. Some of the mathematician-engineers of Alexandria understood progress but, in terms of their own research interests, concrete, not abstract from the perspective of society.

NUMBER

Abstraction had different levels or stages. Number is a prime illustration. The first numbers referred to specific objects. A number system without reference to specific objects was the first stage of abstraction; it consisted in counting. The second stage was measurement, which might be described as an abstraction from counting. It was a response to needs for information on length, area, volume, and weight, themselves abstractions. The first civilizations initiated this step employing practical, empirical rules for land measurement, construction, and the like. The Greeks went further. Geometry was developed as an axiomatic, deductive reasoning method of proof, rather than as a means of solving practical problems. Greek geometry was an analogue of Aristotle's syllogism. What the geometer called an axiom, the philosopher called a premise.

Euclid's (326–265 BC) compendium, *Elements*, is our encyclopedia of Greek geometry and other mathematical achievements, which he standardized. The question is whether this is as far as the Greeks advanced in abstraction. Spengler (1945, 63–65) claims that the Greeks went no further. Their mathematics is geometry of space; their numbers are just about extension, magnitude.

Plato, Aristotle, and other philosophers wrote on many subjects, but what stood out was the role of mathematics not as a practical tool but as cosmology, as fundamental reality. Their concept of number must have been more abstract than measurement. Greek thinking on numbers, as with other subjects, was diverse.

Pythagoras is reputed to have said, "All is number." He might as well have said, "In the beginning, there is number." The thinking of Pythagoras on number is incomprehensible to the modern mind. But he is clear that number is not an attribute of things but rather quite the contrary, that numbers were the building blocks of things, their progenitor, the very foundation of reality. For Pythagoras, numbers are real, not abstract (Schlagel 1984, 94, 98, 101). The distinction between reality and abstraction would come later with Plato.

Pythagoras also discovered a note as a function of the length of vibrating strings or weight of hammers, which were not three-dimensional objects. Their determinants were not lengths and weights, not magnitudes but ratios or elementary relationships.

Three centuries later, we come to Archimedes (287–212 BC), a great mathematician. He mastered the principle of the lever and designed very complex machinery of pulleys and levers, cogs and gears that compounded ratio on ratio—again, a pattern of relations. He was a rare combination of discoverer and inventor. His experiments in designing catapults determined the relation between leverage power and the weight of the projectile or the distance traveled. They went beyond three-dimensional magnitude. They were a crude measurement of energy. Hero calculated how a given weight could be moved by a given force for five different machines, again approximating the abstract concept of energy (Usher 1959, 120).

When Archimedes said that, given a firm foundation on which to stand and a lever long enough, he could move the earth, he was thinking of relations, not measurements. He also discovered the principle of specific gravity, the eureka experience that extrapolated from the existing measures, integrating weight with volume. Relative densities were usually based on water as the medium of density or mass.

Archimedes's palimpsest, discovered in 1906, has been interpreted to advance the concept of infinity to that of mathematicians of the Scientific Revolution. Archimedes and Eudoxus approximated the calculus. But whereas Newton was concerned with change, the Greeks were simply attempting to measure nonrectilinear areas and volumes.

Greek mathematician/engineers, including Archimedes, constructed planetariums, which replicated the motions of the sun, earth, moon, and planets, including eclipses of the sun and moon. This was a more complex pattern of relations not in three dimensions but in four, space plus time. The geocentric solar systems preceding Ptolemy's had many cocentric spheres rotating at different speeds and directions. Building a planetarium would come close to solving a complex set of equations. The Antikythera mechanism, creator unknown, whose fragments were recovered from an ancient Greek shipwreck and which had been described as an analog computer, is in fact the only planetarium we know to have survived.

Greek mathematics were inventions not of the world about us but in the inner world created by our minds. Mathematics, like language, was a grand ongoing invention, still in its early stages at the time of the Greeks, within which they contributed many discoveries (Ochoa and Corey 1995, 10–22). Greek measurement went well beyond three-dimensional space—energy, density; it approximated object-free relationships and patterns. They were conceiving of numbers as relation, as pattern. Although not credited with algebra, they learned how to solve algebraic equations by geometric methods.

There was a fifth dimension along which the Greek people, not just the philosophers, progressed in number abstraction, not time but value ratios. Earlier cultures had advanced from the intrinsic value of particular commodities to a commodity medium of exchange or relative value, such as silver. Each Greek city-state had its own currency. Only that of Athens was widely accepted. There were money changers who charged a percentage and who lent their earnings at interest. They were the predecessors of banks. This was an experience of the population, not just the philosophers. Multiple city-states, an economy of production for export, exposed the average citizen to the value ratios.

The Athenian currency had silver as a medium of exchange. But in 407 BCE, Sparta defeated Athens, capturing the Athenian silver mines and releasing the slaves who worked it. Athens issued bronze coins with a silver coating. The Athenian public hoarded the silver coins, which as a result quickly disappeared from circulation, leaving only the bronze ones. Thus, Athens adopted true money, a system of value ratios, a concept of number as an abstract noun rather than adjective modifying an object.

REASONING AND LOGIC

The early philosophers may have propounded. Their successors, faced with a diversity of opinions on many subjects, had to persuade. Plato's Academy and Aristotle's Lyceum institutionalized debate.

Greek thinkers and their students were engaged in vigorous discussion on the nature of reality and many other subjects. How could they support their views and resolve differences of opinion? They deferred to neither priests nor rulers. There was no recourse to authority in settling disputes. Truth was not the dictate of the palace or temple but abstract knowledge, information, whoever the writer or speaker (Assman 2011, 258–63). Progress toward the truth required acceptance of a process of seeking the truth. Rejection or suspicion of the evidence of the senses meant that logic was the chosen method, that empirical evidence was neglected and mistrusted. Why this was so is part of the mystery of Greek embracement of abstraction. But it was also unavoidable since the knowledge or technology needed to verify or test many of their theories did not exist at the time.

The Greek invention is deductive reasoning, the syllogism its basic process. The simple syllogism contained a major and a minor premise, and the findings deduced from these premises, such as humans, are mortal. Socrates is human; therefore, he will die. The major premise is assumed to be correct; the minor premise is a classification that provides explanation for the conclusion, renders it credible, and— together with the minor premise—offers proof of its truth. However, the major premise is assumed to be true by common consent, not proven by any logical process. The validity of a syllogism rests not just in its internal logic but on the acceptance of its major premise, not on proof. The premise may or may not have been the conclusion of an inductive process.

Deductive reasoning is a method of discovering new knowledge only within narrow limits. The new knowledge must be an inference from the premises, not a new discovery. The syllogism is an instrument of proof. Dialectics is a process of resolving disagreements and contradictions in the search for truth. Today it is called conflict resolution. It is a search for truth by an argument conducted by two, the resolution of differences.

Contradictions could take several forms, including proof that one or both were wrong. It was the ideal of objectivity in the search for truth that characterized dialectics.

Aristotelian deductive logic was a discovery/invention pertaining to the human mind, not nature. It was a cultural development of no apparent survival or subsistence value at the time except for Greek thinkers.

The Greek contribution to the creative act of discovery was the generation of hypotheses about the natural world. A syllogism had a major premise that was an assumption but could be a hypothesis. Some Greek hypotheses were reductionist, abstractions from observed reality, hence testable in principle. What was missing was hypothesis testing. Their very abstraction placed many beyond the ability of the Greeks to test them. Inferences could be drawn, but definitive testing had a long wait. The dedicated instruments and the knowledge did not exist at that time.

Zeno's paradoxes were, in fact, a testing of preposterous hypotheses, proving them false. In a footrace, if a tortoise has a head start, Achilles can never catch up. The proof was based on common empirical knowledge.

How hypotheses are generated is beyond my understanding. Wide knowledge helps. The Greek philosophers were notable for the diversity of their interests, the breadth of their knowledge, and their range of achievements, starting with Thales and Anaximander, epitomized by Aristotle. These characteristics have facilitated the generation of hypotheses and the ability to synthesize. The habit of debate provided a favorable environment. Authority is a curse.

Greek thinkers' reliance on deductive reasoning, their elucidation of the principles of logic, reinforced their disposition to conceive of a static universe and to reject the reality of change, of uncertainty, of irrationality. Yet they were also creators and seekers after knowledge. There was no contradiction since they believed that there was much yet to be learned and explained.

The way toward unbounded new knowledge was induction. The Lyceum was devoted to research, but this was organized observation and collection of data, not experiment or testing of hypotheses. His method of proof was the syllogism, not empirical investigation (Schlagel 1984, 222). Usher (1959, 86–87) wrote that Aristotle, in his biological treatises, recognized the method of observation and inference. McKeon (1949, 17) asserted that Aristotle appealed to perception rather than intuition but didn't use it.

Nevertheless, informal social induction was the basis for the common consent for the major premises of most syllogisms. They laid the foundations for systematic inductive approach two millennia later through their work on taxonomy and their stress on number. Induction can prove beyond a reasonable doubt but not beyond any possible doubt. It did not offer the certainty, the final order the philosophers sought.

The true empiricists, the inventors, came later, associated with Alexandria rather than Athens. They were mathematicians and engineers more than philosophers. They sought to link theoretical, mathematical reasoning to practical applications, endowing it with great social value. There were much systematic experimentation and inductive reasoning rather than casual trial and error or simple observation. There was some testing of hypotheses. Hero of Alexandria disproved Aristotle's belief that there was no such thing as a vacuum via careful experiments (Schlagel 2010, 136–38). The interaction of theory and practice, of science and technology, demonstrated by a number of Alexandrians went beyond the Scientific Revolution; it was the trademark of the Industrial Revolution that followed.

The instruments required to determine whether the empirical applications of Archimedes's law of leverage were confirmed did not exist. Archimedes derived mathematical rules of leverage; he, Ptolemy, and others derived mathematical rules of optics by systematic experimentation. They lacked the instruments to prove that their findings were precise regularities of nature or just very close approximations from an empirical experiment; it was not a testing of hypotheses.

Mention of logic in classical Greece usually refers to formal logic and Aristotle. But logical can mean obvious, credible, or precise. There were other notable achievements facilitating the expression and communication of knowledge. The most important was the adoption of the Phoenician alphabet and its improvement by the addition of vowels. In written language, Greeks invented the sentence, converting a list of words into a coherent and precise unit of thought by introducing punctuation and by discovering grammar. Aristophanes of Byzantium (257–180 BC) standardized punctuation, whereas Aristarchus of Samothrace (220–143BC) wrote the definitive grammar. (He was not Aristarchus the astronomer.) They were both librarians at the Alexandria Library.

TAXONOMY

We observe particulars—objects, events, sights. Sensory experience is disordered. Learning requires the classification of experience. It is the warehouse problem mentioned in the introduction.

As knowledge was accumulated by each generation and transmitted to the next, its growth led to specialization. There were astronomers and physicians, philosophers and engineers. Compartmentalization of knowledge became a necessity; access to knowledge became framework dependent. Taxonomies were developed. They structured the accumulation of knowledge so that any new knowledge would have its proper place in the intellectual universe. Such a system created associations that facilitated the storage and retrieval of knowledge, whether in a human mind or later in libraries. They also imposed some order on the search for information on new objects and ideas.

Language itself is the original taxonomy. It has created the cognitive elements that are to be classified. Vocabulary alone is too long a list; it is a single-stage taxonomy. It must be fragmented and ordered hierarchically.

The phonetic alphabet is an easy and convenient way of classifying, storing, and retrieving what is known. That is a dictionary. But taxonomy, to be useful to the ignorant as well as the knowledgeable, must go beyond a list of particulars. It must go beyond the known to relate particulars to each other and new knowledge to that already known. A hierarchy of classification facilitates storage and recall, reveals relations, and encourages associations. It converts the dictionary, that is, language, into an encyclopedia, that is, knowledge. It facilitates communication and learning.

Speech and writing consist of sentences, not just words. The relations between words are specified by order, prepositions, conjunctions, and pronouns. Verbs are related to other words by tenses. This is grammar and syntax, part of the great invention we call language, although it was not "discovered" until later by Aristarchus (310–250 BCE) (Schmidhouser 2010, 11). These relation words represent a higher level of abstraction than object-specific taxonomy. They give structure to speech and then to writing. Vocabulary is a catalog; grammar and syntax is the structure that gives meaning to statements.

Particular taxonomies were commonplace in every culture—lists of manuscript in a library and of objects serving a common purpose or sharing a common trait, such as fruits or medications. What was different in Greek taxonomy was its generality and its hierarchical structure, its object- or function-free nature. It represented a higher level of abstraction than the particular groupings of everyday life.

The four elements of cosmology, already mentioned, were the basic elements or states of matter—earth, water, air, and fire—with multiple subdivisions (such as dry and wet, hot and cold) and can be viewed as a primitive taxonomy of physics and chemistry. Greeks identified some elements, some compounds. But there would be a long wait for the periodic table of elements.

What is the reality that needs to be ordered and classified? How do we order or classify the near-infinite variety of reality as observed by our senses and conceived by our minds? The ideal taxonomy has two characteristics, universality and exclusivity. Every item in a classification shares a significant characteristic with every other item, and no other classifications share this characteristic. It must be hierarchical; the material world is divisible into animate and inanimate, animate into animal and vegetable. This is feasible in the inanimate world. In the animate world, it is not clear that the logical requirements for classification can be met in lower levels of hierarchy. It becomes almost impossible to avoid overlap missions.

It is the categorization of Aristotle that prevailed. In addition, with four (or five) elements of taxonomy, he sought to order all objects in the universe. He divided them into the living and the nonliving. The living, in turn, were subdivided into animals and plants. By observing the characteristics of every species, he identified commonalities and differences, both structural and functional. Employing this dual criterion, he generated partitions and subpartitions, a multistage hierarchy of animal and plant types. Aristotle believed that every species was separate, distinct, and permanent. His taxonomy was the standard almost until Linnaeus in 1735. Theophrastus, Aristotle's successor, continued his work on plants and initiated the taxonomy of minerals.

Pythagoras saw reality in terms of number, without reference to sensory reality. His taxonomy and that of Democritus were pure imagination.

Plato's types of government was a small beginning in the classification of ideas. Plato defined reality as ideas; taxonomy would be a classification of ideas. They had no sensory basis, perhaps no observable reality. In the realm of ideas, boundaries were poorly demarcated, without laws, perhaps without order; domains overlap. The great libraries in Alexandria and elsewhere had to have a catalog. Today we have advanced to the Dewey decimal system.

ON THE ORIGINS OF ABSTRACT THINKING

The three areas in which Greek accomplishments had no counterpart in other cultures of the time, according to Goody and Watt (2002, 330), were logic, taxonomy, and epistemology, or the search for an understanding of fundamental reality. All were characterized by abstraction. Other cultures did not lack for imagination, but Greek abstraction conceived of nature as self-ordered; it was a simplification of complex reality, a rejection of reality as perceived by the senses. The abstractions of other cultures, and of fellow Greek citizens, were overpopulated with spirits and agents. They were myths.

What drove a significant number of Greeks to reject a cosmos populated and governed by a host of anthropomorphic deities for an insentient universe self-governed by abstract principles? Perhaps they were unwilling to accept authority, even divine, whereas other civilizations craved it and felt little urge to decipher God's mind.

What led them to reject the rich variety of matter on the earth, the overwhelming evidence of the senses, for a pattern of numbers, an ordering of featureless, invisible atoms? Certainly, a search for order. But also a passion for simplicity? Why should they argue about the number of worlds, their extent in time and space in a world beset by more pressing issues? Why should physicians argue over theories of disease instead of concentrating on better diagnosis and treatment?

If there was a place of origin, it would be Miletus in modern-day Turkey, home to Thales and Anaximander. Thales was reported to have said that he had many predecessors. Perhaps they did not write. An indication that he was right was evidence of the rapid evolution of the Greek language. Homer's epics were first written in the eighth century. Their vocabulary, although rich in comparison with the early civilizations, was lacking the abstract nouns and other words required to express the thought of Thales and the Silesians (McGilchrist 2009, 163–64). But two centuries later, many such words had been incorporated in the vocabulary available to the Milesians for thinking and writing. This was an incredibly rapid evolution. We do not know who were the people who created all these words.

Major thinkers came from many Greek cities from Italy to Turkey. Only Plato was from Athens. The major achievements of the philosophers were incredibly concentrated in time, a mere two centuries, suggesting a true community of thinkers. It was the institutions founded by Plato and Aristotle that maintained Athens as a center of scholarship for nine hundred years; the Academy and the Lyceum were established late in the period of highest achievement.

Plato's Academy, a private foundation, first institutionalized advanced education. It was soon joined by Aristotle's Lyceum. They provided for the transmission of knowledge down the generations, but in argument and debate, they were also quasi-research institutions generating new knowledge. Their contribution was facilitated by the fact that Greece was a literate society, the first in history.

The scholars in Alexandria, likewise, were from the far-flung Greek settlements, not all of them Greeks by ethnicity. Their achievements were also highly concentrated in time. Their location was a product of the institutions created by the Ptolemies, Greek monarchs of Egypt; the library; and the museum. The Ptolemies also provided financial support.

The temporal and spatial concentration of achievement raises the question of what came first, the culture or the mind? What was the direction of causation? Brains, we are born with; mind is what we make of our brains. Experience generates structural and functional changes in the brain (McGilchrist 2009, 243–56). Mathematicians develop dedicated bundles of neurons not found in most people. When large numbers of educated and able people congregate, there is an evolution of mind. Concentrated intellectual effort has shaped culture, or has it been a cabal of Milesian minds that has generated the subculture?

Abstract thinking arose for no particular evolutionary reason that we can tell. It conferred no survival value at the time. Perhaps it should be conceived as a spandrel—a mutation (cultural in this case, not genetic) that had no function but somehow persisted and eventually came to be the key to progress, if not survival of the species.

Stephen Mithen (1996, 215) does not believe that thinking or religion, or art, can be explained as an evolutionary response to challenges. Merlin Donald (1998, 61) agrees since adaptive genetic changes tend to be very specific, narrow in focus, whereas religion, art, or other abstract thought is very general. But they are referring to genetic change. The experience of Greece was cultural, not genetic.

The cognitive abilities involved in mathematics, science, religion, or art do not appear to have survival advantage in the hunter-gatherer stage of human development. They became relevant and important after humans created complex societies with hierarchy and specialization. Their existence is simply a fact in itself, which had no explanation and required none. Humans had been endowed with mathematical ability since they acquired linguistic ability. But they found little use for it until the birth of agriculture. And then their needs were practical—trade, taxation, irrigation—not the abstract mathematical reasoning of the Greeks.

Europe retrieved much of the Greek legacy and went ahead with the Scientific and Industrial Revolutions. Rome and the Arabs, who shared that legacy, did neither. So there is no Darwinian explanation for the advent of abstract logical thinking among the Greeks. Would it have arisen elsewhere in time? It almost did in India. The Mohists, Chinese logical school, vanished without a trace. In the two millennia since the golden age of Greece, China did not attain their mastery of logic or conception of an agency-free, coherent natural world. One example proves nothing.

The short answer is I don't know. But numerous explanatory hypotheses have been proffered, which will be considered after reviewing the accomplishments of the inventors centered in Alexandria. A separate question is the brevity of the golden age of Greece.

INVENTION AND EXPERIMENT

The Greeks learned from earlier cultures, improving on the inventions of others. Their alphabet was borrowed from the Phoenicians, to which they added vowels. Their triremes also were a Phoenician invention. But their major achievements had no ancestry. According to McKeon (1949, 21), the Greek achievement associated with Athens consisted not of objects or processes or data but in ideas and concepts, not only space, time, and matter but also mechanism, order, organism, structure, pattern, and function. One might label them inventions.

Neither the palace nor the temple contributed to invention or provided a ready market. But property rights and a degree of affluence provided the resources for invention and freedom and affluence a market for innovation. What was lacking was the motivation. The best minds were interested in idle speculation, not in practical accomplishments. The Greek thinkers engaged in abstract theorizing, and logical debate had no interest in inventing tools, weapons, or processes. Some had a low opinion of craftsmen and artists who might engage in problem-solving or product-improving inventions. What distinguished them was invention in the realm of ideas and hypotheses and their capacity for abstraction, their progress in reasoning. Their main practical inventions were instruments for observation and measurement. There were improvements on objects and methods first developed in Egypt and Mesopotamia. This was the Greece centered in Athens, whose best known thinkers were Plato and Aristotle.

There was another Greece, a later Greece, the Hellenic period, when Alexandria had surpassed Athens as the center of intellectual activity. Alexander conquered Egypt in 332 BCE. It was ruled by Greek kings, the Ptolemies, who were interested in promoting scholarship. They built the famous library and the museum, the latter exclusively for research. They also funded many of the scholars who came to work in these and other institutions. The scholars, like the Athenian philosophers, were primarily interested in theoretical knowledge, but they did not share the aversion to empirical testing or the disinterest in practical results that characterized the Greek thinkers of its golden age. They initiated empirical experimentation in physics and medicine (Schlagel 1984, 250–62). If Athens was the center of academic debate and instruction, Alexandria was the home of research and government research grants. Aristotle himself had taken a step in that direction, not as an inventor but as one who was concerned with facts as the final arbiter of reason.

In Alexandria, scholars were supported not by student fees but by the Ptolemies and also by private patrons (Lloyd and Sivin, 99). Some patrons were interested in practical results from their intellectual activities; perhaps so were the rulers. They provided incentives for inventions and perhaps attracted a somewhat different breed of scholars. It was not so much a change of perspective as a change of support and opportunity that altered the culture of inquiry, involving practical applications, not just ideas. Physicians and architects, with private patrons, also had motivations different from those of the philosophers.

The Ptolemies were succeeded by the Romans in 31 BCE, who had little interest in the pursuits of scholars other than military weapons and infrastructure engineering. Egypt remained under Roman, later Byzantine, rule until the Arab conquest in 641 CE, but Emperor Justinian closed the Lyceum and the Academy in Athens and other institutions of scholarship in the belief that their work was subversive of Christianity.

The training of mathematicians and engineers continued under Byzantium, with some further progress. Their achievement was crowned by the Hagia Sophia in Constantinople, whose designers and architects demonstrated an amazing understanding of the physics involved and engineering know-how, as well as the chemical properties of the materials used (Mark and Çakmak 1992, 12, 38). Its two architects were Greek—Isidore the Younger of Miletus, who taught math and physics in Alexandria, and Anthemius of Tralles, mathematician-engineer who taught in Constantinople. The materials and methods used imply experimentation in the modern sense, to acquire knowledge needed for the task.

The Inventors and Discoverers

Who were the inventors? In Athens, the philosophers invented ideas, but some practical inventions were the work of artisans and craftsmen, poorly regarded by the thinkers. We do not know the names of most of them. But inventors and discoverers associated with Alexandria were predominantly from the educated elite, scholars very similar in background to the philosophers in Athens. They were mathematicians and engineers, typically characterized by their breadth of knowledge and diversity of interests, masters of the achievements of their Athenian predecessors. In most cases, we know their names. They were markedly different from the inventors in the founder civilizations of Sumer and Egypt, who were unknown illiterate artisans. Some were affluent and did not invent for a living.

Almost without exception, their primary interest was theory, and their inventions were applications of their theoretical understanding. The leading inventors were, in fact, discoverers of natural phenomena who found ways of putting their knowledge to practical use. They were not testing hypotheses, but the process of application was analogous to testing. They were gifted experimentalists.

Archimedes, the greatest inventor, made it clear that he had little interest in his inventions. His interest was in mathematics, in the discovery and invention of ideas, not in practical inventions. On his tomb, he wanted a sphere encased in a cylinder because his proudest achievement was the calculation of the ratio of volume of the cylinder to the sphere. Nevertheless, he was a problem solver known for his practical inventions. He was motivated more by circumstances than by choice. He discovered the principle of the lever and used it in the defense of Syracuse from Roman attack and for multiple other uses. He applied his knowledge of optics to develop a "heat ray" for naval warfare by focusing sunlight with curved mirrors. And his eureka experience, the discovery of the principle of relative gravity, was the solution to the problem of detecting the adulteration of gold with base metals. Other leading inventors were also discoverers who searched for applications of some discovery they had made. They had solutions in search of problems. Who needed Hero's wind-driven organ?

Other Greek inventors who also derived their inventions from their own discoveries included Ctesibius (285–222 BC). A contemporary of Archimedes, he applied his discovery—the elasticity of air—to practical use, inventing a number of mechanisms powered by compressed air, including a cannon. He was the founder of pneumatics. Hero (AD 10–70) discovered the power of steam and applied his understanding to inventing, a crude steam engine. Philo of Byzantium (280–220 BC) was a student of Ctesibius, suggested a number of uses for compressed air and water pressure, and made improvements to the catapult. He was the first to mention a water mill and may have invented it. Ctesibius, Hero and pneumatics, and Archimedes and the lever are outstanding examples but not the only ones.

Leading discoverers-inventors had multiple inventions to their credit. They were able to transfer the technology of the original invention to different domains. A leverage machine can lift and move, toss, or batter. And there was cognitive transfer between domains. Hero understood pressure and could compare wind pressure on sails to pressure of falling water or steam. This was cognitive transfer. It multiplies the impact of a discovery or invention.

Archimedes and other inventors did not personally construct huge catapults, steam pressure chambers, or windmills. They employed skilled artisans. Invention was a collaborative effort with skilled artisans.

The proliferation of practical inventions would not have been possible had there not been a market for many of them. Affluence was a factor. Some inventions were responses to the demand of patrons. But the dominant factor on the demand side must have been cultural, the Greek's love of novelties.

Euclid's compendium of Greek mathematics and Ptolemy in astronomy was more in Athenian than Alexandrian mold. Although they were inventors, their main accomplishment was synthesis—the collection, emendation, addition, and summation of their field for posterity. Ptolemy (85–165 CE) had a very wide range of interests, knowledge, and accomplishments. He made contributions to music theory, optics, geography, and other subjects but is remembered for his astronomy, the invention of a complex geocentric model of celestial mechanics. It was incorrect, but its predictions were close enough to grant it survival value until Copernicus. Aristarchus (310–250 BCE) had hypothesized a solar-centric cosmos, a radical idea at the time. His logic could not prevail over an entrenched belief and the evidence of the senses. It was forgotten, and Ptolemy's model prevailed.

The Inventions

We know little about the actual process of invention. It is clear from the nature of many of the products that the inventors did not themselves make them. The inventors often employed artisans to make their inventions. The leverage machines of Archimedes were too big for him to make himself; the intricate metalwork of some of others was outside the expertise of the inventor. So much invention was teamwork. Some of their products, such as cranes and catapults, required the labor of many workers to build. Complicated mechanical devices required craftsmen with diverse, high-level skills. This division of labor—the invention proper and its actualization in a product—was rare in the founder civilizations but would become the rule in the future. Archimedes was a manager as well as an inventor.

Their inventions drew on their understanding of physics and knowledge of mathematics. It was unlikely that a craftsman without Archimedes's knowledge of the principle of the lever could have designed the complicated machine that lifted Roman warships from the sea, spun them around, slammed them against cliffs, or dumped them back to the sea (Schlagel 1985, 261). Nor could they have created the complex catapults capable of tossing heavy stones great distances with accuracy or the screw for pumping water, which remained in use until the invention of the Newcomen engine in 1712. Archimedes's heat ray, the use of concave mirrors to concentrate sunlight to set ships on fire or at least heat them beyond human tolerance, required his knowledge of optics.

Greek inventions were predominantly mechanical. Greek fascination with mechanism preceded its period of intellectual achievement. This mechanical bent was found in Greek mythology. The god Hephaestus made many human statues of bronze and precious metals as workers, guardians, and dancers, as well as animals—bulls, dogs, horses, eagles— each also endowed with life and function. The mythical Athenian sculptor Daedalus also created metal statues brought to life. There were self-regulating inanimate objects as well—tripods, tables, self-propelled, operated vehicles (Kalligeropoulos and Vasileiadou 1984).

Mechanism was compatible with the Greek concepts of reality, whether it be Pythagoras and "all is number," Democritus and atomism, or Aristotle and causality. Even in medicine, although there were advances in diagnosis and treatment, the major achievement was in anatomy and physiology, discovery rather than invention. Had the Greeks been less obsessed with mechanism and more concerned with organism, they might have made more progress in chemistry and medical treatment.

Mathematician/engineers devised levers, pulleys, screws, and cogs to operate a wide range of machinery, whether siege artillery and catapults, hoists, cranes, pumps, or grain mills. All components of a steam engine were made but not combined (Landels 1978, 28). Many laborsaving mechanical devices were invented—leverage machines, water-powered grinding machines. There were improvements and new uses for wind and waterpower. Hence, the argument that there was no demand for steam power because slave labor was abundant and cheap was not valid. Few owned slaves. The scale of production in place that could have made steam power economical did not exist. Production of most goods was craft, not factory organized. The needs for draining mines and irrigation were met by Archimedes's water screw, which was used until the invention of the first steam engine, the Newcomen mine-pumping engine, in 1712.

In addition to inventions responsive to the needs of society—machines designed for power to lift, to heave, to pound—some of the same mathematician-engineers designed machines for measurement and prediction—an odometer, improved water clocks, astrolabes, a thermometer. Such inventions were more responses to the research needs of the scholars than the practical needs of society.

After Alexander's conquests, engineers were also engaged in city planning, improvements in roadbuilding and supply of urban utilities. But they were subordinate to planners, who reasoned synthetically. A city was a hybrid of mechanism and organism.

Another difference between some Greek inventions and those of earlier civilizations was that some of them could not be said to be responses to the needs of their society or of the inventors but represented novelty for its own sake. The mathematical engineers created automatons—devices simulating humans or animals designed to perform simple actions appropriate to their appearance on their own once activated by their inventors. They were intended for entertaining the public and demonstrating their inventors' cleverness. Both inventors and their public were interested in novelty, an interest that was also an incentive to invent. Mechanical automatons as the currency of novelty also told us of the arena and goal of novelty seeking. Historically, they were replicating their mythology. Philo of Byzantium, contemporary of Archimedes, was best known for his comprehensive description of Greek mechanical achievements. Since most of his book on automatons was lost, there was uncertainty about his own accomplishments. Hero used the pressure of heated air to power a mechanism opening temple doors. He invented a windwheel and used one to operate an organ. He was also a prolific inventor of automatons—complex, self-regulating machines more for entertainment than for useful work.

Whatever the purpose of these diverse, ingenious mechanisms, the multiple means of powering them came close to the concept of abstract power or energy. It was not just the muscle of human or beast or the passive role of sail but could be metal spring, twisted cord, steam, compressed air, or gravity as well. About their only predecessor was the water mill.

The automatons had another implication—the early idea of the robot. Many of these mechanisms functioned on their own once activated after purposeful sequences of action. They were advancing from mechanics to robotics. What they lacked was the power of autonomous decision. The idea of the robot was an abstraction of the human agency, predetermination.

What the mathematician-engineers accomplished was not just transfer of cognition and technology to diverse domains but also the combination of science and engineering two thousand years before the Industrial Revolution. One other distinctive characteristic of Greek inventions should be noted. Most of Archimedes's inventions were practical solutions to problems, but most of Hero's were not responses to needs but exercises in novelty.

The planetariums, already mentioned, could be used to predict eclipses, which had significance in popular culture. They would demonstrate the mastery of their designers. Could the geocentric models of the time yield predictions good enough to satisfy the best mathematical minds of Alexandria? Could any of them have been a solar-centric mechanism, an implicit test of the geocentric hypothesis and confirmation of the heliocentric model, such as proposed by Aristarchus?

Not all achievements were in physics, mathematics, and engineering. Galen (130–210 CE), the greatest Greek physician, was more a great discoverer than an inventor. Through dissection of animals and humans, he learned much about the human anatomy and its physiology—the circulatory system, the nervous system, the function of organs. As physician to gladiators, he was able to observe natural experiments that led to understanding the relations of the spinal cord, brain, and nervous system. Observation and experimentation were his approach. The knowledge gained placed much diagnosis and treatment on a sounder factual basis. His writing was standard reading for physicians for 1,500 years. He was the last of the great Greek protoscientists.

What is amazing to me is the longevity of Greek inventions. The Archimedes screw for draining mines and quarries was in use until the Newcomen engine. Ptolemy's astronomical model prevailed until Copernicus. And Galen's medical text prevailed even longer. Euclid's geometry is still taught.

In the case of Ptolemy, there was a better alternative—Aristarchus, whose heliocentric theory was based on detailed empirical data and careful reasoning. His writings were lost, but his achievements were reported by Archimedes. In measuring the size and distance of the sun and moon, Aristarchus learned that the size of the universe was immensely larger than conceived by others at the time. Archimedes, who told us about Aristarchus, built a planetarium—a working mechanical model of the solar system known at the time. Was his model perhaps heliocentric?

Theory and Application

Did the Greeks experiment? There are differences of opinion (Schlagel 1984, 25354, 263–66). Trial and error is older than civilization, older than the human species. But the mathematicians of Alexandria were better informed and more focused in their experiments, in their choice of trials, than their predecessors. Experiment directed toward solving a problem, achieving a goal, was certainly evident. When trials are clearly focused, even errors are learning experiences.

Hero invented the windwheel (a windmill minus the milling apparatus), initially using it to power an organ. He considered several designs for the wind vanes, experimentation to be sure. One consisted of sixteen short wide rectangles. Another was four long narrow vanes that looked much like the modern three-vane wind turbines. Both spun on a horizontal axis. But a third consisted of eight wide and long vanes at different angles, looking like so many sails circumventing a mast, spinning around a vertical axis. I think that Hero adapted the concept of a stationary sail as a wind foil for ship propulsion to a rotating wind foil for compressing air. He went further, learning to dispense with variable winds altogether. He compressed air by heating it and by steaming water and proceeded to employ compressed air and steam energy to diverse, unrelated uses.

It was the mathematician-engineers associated with Alexandria who were best prepared to convert the assumptions of the Athenian philosophers into testable hypotheses and proceed to test them experimentally. But experiment as hypothesis testing toward discovery of knowledge was not the Greek way, which was premise or assumption and implication (Usher 1859, 86–87, 95–96). But the mathematician-engineer inventors of Alexandria were extending the Athenian method of assumption and implication to the material world, seeking ways of applying theoretical understanding to some practical use. In so doing, they were also testing their theorems, though testing was not their objective. Hero did test and refute Aristotle's assertion that nature abhors a vacuum, that there is no empty space. He proved experimentally that what Aristotle regarded as space filled with air or ether was, in fact, mostly empty (Schlagel 2010, 136–38).

Archimedes, a great mathematician and great inventor, combined theoretical reasoning and empirical application that would characterize the Scientific Revolution and industrial age, which was to come much later (Schlagel 1984, 261–63). He experimented with nature not just to understand it but also to exert control.

What the mathematician-engineers associated with Alexandria accomplished was the application of some scientific understanding to a diversity of uses—cognitive transfer, technology adaptation—more than just isolated inventions. Some of them were both discoverers and inventors.

The Athenians generated hypotheses in many areas, which they could not test. They searched for order in the universe. The Alexandrians were the inventors. To the extent that their inventions were based on their theories, they were an implicit test of their theory, which could be a discovery—the mathematics of leverage—or refinement and application of older discoveries, such as the expansion of air when heated and of water when steamed, wind pressure, the power of falling water, gravity, and the concentration of light and heat, whose precise measurements were not yet possible.

The philosophers of Athens were two steps removed from the collusion of theory and practice that resulted in the Scientific and Industrial Revolutions. It was the great inventors of Alexandria and Syracuse and Byzantium who were just one step removed—the systematic testing of hypotheses.

EXPLANATIONS: WHY THE GREEKS?

A number of explanations have been suggested for Greek achievement. They should be regarded as contributory, not causative. Nor are they mutually exclusive since they differ in what they explain. All deserve consideration. In my view, they are correlated; it is the pattern rather than any component that comes closest to the explanation. These can be classified as geographical, economic, social, political, psychological, linguistic, and technological. The technology to which some attribute Greek achievement is the alphabet.

GEOGRAPHY AND ECONOMY

Sumer and especially Egypt were river valley civilizations surrounded by desert or semidesert. They had boundaries. Greece was a peninsula and numerous islands, plus city-states in Asia and Africa. It had no fixed address, no permanent boundaries. This difference may help account for contrasting attitudes toward change and novelty. Greece was a civilization without frontiers.

How does one explain the Greek worldview and the different worldviews of the early civilizations? A laborer who is part of the large workforce of a vast agricultural enterprise has little need or opportunity for decision-making. A fate at the hands of natural and human forces beyond one's understanding or control is conducive to conservatism, to fear of change, which is more likely to be viewed as a threat than as an opportunity. By contrast, a small farmer who sells his crop and uses the proceeds to buy necessities has both need and opportunity, as well as the incentive for practical inventions. Independent farming, trading, seafaring—this is a society in which the decisions are decentralized and individual; it has an entirely different attitude toward change and a different understanding of the relation of man and nature, of the individual and the group. Such a society does not live in isolation but is in constant contact with other peoples, places, and ideas. This is more speculation than observation; there are too many variables, not enough cultures that we may classify as civilizations with which to compare.

A seafaring people relying on trade and in contact with many others speaking different languages would have a strong incentive to adopt a script that could be used for any language. In fact, it discarded its early script—undeciphered but possibly ideographic—and adopted the Phoenician alphabet, adding vowels. This allowed the visual representation of speech in any language. Exposure to other peoples and practices contributed to interest in novelty—novelty seeking, a trait notably absent in Egypt.

Greece also lacked a characteristic common to all the earlier civilizations—large-scale water management for agricultural production, which entailed labor drafts and a powerful bureaucracy to direct the process and store and distribute the product. This lack made possible individualism and the free, nonauthoritarian state and society in which they lived. It meant that land was private property. The landowner had autonomy not available to most people in a hydraulic society.

The contribution of Greek geography and economy to its intellectual achievements was indirect—individualism, an acceptance of novelty and change, an absence of central authority—perhaps to the adoption of a phonetic alphabet. Greek cities were also affluent enough to support the intellectual elite for generations via student fees.

The acceptance of novelty could be the most important factor. It means that Greece was open to innovation, to the adoption of new ideas and new things. Without it, discoveries would be forgotten, inventions not adopted. The Greeks did not have the idea of progress, but their favorable attitude toward novelty was an essential ingredient, perhaps the seed of the idea. While the Greeks were open to new ideas and new experiences, they had no taste for change in institutions or ways of life.

Such change was destabilizing; they wanted order and stability. Change, for them, was diversity of experience, not temporal change.

LAW AND POLITICS

Muller (1957, 103–11) recognized the contribution of geography and trade but noted that other cultures had similar advantages but not achievements. What Greece had that no other previous or concurrent had was freedom.

A second set of explanations focused on the political structure and legal system. A key aspect was the prevalence of city-states, the absence of a single overall ruler or state. Perhaps the multiplicity of city-states can be explained, in turn, as geographic determinism—rugged terrain, indented coastline, multiple islands. But the legal system prevailing in Athens and some other city-states was not self-explanatory. Sparta was a city-state also. Plato was one thinker whose political views were more in line with Sparta than Athens. He opposed freedom and equality but lived in Athens. Multiple city-states, whatever their form of government, offered refuge for dissidents from any one city.

Authority has two dimensions: vertical and horizontal. Vertical authority may be top down, which we call dictatorship, or bottom up, which we call democracy. The horizontal dimension refers to the range over which authority can be exercised. If vast or unlimited, we call it totalitarianism. If the range is small, we call it limited government, which may coexist with a number of private authorities with specific jurisdictions.

Under a totalitarian rule, the emperor or pharaoh is the final decision maker on all matters and exercises his personal preferences or follows the guidance of the heavens, with which he is the only communicator. There is no institution independent of authority, where diverse ideas are discussed. There is no free space and no commons, social or intellectual, whether authority is secular or sacred. Few resources are available for autonomy and creativity. It is autocracy if authority is top-down, democracy if bottom-up.

Democracy is a matter of degree; who is the electorate, and what are the limits of authority? The electorate is limited by age and usually by other criteria. What is the scope of authority? It may be limited to common goods—security, defense, roads, or other utilities—or extend to the realm of ideas—education, information, or religion. It is limited by law and subject to it.

Democracy in Athens was limited by our standards; the electorate was restricted to free males. The scope of authority in practice more than theory was quite limited. The state was subject to the rule of law. There was much opportunity for dissent, the key requirement for creativity. Participation in the intellectual community discourses and debates was open to all, including women, even slaves. Personal authority was earned but provisional, tentative, and always subject to challenge and dispute. The intellectual community was far more democratic than the political community. How student fees were assessed and collected, I do not know.

What were the conditions for the establishment of democratic polities? We can specify the absence of conditions for a despotic rule. In Greece, there were no water management public works on the scale of Sumer and Egypt, labor draft, and a vast bureaucracy for their maintenance and management of the product. Also absent was a hereditary hierarchical ordering of society. Near-universal literacy, at least among freemen, meant that everyone had the opportunity to participate. It was a meritocratic society. But the argument was circular; democracy promoted universal literacy and vice versa. The individualism that characterized Greece, also favored by its geography and economy, precluded authoritarianism as a viable system of rule. Ultimately, democracy was the residual political system that prevailed by default, if not by choice. Not all city-states were democratic, but original thinkers from such states could and did seek freedom in Athens or, later, in Alexandria.

The city-state was the origin of democracy. It was small enough in area and population for its residents to meet and discuss their problems. Cities require public services. In the absence of a higher authority, some of its residents would get together and organize the beginnings of a city government. Such cities would lack tribal authoritarianism or self-sufficiency. Many of its residents produced for or traded with distant markets.

The independence of individuals was assured by the multiplicity of city-states, by the small scale of farming and craft enterprise. An economy left in private hands provided such autonomy and the resources to exercise it. Established property rights enabled enterprise. The love of novelty that favored diversity and experimentation could only flourish in such a society.

It was the structure of authority and representation that distinguished Greece from other cultures. All others featured a top-down authority. In Greece, authority was embedded in the people, or freemen, who delegated it to officials elected to represent the people. Authority could also be withdrawn. This structure, which we call democracy, gave people a sense of empowerment, an opportunity to exercise initiative, which was denied to those living in a top-down authoritarian system. The rule of law, instead of kings and pharaohs, provided a secure environment for a wide range of individual enterprise. Sumer was authoritarian, but Egypt was totalitarian.

Although creativity is much more likely in a democratic than in an authoritarian regime, democracy is not a guarantee. The essential requirement is the limitation of authority. Autocracies do not tolerate open debate and dissent. Democracies are not necessarily open minded either. Each city had limits on what could be said or done; there have been gods to placate and, initially, oligarchs to consider.

The authority structure is important at the family level, not just at the state or political level. If the head of a family remains an authority figure until he dies, there is little room for individualism or democracy. The Greek landscape and economy promoted geographic and occupational mobility and individualism.

Freedom told us nothing about its uses or its direction and destination. What Athenian democracy contributed more directly was the involvement of citizens in its institutions, in particular their role in the administration of justice. All citizens were participants in decision-making. They witnessed and participated in argument;

they were familiarized with issues of credible evidence and plausible reasoning. They were exposed to conflicting evidence and views, facts and reasoning, and were required to reach a verdict and to accept the outcome. They learned to accept decisions not always to their liking but in which they had participated. I suspect that this experience would help account for the tolerance of the government and the people for the radical views of some of the philosophers.

Thomas (1992, 129, 138) describes an analogy between the city governments, law courts, and legal procedures and the culture of the intellectual community. She goes further and attributes genesis or causation to the legal system. The participation of citizens in every aspect of government, judicial in particular, prepared them for debate and predisposed them to reasoning. Lloyd and Sivin (2002, 184–87) share much the same views; multiple city-states, the absence of authoritarian rule, the prevailing system of laws, and their administration have been the propitiating conditions for intellectual achievement.

Democracy and a climate of discussion and debate were mutually supportive and essential. But it was the discussion, debate, and agreement that came first and gave birth to government. Elsewhere, the emperor was far away and all-powerful.

The laws of Athens extended into the sphere of religion. In the days of Pericles, the propagation of astronomical theories was an impeachable offense (Schlagel 1984, 51). Anaxagoras was exiled because he claimed that the sun was made of stone and the moon made of earth and inhabitable. Socrates was sentenced to death for impiety.

The Greek philosophers, starting with Anaximander and Pythagoras, utterly rejected the religious beliefs prevalent among the people. They had no place for deity, or for agency, in their cosmology. Yet they were highly respected and secure members of society. Plato's Academy and Aristotle's Lyceum flourished for nine hundred years.

Why did not the priesthood rise in arms and motivate the people to turn against them? Why did not the people themselves, the government, turn against the infidels? It was not a competing religion, but it was a rejection of prevailing beliefs. Were the views of the philosophers so abstract that they were not seen as a challenge to popular beliefs?

Popular religion occupied little intellectual space. The humanoid gods had limited power and jurisdiction and were humanlike in personality, with whom they could negotiate (Muller 1957, 138–40). There was minimal overlap with the abstract cosmology and causality of the philosophers. But ignorance could not explain the respect and support accorded the scholars. Only tolerance of differences could do this.

The survival and prosperity of this subculture for so many centuries admitted of only one possible explanation. Ordinary Greek people shared the tolerance of dissent of the philosophers despite their polytheistic beliefs. Tolerance was the product of citizen experience in the judicial process, familiarity with the argumentative process, and acceptance of judicial (and electoral) outcomes.

The closest analogy is the experience of Akhenaton, who imposed a more advanced monotheistic creed on the Egyptians. It was nowhere as extreme as the views of the philosophers, but the priesthood had everything to lose; it rebelled and, after Akhenaton's death, sought to eradicate every trace of the new religion and of Akhenaton's very existence. His tomb was unknown. But he sought to destroy the established religion.

ADVERSARIAL CULTURE

A private enterprise economy and a free and democratic society provided the opportunity for wide participation in the research endeavor of the Greek intellectual community. The participants were enabled to contribute by the democratic nature of the state on one hand and by affluence in a free economy on the other. Literacy, in particular, promoted participation and enlarged the potential audience. Who were the individuals and groups who contributed to Greek intellectual and scientific achievements? What was their motivation? What was their support?

The Greek intellectual community was a highly competitive enterprise. Participants were self-selected. Contributors were those who could convince others of their sagacity but particularly of the correctness and originality of their views. It was highly individualistic and meritocratic as judged by participants and by students in particular. There were no formal qualifications or requirements of class or occupation. There were women among the participants, even slaves (Lloyd and Sivin 2002, 90–92, 97–102).

Philosophers strove for reputation for its own sake and as a means of economic survival. They acquired a following, sought student fees from lecturing and tutoring, and supported themselves in this fashion. They had to differentiate themselves from other philosophers, to distinguish themselves by challenging prevailing views and proposing radical hypotheses and speculations of their own. Even physicians engaged in vocal dissent about theories of disease and treatment.

There was no state involvement and few wealthy patrons (Lloyd and Sivin 2002, 85–103). Only later, in Alexandria, was there support for scholars from the Greek kings of Egypt. Thinkers specializing in medicine, engineering, and architecture had an easier life since they had patients and clients, if not students.

This was a subculture of creativity. The schools in the fourth century BCE were better described as debating societies than educational institutions. They were arenas for the competition of ideas. Participation in and allegiance to any school was voluntary and, for many, transitory. Students clustered around a respected teacher, initially little more than a coterie of students. Institutional development was rudimentary until the establishment of libraries. Later, Plato's Academy and Aristotle's Lyceum evolved into universities and research institutions.

The competition of ideas helps explain the vigor of Greek intellectual activity, its diversity and creativity. Debate was the process of Greek learning. It promoted a cognitive selection, an evolution of ideas, many minds being better than just one. The process was both oral and written—lecture, discussion and debate, text and commentary. Rival schools of thought—Stoics, Epicureans, and Cynics—as well as individuals propounding conflicting views competed for influence. It was the adversarial culture's stress on logic that must have required abstraction and objectivity.

Participants in this subculture were exposed to a wide range of subjects. Some of the leading thinkers were not specialists but made contributions on diverse subjects. This was clear with Aristotle, who wrote on everything, and Plato, who ranged from political scientist to epistemologist. But there were many others. Such a wide range of knowledge and interest was almost a prescription for the ability to hypothesize.

Argument or debate was associated with the absence of an attitude of obedience and subservience, a lack of respect for authority, be it secular or sacred. Democracy was probably essential. Debate could stress empirical facts or logic or neither, just personal opinion and individual experience. The institutional structure for intellectual activity guaranteed diversity, novelty, and creativity; it also provided a limited reality check—logic but not empirical verification.

The absence of sacred authority in the minds of the Greek intellectual elite induced, if not required, the invention of an alternative source of order and authority. Their choice was logic. Abstract reasoning ruled in the absence of another authority. Scholars were certainly testing one another's assumptions and implications but did not employ experimental methods. Although the process was competitive, the enterprise or the results were collaborative. The Greek method was less efficient than the scientific method inasmuch as no road went untraveled, but eventually, it led in the same direction, even if the destination of teachings and discoveries remained beyond reach.

How such a minority came to exist and persist for a millennium in Greece and Greek-dominated areas and nowhere else in antiquity, we do not know. But writing that preserved classic texts for successive generations was essential. The leading scholars wrote.

THE ALPHABET

The characteristics of Greek culture described so far are geography, economy, individualism, taste for novelty, experience in self-government, limitation of authority, and debate. They were the conditions for the vigorous intellectual enterprise, a competitive search for knowledge that persisted for centuries. But it tells us nothing about the direction of that search or its achievements. Why such concern with the abstract nature of reality? Two elements of Greek culture have been suggested as conducive to achievements and its character: the alphabet and the language itself.

The phonetic alphabet is the most widely stressed explanation of Greek intellectual achievements. No one claims that it accounts for Greek achievement, only that it was a major contribution. It is not the alphabet per se but the uses to which it was put and their consequences. Only a tiny minority in Egypt could read and write its hieroglyphic script; not many more in Sumer were familiar with cuneiform after years spent learning. But in Greece, most citizens were literate by the sixth century BCE. A literate population is one of many potential readers. Much more is written. Libraries had been created. Individual achievements were disseminated and preserved.

The Greeks had an earlier script. Linear B, which was a mixture of syllabics and ideographs, was abandoned, whereas the founder civilizations clung to their complex old script. The virtue of this explanation was that it raised no further questions since the Greeks did not invent the alphabet. They adopted the Phoenician alphabet and added vowels. Living for centuries without a script allowed the language to evolve and grow.

The signal cognitive characteristic of a phonetic alphabet is abstraction and representation. Writing is the visual version of speech. Reading and writing require the analysis and synthesis of letters and words. They are facilitated by punctuation marks, themselves abstractions of relations rather than words. But punctuation did not come into common practice until late in the history of classical Greece. The practical characteristic of a phonetic alphabet is that it is easily learned. A logograph abstracts from a pictograph, which is an abstraction from an object or just imaginary, a construct. Languages with logographic scripts grow slowly, and the written language is never fully equivalent to speech.

Sumerian cuneiform and Egyptian hieroglyphs have had only about one thousand characters. Even considering the fact that almost every symbol has multiple meanings, they were small compared with classical Greek. Since the unit of measure is meaning, not character or word, it is nearly impossible to make quantitative comparisons. Abstract words used in speech that lack a visual association are unlikely to acquire a character and be perpetuated in the script. Characters or logograms are abstract too. A phonetic script is abstraction from speech; a logogram is a likely abstraction from a pictogram, which is an abstraction from a specific object or concept. Otherwise, it is arbitrary in form. The difference is that a phonetic script is a system, and a logographic script is a collection; the ability to read one character is unrelated to the ability to read other characters.

The ease of reading and writing with an alphabet was a factor, but it was more than that, a cultural expectation. Consequently, much of the population was exposed to the cognitive gains of literacy previously described. Greece was the only literate society. No society with a logographic script achieved literacy until the twentieth-century China and then only to a small portion of the total written vocabulary. Writing materials—whether parchment, papyrus, or wax tablets—were much more widely available in Greece than in earlier civilizations, and so were manuscripts to read. Libraries were invented in Sumer, but there were not many patrons. That of Alexandria was world famous. Some individuals had their own libraries in Greek cities.

The question is the role of literacy in Greece's singular achievements. Goody and Watt (1963, 320–33) consider Greek alphabetic literacy as an essential enabling factor in the democratic ordering of society and politics, in the development of logic and of analytical and critical traditions in the study of nature and history, and in the externalization and objectification of notions of time, space, self, and nature. They note that some of the Greek achievements in logic, taxonomy, and cosmology could not be found in other early cultures.

Writing and literacy accelerated the growth of vocabulary and of knowledge by preserving words rarely used and knowledge few shared, enhancing the linguistic and cognitive resources of successive generations. Vocabulary is the dominant raw material of rigorous thinking. Knowledge of the past widened the cultural repertoire of the present. The growth of knowledge led to specialization.

Logan (1986, 17–25, 99–123) stresses the role of writing. Its separation of knowledge from the knower leads to the concept of objectivity, universal truth, and abstraction. It contributed to Greek objectification of nature, the search for fundamental elements. The alphabet is also an instrument of division and partition and an efficient means of classifying information. This aspect he associates with deductive reasoning, with codified law, abstract science, and individualism. The very process of abstraction may carry over to other cognitive activities, including creativity.

The character of phonetic writing is consistent with the Greek objectification of nature in its taxonomy of knowledge and in its bias for abstract reasoning over empirical verification. However, it is reasoning by analogy or association. All Logan can claim is the correlation or the historical association of these characteristics of society and cognitive style, which may differ from one society to another. It is the cognitive style that is closely associated with the alphabet since there are differences between literate and illiterate individuals in the same society. The abstraction of phonetic writing involves a frame of mind that apprehends the distinction between sensory observation and fundamental reality.

Written language separates information from communication. Assman (2011, 3–21) stresses the institutional framework that will preserve representative texts and maintain a tradition that retains their relevance. It is this tradition, rather than any particular writer or text, that constitutes the Greek intellectual achievement. There must be social memory as well as individual achievement. The perpetuation of relevance requires what he calls a concept of truth or information, a criterion for judging the tradition, which for the Greeks was logic.

Texts can be written in any script. But a phonetic alphabet promotes far more prolific writing, many more copies, and a universe of potential readers. With writing, there is remembrance and evolution, without it, amnesia and repetition. The alphabet has also made possible the organization of written materials for easy storage and retrieval by any literate individual. Without it, access depends on the memory of librarians, their individual taxonomy.

Rosalind Thomas (1992, 3–14) took issue with phonetic literacy as an explanation of achievement. She stressed that Greece was a predominantly oral culture, even at the peak of its intellectual achievements. Although Athenian citizens learned to read at school, after school, there was little for them to read. Literacy was not a requirement for living. The supply of reading material other than monuments was very limited centuries after some of their great thinkers had lived and died. Few people wrote; papyrus was expensive, not used for casual messages or scribbles. Even some of the highly literate preferred to have texts read to them. In fact, reading was rarely silent; more often, it was aloud. Some scholars preferred listening to manuscripts being read aloud rather than reading them.

But we are not talking about most people but a small creative minority. The cumulative volume of writing was large. So was the reading public compared with any previous civilization.

If not phonetic literacy, then to what does Rosalind Thomas attribute Greek achievements? She does not offer one as such but suggests propitiating conditions—the absence of bureaucracy, the prevalence of the rule of law, the involvement of citizens in the enactment and in the implementation of law (Thomas 1992, 129–30, 138).

I would add that reading handwritten manuscripts until late in the Hellenic period was a slow and difficult enterprise, quite unlike reading today. Handwriting is not print; the quality of calligraphy was not always highly legible. There was little or no punctuation to structure clauses and sentences. Punctuation was not standardized until the second century CE by Aristarchus, librarian of Alexandria. Also, there was little separation of words. Reading was puzzle solving, word by word. Few literate people did any writing. Thus, the cognitive gains implicit in the use of alphabetic reading and writing today were limited in ancient Greece. A cognitive advantage particular to a phonetic script was that reading can proceed in gestalts—the swift grasp of phrases, clauses, and sentences—but not until print and Gutenberg.

Literacy usually means "reading ability." It can also be defined as "writing ability," which assumes reading ability but is not implied by it. It is the difference between recognition and construction. In writing, one has to select the symbols corresponding to the words and sounds one wishes to convey, instead of merely recognizing them and the words they represent. With the alphabet, the difference is small since the symbols used are few and simple. With ideographic script, writing is much more difficult than reading inasmuch as the symbols are many and complex. But composition is cognitively more demanding than comprehension, whatever the script. Reading literacy is more easily mastered and more widespread than writing literacy. Writing is creative; reading is not. How much writing was done? Probably not much. There was no writing surface that was both cheap and easy to use.

The availability of written texts has consequences, whether the texts are read by individuals alone or read to assemblies of individuals. The message is preserved intact, and it is amplified by reading to groups and multiplied by copying manuscripts. What is missing is the cognitive gains the listeners are forgoing by not reading.

What mattered most was who wrote and what was written. As a continuing process of development and dialogue across generations, it avoided the veneration of tradition. It was the writing, not the reading, that propelled and perpetuated Greek achievement, even if it was mainly an oral society. Greek thinkers had a market for their ideas, including students paying tuition, an audience for their disputes, and a readership for their writings. Widespread literacy was a necessary condition. Great thinkers may have lived in other cultures but lacked intellectual company or progeny.

The historical case against the dominant role of the alphabet was that the early Greek thinkers, such as Thales and Anaximander of Miletus, lived not long after the alphabet was adopted. At a time when Greece was strictly an oral culture, literacy was rare. There was little writing, almost nothing to read, and texts were very costly. A large amount of diverse reading material was not available until the fourth century BCE, long after Pythagoras, Parmenides, Empedocles, even Democritus. Whether these and other individuals would have achieved what they did had they been illiterate, we will never know. The alphabet, minus vowels, had been invented and used by the Phoenicians without the consequences asserted in Greece. But any script was better than none.

One must distinguish here between invention and discovery. Most invention is not a linguistic process at all, one reason it is found in all cultures. Language is not needed to invent the plow or the wheel or to transmit this knowledge to others. Only for the invention of ideas is language a near necessity. How does one identify or isolate an idea unless there is a word for it, or a word is created to express it mentally and in communication? The product of discovery, which is knowledge, is rarely an object, more likely a pattern or relation, an intangible. Even if a discovery requires no language, its perpetuation is in words or formulas; the Pythagorean theorem or pi has no other tangible form. With an alphanumeric system, it is easy to create words or formulas for every idea, material, or species. With logograms, it is nearly impossible; the store of knowledge available to an individual investigator cannot match that available to a user of alphanumerics. We know how inadequate the Egyptian hieroglyphs were because the conquest by the Greeks and Romans was followed by addition of another three or four thousand characters until the sheer burden of learning to read has led to their abandonment.

McGilchrist (2009, 179) argued that the invention of money was just as plausible as the alphabetic script as a stimulus for abstract reasoning. I question this view. First, abstract money—devoid of a commodity medium of exchange—was not introduced until late in the golden age of Athens, some four centuries after the alphabet. Second, the domain of prices was tiny in comparison with the domain of written language.

LANGUAGE

Alphabetic literacy contributed to abstract reasoning, but so did the structure and vocabulary of the Greek language. The language favored adoption of such a script because it was highly inflected.

In addition to changing a vowel and adding a letter or syllable to a noun or verb to reflect mode, number, and sex, it had cases—normative, genitive, dative, accusative—each of which provided multiple relations of the noun to other words as determined in the context of the sentence. Greek also was rich in prepositions, pronouns, and conjunctions—words that express relations between different words that facilitate organizing them into phrases, clauses, and sentences. It had an abundance of modifiers—adjectives and adverbs—as well as abstract nouns, giving it a range and precision of expression difficult, if not impossible, to achieve in Sumerian or Egyptian. In fact, Greek was both a synthetic and an analytic language. Without these qualities, it would have been difficult for its thinkers to conceive of the ideas they promoted and nearly impossible to communicate them. How this came about we do not know. Did they precede widespread literacy or result from it?

This linguistic versatility was not evident in Homer, whose Greek was spoken before the adoption of the alphabet. Homer's epics, when first written down in the eighth century BCE, lacked the abstract vocabulary required and employed by the philosophers, starting with Thales in the sixth century. Havelock and Herschbell (1978, 3–21) compared Homer's *Iliad* with *Gilgamesh*, finding that the Greek text already had many more different words and different meanings than the Sumerian text.

Nonphonetic scripts found it very difficult to create a character for a word that had no pictorial reference. Assman (2011, 235) believed that the small vocabulary in Sumerian and Egyptian scripts was nevertheless quite efficient in reflecting speech, implying that spoken vocabulary was similarly limited. Early Greece was an open society; it had a wider range of experience and needed a larger vocabulary. The scripts that replaced the original writing in that part of the world had a phonetic component—syllabic rather than alphabetic. With the adoption of the Phoenician alphabet, Greek became much more inflected by the time of Thales.

Connecting and relating words—conjunctions, prepositions—convert a series of separate words into coherent speech. So do tenses, cases, number, and gender. Writing does not fully replicate speech; it comes closer with the development of punctuation. A large vocabulary of abstract words facilitates abstract reasoning. The consequences for cognition apply to the illiterate since they are part of the language of speech and thought.

The cognitive process of speaking and reading in highly inflected, analytic languages differs from that in languages with no inflection or purely synthetic—changes in the sound and spelling of nouns and verbs to express relationships. Reading and thinking in uninflected languages is word by word; the reader must surmise how successive words relate to one another in context, but what is the context, the sentence? In inflected languages, the unit is the sentence. Prepositions, pronouns, conjunctions, and tenses allow the reader to identify sentences long before punctuation was invented. Language structure matters.

Language structures evolve. With writing, the pace of evolution is dictated by the script. A phonetic script facilitates inflexion, an analytic structure. In the short run, the existing language is the dominant resource for thinking and communication. It shapes the way we think. If verbs lack tenses, we have difficulty in conceiving of and communicating a precise sense of time. If language is poor in abstract nouns, so is our thinking. Benjamin Whorf (Hoijer 1954) argues that thought is shaped by language, but historically, one might argue that language is shaped by thought. The meaning of a word must exist in some mind before the word can be created to communicate it and to recall. It must be used to survive.

THE DECLINE

Greek culture was not destroyed as were the civilizations in the Western Hemisphere. Its intellectual progress slowed; institutions that once housed debate and accomplishment regressed into transmission of past achievements to the next generation. Civilization ended; culture persisted. The knowledge of the Greeks was passed on to the new Islamic civilization, which initially accepted and advanced it but eventually rejected most of it.

Perhaps we can learn something about the conditions for discovery and invention from the end of the Greek experience. Alexander, pupil of Aristotle, greatly expanded the boundaries of Greek influence.

For hundreds of years thereafter, there were more people of Greek culture and language than in the golden age of Athens. Some of the late achievers were not ethnically Greek. The most important addition from our standpoint was Egypt, conquered in 332 BCE. The city of Alexandria was built on the delta of the Nile. Egypt was ruled by Greek royalty until the death of Cleopatra in 30 BCE. It became a Roman colony thereafter and part of Byzantium after the fall of Rome until the Arab invasion of 641 CE. Nearly all achievements late in Greek civilization were associated with Alexandria.

Alexander converted the Greek world into an empire that fragmented into monarchies often at war, followed by Roman conquest. What had been independent city-states were reduced to small components of a large empire, leaving them with less autonomy and little independence. Citizens were no longer active participants in their own governance. Strange peoples with whom the Greeks traded and sometimes fought were now incorporated in the same empire. Many of them were Hellenized. Perhaps the quest for order displaced the passion for knowledge. The empire itself created a new set of occupational opportunities for the able and ambitious as officials and administrators. Patronage declined. Opportunities for economic advancement and professional prestige shifted to other occupations. Roman government interest in scholarship and research was largely limited to contributions to military power and public works. Most likely, the quality of scholars and researchers declined over time.

Most of the achievements associated with Alexandria were during the period of Greek rule. But there were a few important inventors during the first two hundred years of Roman rule—Hero, Ptolemy, and Galen, little of note thereafter. Alexandria remained in Byzantium and continued as a center of scholarship. After the fall of Rome, much of the Greek cultural area remained within Byzantium. The two builders of the Hagia Sophia were both Greeks.

Symbolically, it ended with the closure of the Academy and the Lyceum by Justinian, who regarded these institutions created by Plato and Aristotle as pagan. But long before closure, they had ceased being arenas of discovery and become educational institutions, bequeathing the past to the future. Remnants of Greek culture and accomplishment lingered on another thousand years in Byzantium and, more significantly, in the Islamic civilization in the eighth and several subsequent centuries.

We cannot quantify the influence of these trends or rank them in importance, but taken together, they amounted to an environment much less favorable than it had been in city-states or under the munificence of the Ptolemies in Egypt. But there was nothing to preclude careers in the tradition of Athens or Alexandria. Private property and the rule of law were maintained.

There was another possible explanation, not external or environmental but internal to the Greek intellectual enterprise itself. It was self-limiting; its job was done. The corpus of Greek thought, capped by the prodigious writings of Aristotle, had become so large that what had been an arena for debate became a classroom for learning. Later generations of scholars devoted much of their time to mastering the works of their predecessors. Communication of knowledge alone became a drag as well as a springboard. New generations spent more time mastering the achievements of their predecessors. New ideas had to struggle against established beliefs.

The Greeks accepted that the evidence of the senses was not fundamental reality. They debated the nature of this reality but had no means of testing their hypotheses or of probing beyond the senses. What was missing was opportunity. Further progress depended not on the speculations of the philosophers but on experimentations of the mathematician-engineers of Alexandria. They required the means of testing hypotheses or the information to generate new hypotheses. Failing these, their job was done.

The hallmark invention of the Scientific Revolution was Galileo's telescope. Archimedes and Ptolemy studied optics. Magnifying lenses were available, initially carved from quartz, later made of glass. They were used for close-up magnification and as burning lenses to start fires. Ptolemy could have used a telescope. Perhaps a flash of insight was missing, that a telescope required two lenses at opposite ends of a tube. More likely, the precision needed to create lenses that magnified with limited distortion did not exist; neither did colorless glass. A simple telescope or microscope would have multiplied the information of the senses and opened up new opportunities for research.

Hero opened the temple door with steam power, the emblem of the Industrial Revolution. He understood energy, whether steam, compressed air, wind, or the force of gravity. There were opportunities to mechanize the labor of humans or oxen, such as the Archimedes screw pump. Greeks knew mechanics as witnessed in their planetariums and robotic toys. But could Hero have generated and maintained the high pressure needed for an efficient, laborsaving device? The quality of the metals and the precision machining required did not exist. Technology was not ready. The Archimedes screw survived for two thousand years and Galen's medical textbook for fifteen hundred years, and Ptolemy's cosmology prevailed until Copernicus.

There was some progress in materials and methods. But the contributions of mathematician-engineers required a demand for novelty, and perhaps this too was missing in the final centuries of the Roman Empire. The Islamic civilization that inherited the accomplishments of the Greeks eventually became introverted and retrogressive. But that is another chapter.

I suggest that its job was done. Greece had accomplished most of what was possible with the tools it had—Greek mathematics and human senses. They did not accept the reality as revealed by the senses but lacked the tools to probe deeper into fundamental reality, beyond the discriminatory power of the senses, and beyond the spectrum of human sensory dimensions.

One area in which the Greeks fell short of what was possible was the study of change. They could have performed the experiments on acceleration, which Galileo carried out much later. The mathematics developed to measure curvilinear areas and volumes might have been adapted to measure acceleration and deceleration. But then I think of the catapults designed by Archimedes, some of which propelled projectiles of a specific weight and specific distances with high accuracy. He must have understood ballistics, and he invented the geometry of curvature.

SUMMARY AND CONCLUSION

The accomplishments of the Greek civilization in discovery and invention were, first, a concept of the cosmos that was agency-free, whose constituents were causally related, a search for reality beyond the evidence of the senses; second, logical processes to guide the search for knowledge; and, third, a beginning effort to order, to characterize reality. Their common element was abstraction. There were numerous practical inventions derived from the principles of reality as conceived by their mathematicians and engineers.

Greece was a latecomer. It was a hunting, gathering, and fishing society well after the adoption of farming to the east and south. It was illiterate when the first works of literature were being read in several other places. Its alphabet was adopted from the Phoenicians. It contributed none of the major inventions before the first millennium BCE. Yet it forged far ahead of all the others in contribution to human knowledge and understanding. Why did abstract reasoning, cosmology, logic, taxonomy, and the elements of discovery flourished in Greece, not among the Phoenicians or the more advanced older civilizations of Egypt, Mesopotamia, and China?

Thomas Kuhn (1962) has answered this question with regard to scientific communities in the modern world—why it is so often an outsider, not the leading thinkers of the current scientific orthodoxy, who makes the breakthroughs. It is the young, whether individuals or civilizations, that are most creative because they are not burdened with the legacy of culture or constrained by intellectual habit. Ultimately, it was not the civilized peoples of the Roman Empire or the succeeding Islamic world who carried forward the Greek achievements; it was the barbarians to the north and west.

Numerous explanatory variables have been proposed. These explanations are not alternatives; they are complementary because they attempt to explain different aspects of Greek achievement. Nor are they additive. They may have structure, a hierarchy. One must ask of each explanation, what is its own explanation?

Numerous factors favorable to Greek discovery and invention or achievement in science and technology have been considered so far. But they are just a list. How should the diverse factors be ordered or ranked? Is there a pattern? First, which are self-explanatory, and which require further explanation for their influence? Second, which are merely contributory, and which are essential?

Geography and the alphabet require no further explanation. Geography is given, and the economy is largely derivative. The alphabet was inherited from the Phoenicians; it enabled the evolution of the language into a means of abstract thinking and communication. Their influence on other factors is one way. The others—polity, logic, language—interact, making it difficult, if not impossible, to assess their relative importance. They require explanation, the political structure in particular. Why the bottom-up authority in some city-states, whereas top down prevailed everywhere else? Why a limited scope of authority? Then there is the culture of debate. The reliance on logic to resolve disagreements was both a product of Greek thinking and a condition for its achievement.

Geography and economy were simply favorable conditions. Geography is many things—location, topography, climate, soil, and other resources, none of which is essential, but the combination is important. Economy also is multidimensional, but extensive and diverse trade with other places and peoples is the important feature. Exposure to other cultures, ways, and ideas must have influenced attitudes toward novelty which characterized Greek society and its intellectual life. But trade was not the only way. The Greeks were often at war with other peoples.

Economy and trade provided the affluence for intellectual pursuits and enabled some individuals to devote their lives to philosophical inquiry. It also encouraged individualism. But a case has not been made that any particular feature of geography or function of economy is essential. Some affluence and exposure to diverse peoples, ideas, and practices may have been necessary, but they do not foretell or condition the uses to be made of these resources.

A different explanation is the character of Greek polity. Polity, unlike geography, must be created and maintained. What aspects of polity were essential, and essential for what? The city-state, bottom-up authority, limitation of authority, the process of administration of justice, and election of officials?

Much of Greece was partitioned among city-states. But Alexandria was part of Egypt, not an autonomous city-state but a new city, a transplant of Greek culture. It was their multiplicity that ensured freedom from authority. But there must be at least one haven. Other cultures, including Sumer, had city-states but no haven.

Bottom-up authority was not needed. We know this because the originators of the Greek intellectual enterprise were not in Athens but in Miletus, well before the establishment of democracy. Only Plato among the leading scholars was Athenian. Democracy, as practiced in Athens, was not in place at the beginning. Thales was worshipped as one of the great sages of antiquity. Together with Anaximander and other Milesians, they initiated a subculture of inquiry. Limited authority was enough. In the case of Alexandria, as long as the kings were Greek, creativity was encouraged and subsidized.

What was necessary is the tolerance by the people and the state for the philosophers, mathematicians, and engineers. Tolerance for differences may be enhanced by the practice of democracy. But it is best regarded as a condition for democracy. It precludes tyranny of the majority. Tolerance and limitation of authority can be considered as opposite sides of the same coin. Either is possible without democracy.

Athenian democracy involved citizens in the administration of justice and other public decisions. It exposed them to reason, to evidence and logic in the judicial process, to debate and conflict resolution. This experience was training for a subculture of dispute and discovery, to the size of membership in the intellectual community and its enterprise, and may account for its longevity. It must have contributed to the adversarial culture among scholars and to logic as the final authority. Citizenship and scholarship were complementary, but neither was causal. Debate, with reason as arbiter, was practiced by the scholars in Miletus without the benefit of citizen participation in government.

The adversarial culture and tolerance of differences was the method of intellectual advance and discovery at the time. It is the only explanation that itself needs explaining.

The alphabet was necessary. It contributed to literacy, which in turn contributed to democracy. But it was essential for the evolution of the language into a vehicle capable of expressing and communicating ideas. The alphabet enabled Greek language to develop a large repertoire of abstractions as resources for thinking and communication. It was necessary but not causal.

All languages written alphabetically evolved because they could. But cultures retaining a nonphonetic script had languages that were concrete; none developed a rich vocabulary of abstract terms or of relational terms because they could not.

Literacy also provided a market for new ideas and preserved them for succeeding generations. The gains of literacy were not fully achieved until Gutenberg. In Athens, it was state policy that generated a literate citizenry.

Why did Greece adopt such a script, whereas Egypt and Sumer did not? One plausible explanation is that far-ranging trade and travel promoted a script that was not language specific but could be used to write any language.

Natural experiments are going on in our time on script, language, and authority that may shed light on their influence. Many Chinese are using pinyin, Chinese written in the alphabet, for communication via electronic devices. Will the pinyin writing develop words for which there are no characters? Vietnam changed from the Chinese script to the Latin alphabet under French rule, but widespread literacy is a very recent development. In several Asian nations, top-down authority has been replaced by bottom-up authority as a consequence of WWII. But behavioral changes are measured in generations, not years. South Korea also shifted from the Chinese script to its own syllabary. Is it mere coincidence that South Korea, since 1953, has advanced more rapidly than any nation in history?

In the final analysis, how do I order these diverse explanations? The phonetic alphabet, the Greek language, the limitation of authority, and a culture that has valued novelty are the four characteristics most directly related to creativity. The alphabet and language are the two most relevant for abstraction. Geography and economy promoted individualism and provided the means. Argument is the method, the political structure, the experience of search for truth, knowledge. None of these contributions to Greek creativity can be regarded as causes. But their combination has been causal. What remains to be explained is the agenda of abstraction, the search for fundamental reality, rather than subjects more closely related to the needs and interests of the society.

What characteristics of Greece that appeared relevant for its intellectual efflorescence were not found in any of the civilizations or cultures at the time, before, or for a millennium after? There were other trading, seafaring cultures. There were others with a phonetic alphabet, a fairly high level of literacy. Other languages had extensive vocabularies, not lacking abstract words.

The inventive Sumer may have prized novelty. If there were any facilitating condition not found elsewhere previously or at the time, it was the limited scope of authority and its bottom-up direction that provided scope for freedom of opinion and behavior. But that freedom still told us nothing about the uses made of it. Another may have been the passion for novelty. Greek inventors were not the artisans but the most educated individuals and discoverers, some of whom put theory to practical use. They were able to apply cognitive skills developed or exercised in one context to other domains. Some civilization had to be the first, and the Greeks were first.

There are other questions to which, I think, there is no answer. Why the passion for abstraction and discovery that created the world in which we live today? Why were the subjects debated by leading thinkers so esoteric, and why should they be so highly regarded? Why did Greek intellectual effort not focus on invention rather than discovery, on engineering rather than physics, on improving conditions of everyday life, on ethical issues instead of debating the fundamental structure of matter and the dimension and duration of the universe? Yes, they were concerned with disease and its treatment; but even here, there was a bias toward fundamental explanation rather than practical experimentation. It was a search for Occam's razor before puberty.

All early cultures stared at the starry night sky, observed the orbits of the sun and moon, and noted other regularities of nature. They invented polytheistic myths as explanations. Only the Greeks advanced from myth to an agency-free concept of reality.

A search for understanding of astronomical reality meant discovery of the laws of physics. Bottom-up cosmology, theoretical physics, and applied mechanics were the Greek prelude to the Scientific Revolution. What if they had focused on earthbound chemistry instead or sought to understand the subjective mind instead of the objective matter? Was there an alternative access route to the Scientific Revolution? I think not. To the Industrial Revolution, there was no other way. Only physics could invent the instruments and knowledge needed to advance in other domains.

REFERENCES

Annas, Julia. 1975. "Aristotle, Number and Time." *Philosophical Quarterly* 26 (99): 97–113.

Assmann, Jan. 2011. "Greece and Discipline Thinking." In *Cultural Memory and Early Civilization*, 234–75. Cambridge: Cambridge University Press.

Cahill, Thomas. 2003. *The Wine-Dark Sea—Why the Greeks Matter.* New York: Nan A. Tolese, Doubleday.

Bittle, Celestine N. 1950. *The Science of Thinking.* Milwaukee: Bruce Publishing Company.

Donald, Merlin. 1998. "The Prehistory of Mind: An Exchange." *New York Review of Books* 45 (9): 61.

Goody, J., and I. Watt. 1963. "The Consequences of Literacy." *Comparative Studies in Society and History* 5 (3): 304–34.

Havelock, Eric. 1978. "The Alphabetization of Homer." In *Communication Arts in the Ancient World*, edited by Eric A. Havelock and Jackson E. Hershbell, 3–21. New York: Hastings House.

Hoijer, Harry. 1954. "The Sapir-Whorf Hypothesis." In *Language in Culture*, edited by Hoijer, 92–105. Chicago: University of Chicago Press. See Whorf, Benjamin. 1952. *Collected Papers on Metalinguistics*. Washington DC: Department of State, Foreign Service Institute.

Kalligeropoulos, D., and S. Vasileiadou. 1984. "The Homeric Automata and their Implementation." In *History of Mechanism and Machine Science 6*, 77–84.

Kuhn, Thomas. 1962. *The Structure of Scientific Revolutions*. Chicago: University of Chicago Press.

Landels, J. G. 1978. *Engineering in the Ancient World*. Berkeley: University of California Press.

Lloyd, Geoffrey, and Nathan Sivin. 2002. *The Way and the Word—Science and Medicine in Early China and Greece*. New Haven: Yale University Press.

Logan, Robert K. 1986. *The Alphabet Effect—The Impact of the Phonetic Alphabet on the Development of Western Civilization*. New York: William Morrow and Company, Inc.

Mark, Robert, and Ahmet Çakmak, eds. 1992. *The Hagia Sophia from the Age of Justinian to the Present*. Cambridge University Press.

McGilchrist, Iain. 2009. *The Master and His Emissary—The Divided Brain and the Making of the Western World*. New Haven and London: Yale University Press.

McKeon, Richard P. 1949. "Aristotle and the Origins of Science in the West." In *Science and Civilization*, edited by Robert C. Stauffer, 3–29. Madison: University of Wisconsin Press.

Mithen, Steven. 1998. *Creativity in Human Evolution and Prehistory*. Thames & Hudson.

Muller, Herbert J. 1957. *The Uses of the Past—Profiles of Former Societies*. New York: Oxford University Press.

Ochoa, George, and Melinda Corey. 1995. *The Timeline Book of Science*. New York: Galantine Books.

Schlagel, Richard. 1984. *From Myth to Modern Science—A Study of the Origins and Growth of Scientific Thought*, vol. I. New York: Peter Lang.

———. 2010. *Seeking the Truth*. Amherst, New York: Humanity Books.

Schmidhauser, A. U. 2010. "The Birth of Grammar in Greece." In *A Companion to the Ancient Greek Language*, edited by E. J. Bakker. Oxford: Wiley-Blackwell.

Shipley, Graham. 2000. *The Greek World after Alexander, 323–30 BC*. London and New York: Routledge.

Spengler, Oswald. 1945. *The Decline of the West*, vol. 1. New York: Alfred A. Knopf.

Thomas, Rosalind. 1992. *Literacy and Orality in Ancient Greece*. Cambridge University Press.

Toynbee, Arnold. 1947. *A Study of History, Abridgement by D. C. Somervell.* New York and London: Oxford University Press.

————. 1952. *Greek Historical Thought.* New York: Mentor Books.

Usher, Abbot Payson. 1959. *A History of Mechanical Inventions.* Boston: Beacon Press.

VI

Chinese Civilization and Culture

INTRODUCTION

The question is often asked, how is it that China, leading the world in technological achievement until 1500 or so, has lagged ever more behind thereafter? That is not the right question. After all, other civilizations have also led and then fallen behind. The real question is how and why the West has forged ahead with its Scientific Revolution, followed by the Industrial Revolution?

China's case was simple; it led because it was a civilization uninterrupted for millennia, until modern times, whereas other civilizations declined or disappeared. It was geography—the Pacific on the east; Himalayas on the southwest; Siberia, scarcely populated, to the north; and desert and semidesert to the west. The Chinese heartland had the soil, water, and rice to result in a very large and densely settled population, which easily digested any conquerors from its less populated periphery. Yet in its long history, it never matched the achievements of classical Greece in abstract reasoning and decipherment of the laws of nature. More striking perhaps is its persistent lag in the past half millennium despite repeated exposure to European science and technology, including military conquests.

China lagged in recent centuries because it did not experience a scientific revolution and the resulting Industrial Revolution. Neither did anyone else, except in Europe. Technological progress can precede only so far by chance, serendipity, and trial and error. Eventually, it became dependent on scientific understanding. Science, in turn, can advance only so far without improved instrumentation to magnify and supplement the senses.

Unlike other civilizations, it was never brought to an end by foreign conquest or internal dissolution. It alone, among civilizations, persisted invulnerable for thousands of years, until the arrival of the Europeans in the past two centuries. It, of all civilizations, might have been expected to lead the way to the modern world. China, rather than shorter-lived civilizations, can best provide information on the deterrents, disincentives for discovery and innovation in particular but also in technological invention.

What is China? In the days of classical Greece, it was the middle kingdom, largely the area between the Yangtze and the Yellow Rivers. Comparing it with Greece would be appropriate, but there was a large difference in population: China's was estimated at sixty million in 1 CE (Lloyd and Sivin 2002, 11), whereas the Greeks were scattered around the eastern Mediterranean as well as in Greece but probably totaled no more than one-tenth of China.

At the time of the Scientific and Industrial Revolutions, it was a much bigger China, much of it not Chinese by ethnicity. But *China* and *Chinese* referred to the culture more than the ethnicity. Thus, it is appropriate to compare it with Europe rather than with a particular European country. Some of its achievements were by members of different ethnic groups but of Chinese culture. It is the culture that concerns us.

Lloyd and Sivin (2002) compared Greece and China for the same period, 800 BCE–200 CE. But if we used the development of writing as a starting point, China was well ahead of Greece. Some four thousand years ago, its logographic writing was well developed. We do not know how far back its beginnings were. In any case, with logographic script, development of writing was a prolonged, endless process, whereas with a phonetic script, it can be almost instantaneous. Greece adopted the Phoenician alphabet, adding vowels, around 800 BCE. It had been illiterate for centuries but previously had used a combination of logograph and syllabary, Linear B. Thus, it was not clear by how much Chinese civilization preceded the Greek but by at least a thousand years.

The status of China in the sequence of civilizations differed somewhat from that of Greece. Greece was not a founder civilization; it drew a great deal from neighboring cultures and civilizations with which it traded and against whom it sometimes fought. China was a founder civilization with qualification. It lagged the other founder civilizations, and some of its achievements were imported. But it was relatively isolated by geography and by choice, never part of a cauldron of culture as was the eastern Mediterranean. The Great Wall is symbolic of Chinese mentality.

In comparing China with Europe, the relevant period for Europe could be the thirteenth through the eighteenth century. For China, the same period is appropriate, although China changed so slowly and so little that precise periods are meaningless. The last four centuries are out of bounds.

It was too late for China to develop its own scientific revolution, never mind a subsequent industrial revolution. All it could do was to imitate, to catch up. Its contacts with Europe were almost nil until the sixteenth century and quite limited for centuries more so that independent development remained a possibility. But there was no flow of discoveries, and the flow of inventions—paper and gunpowder—was in the opposite direction. Since it took Europe more than five hundred years from the beginnings of the Scientific Revolution to the Industrial Revolution, China could have had its scientific revolution centuries after Europe and still forged abreast or ahead. None of its invaders until the arrival of the Europeans were advanced enough, or numerous enough, to cause a discontinuity.

How much have changed in values and attitudes during the twentieth century, from Sun Yat-sen to Chiang Kai-shek to Mao and to the current infiltration of Western values and attitudes? China is still stuck with hieroglyphics and retains traditional medicine, superstitions of primitive religions, numerology, and fortune-telling while also adopting the culture and technology of the West. China's future is not our subject. There are too many different influences in China, no generalizations can be made, and the eventual outcome is unknown. Much has changed in Japan, which shared some of China's shortcomings. But that is another topic.

What needs to be explained is not just the absence of continuous progress but also the failure to exploit what achievements it had, even the failure to preserve. Some were forgotten and lost, suggesting they were not the products of the literate Chinese, but some that only the literate Chinese could master were forgotten. At several points in its history, there were modest steps toward a scientific revolution—periods of innovation, people with protoscientific insight—but these achievements did not evolve, left no progeny, and in some cases were forgotten. So there were false starts rather than simple stagnation. Knowledge of the workings of the solar system learned from foreign astronomers was forgotten. So was the immense tomb of the first emperor of a united China, built by hundreds of thousands of workers over several decades, entombing thousands of workers and hundreds of concubines?

It is not just that China did not have a scientific revolution but also that it regarded its history as regression rather than stagnation. Achievement was not advancement but recovery of the knowledge of the ancient sage-kings or deciphering Confucius. This view of the past was not another version of the Garden of Eden. Adam and Eve were not sages. There were regressions in fact, but the belief preceded the historical facts. Such beliefs discouraged progress.

In a large population, in a very long-lived culture, one is likely to find examples of almost every concept and idea, practice, and belief. But a series of isolated examples does not stretch to any conclusion. Joseph Needham, in his thorough search through surviving texts going back three thousand years and careful interpretation of the meaning of words used by scholars in different ages, finds Chinese examples of almost every concept or idea believed to have contributed to the rise of modern science. Even admitting that a few examples do not establish a pattern of thinking, his work makes it all the more difficult to understand why Chinese protoscientific efforts never bloomed into modern science.

Our purpose is to understand the conditions for discovery and invention, not conditions precluding or deterring. We look at China not just because of its longevity but because, over its long history, it has been responsible for many discoveries and inventions, some which we might consider complex or advanced. They lead us to expect a sequel. But China is unique in other ways. Its resistance to change is without peer. Other fairly long-lived civilizations have evolved. They have developed or adopted phonetic scripts. They have created or adopted cosmologies somewhat less primitive than that prevailing in China throughout its history. Their reasoning processes have tended to advance beyond the similarity qua analogy prevailing in China.

What follows is not a history but a discussion of those aspects of Chinese culture that may be relevant for the progress of discovery, invention, and innovation. An explanation of what did not happen is inevitably short on facts and long on speculation and hypotheses. There will be some references to behavior in the twentieth century as evidence of the incredible persistence of Chinese culture but no implication to their prevalence. All one can say is that traditional beliefs and behaviors that persist in the twentieth century must have been even more prevalent in the past. Undated generalizations refer to the more recent period.

CULTURE

Philosophies

China, during its early history, was not united under a single ruler. There was a period of contending states, often at war, 481–221 BCE. This situation was not quite comparable to Greek city-states. There were ethnic differences, no hint of democracy. These states represented different cultural origins and combinations. There was much diversity (Lawler 2007). Among them, there were multiple sponsors and patrons of scholarship, a period also described as the Hundred Schools of thought.

The rulers of the contending states were interested primarily in the art of government and the art of war; these and ethics were what most schools of thought provided (Lloyd and Sivin 2002, 27–33). The people were confronted with contending schools of thought or personal behavior, which might be called secular religions. In terms of lasting influence on Chinese culture, there were not one hundred but only four schools: Taoism, legalism, Buddhism, and Confucianism. Buddhism did not come to China from India until 65 CE, after the country had been unified. There was a fifth, Mo-tzu and the Mohists, who had no influence and represented China's opportunity lost. In this period, there was diversity. That window closed with the unification of China by the Qin in 221 BCE and the standardization of state doctrine by the Han, who replaced the Qin.

What was lacking was a multiplicity of city-states or autonomous regions competing in culture, values, technology, and trade. A dynamic civilization became a static culture. To Spengler (1945, vol. II, p. 109), Chinese history ended early in the Han dynasty. Toynbee (1947, vol. I, p. 549–50) held a similar view. The next historical event was the revolution of 1911, ending the Manchu dynasty and introducing Western political institutions and ideas.

The Qin dynasty was brutal and short lived. It was best known for its great burning of the books (Fitzgerald 1973, 80–84). The legalist school, which stood for the undisputed authority of the state and strict laws, gained the upper hand. The legalists tried to destroy the books of all other contending schools of thought. They sought to erase history. Scholars hiding copies from the bonfire were beheaded. So much for tolerance of diversity. Confucian writings mostly survived; his works were widespread. But nearly all the work of the Mohists was lost so that we do not know for sure the extent of their achievements, only the direction of their efforts.

The Qin was overthrown and succeeded by the Han dynasty (206 BC–221 CE), which rehabilitated Confucius. His views on the family were generalized to society and the state as the doctrine of the land, with the emperor as a father figure. From the Han dynasty forward, it was Confucianism that mattered. It did incorporate some elements of Taoism and Buddhism and underwent corruption and reform but remained the dominant way of thinking of the Chinese people into the twentieth century.

A single unified state has persisted to the present day and a single state doctrine, Confucianism. There were conquests by Mongols and Manchu, which were just changes in dynasties. Rampaging warlords eager for subjects and spoils were no substitute for stable, independent communities.

Belief in China was never of the either-or variety prevalent in the West but decidedly both-and. The culture embraced contradiction. Most Chinese would participate in the rituals of more than one school of thought or religion. Our question is, what influence did each of these traditions have on discovery and invention, on science and technology?

Taoism, originating perhaps in the third century BC, was fundamentally opposed to participation in society, to government and civilization. It advocated a return to simple, primitive life in communion with nature. Taoism was a philosophy of austerity and self-discipline in life, of nihilism in mind (Fitzgerald 1973, 78, 84–88). It was well suited to a people with little to spare and little prospect or hope. Many Chinese led a Taoist existence by necessity, if not choice. For those who chose, there was ample evidence of extravagance and faults of power and civilization against which to rail and rally. Taoism exerted some influence on Chinese thinking until modern times.

Taoists were opposed to learning, to progress of any kind. Since they did not believe in the power of reason, only in intuition, they opposed education and research. Nevertheless, unlike Confucians, they had a deep interest in nature. Despite their nihilism, their observation of nature resulted in numerous contributions to herbal medicine as well as discoveries in alchemy. But they were alchemists who did not carry out systematic investigation and whose work was despised by the scholars. They could not advance to biological or chemical science. Later, Taoism blended with the popular religion of many nature gods, rites, and offerings by incorporating the agenda of the alchemists, in particular the search for drugs offering immortality and formulas for converting base materials into gold (Fitzgerald 1973, 265–74).

The legalist school was not a people's faith but more the doctrine of the elite bureaucracy. It built no temples. It assumed that humans were bad by nature. Hence, it believed in the necessity of draconian laws rigorously enforced, equally applicable to all, as the only way to assure security and stability. Otherwise, it was devoid of ideas. The main functions of the state were war and agriculture. Bureaucratic authoritarianism had been tinged with legalist tendencies periodically throughout Chinese history.

Confucianism was not against civilization, far from it, but it was against progress, against change, against the pursuit of new knowledge. It was withdrawal to the family and to the past, ancestor worship. If I would define *civilization* as "evolutionary and progressive" and *culture* as "static and backward looking," then Confucius was against civilization but, unlike Taoism, not in favor of return to the primitive. Unlike legalism, Confucius viewed law based on fear of penalties as cruel. As the dominant philosophy starting with the Han dynasty, Confucianism was a major factor in China's failure to evolve.

The three Chinese schools were mundane; they dealt with human affairs, proper behavior, and the legitimacy of authority. They were policy advisers more than philosophers. Buddhism was different. It did not reach China until Confucianism was already entrenched as the prevailing doctrine.

Buddhism was a philosophy of contemplation; it was escapism but positive, unlike Taoism, which was negative. It stressed knowledge for its own sake, not as a means to worldly ends. Buddhism was otherworldly. It regarded the visible universe as illusionary. Such an attitude was incompatible with scientific progress but so alien to China that it had no effect (Bodde 1991, 158). The Chinese, by contrast, were interested in practical knowledge. The Buddhist search for knowledge was neither empirical nor logical. Buddhist contemplation was compatible with Chinese intuition; one was a process, the other a product, but its level of unworldliness was much too high. Whereas Confucianism was Chinese and hierarchical, Buddhism was universal and egalitarian and favored the monastic life rather than the family. It survived in China and transformed into a more acceptable creed. The typical Chinese Buddha was little more than a caricature of the Indian original. It was banned from China during the Sung dynasty but never left.

But there was a striking exception—Mo-tzu, contemporary with Athens's golden age, and his followers, the Mohists. They were idealists against war and then a major, if not the main, function of states; they preached universal love and equality regardless of ethnicity, Chinese and barbarians alike. Mo-tzu denounced lavish rites, rituals, and donations to ancestors and assorted deities practiced by other belief systems as of no value and of high cost, a waste of resources better used for the relief of poverty (Muller (1957, 350).

Mohists believed in the pursuit of knowledge through the study of nature and made contributions to physics, including optics and astronomy, seeking to arrive at natural laws. And they developed logic (Bodde 1991, 166–70). There was much in common between the Mohists and the Greek philosophers. Had Mohism survived, Chinese history would be different, and so would China.

This school was an anomaly—secular, logical, objective, rejecting superstitions of the time. Although it persisted for centuries, it had no impact on Chinese culture. Some considered it treasonable as it pursued truth independent of the emperor and his direct line to the heavens. The Mohists' search for knowledge could be seen as a rejection of the omniscience of the ancient sages and a challenge to the authority of the emperor as the final arbiter of truth. The Mohists were rejecting the core of Chinese culture and ideology. It was the only school of thought contributory to discovery and invention. The Mohists looked forward, not backward; sought new knowledge; and employed reason rather than intuition in the pursuit of knowledge. They had a mechanistic, not an organic, concept of reality. They posed a threat to all contending philosophies. They had few followers and never had a chance. Their writings were burned, their achievements rejected.

All other schools of thought were antagonistic or indifferent to discovery and invention and to the processes involved. But it was Confucianism, as the ruling orthodoxy, that mattered.

CONFUCIUS AND CONFUCIANISM

It was Confucianism that dominated Chinese philosophy for two millennia. The writings of Confucius and his followers were required reading for candidates to bureaucratic positions throughout that period. We do not know to what extent Confucius simply reflected, to what extent he shaped culture. The dominance suggested that it was an articulation of Chinese values. For this inquiry, it is behavior that matters.

Confucianism was the product of the writings of Confucius himself and those of his descendants, colleagues, and followers over two centuries. It is not always possible to distinguish the words of Confucius from those of other authors. Thus, there are some inconsistencies as well as doubt about authorship. Confucius himself wrote on many subjects, but his work focused on the ethical training of leaders for the state. There is evidence suggesting that later followers of Confucius held views reflecting the influence of Greek philosophers, possibly transmitted by way of Alexander's conquest of Bactria (Brooks 1999, 4–12), a transit for trade to and from China. They condoned argument to convince those with whom one disagreed and the resort to logic for that purpose, whereas Confucianism frowned on disagreement and abstract reasoning. And there was a hint of democracy, a close relation between the lower and the higher strata of society, instead of a rigid hierarchy. The ethical teachings of Confucius himself were more ecumenical than either the ideology or the doctrine of Confucianism.

Confucianism as popular ideology should be distinguished from the state doctrine. Popular Confucianism focused on the unity of the family over time and ancestor worship. The state doctrine of Confucianism stressed authority, loyalty, and obedience by analogy with popular Confucianism. It was the civil servants, not the people or the state, who knew Confucianism in its entirety and embraced it in part.

Family. Confucius stressed the central role of the family in society and ethics. His family was small—little more than the nuclear family—but extended in time through ancestor worship. He preached obedience and respect to one's elders, veneration of ancestors, and total commitment to members of the family. Here, Confucius was very successful. Family commitment was carried almost to the exclusion of concern for everyone else. Rites and offerings to ancestors were lavish. Confucius was reinforcing existing beliefs and practices. One consequence is that when the father dies, his children—perhaps fairly elderly themselves—become the authority figures, although all their experience has been obedience.

Confucius taught that if people cultivated the Tao in themselves, family and society would achieve harmony, which was his primary objective. He extended his concept of the family and his advice on manners and morals by analogy to society and the state. The emperor was the father figure, and piety and obedience were directed toward a hierarchical and authoritarian bureaucracy. It was his vision of utopia, in which each individual was content with his station in life. Inequality, according to Confucius, was both a fact and a desideratum.

State. The state, starting with the Han dynasty, attempted to transfer Confucius's family values to the state as official policy. The bureaucracy and society was a hierarchical structure, like a multitiered pagoda. The emperor at the apex was a godlike father figure providing access to the heavens. The family hierarchy of generations was equated to a hierarchy of status.

Confucianism at the state and societal level I regard as a calculated face-lift for oriental despotism (Wittfogel 1957). It dignified subjection. The virtue of obedience was displaced by the fear of disobedience. The focus on the family, including ancestor worship, remained an integral part of Chinese culture for the next two thousand years, but its extension to the state and its hierarchy and to society can be questioned.

The plastic surgery did not succeed in preventing numerous revolts and a long succession of dynasties. Somehow the new rulers, whatever their original status, soon became accepted as near divinities monopolizing access to the heavens. It was the position, not the individual occupying it, that was semidivine. But this pattern predated Confucianism. State and social Confucianism was an example of the analogical thinking that permeated the culture.

The state and the family power structures represented a double dose of authoritarianism—a culture of authority and obedience, deference, and servitude. It may well have been one source of a lack of curiosity.

Learning and Knowledge. When reference is made to Confucianism as a deterrent to creativity, the primary meaning is the structure of authority he propounded, followed by his ethical teachings and ancestor worship. This was the view of the common people, who were illiterate.

Confucius had much more to say that would be relevant for progress to those who read his writings. These were the mandarins of the civil service, his principal disciples. Their access to office required passing examinations based on careful study of his and other ancient classic texts. They were the individuals who—by ability, opportunity, and experience—were most likely to contribute to major discoveries and inventions. Of all versions of Confucianism, it would be their view that most mattered for the culture.

Confucius certainly encouraged learning and knowledge. But he believed that everything worth knowing had already been learned in the past; much had been forgotten. Thus, learning was recovering lost knowledge. There was no need to seek new knowledge by observation and experiment. He opposed a logical process of seeking knowledge. He disapproved of universals or generalities and abstractions. He distrusted reasoning (Bodde 1991, 179, 186, 191, 258, 328). The appropriate process was intuition, not logic or research. Intuition admitted of contradictory beliefs; logic did not. He opposed the search for knowledge about nature. Nature was as we saw it; there was no purpose in inquiring how or why it was.

With these restrictions of learning process and scope of inquiry, there can be little new knowledge. And what new knowledge may be gained by chance or intuition is self-limiting. Implicitly Confucius opposed a scientific revolution, which is not a response to practical needs or opportunities but simply a response to a need to know, a product of idle curiosity, its initial accomplishments of no practical relevance. The quest for certainty may be part of the human genetic identity, but the scientific need to know is a rare mutation. By contrast, industrial revolutions are problem-solving responses to needs and opportunities.

Their cognitive abilities and perspectives are built into the species that must struggle to survive.

The Confucian ideology of the mandarins militated against creativity or the adoption of new ideas of others. Confucianism opposed change, opposed novelty, and lacked inquisitiveness. They were disruptive. In particular, he rejected inventions that were too theoretical. He was not a proponent of the status quo but of regression. He praised antiquity, disparaged modernity, and was negative to new ideas (Bodde 1967, 27–36, 44–51).

His teachings reinforced two other features of Chinese culture that are relevant for discovery and invention. One is the perpetuation of ancient customs, rituals, and teachings. The other is a negative attitude toward the observation of nature.

By analogy, the Confucian ethic applied to scholarship. Confucius himself and his writings, as well as other ancient sages, were not to be questioned. Scholarship was the mere reiteration of the past, a never-ending effort to discern the true meaning of their words. He was a great teacher who advised rulers and trained his students to be high-level administrators and advisers to the state. Shortly thereafter, another great teacher, Aristotle, opened the Lyceum in Athens. But it had a different pedagogy—debate—and a different curriculum—stressing physics, logic, and mathematics and seeking new knowledge.

Harmony. Confucius was born in 551 BCE. The China of his day was a corrupt society, and Confucius sought to establish high moral standards. He believed that if people followed simple rules of kindness, respect, selflessness, and obedience, China could be a harmonious society.

One of his basic principles he called shu, or reciprocity. Through shu, Confucius meant, "What you do not want done to yourself, do not do to others." This negative version of the golden rule was not about ethics but a guide to behavior toward others. It was equilibrium. What others saw as ethical teaching and some as religion was, in fact, not about abstract moral principles but about stability. Social stability in practice meant opposition to change. Mutual neglect, as much as any other relation, was the preferred policy within the empire and isolation

from the outside world. In Confucian philosophy, there is no worship
or prayer dedicated to any gods.

Confucius opposed debate and dissent. Disagreements were not
resolved, just accommodated. Conflict resolution was just conciliation—
no winners, no losers—facts or logic was secondary, if not irrelevant.
No progress was possible under these rules of engagement. The lack
of concern for human rights was another consequence of the pursuit
of harmony. The stress on duties, not rights, and on piety and peace
of mind was also a deterrent to opportunity and progress (Muller
1957, 351).

The teachings of Confucius on society should not be equated with
Chinese behavior or belief or with Confucianism. He lived in troubled
times, and his stress on harmony was a reflection of his times. He
believed in a hierarchical society, with acceptance of one's status and
mutual respect, but Chinese society had magnified status differences,
engendering more status anxiety than acceptance. What one must ask
at every point would be whether Confucius shaped Chinese culture or
merely enunciated it. Later, Confucianism at the state level was policy,
not faith or philosophy.

Chinese culture—according to Wittfogel (1957), oriental
despotism—was shaped by the need for large-scale water management.
(War and defense needs were more universal and perhaps more
important than rice irrigation at the time.) It was autocratic, based on
fear and obedience, supplemented 2,500 years ago by another culture
of authority and obedience. Confucianism replaced subservience with
obedience and based authority on honor, a positive veneer on oriental
despotism. What was new was his stress on learning. One learned and
memorized what the teacher said; one never questioned the teacher or
his teachings as though he were a living ancestor.

Thus, Confucianism contributes to an explanation of both
achievement and also lack of creativity—why the Chinese lead
in technology rapidly became a lag, why it failed in discovery and
invention, which requires hypothesizing, theorizing, and questioning.
It is a culture looking backward in time.

SOCIETY

The Confucian ethical universe remained very small. One can observe its boundaries today—reports of humans in distress, hit by a car, and lying in the street, with Chinese passersby looking but doing nothing; only foreign tourists come to help. The excuse is that anyone who helps assumes responsibility for that person. Of course, that is exactly what someone does who comes to the help an injured person. If the passersby mean a long-term responsibility, this is another way of saying their ethical universe is small, bounded by the family, little else, and that they live in a society that lacks the institutions and whose members lack the morality and will to help. But even numerous such reports do not tell us about the prevalence of such attitudes in the past millennium or quantify current attitudes.

The key question is not what the Chinese believed, but how the people acted. What do belief systems have to do with behavior? In the Chinese case, not much with regard to social empathy, cooperation, or trust but a great deal with regard to obedience. In the past, China could not accept the universalism of Buddhist philosophy, converting it into a Chinese system of rituals rather than personal behavior. It had no interest in the Mohist doctrine of universal love. The teachings of Confucius are not compatible with the absence of trust and the absence of concern for others beyond the immediate family and social group.

China has always been communal; the West is individualistic? No and no. This dichotomy is simplistic and unrealistic. There are degrees of "otherness," multiple self-identifications.

Lin Yutang (1935, 172–76), who personally witnessed the last decades of the Manchu dynasty, stressed one feature of Chinese society rarely understood and often contradicted. It was not communitarian, in contrast to the individualistic Western society. In some respects, the opposite was a more accurate description. To find a communitarian society, one must travel to Japan.

The Chinese sense of community did not extend much beyond the primary family, including ancestors. It did not extend to the neighborhood, the face-to-face community, much less to the nation, ethnicity, or sect. Nakamura (1964, 247–48) notes a lack of teamwork and cooperation, a weak sense of membership. Beyond this tiny social and ethical world, despite an "organic" concept of reality, there was no concern for or obligation to others, to the commons. On the contrary, kleptomania was no vice and was consistent with honesty (Yutang 1935, 180–82). Government officials did not hesitate to steal or to practice nepotism (another term for a small community), which was more a duty than a misdemeanor. It was a hierarchical society whose members devoted much effort to revealing their status and maintaining social space.

The perspective was on the past, on family relations in terms of generations, a vertical and hierarchical mentality rather than horizontal and collateral. There was a tendency to objectify "others," to place little value on other people (Nakamura 1963, 250). Any visitor who has had the uncomfortable experience of having a Chinese stop and stare would understand.

So the Chinese are individualistic, but for them, the individual is not one person but a nuclear family. Thus, the person lacks the sense of autonomy and independence typical of people in the West, as well as a sense of attachment to the wider community. Identity in China was different from identity in Greece or in Europe. In the West, and presumably in classical Greece, the individual has been self-defined, in and of himself. In China, there were no sharp boundaries between the individual and others. Ask a Westerner who or what you are, and the answer is likely to specify an occupation, work, or main interest, sometimes place of origin. It is all about the individual and mostly about choice. The stress is on the present and sometimes, for younger individuals, on the future. Ask a Chinese—note that the proper name comes last in Chinese speech; the first name is family, not individual— and he is likely to stress "son of Tzu, who was son of Yang." Beyond the family, Nakamura (1963, 259) reports a lack of discrimination between an individual and the organizations to which he belongs.

The family system was one reason for the weakness of a sense of autonomy; the dominance of the state was an additional constraint. What Chinese society valued was not community but harmony.

Individuals valued security and serenity rather than high aspirations and expectations (Hsu 1981, 109).

The objectification of others explains why there was no sense of guilt or sin in corruption, theft, and forgery. There was little acceptance, limited understanding of human rights. By contrast, in the West, the social and ethical universe was much broader; individualism was tempered with empathy and responsibility for others. One consequence or correlation is that the ability to work together, to collaborate, found in the West was missing in China, where in the absence of trust, secrecy prevailed. It is a mentality not conducive to collegial efforts, social action, or responsibility.

In recent decades, many producers have not hesitated to adulterate their products. Government officials have shown disregard for the health and safety of their constituents. Common people strew their garbage in the commons. We have no way of knowing their frequency, but modern behavior is consistent with traditional attitudes toward others.

The essential condition for community is trust—trust in public officials, trust in the rule of law, trust in the products and services of industry, trust in human beings other than immediate family and close friends. China has a long history of secrecy and mistrust of arbitrary officials and corrupt administration. Nakamura (1962, 247–48, 301–8) stresses the lack of teamwork and cooperation and a tradition of limited human relations. Morality is limited to particular relations; there is a lack of general moral principles.

Yutang and Nakamura were speaking of recent centuries but implicitly about classical China as well. Lloyd and Sivin (2002, 9) confirmed the social spacing in the early years practiced by the dominant bureaucracy, whose members avoided social mixing and lived in separate housing. They craved for distinction by their parasols, garb, demeanor, speech, and transportation. Ostentation of their wealth made sure they were not mistaken for common people. This was not what Confucius taught; he would extend the same ethic and behavior he prescribed in the family to the larger society. But what was practiced was the unintended consequence of what he preached. The supply of empathy, mutual support, was finite. Beyond some level of commitment to the family, it became exclusive. That may be why Confucius preached community. What prevailed was neither the sense of community found in Japan nor the sense of personal autonomy, freedom in the West. But Confucius also preached authority and obedience, status differentiation, and inequality. He did not believe in equality or ecumenicity but in hierarchy. Inequality was accepted as a fact of life but was not enjoyed by the common people.

The state historically opposed private organization of any kind as a threat to its monopoly of authority. The elites did their best to distinguish themselves from the common people and from lower ranks. Under these conditions, despite Chinese tolerance of contradiction, the Confucian dream of community with inequality could not be realized.

Hsu (1981, xiv–xv) exemplifies the opposite and admittedly the majority view that Chinese society was communal. But he agrees with the authors cited above. The Chinese are unable to form voluntary organizations with nonkin members. Parents are intolerant of their children's social contacts with nonkin (394–98). They lack concern for human rights, for any cause (374–75, 394–98). Nevertheless, he regards the community as large. There is a problem of definition with regard to individualism and community; reality is far more complicated than this simple polarity. Apparent contradictory views are simply different definitions of community. Hsu sees communal and individualistic cultures as group centric versus egocentric, in both cases indifferent to the rest of the world. I define them in terms of concepts of identity, without regard to outlook, which is a separate issue. So is group size.

What difference does the structure of society make for discovery, invention, and innovation under the Chinese family system? First, there were almost no voluntary private organizations, and the few were small and local. Accumulation of capital, even short term, to gain the economies of scale or specialization was nearly impossible. Second, there was no general labor market opening up opportunities for good workers. The labor "market" was highly segmented; the principal hiring criterion was nepotism. Third, knowledge and information sharing was limited by the penchant for secrecy, the shortage of private organizations, and the microcommunitarianism that prevailed. Inventors were reluctant to share their knowledge with others, to transfer it to the next generation. An invention that was lost or forgotten might have become the starting point of a technological trajectory (Landes 2005, 15–17).

Religion

Religion is a discovery for believers, an invention or speculation for others. One can examine the goals of a religion and determine whether it is a relevant means toward them. With regard to eternal life, there is no evidence. But as far as human behavior is concerned, one may distinguish between followers of different religions and of none and detect a difference in behavior. With religious freedom, it could be that individuals of a particular bent adopt the appropriate religion rather than the religion affecting the behavior of its adherents.

One can also consider who the creators of a religion were, how they proceeded, and what their purpose was. Did the creators believe their faith as a discovery, or was the faith simply manufactured? What religion should tell us would be popular thinking about the nature of reality, their cosmogony, and something about the role of reasoning. In China, it was hierarchical in a way, with a religion just for the emperor, others for everyone who chose, and the family religion—ancestor worship.

What is the content of religion? First, religion has ethical principles, behavioral guidelines, and perhaps reward and punishment, a moral math. Second, religion is an explanation of reality, perhaps origins and destinations, a cosmology; what has been described as philosophy or ideology can also be viewed as theology, which in turn in some cases is cosmology as well. There is overlap between creeds and concepts. Third, a religion is social as well; it must have followers. The creeds mentioned below have ethics and followers. Some, such as Confucius, lack a cosmology.

There was popular religion before Taoism and Confucianism were conceived, which consisted of two top gods, earth and sky, and a multitude of lesser gods in a vast bureaucracy that ruled the world, a heavenly equivalent of the hierarchy of their own society (Hsu 1981, 240–41). This popular religion was in continuous evolution as new gods were created as needed, city gods in particular, to whom sacrifices were made and from whom favors were sought. Some humans were deified and added to the celestial bureaucracy. What is striking was the ability to generate credulity. It would reflect the need for agency as the principle of order. The heavens, the gods, were not so much objects of worship as sources of information, omens, and potential benefactors.

Deity in China was different from deity in the West. Humanity and deity converged. Early mythical emperors were gods; emperors were godlike. Humans were able to create new gods at will, and deserving humans could be deified.

Most Chinese gods (lowercase) had the power of agency but were highly specialized, with limited jurisdiction. Buddha and Confucius were worshipped as gods but were mortal men. The emperor was the Son of Heaven. He had the power to deify mortals.

What is missing is any explanation of reality. There is little concept of origin, purpose, and destination—another instance of the absence of curiosity. They are, at best, passports of life.

Chinese religion was pragmatic, not worship so much as pleading, flattering, and presenting offerings to several deities in the hope of obtaining their favor. This is a legitimate transaction in the supermarket of destiny, not to be regarded as a bribe. Chinese payments to worldly officials for favors, which Westerners regard as corruption, are seen in a different light by the Chinese accustomed to voluntary donations to quasi deities. They lack a sense of control over their own destinies.

For a people said to have had no religion, China had an abundance of temples, a multitude of worshippers, a proliferation of rites and rituals. One might as well describe China through millennia as polytheistic with numerous quasi religions and deities with limited domains. Domain overlap was no problem for the Chinese. They paid their respects to, followed the rites of, make offerings to, and obeyed the precepts of Taoism, Buddhism, and Confucianism. Further, those in the countryside made offerings or paid bribes to the local gods of grain, soil, and water. Spirits seemed to inhabit every nook and cranny. The forces of nature were personified and then deified. City gods were created and honored. The Chinese followed rituals and made offerings to many deities.

Some of the philosophies previously discussed donned the trappings of religion—temples, rites, worshippers. Confucianism and Taoism were quasi religions. Today one might call them secular religions. Confucianism provided the ethics and the social cohesion that was part of the role of religion. Taoism, initially a philosophy, which it remained for many, was also transformed into a religion with priests, temples, rites, and offerings by incorporating the agenda of its alchemists, offering the prospect of immortality by the discovery of a wonder drug.

Buddhism was the only imported religion. It was influential in the fourth and fifth centuries (Fitzgerald 1973, 278–83). One emperor became a Buddhist and entered a monastery. But it was sinified; the boundless quest for knowledge of Buddha was redirected toward the past, rituals added, and its universalism neglected. It was banned by the Neo-Confucians in the Sung dynasty but survived thereafter in its Chinese version.

Then there was ancestor worship. It can be called religious because it was based on the belief that there was an afterlife. No one really died, simply became a spirit who had needs and wants analogous to those of their descendants. They also had the power to influence the present and future of their descendants. Spirits must be honored and petitioned, or ancestors might not survive (Fitzgerald 1961, 42). Ancestor worship was often really a transaction, offerings by the living in the expectation of favors from the spirits. Their jurisdiction was family based, more like the emperor's religion, rather than to socially shared faiths. How family-based jurisdiction was integrated with jurisdictions based on place, function, or whatever would be beyond comprehension. The question simply never came up.

Early religion of the palace is revealed in the immense burial grounds of the first Qin emperor, an afterworld for an afterlife, peopled with a terra-cotta army and the corpses of thousands of workers and hundreds of concubines, who would be resuscitated to serve the emperor in the afterlife. The emperor created his own afterlife. It was more than the emperor's lust for immortality. Many others also believed that all these artifacts and corpses would come to life in the afterworld and continue to serve the emperor. If this was religion, it was the emperor's, not the destiny of lesser humans. The afterworld was a replica of the emperor's capital and realm. Let there be no change.

The emperor, Son of Heaven, had his own religion, of which he was the only follower. It underwent substantial changes during the Han dynasty, which were explicitly designed and created step by step by members of the court (Fitzgerald 1973, 219–23). The emperor was the sole recipient of messages from the heavens. It was public policy. How it managed to obtain the credulity of the people and of the court itself is a mystery. But it did. Early emperors were of divine ancestry; the later usurpers were accepted. Heaven needed a parishioner. He alone made sacrifices, performed rites, and presumably was delegated the right to deify deserving humans.

The emperor was the intermediary between the heavens and the people. As head of both state and church in a hierarchical society, he had a monopoly of access to the heavens (Lloyd and Sivin 2002, 194–96). But the heavens, singular or plural, was ambiguous and remote. They had agency but did not control events on earth. There was no order. They advised the emperor and may reward or punish. Communication with the heavens was sporadic, rare, ambiguous, and one way. The emperor employed a corps of astronomers to scrutinize the sky for any unusual events, such as eclipses and comets, which were messages from the heavens, omens that then had to be interpreted by astrologers. Thus, the emperor was, and was not, in communication with the heavens.

What do so many beliefs and practices have in common? One is the fact that they share believers. Many, if not most, believers have not made up their minds; they have practiced more than one belief system. There is a lack of certainty, of a sense of security.

Another widespread attitude was the absence of a sense of autonomy, of control. They did not worship as much as seek security. There was no interfaith struggle or war, other than the short-term banning of an imported creed, Buddhism. A third was implicit; commonality was the prevalent ability to hold diverse, sometimes conflicting, beliefs

Regression

Classical Greece and the European Scientific Revolution were two thousand years apart. But the China with which we compare them—China in culture, society, and mentality—was much the same. The Chinese prized stability above all. Despite imperial expansion and major new inventions, the culture remained backward looking, closed, and static.

Ancestor worship is part of the Confucian heritage. Obedience is not just to one's elders but also concern for one's ancestors. It is an integral part of a culture of regression, a culture dominated by hindsight, not foresight. In a sense, no one dies; the spirit is still around, it needs to be honored, and it may have some influence on the fates of the living. The past is never over. The worship of the dead has taken many forms. Plagiarism—copying words of ancient texts, the brushstrokes from ancient painting masterpieces—is an honored occupation.

Knowledge was also an ancestor; everything worth knowing was known to the sages, much had been forgotten, and knowledge was retrieving. The early emperors, mostly mythical, were the sage-emperors; the Yellow Emperor knew everything (or everything worth knowing). Learning meant an effort to retrieve the knowledge from the past.

China's ideal world was in the past. Accordingly, there was no interest in the study of nature as a means of building new knowledge nor in logic as a process of arriving at knowledge. Thus, Confucius discouraged the exploration of nature; anything approaching scientific investigation or logic was a waste of time, and he recommended ancient practices. For the sake of harmony, Mencius—his noted follower—discouraged debate.

If a civilization lived long enough, there would be a lot of rearview mirrors. But China was backward looking almost from the start. Hence, China always resisted change, never developed the idea of progress. Its view of history was cyclical, a series of repetitions. It never looked forward to advance, only backward.

I have not forgotten Chinese writing and language. The difficulty of learning the script is common knowledge. During the period under consideration, the script shaped and constrained the evolution of the language. Discussion of their implications for discovery and invention is deferred to the final section of this chapter. All scripts started as pictographs (the Incan quipu could be an exception); they have evolved into abstract phonetic symbols. China never made a transition by choice. Why, I do not know. These are the principal vehicles of thought and communication. It is another aspect of resistance to change. It is a correlate of a culture of authority, hierarchy, and subservience. China resembles Egypt—hostile to novelty, delinquent in adopting technologies developed elsewhere. There was no desire for widespread literacy (Lloyd and Sivin 2002, 49). Confucianism may have codified the culture rather than created it.

The Chinese lunar calendar is another example. Nature operates on the solar calendar, so New Year is a different solar date each year; so are the dates for planting and harvesting and all calendar-related occasions. Calculation and printing of the annual calendar was a major palace responsibility. Private individuals were severely punished for publishing their own.

Grandiosity

A sense of grandiosity with respect to itself and superiority to other peoples had been characteristic of the Chinese elite, if not of its people, throughout the period of a unified nation. China regarded itself as the center of the world. Since the early sixteenth century, the belief may have been tempered with pretense. But this attitude was passive; there was no desire to change the ways of inferior peoples (Hsu 1981, 103).

The burial site of Shihuangdi—the first emperor of a unified China—is, if anything, more grandiose than the pyramids of Egypt. The army of terra-cotta soldiers, horses, and chariots is only a small part of a complex covering thirty-eight square miles. The tomb proper is untouched. Shihuangdi died in 210 BCE, his tomb still unfinished.

Harems of emperors were as grand as their tombs. Emperors needed multiple wives and concubines to assure succession, but three thousand?

In 97 CE, a Han army was on the shores of the Caspian Sea, and court emissaries on the Black Sea were considering a crossing. They were dissuaded by false information on the length and perils of passage by people fearful of Han dominance (Fitzgerald 1973, 196–97). This expedition reminds one of Alexander the Great's expeditions nearly four centuries earlier. There was a big difference. Alexander's conquests were a very successful missionary project, Hellenizing North Africa and the Middle East and extending the Hellenic culture as far as India. The Han expedition had no such interest or achievement.

The Great Wall, for all its claimed purpose of defense against invaders, was more a grand symbol of separation. The Grand Canal was different, a valuable artery between north and south, linking the Yellow and the Yangtze Rivers.

In the early fifteenth century, Zheng He led several maritime expeditions, the last of which went well beyond the world known to China, to the Red Sea and down the east coast of Africa. They were an anomaly in Chinese history, the only maritime venture. But the idea that the world was much larger than China and perhaps worth knowing did not imprint.

The fleets were large, some ships were huge, and they carried seventy thousand men, with twenty-six thousand soldiers on board. Sail-driven ships over four hundred feet long were underpowered, slow, and not very maneuverable but impressive. A National Geographic expedition it was not. "[T]he main purpose was to display the power of the Ming Empire and win nominal suzerainty of China in these regions. Kings who acknowledged the over lordship of the Ming Emperor were helped against their rivals who refused such homage" (Fitzgerald 1973, 473–74). It was undiluted grandiosity display, this time to the rest of the world. They were not initially driven by curiosity, but the last trips were exploratory. Incidentally, the admiral who led it was not Chinese at all. His relatives were Muslims of diverse ethnicities involved in the trading routes between China and the West, a prisoner of the Chinese captured in war. His curiosity was understandable.

After Zheng He's death, there was a power shift at the court from the eunuchs to the mandarins. Claims were made that the voyages were inappropriate, even illegal. China had no business going out into the world. Voyages were banned, the ships were burned, and no new seagoing vessels were to be built. Official records of the voyages were destroyed.

These voyages were the one episode of Chinese history favorable to discovery and invention. But they came to nothing, and they came too late. The Portuguese simultaneously were exploring the west coast of Africa, and the early Scientific and Industrial Revolutions in Europe were well underway.

In the early 1600s, the Ming dynasty was so ignorant of the overseas world that it thought that its empire encompassed most of the planet. The court was uninterested in the world beyond its borders, believing it unimportant, more than a century after the arrival of European ships on China's shores. Aristarchus had measured the dimension of the planet fairly accurately long before, and some of the court astronomers must have known its dimensions.

Two centuries later, in 1793, Emperor Qianlong dismissed the British request for diplomatic representation because the greatest empire on the earth was a small country far away, and China had no need for anything from any other country. This denial came two centuries after the end of any possibility of China having its own scientific or industrial revolution; it was already condemned to a copycat role. Even given the reluctance of officials to displease the emperor, I find it impossible to believe that, by then, he did not know that China had missed the boat.

Even toward the end of the twentieth century, the Chinese ambassador to the United States reflected the attitude of the Ming emperor when he seemed insulted at the suggestion that the Chinese had spied on America for nuclear secrets. *China has no need to spy. It can develop science and technology on its own, thank you.* There was a slight difference; the Ming emperor was guilty of hubris, and the modern Chinese ambassador was trying to save face.

What I find most astounding about these examples and Chinese civilization is the absence of curiosity and interest and the repeated amnesia after exposure to new experiences. There has also been an obsession with size; bigger was better.

Its conviction of superiority with respect to other peoples meant contempt for their achievements and little interest in imposing its own culture on others. It was others, whether conquered and assimilated, who were willing to learn, who adopted various aspects of Chinese culture. Grandiosity at home was hierarchy with steep gradient. The emperor at the top was godlike. The bureaucrats distanced themselves from the common people in every way, and within the bureaucracy, mandarins separated themselves from lower ranks in the most visible ways. Grandiosity was in conflict with community.

A passion for control was a counterpart of grandiosity. The state was beyond authoritarian, verging on totalitarian. The hierarchical order required detailed control of what people may do, own, wear, think, and say for stability. A siege mentality prevailed.

Today a grandiosity syndrome is deeply entrenched in the Chinese psyche, reinforced by centuries of subjugation to foreign powers.

Isolation

China was geographically a very large contiguous area, isolated and economically self-contained throughout the period under consideration. Before the Silk Road, there was the Jade Road, but China did not depend on them, and it was not the Chinese who transported goods to Europe. Other peoples ran the Silk Road. There was minimal exposure to other peoples and other ways. On the contrary, as it expanded its borders, it exported its culture and customs to other peoples on its periphery. Its isolation was also a matter of location. Whereas Greece was in contact with older and initially more advanced civilizations and took advantage of their achievements, China was neither so fortunate nor so enterprising. It did not believe it had anything to learn from anyone else. Its international relations department was the office of the barbarians.

This self-imposed isolation was a condition for a backward-looking society. It was also an expression of grandiosity. China's only significant import was Buddhism. When it came to China, there was some flow of scholars to India; but in time, it was converted to Chinese rituals, universalism, and the unbounded search for knowledge forgotten. China had little interest in libraries except as repositories of its heritage nor in travel. Block printing had limited consequences (Huff 1993, 319).

China showed little curiosity about distant lands. We know of the lack of interest of the Chinese court in the Western world and in the artifacts brought to them by missionaries and royal representatives, products of the Scientific Revolution, later of the Industrial Revolution, dismissed as useless trinkets. Matteo Ricci was able to interest the emperor and many others in clocks and calendars, which fit in with the concerns of the culture, but little else. Their refusal to accept an envoy from the king of a little remote island, England, in 1797 is hard to understand.

Foreign traders and foreign ships came to China; Chinese traders stayed home. The Ming dynasty sought to ban foreign trade altogether. Neither Alexander's introduction of Greek culture in nearby Bactria nor the later encroachment of Muslim civilization had a lasting influence on the culture.

The lack of curiosity about the outside world is an implication, an unavoidable consequence, of its sense of grandiosity. It is also consistent with the belief that all knowledge was already known in the past and that what should be done is understand the ancient texts in which it is written. It is also consistent with the Confucian opposition to the study of nature. If all is already known, the present and the future must also have been known. This, at least, is the implication of the backward-looking search for knowledge and understanding.

China expanded by military conquest and population pressure, a demographic imperialism. Only for very brief periods was it engaged in exploration. In 97 CE, the Han dynasty had a large army on the shores of the Caspian, with envoys considering crossing the Black Sea. They learned that there was much land and many people farther west. Some of the barbarians could read and write, lived in large cities, built magnificent structures, and mastered diverse arts and crafts. This information may have reached some in the royal court, but it did not imprint. Neither did Zheng He's naval expeditions or the Ming naval expeditions to Africa and the Red Sea. Preservation of its cumbersome script was a choice for isolation.

The Chinese elite had little grasp of the dimensions of the inhabited world and little curiosity about it. The court had hired astronomers from various countries to the West, and astronomers had a good idea of the dimensions of the planet and must have known that China was a very small part of it, but this knowledge did not transfer beyond the observatory. Foreigners from many lands not only visited its ports but also lived in several cities. What to make of this attitude? Was it truly ignorance, the result of the Chinese penchant for secrecy, the reluctance of adventurers to provide information to authorities, who did not want to hear it? How much was just pretense?

At some point, the illusion of grandiosity was replaced by a profound feeling of humiliation, but we do not know for sure when this happened at different levels of Chinese society nor even at the top. The most plausible explanation would be that the Chinese were so incurious about the outside world that the record of its contacts had not imprinted in the cultural mind and had been forgotten. Narcissism was a late development, grandiosity in retreat.

THE STATE

Authority

How would one account for the authoritarian state and its bureaucracy? It was the evolution of agriculture into settled farming that required organization to protect immobile farms and towns from plunder. China, during its early history, was not united under a single leadership. There were contending states; it was not a peaceful place. To the north and west lived seminomadic tribes with a hunter-gatherer mentality, who viewed Chinese farms and towns as prey in time of need or greed. They were warriors on horseback. Chinese survival demanded an organized military. The multiple Chinese states were frequently at risk. The unification of the diverse Chinese states into an empire was probably necessary for survival as they combined forces to fight common enemies. The need to conscript the peasantry to fight off invaders was the foundation of authoritarianism. A sense of encirclement by enemies had been a permanent feature of the Chinese psyche. The emperor, the dynasty, and the state lived in fear for its own survival. The need for state authority and organization for hydraulics was later and limited. With three river basins not surrounded by desert, it did not need a central government. It was war and preparation for war that dictated an authoritarian central government.

Authoritarianism would not be the proper term. The scope of authority was unlimited; it was totalitarianism. The exercise of unrestricted authority was despotic much of the time. There was no sphere of private initiative beyond the reach of the government. Alternatively, what was lacking was a multiplicity of autonomous cities and regions competing in culture, values, technology, and trade. Rampaging warlords eager for subjects and spoils were no substitute for stable, independent communities. From the Han to the present, there were no alternative authorities. There were conquests by Mongols and Manchus, which were just changes in dynasty.

The influence of authoritarianism should be viewed from several perspectives. First was the dominance of the state over society that prevailed before any doctrine. Second, Confucianism promoted authority and obedience in the context of the family and by analogy to other social groups. Third, the state adopted Confucianism with the emperor, whatever his age, as the national father figure and the bureaucratic structure as the equivalent of generations.

The basis of authority was power and position. Usurpers who overthrew a dynasty were promptly recognized as emperors, their semidivine character transferred. It was the position, not the person, that was divine. Only the emperor's religion set limits on power. Authority was self-selected at the top, appointed otherwise. It was strictly top down; responsibility was bottom upward.

In China throughout its history, the state had dominated the society and economy. Its authority recognized no limit. No sphere of activity was autonomous in principle and few in practice. It allowed little scope for private organization and enterprise. There was little organization

VI. CHINESE CIVILIZATION AND CULTURE

outside the state and beyond the primary social group that could command capital, which could provide a demand, a market for new products or new ideas. Potential sources of private capital, large private enterprises, tended to be monopolies awarded by the state. Private property was limited and contingent on the will of the emperor and his officials.

Discovery and invention were the business of the state and no one else. How did the state exercise this monopoly if it remained resistant to change? It would focus on military technology and infrastructure development. Paper and movable type were for bureaucratic communication and information; gunpowder was for defense against barbarians and against evil influences and demons. Only the state bureaucracy itself, given its high income, exercised a semiautonomous demand, but it was not for novelty but primarily for the luxury goods required to maintain the lifestyle appropriate to their rank.

In the past, discovery and invention was the work of individuals. What top-down authority did was to limit individual autonomy and initiative. Individuals lacked the freedom to create or the access to the resources needed and the means of profiting from their work. The scope of authority was so extensive that there was little opportunity for change or novelty. What also mattered, and was in short supply, was a demand, a taste, for novelty, acceptance of change. But Chinese authoritarianism also discouraged new ideas. It rewarded obedience, not originality. The state philosophy, Confucianism, discouraged search for knowledge. Achievement motivation was directed toward the civil service examination system.

Did officials have a sense of responsibility for the well-being of those over whom they ruled, if they did not represent them? The answer should be yes, if they were to please their masters. The mandarins were very able individuals, many of whom learned on the job what they should have known before appointment. A full granary and security were conditions for social harmony.

The reverse question is, is bottom-up obedience motivated by respect, by fear, or just by habit? It is impossible to answer these questions for the people and for officials two millennia ago or five hundred years ago. All we can say is what appeared to be the situation in the century just past and assume that it had characterized the more distant past.

The sense of responsibility of officials for their charges was weak. The obedience of the people was driven more by fear than by respect. Protest and revolt were the only ways of expressing one's own views or promoting such views, and these were frequent.

The state doctrine of the short-lived Qin dynasty, which unified China, was legalistic. It sought to destroy the past without providing an alternative vision of society. It was domination without doctrine. It would be best remembered for the burning of the books. The Han dynasty, which succeeded it, restored Confucianism as state philosophy. Confucianism was the moralization and justification for despotism. It replaced subjection with submission, chaos and confusion with order and stability. It internalized authority and obedience and divorced them from fear. The particular indoctrination of civil servants was helpful but not necessary for the survival of the state. But like authoritarianism, it survived virtually unchanged into the twentieth century, long after it had ceased to be an asset and become a liability for the Chinese people.

The people did not behave as Confucius preached. Their sense of community did not extend to the community. The civil servants practiced separation and segregation. Nor was the state Confucian. Had it believed that humans were naturally good, there would have been limited need for laws, for government. Instead, the state was totalitarian, attempting to regulate or control almost every aspect of human behavior. In fact, it was legalistic, with no trust in human nature or in the teachings of Confucius—legalists in Confucian clothing.

The attempt to nationalize Confucius was nation building by the Han dynasty early in its reign. It had been preceded by constant wars between the states, which were united into one empire by the Qin, whose brutal rule was very short lived. These states differed in language, customs, and culture and regarded themselves as distinct from other states in the empire. There was no Chinese identity; there were regional identities and overlapping of identity, which we call Chinese. For many of the provinces, regional identity was paramount, interprovincial relations not always amicable. For some provinces, there was only regional or ethnic identity, no sense of a Chinese identity. But regional and ethnic identity cannot fully explain the miniscule scope of the sense of community.

Legalist thinking persisted in state practice and occasionally prevailed—distrust of human nature, the need for total control. Behavior and attitudes were also circumscribed by detailed rules as well as by the will of the ruler. These were limits on choice. The state was concerned with social stability, not in the well-being of individuals or families. This was political, secular authority that required obedience. Confucianism was intellectual authority, imposing belief, and sacred authority, belief beyond question. The former was a constraint on opportunity, the latter on creativity.

Bureaucracy

Government positions were initially filled by high-status individuals, and scholarship was the major criterion of status. Subsequently, they were filled by lineage, inherited. Appointees had no specialized training or experience. The Han dynasty initiated civil service exams as a means of access to bureaucratic positions, but most positions were still filled by district officers. Scholarship and the Confucian ideology had been a major qualification in the selection of scholars for political leadership before the exams. It became the dominant route to bureaucratic positions during the Tang dynasty (618–907), which also opened local schools to prepare candidates for the exam. It concentrated authority in the palace.

The content of the exams was memorization of literary classics, the writings of Confucius among them. They institutionalized what Confucius had done in his lifetime as a teacher. The pursuit of technology and science was relegated to the lesser classes; later, there were some additions to the exam content. In the Sung dynasty, special exams for medicine and mathematics were introduced. There were also efforts to reform the civil service exams and end favoritism and nepotism. But reforms did not survive (De Bary 1967, 92–94). Candidates for the civil service in the nineteenth century were still being examined on the same ancient texts, and civil servants were commenting on them and seeking to decipher their meaning.

Exams at the provincial, national, and court levels qualified successful candidates for different ranks in the bureaucracy, but the number who qualified did not match the number of positions available. Waits for an opening, or a position at one's level of qualification, created opportunities for corruption. For candidates, they were a cost in addition to the long years spent studying for exams.

The characteristics of the bureaucracy that discouraged a scientific revolution were, first, the authoritarianism of the state and its dominance of society and, second, the mind-set of the bureaucrats, indoctrinated in the ancient classics, Confucius in particular. The influence of Confucianism on the education of the elite was not just the civil servants but also the many who tried and failed, as well as those who passed but did not obtain a post.

Hsu (1981, 187–88) tells us that the salary of the lowest official was ten times that of a highly skilled artisan; so, no doubt, was the difference in status. Thus, the long years of study in preparation were worth the effort. Besides, the civil service was almost the only road to achievement. The children of bureaucrats would be grossly overrepresented because they could afford the preparation. Thus, even without corruption, the bureaucracy was self-reproducing, inbreeding.

The process of selection for admission to the civil service was itself badly biased. First, the ideographic system of writing precluded widespread literacy. Only literate individuals could be considered, and they remained a small minority into the twentieth century. Second, many of the literate minority could not afford to spend the years of study required in preparation for taking the civil service exams. Third, the content of the exams themselves—focusing on traditional literature and philosophy, the Confucian classics—was irrelevant for the selection of candidates with scientific, technical, cognitive, or managerial ability or accomplishment.

Whether one defines *meritocracy* as admission to the civil service or appointment and promotion within it, in fact, the bureaucracy was meritocratic more in theory than in practice. Office eligibility already in the Han dynasty was mainly by birth; offices were inherited (Lloyd and Sivin 2002, 16–18). By 100 CE, advancement in the civil service was based not on knowledge or performance but on lineage, behavior, and ritual (Sivin 1990, 187). Even admission to the grand academy, which prepared candidates for the bureaucracy, required influence, bribes, or lineage. There were private academies and tutors for those who could afford them. Under these conditions, it would be difficult to judge how corrupt the system was or whether corruption made much difference to performance.

Lineage can be considered a Chinese version of meritocracy. In a culture of authority and obedience that believes that the best is in the past, worships ancestors, and opposes change and novelty, in a culture in which identity is not individual but a collective called family, lineage may seem a better way than an exam prepared and graded by a committee of strangers.

The civil service exams and employment of the meritocracy were a national misdirection of talent (Huff 1993, 308–9). Changes in dynasty and wars reshuffled the bureaucracy with little regard to test performance, but the system replicated itself.

The bureaucracy sought to distance itself from the common people (Lloyd and Sivin 2002, 18–19; Hsu, 173–74). For the common people, there was contempt; and in return, there was not always respect but often fear. This segregation was not what Confucius had in mind for his administrators. It distinguished itself in housing, dress, behavior, and lifestyle. Each status had its own standards, its own needs for ostentation, and conformity was the rule. The lowest rank rode horseback, the next higher traveled by sedan chair with four carriers, and a promotion meant eight carriers and an announcer. Its lifestyle diverted too much of China's resources to supply of luxury goods and services. Many a mandarin had to supplement his official income by corruption—demanding bribes, misusing funds and extralegal levies—to maintain his expected standard (Hsu 1981, 209–16). Those who bought their positions were likely to seek to recover their costs. Corruption bred more corruption and influenced their policies and practices.

Bribery was found everywhere. By 124 BC, admission to the grand academy to prepare for the exam required a sponsor or a bribe (Lloyd and Sivin 2002, 49–50). Exam grades and admission to the civil service could be bought, as well as promotion. Or they could be arranged by marriage. Marriage to gentry was highly correlated with subsequent passing of exams (Huff 1993, 277–82). What cannot be known is the scale or the extent to which it altered admission to the civil service or the careers of civil servants. There were repeated attempts at reform, reflecting concern at the extent to which the intent of the meritocracy was being circumvented. If bribery of government officials was a standard practice, it would become difficult to distinguish a bribe from a legitimate market price or from offerings to the gods, spirits, or ancestors. As to nepotism, it could be considered a Confucian duty rather than a misdemeanor.

The question is to what extent did corruption water down the quality of the bureaucracy or perhaps add talent not recognized by examination? China's great admiral was not a mandarin but a prisoner of war of Muslim ancestry. Some of the chief astronomers were foreigners; now that was a real meritocracy. Corruption, like lineage and imperial discretion, simply provided an alternative but highly selective entry and advancement. What was missing in the Chinese meritocracy was not selectivity of civil servants but a criterion of performance.

Technical workers were outside the civil service exam system; their selection was dominated by a different lineage, not family but teacher-student or master-apprentice, and so was the evaluation of their performance (Sivin 1990, 207–8). The question remained, how was a lineage first established, and how did the first one qualify as a master?

Who were the architects, engineers, technicians, and craftsmen? How were they chosen and trained? Surely, not through civil service examinations. Most of them were illiterate. Their occupations were largely inherited. Their training was on the job. They were selected on the basis of "lineage"—their teachers, masters, tutors. Their success was judged on the same basis as the mandarins, not on performance. Status was ascribed as much as achieved.

There was another hierarchy centered in the imperial court that was not selected by competitive examination and was not conversant with the Confucian classics. They were an alternative bureaucracy untainted by many years of memorizing the Confucian texts. Its selection, appointment, and promotion did not involve lineage. They were the eunuchs, in particular the palace eunuchs (see Anderson 1990). They always had influence and sometimes had power. It is difficult to assess their role since Chinese history was written by the mandarins, who despised the eunuchs, with whom they often competed for position and power. The introduction of civil service exams exacerbated resentment since civil servants who spent long years preparing for the exams and more time waiting for appropriate posts were in competition for influence and sometimes for posts with eunuchs, who had done neither.

According to the mandarins, the eunuchs were corrupt, conniving, and murderous. Some were. But if this were the full story, the mandarins or emperors would have turned against the institution and eliminated it in the Han dynasty, an egregious example of their worst fears. But they did not, and the institution persisted until the last dynasty.

This is a striking contradiction. What is the other side of the story? We will never know in full.

Eunuchs did not write memoirs. It was not good performance that made the headlines. They were valued by some of the emperors, to whom they were the only males with daily access, and by some of the princes and top administrators and wealthy families who also employed eunuchs. They were complementary with the civil servants, not just competitive.

What is overlooked is that much of the misbehavior of palace eunuchs was as agents of the emperor, princes, consorts, or ministers or in collusion with them. One would suspect that failures were outsourced to the eunuchs, which should be shared, if not monopolized, by others. Criticism can also be interpreted as backhanded recognition of initiative and ability.

The history of palace eunuchs would potentially be a natural experiment. To my knowledge, no scholar or mandarin ever discovered anything before 1500 or invented anything other than five-element trigrams, pentagrams, and the emperor's religion. Some eunuchs did. But one cannot generalize from one or two examples. But it is worth noting that the great naval expeditions of 1405–1433 were basically a eunuch enterprise, led by a eunuch and opposed by the bureaucrats. Once the eunuch admiral Zheng He and the emperor who supported him were gone, the bureaucrats burned the ships and banned the construction of any seagoing vessel. The hypothesis is that there was a difference in inventive achievement, correlated with the difference in education, that Confucian scholarship discouraged invention as well as discovery.

The inventor of paper, the greatest invention, was a eunuch. (He had been a mandarin who became a criminal.) Eunuchs were predominantly criminals and POWs until the Qin dynasty, whose first emperor engaged in huge engineering projects and expanded his harem to three thousand concubines. The state conducted a recruiting and selection program, seeking for able candidates for castration. Some poverty-stricken adults volunteered to become eunuchs; others were boys sold by their families. Those selected were assured security and the prospect of affluence. They were trained by the government for the diverse occupations required. Talents were noted in training and in subsequent work experience. Whenever the death penalty was reduced to castration, the number of candidates would rise. The number of eunuchs was large, estimated as high as one hundred thousand, although these numbers are considered exaggerated.

The role of eunuchs varied with the emperor and the dynasty. They always had influence, deriving from their position as the emperor's palace office staff, especially in the reigns of weak emperors (Wittfogel, 355–57). Often they also were empowered by the emperor through his choice of advisers, through appointments to important administrative and policy positions. Several times, they were in power as a self-organized group, dominating state policy with its own appointment and policy process. Their role was at the emperor's discretion. The habit of authority and obedience was preserved. The composition of the eunuch workforce—volunteers, castrated boys, criminals—changed over time. All one can infer is that there was a pool of talent, sometimes wisely used, often not, and that some eunuchs showed great initiative, enterprise, and ability to work together.

Law

Law was the will of the emperor. If he was displeased by the news brought to him, he may order the messenger banished or beheaded. The sentence was promptly carried out. There was no concept of law as an independent body of principles—universal, natural law. Law was concrete, ethnocentric, differentiating among Chinese, Mongols, Muslims, and others (Huff 1993, 262–65). It was hierarchical and discriminating by status and occupation. There were special laws for different ethnicities. A law might apply to some members of society but not to others, to most occupations but not to all. The burden of the law and the consequences of violation likewise were not uniform. The penalties for conviction were hierarchical; severity was inversely related to lineage, social status, birth, age, and occupation. Some occupations were exempt from prosecution for particular offenses. Some occupations were exempt from a variety of crimes, penalties, and taxes (Huff 1993, 262–65, 268–69).

It was not a system of law or of justice but a process for maintaining social order to prevent dissension. Civil rights were an alien concept. Dissension and disrespect were unforgivable. The purpose of law was harmony. This was the reason high-status offenders were exonerated or lightly punished and low status punished severely and why there was one law for Chinese and other laws for ethnic minorities. The abstract concept of law, of justice, was missing. The legal system was an illustration of the absence of abstraction and of generalization and the dominance of the particular, which characterized Chinese culture.

An emperor might change the laws of his predecessor upon ascending the throne or anytime thereafter. It was the will of the provincial governor, of the bureaucrats who ran the affairs of state. There were no constitution circumscribing the power of the state, no law circumscribing that power, no civil rights, and no judicial institutions as we know them to enforce and adjudicate the law (Huff 1993, 255–61). The teachings of Confucius were the equivalent of a constitution.

In a system of top-down authority, there was an inclination to assume guilt of anyone charged with an offense by the authorities. The burden of proof fell on the accused. In such a system, to question the authorities can border on treason. One dared not assume that the authorities may be wrong. There was logic to the Chinese way of thinking. If authority was top down, then responsibility was bottom up. Such wide judicial discretion was an invitation to bribery.

The legal system was designed and employed to perpetuate stability or stagnation rather than to lubricate the wheels of society and the economy. The goal of harmony is a barrier to discovery and invention, to change. Ethically, it implies that good and evil are of little concern. Cognitively, it rejects truth as the objective or even as a criterion. There must be no disagreement. Law is not a search for truth since it is not a search for justice. The wide range of discretion and discrimination in the administration of law is a climate of uncertainty for the citizen.

Regulation

Law is negative; it stipulates what you must not do, say, be. It punishes misdeeds and wrongdoers. It sets limits to individual behavior. Regulation is largely the positive—what you are permitted to do, to own, to be. Regulation draws the boundaries of state authority. It is the license to practice medicine, to operate an inn, to mine salt, to trade. The regulator has something to sell. It is regulation that deliberately minimized and imprisoned the private sector, the autonomy of individuals and groups. The default position is denial; without state permission, there is no scope for enterprise.

There were no rights; there were permissions—to travel, to move, to organize, to produce, to sell. The individual needed the approval of the bureaucracy. To this day, many million workers in cities remain legal residents of the rural communities they left many years ago and are deprived of the rights of legal residents in the cities where they live. There was no right to emigrate, and returning emigrants were subject to beheading in the Ming dynasty. The result was immobility and isolation. Trade was the occupation most adversely affected.

Intergenerational immobility was promoted by equal inheritance. Farms were subdivided; living levels were under pressure from population growth. Primogeniture would have driven younger sons to seek or create new occupations. Most important was the regulation of the purchase and sale of land and of its inheritance.

Restricted mobility of population limited the market for land and atomized markets. Restrictions on its sale hindered the accumulation of larger tracts permitting the use of technologies and increasing the productivity of workers. These restrictions were supplemented at various times by policies to reduce the size of large landholdings (i.e., the accumulation of capital).

Throughout the period considered, agricultural land was the main form of wealth, income from agriculture the principal source of income. The absence of a competitive market for land was a deterrent to the accumulation of capital and to investment (Hsu 1981, 313).

The state monopolized the production of staples such as salt, wine, and iron—the most important markets. In some periods, it authorized private production and sale, but these were monopoly permits rather than authorization of competitive markets. Furthermore, the extreme inequality of income throughout history meant that the common people had little to spend beyond the staples. There was private production of luxury goods for the mandarins. The state also restricted the practice of medicine and other occupations. Independent institutions, private organization of any kind, were rarely tolerated (Huff, 310–13, 318–19).

The state also directly and intentionally restricted private ability to discover and invent and the dissemination of new knowledge. The great book burning of the Qin dynasty was not the only one. Already mentioned were numerous book burnings on many occasions, most extensive in 1772–88 (Bodde 1991, 186, 191) during the Manchu dynasty. There were severe penalties for ownership of forbidden writings. The law code in 653 prohibited the possession of all instruments, writings, charts of astronomy, and calendars, a prohibition lasting to the end of the Ching dynasty in 1911 (Bodde 1991, 191). Private publishers of calendars were executed. These were restrictions on what one could read and on tools available in the search for knowledge.

If property rights in land were limited, those in intellectual property were nonexistent. The Chinese had honored, almost venerated, their inventors and discoverers. What was different was the attitude of the consumer toward the property rights of the inventor, the creative artist. Chinese scholars felt no compunction in copying the work of others without attribution or compensation. There was no recognition of exclusive rights of others to their intellectual product. This is one explanation for the penchant for secrecy and its negative implication for invention and for social cohesion. Copyrights and patents were not legal constructs erected in a vacuum; they reflected attitudes of the societies in which they were developed. Incidentally, in a culture that regarded copying old masters as the highest form of art, what we regard as plagiarism or fraud can have a different implication—praise.

The scope and detail of state regulation of every aspect of life peaked during the Ming dynasty (1368–1644), which required permission to move, sought to ban all foreign trade, and regulated the style and color of clothing and details of housing size and structure. Not even time knowledge was a personal right; ownership of timepieces was a rare privilege (Landes 2005, 6–8, 12). It is no coincidence that there was no progress in technology well before science became an essential ingredient of invention.

Authoritarianism deprived the people of initiative, incentive, and opportunities for discovery and invention and almost precluded innovation in the private sector. Regulation of what could be printed and read, of what products might be made and sold, on the purchase and sale of land, and on the pursuit of particular occupations restricted opportunities. Uncertainties associated with the absence of a rule of law also discouraged enterprise. The state was basically the only market for discovery and invention and the sole agent sponsoring investigation but only that which was responsive to its own needs.

Change without Direction

Over a period of two thousand years, there had been numerous changes in laws and regulations, property rights, the range of authority, and the scope for personal initiative. The exercise of authority varied between dynasties and emperors, from the more restrained rule of the Sung to the totalitarian rule of the Ming. So did progress, however defined. But if there was any direction, it was toward greater complexity and authoritarianism. Progress was not what rulers and administrators had in mind but rather social needs—stability, security, and status (Hsu 1981, 108). The supremacy of the emperor and court and the subservience of its subjects had persisted to the present day. The eunuchs are now gone, and so is the palace harem.

Agriculture evolved between the seventh and fourth centuries BCE from slash and burn to permanent fields. Land became property; there were technological advances, increases in productivity, growth of trade and markets, urbanization, and improvements in communication and transportation. The country became settled. Then came the period of the warring states. The land and its harvest had to be defended from plunderers and invaders, and collective efforts were also needed for water management, especially irrigation, and transportation. Government grew in power and scope. Labor was drafted for public works and for the army, and taxes were collected. This period of growth and change came to an end with the unification of China under the Han dynasty (Elvin 1973, 23–26). There were growth in territory, changes in dynasties, and the Mongol conquest; but when the Europeans first arrived, China was much as it had been during the Han dynasty and so remained for another four centuries.

Under the Han, the state became the biggest landowner. Large private holdings were confiscated. Land redistribution was repeated and evaded in later dynasties. State rule became and remained intrusive, allowing little space for an independent, private sector in any field of endeavor, with a brief hiatus during the first Sung dynasty.

The expanding Islamic civilization came into contact with China during the Tang dynasty. Many Arabs, Persians, and other ethnicities, mostly traders, came to live in China, which became more interested in the outside world and subject to its influence (Fitzgerald 1961, 325–40). But starting in 683, the state turned against all foreign creeds, persecuting them, implicitly rejecting foreign influence.

There was a period of economic development and relative openness during the Tang and Sung dynasties, from the 600s to the late 1200s (see Elvin 1971). Agricultural productivity increased with better seed, tillage, and water management but with diminishing returns. With an upward trend in population, higher yield per hectare did not translate into higher output per capita. Agriculture remained the dominant employment and output. There was technological progress in transportation with better roads. Sea transport was much expanded and improved and in private hands, which until the Sung had depended on foreigners. Private sea transport was evidence of the liberalization of the private sector as it evolved. Sea voyages with merchandize to and from foreign lands required complex management and financing and much capital.

The introduction of money and credit starting in the third century had created one condition for growth and development of the economy. Urban population promoted the development of a private market structure and transportation systems, and ships engaged in international trade. These activities required private capital and facilitated its accumulation.

There was a boom in invention. Porcelain was first made in 700. Woodblock printing was invented, and the first book published this way, in 868. Movable clay type was introduced in around 1041, the pivoting needle magnetic compass in 1000. The uses of gunpowder advanced from firecrackers to propellant and explosives almost to impact delivery. There was much progress in medicine, a field in which alchemists came close to creating scientific chemistry and biology, adopting the experimental method. They did dissection and sought to understand the body, disease, and treatment in natural terms.

During the Sung dynasty (960–1279), there were beginnings of what might have become a scientific revolution. There was freedom for enterprise, resources for invention, and the possibility of novelty and innovation. There were protoscientists conducting experiments, exploring nature, seeking new knowledge, inventing, discovering. There was something of an intellectual awakening as well as economic progress (Elvin, 179–95).

The state encouraged dissemination of technical and scientific as well as practical knowledge through its publications. It sought to democratize knowledge, but interest was limited, and the spread was slow. The government also published a large number of scientific texts and sponsored education in prefecture and large county capitals. It distributed health information and adopted public health measures. Its manuals stressed prevention as well as treatment. There were state schools of medical education and qualifying examinations.

But the Sung dynasty also promoted Neo-Confucianism, returning to the original doctrine, stripping Confucianism of accretions from other philosophies, and banning Buddhism. It reaffirmed the backward-looking aspect of Chinese thinking, the negative attitude toward change (De Bary 1967, 84–88). There was economic growth and relaxation of constraints on private behavior but no fundamental change in values and attitudes. It was light authoritarianism. Its economic accomplishments were perhaps a window of opportunity for an industrial revolution, but that window slammed shut with the Mongol conquest, followed by the Mings. The progressive protoscientists were unable to change entrenched values, beliefs, and behavior. The researchers themselves may not have been sufficiently liberated from tradition. Bodde (1991, 185–86) notes that their work was still focused on particulars, lacking generalizations, and loaded with references to the ancients. Elvin's conclusion was that nobody tried.

Late in the thirteenth century, Chinese civilization stalled. Achievement in invention and discovery came close to an end. There was regression; the inventors of positional algebra were forgotten, and no one understood their works till late in the seventeenth century. Advances in textile technology stalled and were abandoned (Elvin 1973, 193–95).

One hypothetical explanation for China's stagnation is that further invention and discovery required a scientific approach. Landes (2005,

6) rejects this explanation because stagnation preceded the Scientific Revolution by two centuries.

I do not understand; it was the absence of scientific knowledge that mattered, not when it arrived in another continent. Greece had a similar experience; so did Islam. I would argue that there was no date after which a scientific input became required. Some invention and discovery continued without scientific input after Galileo or Watt, not in China. But the big technological advances did require scientific input. Could there have been an industrial revolution without a preceding scientific revolution during the Sung dynasty? The Industrial Revolution was about energy and its costs. No other invention could have had so wide an impact. But large gains in agricultural productivity and elsewhere were possible.

The Sung adopted policies relaxing controls over individual initiative, providing opportunity, resources and incentives for invention. But scientific discoveries and technological breakthroughs were not made by illiterate artisans but by people like Archimedes and Galileo. It was the culture and education of the elite that needed change, and there was none. The Sung did not adopt a phonetic script nor replaced the civil service exam by a performance-related procedure for selection and promotion of government workers. The dynasty improved transportation and communication across the empire. But transport was still on foot, horseback, wheelbarrow, or barge; communication was still word of mouth or bundles of logographic script. The Sung revolution was about more of the same—roads, canals, farmland. It was a dead end. There was growth but no technological trajectory.

What was missing was a critical discovery or invention to propel a technological trajectory and technology spillover into other sectors—what economists called a Kondratieff wave, such as fire, agriculture, and more recently the Watt steam engine. It need not be cheap power. Any number of discoveries, inventions, and policies might have terminated its cultural lethargy and changed the course of Chinese history.

There were two inventions that had dramatic consequences in Europe, although of Chinese origin. The significant technological advance in the Sung dynasty was in printing, but 1,500 copies of a book in that vast country constituted a best seller. The reading public remained tiny for obvious reasons. In Europe, the Gutenberg press led to mass literacy. Gunpowder was another opportunity, not just in war but also in civil engineering. It was the Europeans again that took advantage.

The Sung was succeeded by the Mongol dynasty and then the Ming, a regression to the passion for control. The Ming dynasty was particularly hostile to enterprise of any kind. Since it had already been contacted by Europeans and exposed to their superior knowledge and superior technology in fields important to the court, military, and astronomy, it is difficult to understand its history. It was incredibly intrusive. Movement was subject to government control; emigration was punishable by death. Foreign trade and all contact with foreigners were nearly eliminated. It regulated clothing, construction, house dimensions, colors worn, and music heard. It controlled time; few were allowed to own timepieces. It was for the state to inform the people (Landes 2005, 6–8, 12). It left little to chance or choice.

Major changes are propitious; think of the agricultural revolution and urbanization, all the demands they have imposed on invention. So it is not surprising that the near end of invention in China has occurred in the Ming dynasty, which more than any other was opposed to change. Had there been no Europe, what would have happened after the Ming? Probably nothing. Even with Europeans present, that is what happened until 911.

COSMOLOGY

Why consider cosmology, the concept of reality, in a study of discovery and invention? In brief, because cognition is a function of cosmology. Our cognitive approach in a search for order, in problem-solving, is influenced, if not shaped, by our concept of reality. A follower of the polytheistic cosmology of popular religion does not seek favors from a city god by argument, evidence, or logic. He flatters the deity, performs rites, and makes offerings. A believer in Democritus and his atomic theory does not worship or communicate with the cosmos.

For society, thought patterns and beliefs are reciprocally causal. For individuals, cosmology shapes cognition.

Cultures first asked, "What is reality?" and then sought to explain reality. In China, it was the evidence of the senses. The Chinese believed that what they experienced was reality but not its entirety. In other cultures, the search for reality led first to religion and then to astronomy, physics, and the other sciences but not in China.

Neither the culture, notably Confucianism, nor the state was interested in discovery, and the state's interest in invention was quite limited in scope. Yet there were notable discoveries and great inventions.

How does the universe function? There were three cosmologies widely, if not universally, accepted by the Chinese people throughout the period from the Han dynasty to 1500, three versions of reality. First was the abstract cosmogony of yin-yang and the five elements; second was what I would call the geogony of feng shui—a mix of agency and abstraction. The third, encompassing both heaven and earth, was a vast hierarchical bureaucracy of deities, at the lower level city gods and gods of rain and harvest, some of whom may be ancestors deified. This was agency dominated. I included it among religions since rites were performed and donations and pleas made to these lesser gods. It was yin-yang and the five elements that dominated Chinese worldview.

YIN-YANG AND THE FIVE ELEMENTS

The Chinese cosmos is *one*, self-creating, and self-functioning. All components are interrelated and interdependent as though the cosmos were a living organism. In the Chinese worldview, there is no thing "in itself." Everything is interrelated, but whereas in the West things are discrete, and interrelations are patterns and precise, in China, they are ambiguous and amorphous. The Chinese philosopher's stone is a three-dimensional Rorschach tool of contemplation, not of analysis. The ink-and-brush landscape paintings of the Chinese are exercises in ambiguity, by contrast with the precision of Japanese woodblock prints.

The Chinese saw the cosmos as eternal change but change without direction, a cyclical order of dominance and submission of yin and yang, reconciling contradiction and continuity, change, and stability. Attributes are not isolated but come in pairs with opposite values, the yin and the yang, which roughly translate as negative and positive. All objects have both yin and yang. These values are neither contrary nor equal; they are complementary. Yang is more potent than yin; their confrontation does not cancel, but they amalgamate. Higher reality is a harmonious compromise between opposites—light and dark, male and female, heat and cold, and so on. (These are the characteristics of a continuum rather than opposites.)

The unity of yin and yang make up the universe. Some conceive of yin and yang as a second step in the sequence of creation, themselves generated by the supreme ultimate, the first cause of the universe (Fitzgerald 1961, 411–12), analogous to Aristotle's principle of order. The human search for order in the universe, which in Greece and Europe was a search for knowledge, in China was a search for stability, harmony.

Yin-yang may have evolved from the primitive concepts of earth and sky gods. But yin-yang and the five elements is not a primitive belief such as the worship of local gods and a heavenly bureaucracy. First, it was developed late, probably during the period of Warring States; second, it was agency-free, abstract. My hypothesis is that it is a two-step abstraction—first from innumerable dichotomies, second from these dichotomies, which are end points of continua in most cases, to the continuum that most of them represent, not black and white but a continuous variation in shades of grey. Their reality is a continuum of continua. Their cosmogony is abstraction of change to order, process to pattern.

These primordial forces in their perpetual cycling generate the five elements—water, wood, metal, fire, and earth. These elements are not separate but, like yin and yang, interactive. Each of these elements is associated with a specific color, tone, direction (space), and season (time). The elements, in turn, generate all the content of the cosmos. But the process involved is not causal, nor does it involve agency.

The Chinese five elements are not comparable to the Greek four (or five) elements. The Chinese are fundamental cosmogony that generates all other reality. The five elements themselves are collections of characteristics not limited to matter, with no commonality other than yin and yang. There will be stories about the correlations of any pair but for each pair, a different story. These "elements" lack coherence; they are miscellaneous collections. Hierarchies lack a characteristic in common. They are not an early taxonomy.

The Greek elements are really not about elements but about states of matter—solid, liquid, gaseous, and fire. They can be regarded as an early stage in the analysis of matter. The Greek fundamental components of reality are the atoms of Democritus and the numbers of Pythagoras, and their combinations into the cosmos are expressed geometrically.

The Chinese cosmos is a huge matrix connecting every item to yin and yang and to every other item. Philosophers have developed elaborate associations and categories to classify every object, process, and idea in the universe. They are explained in terms of similarity. This is a vague concept, lacking empirical or logical precision. The "correlations" between the elements and other items are mostly arbitrary and ad hoc (Bodde 1991, 97–99). They lack a shared empirical foundation, hence cannot be described as an abstraction. Many of these associations, as well as the categories, seem very strange to non-Chinese minds; some seem absurd (Lloyd and Sivin 2002, 215, 221–22). Why metal is white and related to a particular season is beyond most of us. The combination of several or all of these small groupings does not constitute a hierarchy nor different perspectives on a common reality. They have no common denominator or shared reality; they are so many small files jumbled together in a large cabinet.

What do the correlations have in common? Frankly, nothing. They are different, that is all. The same is true of the categories. There is no pattern, no hierarchy of order, no order at all in this cosmogony. It is a construct of literary imagination, not logic. One could describe this cosmogony as a literary composition. Why five elements? Because humans have five fingers. Therefore, there must be an endless search for or creation of quintets to fit in the train of correlation. Strange quintets were manufactured for this purpose, such as five seasons (summer split in two) and five directions (the four points of the compass and the center). There is a different explanation for each pair and for each step in a hierarchy. Thus, it is not possible, from knowing a particular pair, to infer the component of other pairs that include either of the components of the initial pair. This cosmic matrix is not organic but a composition, a patchwork quilt. What we have is a reconfiguration of reality to fit the composition. Cosmology shapes cognition.

It is often stated that the Chinese view of the cosmos is organic. Perhaps it is better characterized as relational. Interrelations are the essence of its identity. But organism requires that all elements share a common structure and function. Then any change in one component leads to predictable changes in all others. But the yin-yang matrix has no commonality other than yin and yang, no common denominator, no natural laws. An organism has its own "laws," a shared structure and function. The cosmic matrix lacks coherence; predictions are impossible.

It is a top-down concept of reality, characterized by partition and subtraction, versus the Greek and Western concept—bottom-up, addition, and generalization. The concept of "lineage," discussed earlier, is top-down sociology; status is based on relation to masters or sages, not on personal achievement; the individual is not self-defined but part of a greater whole.

Yin-yang is cosmology in the large with reference to the universe and the cycles of history as well as lesser aspects of reality. It seeks harmony and balance at every level of existence, from the solitary to the stellar. It is goal seeking, but is it agency? It implies not subject-object agency but self-agency; subject and object are one. It is incompatible with causal reasoning, which assumes that cause and effect are "things in themselves" rather than bundles of interrelations. More important for the pursuit of knowledge, its "explanations" satisfied the need to know, the quest for certainty for most people, undermining motivation to seek new knowledge. It includes and links everything in the universe.

The Greeks generalized. The Chinese particularized. Confucian society, state authority, and cosmology were all top down, hierarchical.

COSMIC BUREAUCRACY

The bureaucracy of the cosmos is familiar. The Chinese version is much more orderly than the Greek or Roman; it is also more hierarchical. The classical gods seem to be impulsive micromanagers, whereas the Chinese delegate. Their universe is agency riddled. A hierarchy of deities with specific jurisdictions runs the universe.

Some gods were distinguished mortals who had been deified. This popular religion was practiced well before Confucius, who complained that rites were being neglected. Mo-tzu complained that people spent too much in rites and donations to these gods, better spent for relief of poverty.

This set of beliefs is better described as a cosmocracy than a cosmology. It does not consider the nature of reality; believers take for granted the evidence of the senses. It is only about how that reality is governed. It is social; rain and grain gods do not reward only the farms of those who have donated in their behalf.

What was the relevance of these beliefs for discovery and invention? It told us first that people lacked a sense of autonomy, a feeling of control over their environment and their lives. Their subservience to the gods preceded Confucius and long preceded the Han meritocracy. The state bureaucracy inherited some of the popular attitudes directed toward the heavenly bureaucracy. The people were predisposed to acknowledge, if not accept, that the laws of the land were the will of the mandarins.

Christianity retained vestiges of this primitive cosmology. The saints were mortals who went to heaven. Sanctification is akin to deification. Patron saints of particular places, nations, and occupations were little different from the cosmologies of other cultures despite the monotheism of Christianity and Judaism. But they were patrons rather than rulers; their domains were limited to humans and animals, and their positions were honorary, not executive.

FENG SHUI

If yin-yang and the five elements and the popular religion of multiple deities are cosmologies, then feng shui is geophilia. It is about this planet, although subject to influence of other heavenly bodies. It is agency riddled but by spirits, not gods. If yin-yang is "organic" and the cosmos is one, then feng shui is best described as animistic, spirits, emanations everywhere and everywhen (Muller 1957, 347). There is no geomatrix; it is space and time specific, particular. The educated were believers.

Feng shui is a set of beliefs and practices that antecedes writing in Chinese history. It was already practiced more than three thousand years ago and greatly elaborated in succeeding millennia; it persists and may prevail today. More than any other aspect of Chinese culture, it reflects its concept of the cosmos. It is separate from the quasi-religious belief in a celestial bureaucracy presided over by a supreme deity discussed previously. The former refers to both the heavens and the earth, feng shui to the earth. The gods are individuals who respond to pleas and bribes for specific ends. The feng shui emanations are impersonal, unresponsive, features of the environment to which a person adjusts to improve chances, not to obtain specific services. Its world is not one; it is not organic. Call it amorphous.

The implicit assumption is that the physical environment is alive and active. Everywhere there are spirits, emanations, and auras that impact on residents. They are not simply positive and negative but multivalent. It seems that subjectively nothing ever ends; in a sense, there is no death. The residents of a house a hundred years ago influence the fates of today's buyers. It is an extreme case of backward-oriented culture. The many other superstitions represented by numerology—lucky numbers, good and bad years—all imply that the environment is controlling, that humans should adapt to the environment for improving their chances. Yes, all cultures have some of this; but in China, it is everywhere and in almost everybody.

Its scope and methods had evolved dramatically over time. The original concern was orientation of tombs with regard to the magnetic pole for the comfort of the dead. The spirits of the dead were sentient and able to affect the fate of the living. The lodestone and magnetic compass were first used for this purpose. Its scope was extended to the orientation and location of dwellings and other structures and environmental features subject to human manipulation. It expanded to include interior arrangements.

What was initially a spatial analysis added a temporal dimension. Places are ridden with good and bad fortune. The location of a house is a critical decision. One does not hire an architect so much as a necromancer in choosing a lot and designing a building. One must know the history of particular places. Events long ago and people long dead have some say on the fates of residents. In the process, the residual autonomy of believers is almost eliminated. They have to improve their ability to read the environment and adapt to it. Even today, many Chinese think that bad things will happen if you drive by a cemetery on the way to a house or if someone who had lived in it long ago had committed suicide or if the house is not aligned with the pole.

The belief has a negative bias; most of its instructions are intended to avoid misfortune, not to promote success. It is analogous in this respect to the negative version of the golden rule pronounced by Confucius. It has incorporated aspects of the yin-yang thinking. There does not appear to be any logical or plausible connection; it is just another item in the tool kit of necromancers.

Feng shui fragmented into different schools with their specialties and prescriptions. Some of this is landscape architecture, aesthetics; some of it is common sense—the direction of sunlight, the location of floodwaters. It is the explanation, the justification, for most of these rules and practices that is nonsensical and primitive. These are the beliefs and attitudes of a people who are not accustomed to making their own independent decisions, who do not believe that they have power over their own fates. The environment is alive; humans must adapt to the environment. One succeeds by luck and by propitiating the spirits rather than by merit and hard work. One advances by propitiating the proper officials, not by achievement.

Feng shui is relevant to decision-making at all levels but in particular on questions of space and time. It is not determinism but weakens personal responsibility for achievement. Success and failure are not personal. Agency-ridden cosmology is incompatible with autonomy of the individual, with the sense of control of one's behavior or conditions. In the practice of feng shui, there is no cause-effect, no subject-object relation, just reduced exposure to unknown adverse events, agents, and phenomena and increased exposure to unknown desiderata. The predictions of feng shui are much too vague to be refutable.

My concern is not with these particulars but with the fundamental—ideas of feng shui that reflect the basic cosmology of the Chinese people. They are the prevailing concepts of space and time implicit in the location and alignment of tombs and houses, arrangement of furniture, and other practices. It is about the future of the past and the particularity of space. It is also about the sense of identity, of autonomy of believers. The individual is not in full control. But the future is not deterministic either. Feng shui, together with numerology and other superstitions, was a way of coping with and explaining uncertainty and misfortune.

The worship of ancestors' spirits is a practice and belief separate from feng shui but similar in its implications for belief and behavior on the scale of a family rather than society. Unlike the celestial bureaucracy, its agenda is responsive to particular individuals and families. It shares the same concept of time and space and implication of immortality and the belief that this practice can favorably influence fate. The practice of burning money or paper objects for ancestors seeks their blessings. It is also performed to preserve the memory of their example for the emulation by the current generation. And the rites perpetuate the spirits of the ancestors, who if neglected might disappear.

Feng shui, like yin-yang, assumes that there is no "thing in itself" nor abstract space or time. The past is never over; it is embedded in the present and influences the future. If there is no thing in itself, categorization is arbitrary, if not impossible. Feng shui discourages all empirical reasoning, which assumes the discreteness of each observation. Like yin-yang and the five elements, it is incompatible with causal reasoning. Belief in its practices has further dampened the curiosity of the Chinese.

SPACE AND TIME

There was no concept of abstract space or time in any of the Chinese cosmologies. These dimensions were always attributes of objects or events, not empty. Yin-yang and the five elements have two concepts of time—the cyclicity of yin and yang and of the seasons. Cycles must contain events, and so must seasons. Space is designated by direction, implying movement or destination. As to the polytheistic cosmology, it is space dominant. There is no place without agency. Even process agency—rain, harvest—which is temporal, is spatially ordered.

Feng shui, at its core, is about the valence of space, the uniqueness of each space, and the absence of empty space and secondarily about the uniqueness of each moment of time. As in yin-yang cosmic cycles, feng shui time has no direction. Every space and every time has a valence; every space has its history. The future is in the past; the past is never over but influences the present and is embedded in the future. There cannot be influence without content.

The spatial aspect of feng shui antecedes yin-yang, but the temporal may have been influenced by it. Space in popular religion is jurisdiction—mountain god, city god. Space is not separable from time. A space is not self-defined but characterized by its content, which can change and be modified by other spaces. These concepts are incompatible with Euclidean geometry, perhaps a reason why it remained unknown despite availability of translations. Matteo Ricci had to get help in coining new words for his translation since there were no Chinese words for some of the concepts.

Bodde (1991, 103, 119) argues that despite the historical consciousness of Chinese culture, two-dimensional space—rather than time—was the dominant dimension. What applied to time also applied to space. Time was not conceived as an undifferentiated extension but attached to particular objects or occurrences. And space was subjected to the concept of centrality, the fifth direction in the five-element space. It was measured with reference to a particular origin. This was not abstract space but situational, relative, "boxed in," or particularized units of two-dimensional space.

Needham (1969, 230, 233) stresses Chinese awareness of time. The concept included a belief in advancement from primitive conditions. But historical time was not perceived as continuous but as a series of dynastic units. Time was an attribute of lives, events, seasons, and dynasties. As to cosmological time, it was cyclical, deriving from both Taoist and Hindu concepts of repetitiveness, endless recurrence. The grand cycles contained lesser cycles in a hierarchy of cycles that finally contained particular events. There was, in the Chinese thinking, a dominant numerological component nesting short cycles—phases of the moon, seasons—into longer cycles of planetary movements, which in turn nested into a grand cycle that was an exact multiple of each of the subcycles. There was no abstract, content-free, empty time within which the hierarchy of periods could be nested.

Chinese historical time has no arrow; it is a turnstile. The process of time passing is revolution from one period to another rather than uniform flow. If you want to know the future, recall the past. For the Chinese, time is an attribute, not a dimension. The past is never over; it is embedded in the present and persists into the future. The present lacks autonomy, and so does the future. Cyclical time, lacking the concept of a future, precludes novelty and change. It is repetition (Needham 1969, 292).

These were the prevailing views. The Mohists rejected them. They conceived of abstract space and time and rejected cyclical cosmological time and the entire yin-yang and five-element cosmology. During the period of the Contending States and Hundred Schools of thought, there were other views of reality, space, and time, but diversity ended when the empire was created.

NUMBER AND NUMEROLOGY

The Chinese had two number concepts: (1) an operational system of arithmetic and abacus and (2) numerological beliefs, whose domain is prediction and explanation. Operational numbers constitute a number system in which logic and deduction is the rule, with no role for ambiguity. On the other hand, calendar cycles—propitious and nonpropitious times and places—lack precision. The former is adjectival, a number system; the latter is substantive, particular, not general, not a number system. In the five-element cosmology, five is the number with the highest valence; it is a noun.

Was there a concept of abstract number free of valence, free of reference to objects or phenomena? If there was neither abstract space nor abstract time, could there be abstract number as a noun, not an adjective? In their cosmology, there were many numbers, hierarchies of numbers; they were particular, not general. Each number five was similar but not equal to other number fives; each had its particular content. They were not abstract number but compositions. Whereas Pythagorean numbers were the structure of reality, Chinese numbers were functional; they counted reality.

Feng shui is particular, not generic. It influences each decision, each circumstance. As in the case of yin-yang, it is also a guide to cognitive activity. Particular spaces have valence with reference to the magnetic pole and centrality. But relations are too vague to accommodate numbers.

In calendar numerology, particular numbers have different valences, with references to dates related to lunar and solar cycles. It is about what may happen in the future, given some behavior at a particular time without reference to location. There are propitious and unfortunate times for birth, marriage, and every important decision.

Numerology that is time oriented is easily refutable but persists anyway. The belief has no rationality, but it is a quest for certainty. Their enormous repertoire of superstitions—numerology, astrology— seems to have done the job with regard to subjective uncertainty and misfortune.

The imperial court interest in astronomy was not in the pursuit of understanding the nature of the universe. The purpose was to predict, detect, and interpret celestial events as guides to imperial decision. This interest preceded the creation of the emperor's religion.

What the prevalence of numerology tells us is the absence of causal thinking; it is about possibilities, not predictions or probabilities. It is the belief that one's decisions must fit this imaginary environment, that there are constraints on choice. One succeeds by luck, by propitiating the spirits, and by chance of time and place rather than by merit and hard work. One advances by propitiating the proper officials, not by achievement; perhaps it is the only way to get ahead.

The Chinese did calculate pi to a record number of digits. They mastered the geometry required for the work of illiterate carpenters and architects. But when Matteo Ricci translated Euclid's *Elements* in the early 1600s, the mandarins were amazed. It turned out that a much earlier translation had languished in the imperial library for centuries, unread. Mandarins did not study math and despised the occupations that needed it.

TAXONOMY AND ORDER

The absence of the concept of a thing in itself discouraged taxonomic thinking. There were lists and classifications, but they were nonlogical (Nakamura 1981, 230). There were practical classifications for storage and retrieval of documents, for government accounting, for dictionaries and encyclopedias, and of particular kinds of objects. But the only global taxonomy of all knowledge, of the contents of the universe, was the five-element matrix. The groupings one finds in the five-element cosmology were based on similarities, not on structural or functional criteria. There was no mutual exclusivity, no either/or. Each item was not separate but a bundle of interrelations based on usually capricious similarities. It was a composition, if not an ad hoc compilation. The taxonomies of Aristotle were discoveries and inventions of order—classification by common and mutually exclusive characteristics.

The quest for order in the West was simply recognition that the universe was orderly, that there were laws of nature to be discovered. In China, there was no idea of universal law or natural law (Huff 1993, 249). The search was for harmony in a quasi-organic cosmos undergoing repetitive cycles. Lacking the concept of law or the principle of noncontradiction, it was difficult to arrive at a scientific truth. But these were not matters of cosmology but of cognition, to which we now turn.

COGNITION

How do Chinese cognitive practices affect prospects for discovery and invention? First, we must ask, how did Chinese culture constrain or bias the reasoning processes prevailing in China? The reasoning involved in its cosmology tells us little. In yin-yang and the five elements, it is "correlation," if we avoid any suggestion of statistical reasoning. "Similarity" is a better description. It does not rise to the level of analogy. In feng shui, the reasoning is "influence" of location, past history, on future prospects. There is neither certainty nor precision. "Influence" does not rise to the level of cause and effect.

Evidence, Logic, and Authority

There are three ways of creating belief. One is empirical—the evidence of the senses, observation, experimentation, induction from the particular to the general. Another is logical—inference from the known to the unknown. But by far the most important is authority.

In primitive societies, authority was dominant. In China, the dominance of authority persisted until the twentieth century. Scholars agree that the Chinese in the period of interest were immune, if not allergic, to logic and very difficult to convince by factual evidence. They were not interested in either. The perpetual question is the foundation of authority. Their beliefs were derived from the sages and ancients, Confucius prominent among them (Nakamura 1981, 204–41, 247). Any belief derived from their writings was immune to contrary facts or logic. Belief and knowledge were the same to them. Those who learned otherwise spoke to deaf ears or chose to go mute. Their writings were burned.

To understand Chinese cognition, it is necessary to distinguish between knowledge, belief, and faith. Chinese learning is sourced almost exclusively on authority, based on faith. But faith itself comes in two denominations. One, common to us all, is belief subject to alteration and refutation on the basis of evidence or logic. The other denomination is absolute; it is inviolate. No fact or reason can change it. The Chinese made no distinction between belief, which requires believers, whether true or false, and knowledge, which is true, whether believed or not. Belief implies agency; there must be a believer. Knowledge is abstraction, self-defined, independent of knowers or believers.

The authority of the sages limited motivation. It dismissed experiment and logic as a means toward learning the truth in favor of authority figures and writings. One did not question them. If Confucius or the sages said so, there was no purpose in seeking evidence or conducting any logical analysis. The doctrine of authority and obedience generalized from the family context to knowledge was a severe constraint on the cognitive resources of the Chinese people. Confucianism—the authority of the emperor and his appointees— simply reinforced these constraints. The cosmologies discussed above were believed by high and low alike with very rare exceptions.

Confucianism is not just about ethics of personal behavior and human relations. It is also a philosophy of knowledge. What is knowledge? What can we know? How do we learn? Knowledge to what end? At the individual level, learning is for the purpose of self-fulfillment, but knowledge should be practical in a utilitarian sense. There is an apparent contradiction here. His disinterest in new knowledge, in theory and in the intellectual methods of discovery and invention, and his preference for intuition as the method of learning and for the immediately practical knowledge amounted to opposition to discovery and invention of the practical.

At the level of society, all knowledge was once known, but much has been forgotten, and learning is but a retrieval of lost knowledge. The classics are repositories of knowledge, if only we could understand them. Authority overruled facts and logic as the source of belief.

CONTRADICTION

The Chinese were noted for their ability to entertain contradictory beliefs (Nisbett 2003, 208, 210) and for the absence of the principle of noncontradiction, the foundation of logic. New knowledge does not displace the old; it is simply added to the repertoire (Lloyd and Sivin 2002, 76). Even in technology, a new invention or major improvement does not displace the old, which may persist for centuries side by side long after it was abandoned in the West. This tenacity hampers innovation, the adoption of the new, hence discourages invention and discovery.

How is this possible? Could it be an internalization of the desire for harmony, the dread of confrontation? One avoids self-confrontation by being of two minds rather than changing one's mind. This is only possible if the believer is uninterested in, not influenced by, factual evidence or logical proof. This is not a way of thinking so much as the absence of a way of thinking. Belief is subject specific; so is knowledge. But reasoning processes are not. It is the absence of cognitive processes in the formation of belief that allows the believer to ignore the principle of noncontradiction, to hold contrary opinions simultaneously.

The ability to hold two contradictory beliefs is enabled by thinking in particulars. It is not their yin-yang ideology, which came later and just legitimized it. Yin-yang can be viewed as an advance that recognizes the difference and converts opposites or incompatibles into complements, resolving the contradiction by amalgamation.

Human cognition initially was highly fragmented. There was no transfer of a cognitive skill from the domain in which acquired to other domains. Cognitive evolution followed two trajectories, progress from judgments of "similarity" to analogy and more formal logic. The other trajectory was extension, consolidation, the ability to transfer cognitive techniques across domains. This required apprehension of a commonality between domains, a process of abstraction. Analogy, as a logical rather than literary process, can do the job, but "correlation" or "similarity" cannot. Since Chinese thinking from the Han dynasty onward remained at the similarity, correlation, poetic analogy stage, contrary beliefs rarely confronted one another in the mind of the believer. At least that is my hypothetical explanation. The principle of noncontradiction was not involved.

This was fragmentation of cognition. The absence of cognitive transfer between domains was enabled by the particularity and concreteness of Chinese thinking. The absence of abstraction in language and thought reduced the likelihood that contrary beliefs would ever meet each other.

The inability to recognize contradiction is in addition to what psychologists call "cognitive dissonance," behavior that assumes a cognitive process in the original domain. (Authority is not cognition, just belief.) In modern times, the Chinese are low in dissonance (Hoshimo-Browne et al. 2005) and presumably have been throughout history. It is both low perception and low concern.

An additional explanation is derived from the Chinese passion for secrecy. The true beliefs of many Chinese are hidden. Noncontradiction, retention of contradictory opinions, ambiguity, and noncommitment are deliberate strategies in a society often intolerant of diversity. It was a cognitive environment of both/and rather than either/or. Yet creativity is often the result of resolving contradiction and debate an effective means of resolution.

HARMONY VERSUS TRUTH

An individual may hold contrary beliefs in his mind, but neither Confucius nor the state were tolerant of diversity at the level of society. In the West, if there are conflicting beliefs, one or both views must be wrong, and resolution is a search for truth. In China, both views have merit, and reasoning is the intuitive process of arriving at some balance between them, harmony or stalemate. There is a compromise, and that is the solution. Interpersonal differences should not be resolved by debate. The process is not a search for truth. Facts and reason are secondary, if of concern at all. The process is closer to bargaining than to analysis. Truth as empirical fact, the Chinese know well; but as an abstract principle of reality, they did not know or regard it as the goal of intellectual search (Nakamura 1981, 204–11, 293).

It was not that people changed their minds but that they shared the ability to be of two minds at once. Since harmony was much more important than truth, one chose not to make up one's mind and to retain contrary beliefs as possibilities. Given the priority of compromise, if a better explanation is discovered or a better product invented, there is no need to discard the old. Progress is not possible under these rules of engagement. Conflict resolution is highly democratic; science is not.

Whether one compares China with classical Greece or with Europe of the Scientific and Industrial Revolutions, the contrast in worldviews is much the same. It can be summed up in three words: contradiction, identity, and resolution. In the West, the principle of noncontradiction is the requirement for rationality; the principle of identity, the thing-in-itself concept of reality, is implicit. China embraces the principle of contradiction (or opposition) in the yin-yang formula and rejects the principle of identity as reflected in feng shui and the relational or "organic" view of reality. There is no thing in itself. The past is embedded in the present; every space has its history. Space and time are event specific and alternative descriptors.

Resolution of contradiction in the West is a search for truth, pursued by argument, debate, experimentation, or testing. The result is objective knowledge. In China, individuals can live with contradiction. Conciliation of opposites is pursued by subjective intuition or compromise; the outcome is harmony. There is no objectivity.

The precedence of harmony over truth was compatible with the Chinese concept of identity. A Greek's identity was a thing apart from the views he might express or from particular actions. Changing his views did not mean a change in identity. Chinese identity was more inclusive; thus, disagreement can involve a clash of identities. What in the case of self-evident individuals was order and due process in the case of individuals as gestalts became harmony and mutual bows.

Truth has little value in China. The individual wishes to save face and to save the faces of family, friends, and associates. One wishes to avoid offending others. These considerations are more important than veracity. One consequence is lack of trust; one tactic is silence and secrecy. So the quest for peace and harmony has unintended and undesired consequences. If telling the truth does not upset anyone or have negative effects on oneself, one tells the truth; otherwise, one concocts a convenient lie—call it fiction. There is little inner compulsion or external pressure to tell the truth.

REASONING

Reasoning in China was bounded by reliance on authority, by the preference for harmony over truth, by the relative absence of abstraction and generalization, and by the relational concept of reality.

Truth is a generalization, an abstraction from particulars. Chinese curiosity was focused on facts, not truths. Particulars are ideographed, communicated, and preserved. Generalities, universals, and abstractions die in infancy (Nivison 1967, 119–21). Their intellectual adhesive was analogy, more literary and poetic than logical or taxonomic. Aversion to abstraction means avoidance of universals and generalizations. But discovery is about universals, and so is science. Their technology could not evolve beyond the limits of the particular, the practical. They could build catapults but not equal the achievements of Archimedes, who knew the principle of the lever.

Our reference is to creative thinking, to invention and discovery, how the Chinese have dealt with the unknown, their learning preferences. We also need to specify whether the reference is to the Chinese people at large or to the literate, the scholars, the mandarins. Yin-yang thinking is the province of the latter; feng shui, more limited in scope, is everyone's presumption. Neither collides with rationality.

The cosmic matrix of yin-yang and five elements does not embody natural laws or broad generalizations. It is a vast warehouse of particular items and relations. It is structured on the basis of numerology and "similarities." It lacks cognitive coherence.

By contrast, the Greek cosmic matrices of Democritus, Pythagoras, Ptolemy, and Aristarchus—the relations identified or imagined—were mathematical and universal. The closest approximations to scientific writing with one or two exceptions were described as cut-and-paste compilations. They consisted of collections of excerpts from previous writers, often verbatim, without attribution and with limited contribution of the author, lacking in either analysis or synthesis (Bodde 1991, 82–88). There was a lack of coherence. The stress was on particulars, not on generalization. In the absence of observation of nature and of experimentation, the latest compilation was little different from its predecessors. Fitzgerald (1971, 213–15) described the work of China's great historian Sima Qian as an uncritical compilation rather than a composition. Scientific thinking suffered from the same particularism as inventions. Then how did the Chinese arrive at new beliefs, at new creations?

The Chinese were eminently practical people. Practical knowledge was not elaborated in the sacred writings. Nevertheless, the Chinese learned. There was no shortage of practical, empirical reasoning—trial and error, learning from experience. They were taught by ordinary people and by personal experience. They learned by imitation. Reasoning was often dictated by the domain. One should note that the fine work of Chinese carpenters and stone masons was not guided by their cosmology but by common sense (Bodde 1991, 122). In this practical domain, there was a place for causal thinking, for conceiving materials and tools as things in themselves. But this was in the realm of things, not ideas.

Practical knowledge is causal; it is either/or, not both/and. Although cognitive styles are not domain specific, practical domains are skill specific.

So they could and did invent, but they could not discover. There were discoveries, but they were accidental, not well understood initially, not discoveries as the outcome of a deliberate cognitive process. What was lacking was generalization (from simple analogy to an inductive process) and abstraction (from observation to derivation of implications).

Analogy

If animals have prehensile trunks, the probability that they are elephants is very high. If they have tusks, the probability is lower; they might be walruses. If they are grey, a trivial attribute, the probability that they are elephants is very close to zero. Most of the "correlations" or "similarities" between items in the cosmic matrix of the five elements are trivial. It is not just that the matrix does not generate logical inferences but also that the Chinese do not draw clear distinctions between correlations that are inferential with high probability and correlations that lead nowhere. Primitive analogical thinking can be found anywhere, but in China, it pervaded the elite. Why did they persist? The answer seems to be the basis of belief. In the West, it is ultimately evidence and logic; it is agency-free. What one reads or hears or who one respects is open to critical examination and subject to change. In China, authority could not be questioned.

Consider a library of a million books. If it was organized on the basis of book size and color, it would be useless. If on the basis of author's name, it would be possible to locate a book. The first was similarity; the second was logical analogy. Chinese use of analogy was biased toward the human body and the human life history as the benchmark. So diverse patterns and processes were compared with human organs and their function, with the human experience from conception to death. This was not just a means of organizing cognition but this was also an alternative or supplement to the five elements as a benchmark for taxonomy. Cognition was severely constrained by these mental biases.

The function of analogy is to compare an unknown with a known to learn about the unknown. They must have something in common, whether structure or function. Analogy lacks the rigor of deduction or the discipline of induction. There is an implicit assumption of replication or repetitiveness in the subject considered. Thus, it is well suited to the Chinese view of time and history as cyclical, of reality as quasi organic.

Analogy is not a method of proof, nor is it evidence in support of a proposition. It is simply an association by some criterion that may suggest hypotheses, point to evidence, or classify a statement.

It is not a logical process, just a fishing expedition. Analogy can be viewed as an incomplete reasoning process, the first step in analysis of objects, processes, and events to be compared to identify apparent commonalities. From this comparison, no logical inferences can be made from the known to the unknown. But the comparison can suggest explanations or forecasts (i.e., hypotheses). Basically, analogy is a first step in a process of induction, a process that approximates but never reaches a logical conclusion. Most Chinese were satisfied with this first step. Induction requires repetitiveness.

There is widespread failure to distinguish between analogy as a logical comparison and similarity as a literary device. Much of the analogy in Chinese thinking is literary, a comparison with no inference. "Her cheeks are pink as a rosebud, her lips are petals, her teeth are pearls" is just poetry, not reasoning. No inferences can be drawn. No hypothesis can be derived. What is an analogy to the Chinese may not be to the Greek and vice versa because they refer to different concepts of reality. The Chinese is organic in an almost literal sense—parts of the body, function of these parts—whereas the Greek pattern of reality is atomistic, each component or event complete in itself.

Logic

It was not that Chinese philosophers could not reason deductively. They could and did but in limited domains (Lloyd and Sivin 2002, 192–93). Even when they used such methods, they did not displace intuition, divination, and other nonrational means of arriving at conclusions.

Arithmetic or mathematics is not intuition or analogy. One of their prized inventions is the abacus, a machine for deductive reasoning with numbers. The number system is definite, not ambiguous. Deductive reasoning provides no room for ambiguity or compromise. But in most domains, the Chinese were concerned with particulars and had no need to resolve any contradictions.

As to inductive reasoning, there was little practice or acceptance of empiricism outside the world of work and everyday living. A series of logical analogies became a process of induction. But if the items to be compared were seen as bundles of relationships, lacking self-identity, the process of induction would unlikely be conducted and its results unpersuasive to the observer. There was no predisposition to explore beyond the known world. This lack of curiosity limits the generation of hypotheses and resort to logic as a means of discovery.

What was missing was the desire to extend the boundaries of knowledge. The very slow development of new inventions compared with the Europeans suggested the absence of controlled experiment, disciplined testing, and induction. In most domains, strictly causal reasoning was absent (Nisbett 2003, 210). The needs for explanation were satisfied by yin-yang or feng shui. It was not just that logic was rarely used but also that it was distrusted and strongly opposed as a method of seeking knowledge (Yutang 1935, 89–90, 110). Belief was based on authority, agency that was beyond question, even when authority was based on hearsay. The believer would not seek evidence and, in many cases, ignored or rejected evidence that came to his attention.

Identity as relational is incompatible with either induction or deduction, both of which assume that identity is self-defined, not relational. In the "organic" view, you must know everything to know anything, whereas in the "mechanistic" view, it is possible to know many things without knowing everything. If the practitioner of the Chinese theory of medical conditions and treatment observes a given result, he may infer a yin-yang "cause." It is not testable, therefore not refutable. This is not causality nor explanation, just imagination. But it satisfies the curiosity of the believer, who seeks no further. They do not hypothesize, preferring to fall back on their imaginative cosmologies for "explanation." Their disinterest in observation of nature and experimentation is also intolerance of induction and testing of hypotheses.

How hypotheses are generated is beyond my understanding. Wide knowledge helps, but too much experience seems to tend toward tunnel thinking. Individualism, tolerance of diversity, and in particular the habit of debate and its institutionalization in law and politics provide a favorable environment. Authority is a curse. Generation of hypotheses is at the heart of the process of discovery. I learned the following from an Asian scientist of Chinese culture, speaking for himself and other students of East Asian culture on their experience in Western colleges. His language is English, not Mandarin. "I got high scores for knowledge content exams, but I was amazed at how my Caucasian classmates were able to come up with ideas and articulate them. Yes, I could memorize facts to pass exams, but I was weak at generating hypotheses." He attributes the lack of creativity to the "heritage of Confucian culture, where we are supposed to accept everything the teacher says without questioning."

Intuition

Intuition, or ideas of unknown parentage, is an essential starting point of the search for understanding and explanation. It is a first step in a process of discovery. Assumptions and suppositions can be hypotheses from which inferences can be drawn, whose validity can be tested. Intuition need not be irrational; it is prelogical, a step toward truth. One can find some empirical support for almost any intuition, but a foundation stone is not a foundation. Intuition followed by a reasoning process may be the best option for discovery. It narrows choices but does not select a single answer.

In China, however, intuition was the preferred mode of cognition of Confucius and most other sages. It was imagination, an alternative to reasoning, observation, and analysis. When Confucius and other scholars sang the praises of intuition, they were denigrating logic and experiment. They saw intuition as both the beginning and the end of a reasoning process. They offered no rational method of verifying an intuition (Muller 1967, 449). Whose intuition should one believe? I would suspect that implicit in its praise was authority as the source of truth. Confucius was on the right track but never left the station. Intuition as insight was not distinguished from sheer imagination or aesthetic, ethical experience. The use of similarity as pretend analogy might be considered intuitive (Sivin 1995, 169).

(What philosophers could not perceive was crowded with spirits, gods, the spirits of our ancestors, and environmental valences. Intuition might be conceived as a means of extrasensory perception of reality.)

Staring at a philosopher's stone generates ideas; call them intuitions. But it is only the beginning of a cognitive procedure. The ideas are disordered. They are but the raw material for cognition. There is no sequence, causality, or other pattern. Ideas with a factual reference need to be distinguished from those that are simply products of imagination. Inferences and implications need to be drawn. Interrelations between ideas must be specified. This analytical process was largely missing from the Chinese cognitive practice.

Intuition as the ability to generate hypotheses is an essential element in creativity, specifically in the ability to discover. But discovery is an ability in which the Chinese appear to have been quite deficient over the past two millennia. Authority does not generate ideas; it is observation, experimentation, thinking outside the box.

Cognitive Transfer

Superstition is antireasoning. One aspect, numerology, has been mentioned. The Chinese, even educated Chinese, are superstitious. They believe in lucky and unlucky years and numbers and guide their behavior by numerous rules for propitious outcomes. The palace itself was often superstitious. They reflect the lack of a concept of an orderly universe governed by objective laws as well as a sense of individual autonomy. The role of superstition in our context is as a means of "explaining" strange, unexpected, and usually nefarious occurrences. It was (is) a substitute for rational inquiry or for confession of ignorance.

What the prevalence of superstition tells us is the absence of cognitive transfer between domains. How could an engineer or a mathematician who understands simple probability believe in numerology, in lucky and unlucky numbers or dates? I do not expect that he conducts research to verify every claim, just that he applies the mental attitude in his work to numerological predictions—what is the evidence?—nor settle for examples of one. The cognition not transferred in this case is general, not domain specific, though acquired in a particular domain. The engineer who is highly superstitious is a modern conundrum. The equivalent occupations in pre-scientific-revolution China worked empirically in the causal world of objects and lacked general logical knowledge. With rare exceptions, there was nothing to transfer.

Cognitive transferability also refers to domain-specific cognition—knowledge. An original invention is rarely the end of the inventive process. It can be and usually is improved. Many new technologies have multiple potential uses. It takes understanding of the technology, beyond observation of its effects, to be able to transfer it to different uses in other domains (Halpern 1998). The process goes back to the multiple uses of fire and flaked stones. Gunpowder is a good example. It is noise and sparks, potentially a propellant, an explosive. But to conceive of such uses, one must understand the invention abstractly, as concentrated power, not in terms of particular effects—noise and fire. Preserving the old technology while exploiting the new is possible in the absence of cognitive transfer.

The term *technology transfer* refers to the adoption of a particular technology practiced in a firm or nation by another. It is replication. The process is copying, and the cognitive requirements depend on the technology. It is innovation but not invention. Technology adaptation involves some creativity, the application of a technology to a new context—a steam engine spinning thread converted to spinning wheels or paddles, a technological trajectory. It was found in Greece, sometimes by the original inventor. It was rare in China, with long delays and different inventors; a mechanical device spinning long fibers converted to spin short fibers was not invented.

The Chinese penchant for thinking in particulars may be the reason why the development of the potential of numerous inventions was very slow to come, if at all. They require thinking abstractly, in generalities that facilitate transfer of cognition from one domain to another (Halpern 1998, 449–55). Such understanding also allows improvement not by trial and error, a slow and uncertain process, but by controlled experiment. An understanding of the role of the diverse components of gunpowder allows an intelligent design adapted to particular uses.

Archimedes mastered the mathematics of the lever, which he then applied to diverse uses. The Chinese did not, so each use of the lever was a new invention and a different inventor. Cognitive transfer was the secret of great inventors and discoverers in Greece and the West, but there were none such in China.

It was not that there were no individuals who were highly capable of abstract, logical reasoning, none who did not ponder on the nature of the universe or of the material world. But such individuals were not numerous and rarely were linked in schools or cults or passed on their interests and attainments generation after generation. The intellectual interests of the literati were human relations and the ethics involved. Their writings were descriptive and prescriptive, not analytic.

DISCOVERY AND INVENTION

Secrecy

A passion for secrecy was an ancient and pervasive aspect of the Chinese culture. It must have had a negative impact on the process of discovery and invention and a very negative impact on the preservation and perpetuation of technological and scientific achievements. One source of this passion was the belief that knowledge was power and that knowledge monopolized was personal power. The master-student relation in many skilled occupations was the trusted and secretive method for transfer of knowledge. Mortality was high; much knowledge was lost. Literacy was very low, another constraint on the preservation of knowledge. Some knowledge was dangerous, it threatened prevailing beliefs, and there were book burnings and also beheadings. But the habit of secrecy preceded the great book burning and persisted to the present. Ultimately, it was the inevitable accompaniment of a highly authoritarian state.

The demand for secrecy went beyond practical concerns. China had many pyramids, but their location and very existence was forgotten and rediscovered by chance. The desire for secrecy by the deceased was understandable; there were grave robbers. The tomb of the first emperor of a united China, filled with ceramic soldiers and much else, required thirty-eight years to build and the labor of hundreds of thousands of workers. On the emperor's death, the tomb was sealed with all the workers inside to operate this afterlife empire. But entombed workers had families, and many workers were needed to bury the tomb and erase all evidence of its existence. How could it have been forgotten? But it was. At the same time, Chinese historians kept very detailed records of current events.

The transmission of knowledge down the generations was not a problem for mechanical inventions. A wheelbarrow can speak for itself. But knowledge of and about some of the immortality drugs is lost. There is considerable uncertainty about when some inventions and discoveries were made and who made them.

INVENTORS AND DISCOVERERS

The bureaucrats despised people who worked with their hands (Needham 1969, 141). They looked down on occupations we regard as professional, such as engineers and architects. Even physicians, although medical schools were developed and licenses required, were not highly regarded. Mathematics was a practical skill; astronomers were also trained in astrology. Mandarins could be knowledgeable about civil engineering projects and facilities within their jurisdiction but nothing else remotely practical.

Several Greeks, notably Archimedes, accomplished more in discovery and invention than, as far as we know, all the mandarins for a thousand years. I do not believe this but lack the evidence to disprove this supposition. There was an exception, Shen Kuo (1031–1095), a polymath in the tradition of the Athenian philosophers but also an inventor, interested in practical applications. This earth pointed to the devastating consequences of long years of being immersed in regression studies required to pass the civil service examinations. It put a damper on creativity and desire for new knowledge. There was imagination; many mandarins may have created new subsets of correlations for the five-element matrix or written poetry. But art and composition are not problem-solving invention or nature-ordering discovery.

Most of the practitioners of occupations that dealt with things and materials were illiterate. These were the occupations most likely to generate inventions. But Bodde (1991, 121–22, 360–61) suggested that this may have been an advantage because they were not influenced by the numerology and yin-yang thinking of the scholars.

The Chinese inventors were craftsmen and artisans skilled in their occupation, mostly trained by the state and working in government workshops. They were not members of the elite, and in most cases, even the engineers and architects were illiterate. We do not know the names of most Chinese inventors. The inventive process involved no theory. The Alexandrine inventors, on the other hand, were mathematician-engineers, whose major inventions involved the application of mathematical reasoning. Some were both discoverers and inventors.

In a culture prizing stability, afraid of change, oriented toward the past, and with no concept of progress, it is surprising that there was much invention. The inventors did not own their product; they had nothing to sell. But self-interest was not lacking. Their achievements would be noted and sometimes rewarded. Workers were interested in improving their products, reducing their labor, and raising their incomes. Their inventions were predominantly practical. State demand for invention and discovery was limited and specialized—the military, the infrastructure, the bureaucracy, weapons, civil engineering and communication (e.g., the crossbow, the wheelbarrow, paper).

In medicine, the discoverers and inventors were the equivalent of pharmacists and physicians. In this area, there was private practice and self-employment. Practitioners discovered new herbal remedies, learned about the structure and functioning of the human body, and invented new techniques for treatment of disease. Some very early inventions and publications on Chinese medicine are attributed to emperors, but this attribution is highly questionable. Emperors were keenly interested in drugs that might confer them immortality. Several emperors died prematurely from ingesting too much of the Taoist immortality drug of the day. Discoverers in biology and chemistry were likely to be Taoists.

In seven volumes (*Science and Civilization in China*, multiple dates), Joseph Needham and coauthors provided detailed, comprehensive, and invaluable history of Chinese discovery and invention. But Needham also, although never compromising his scientific objectivity, devoted much time and effort to demonstrate that the Chinese were the first to discover and invent almost everything; it bordered on propaganda. This position made it incredible that China never progressed to a scientific revolution. It entailed some exaggeration of Chinese achievements and implausible hypotheses of technology transfer to the West. It neglected the possibility of independent invention by dating according to the earliest record of an invention. Since the Chinese had an uninterrupted civilization, much was preserved, which elsewhere may have been lost. Also, they wrote on wood and bamboo, not on perishable papyrus or bark. The past history of technology revealed too many instances of independent and roughly simultaneous inventions—including agriculture, writing, ceramics, and metallurgy—to ignore that possibility. We may never know who was first in many cases, but that is not our subject; creativity and the lack of progress are.

INVENTIONS

Sivin claimed there were several scientific revolutions, but if so, they were all aborted, stillborn, and forgotten. The West had just one, quite enough. Others may be biased in the opposite direction; what they saw was two millennia of stagnation. For them, scientific and industrial revolutions were not possible.

How does one count inventions? How much change in a product or process is required to qualify as an invention? Is the bow and arrow one invention or several? As inventions become more complex, this issue becomes common. And how do we compare inventions? Some are trivial; others are momentous. Even this depends on whom you ask, a beneficiary or a bystander. Some are easy to invent and to use; others are very difficult—a paper clip versus a nuclear reactor.

How does one quantify the technical, scientific achievement embodied in an invention or the importance of its impact on society?

It will take more than one book to consider. The same invention in different societies may have quite different impact and represent different levels of achievement. An invention is not an isolated event; in most cases, it has a history. Comparing inventiveness quantitatively strikes me as an impossible task.

Ochoa and Corey's *The Timeline Book of Science* (1995) sweep with a wide broom, listing many technical accomplishments that do not qualify as inventions or discoveries, for example, calculating pi to five decimal places and again to seven, a calculation no more. They record a number of firsts—observation of comets and novas. Examining all entries for the period covered by Lloyd and Sivin, 800 BCE–200 CE, at first, entries are from diverse cultures in the Middle East; but starting with Thales in 635 BCE, Greek entries dominate for the next six centuries, probably accounting for at least half of all entries, a dominance not found for any culture until the Scientific Revolution in Europe. China is represented, especially in the last two centuries. It has entries long before 800 BCE—medicine, silk manufacturing, writing, decimals, a calendar, a predecessor of the abacus—but does not stand out at any time. The most numerous entries are on medicine, math, and astronomy, the last mainly observations.

The listing from Desmond (1986) is much more restrictive than Ochoa and Corey. For the last six centuries BCE, Greek dominance is still evident. For the subsequent two centuries, China is well represented, as well as Greece and Rome.

There is a problem of comparison. Most Greek inventors and discoverers have names; some of them have multiple inventions. Many Chinese inventors have no names; each is listed for a single invention. So we are comparing an Archimedes or a Hero with centuries of Chinese inventors.

After the lodestone compass in 1115, Chinese inventions and discoveries became a minor share of the total. It is not just that their inventiveness declined but also that its share reflected the explosion scientific and technological inventiveness in Europe. But China produced no big inventions or discoveries thereafter or major technological trajectories. Bodde (1991, 8) notes a gradual decline in science and technology after the Sung dynasty (960–1127 or 1260). Needham listed independent inventions between the first and seventeenth centuries, only two of which postdated the Sung dynasty. This is a puzzle. The Industrial Revolution was not possible without a scientific revolution, but China had not exhausted the potential for invention. It continued in other parts of the world, and even today, many inventions have no scientific prerequisites.

There was a difference in creative bias. The Greeks sought to discover the laws of nature; many of their inventions were applications of their theoretical reasoning. They were biased toward physics, mechanical inventions, and mathematics. Chinese inventions proliferated in chemistry and biology, but there was no shortage of mechanical inventions, such as repeating crossbows, drilling machines, spinning machines, and the load-bearing wheelbarrow. Some were quite complex and ingenious.

Whereas Greek discoverers and inventors had considerable latitude in the direction of their efforts, supported by patrons and students, Chinese had less independence, largely responding to the needs of the state and the mandarins. In considering China's record of invention and discovery, it should be kept in mind that it was not so much a nation as an empire. Some of its signal inventions were claimed by other peoples—the compass by the Mongols, movable type by Koreans. But its boundaries should be defined by culture, not ethnicity.

China is credited with four great inventions—paper, printing, gunpowder, and the compass. Paper was invented in 105 CE. The first woodblock-printed book was in 868. Movable brass type, although not a printing press, was invented in Korea in 1392, well before Gutenberg's printing press in 1451. Gunpowder had been known in China since 221 BCE or 270 CE. The modern compass, developed in Europe in 1269, had a crude lodestone ancestor from China in 1115.

Paper and Printing. Paper for writing was invented in 105 CE by Cai Lun, eunuch director of imperial workshops, after years of experimentation with various materials and processes. It was the beginning of a technological trajectory continuing to the present day. It did not arrive in Europe until 1189. Others had made crude paper at least a century earlier that was heavy and rough, used for wrapping, sanitary purposes, and clothing and layered for armor, not for writing.

Printing was an advance on an ancient technological trajectory. Stamps with symbols and characters were in use in many cultures even before writing. So were signet rings. Movable type could have been bundled much earlier from stamps of clay, wood, and metal that had been used for millennia in several cultures, their symbols impressed on wet clay or ink stained on various materials much earlier. But bundled stamps could not be used to print large numbers of copies of a text on slabs of wood, strips of bark, papyrus, or parchment. Printing had to wait for the invention of paper—flat, absorbent, and cheap. For centuries, paper was used for writing. Eventually, large wood stamps and blocks were carved to produce multiple copies, initially not text but also religious images and decorations. The first book was printed from carved wood blocks in 868, nearly eight hundred years after the invention of paper. Carving characters in reverse on wood blocks was slow, costly, and imprecise. Woodblock was not much of an advance in a technological trajectory.

The use of movable type did not come until 1041, initially made of clay. Movable metal type was first used in Korea in the early thirteenth century. Metal type from molds was an advance in the precision of characters, not possible via multiple wood carvings. This was a late stage in the same technological trajectory going back millennia. But why did it take so long? Gutenberg printed the Bible with metal type in 1454. What took China 1,200 years, Europe surpassed in 265.

Paper was the key invention, a direct response to the needs of the huge bureaucracy. Bamboo strips and wood slats were bulky and heavy. Writing on them was a laborious process of incising characters and rubbing in the pigment. Paper documents were easier to write, carry, and store. But China remained illiterate until the mid-twentieth century. Europe, on the other hand, developed the printing press, produced vast amounts of diverse printed matter in several languages, and proceeded toward universal literacy.

A possible explanation for the delay is based on the difference between Chinese script and an alphabet. The advantage of movable type depends on the repetitiveness of script. In alphabets, letters are highly repetitive even in a single sentence. In logograms with thousands of characters, there is much less repetition. Typesetting with an inventory of multiple copies of a few letters is much easier and cheaper than an inventory of thousands of characters, most of which will not be used in every page. A much larger number of copies would have to be printed to justify the costs than for alphabetic script. The practical alternative is to limit vocabulary to a few hundred characters rather than thousands.

What were the consequences of paper printing, movable type printing in particular? In China, they were modest—a revolution in literary resources for a small elite as most of the population remained illiterate until the mid-twentieth century. The big gain was writing on paper for the bureaucracy—easier to write, read, transport, and store. Blame the script. In Europe, it was dramatic—a great increase in the amount and range of information available in print in many languages, a rapid increase in literacy, the third information revolution, language and writing being the first two. Today we are experiencing the fourth, the Internet offering all world knowledge at our fingertips. They were respectively revolutions in communication, in the preservation and in the distribution of knowledge.

When advances in a technological trajectory take centuries instead of generations, they do not propel the civilization. It was seven centuries from paper to the first book, five more to movable type printing. Europe did it in little more than two centuries. Much of the invention in the Tang-Sung dynasties was simply advances on technological trajectories of much earlier origin. Europe did more than catch up quickly; it leapfrogged.

Gunpowder. What about gunpowder? The explosive potential of a mixture of sulfur, charcoal, and saltpeter had been known since 221 BCE. It was a discovery, probably accidentally, by Taoist alchemists. What most impressed the Chinese were the visible and audible consequences—the light and the noise. In around 600 CE, fireworks were invented. They were used for centuries to drive out demons and ghosts.

In 1067, gunpowder was invented. (Or the formula was first found in writing.) Like paper, it initiated a technology trajectory continuing today. It was first used as a military incendiary rather than an explosive. Soon it was adopted as a propellant for such devices—fire lances, flamethrowers—using bamboo barrels. Only later did they see explosion as concentrated power, bombardment. The first small cannon in China was in 1288. Its bamboo barrel projected small pellets with limited impact and short range. It was the Mongols who first made a metal-barrel cannon. China outlawed the export of gunpowder ingredients, aware of their military potential.

The first mention of gunpowder in Europe, by Roger Bacon, was in 1249; the first cannon was invented by a Franciscan monk in 1260. (The date is uncertain; there are several other later dates. A metal cannon firing an iron bullet is dated 1326, raising the possibility that guns were developed independently at about the same time as in Asia). Before the end of the fifteenth century, Portuguese cannon and muskets proved far superior to any firearms available in Asia. Europe obtained gunpowder a thousand years later than the Chinese, but two hundred years later, they were ahead in its applications. Gunpowder was used in quarrying at about the same time in Europe and China, but in China, it did not replace the ancient technique of fire; both were in use until replaced by dynamite (Needham 1987, 536–44).

The one area in which China faced competition was military technology. China's sometimes hostile neighbors were adept at adopting and adapting Chinese weapons. China was under competitive pressure to improve its weapons, to invent new weapons—repeating crossbow, explosive and incendiary devices, chemical warfare. It was one area in which the Chinese should have been willing sometimes to import ideas. The Japanese bought Portuguese small arms, copied them, and exported. The Chinese never developed any. They did make a grandiose cannon of enormous bore and no military value.

Magnetism and Compass. The compass, like gunpowder, was an invention based on a chance discovery of magnetism or the orientation of lodestone to the magnetic pole. The magnetic properties were noticed in the second century CE, but a crude lodestone compass was not created until 1000 CE. Was there a failure of imagination? Paper and gunpowder were of immediate interest to the state. Magnetism was initially only of interest to practitioners of feng shui for orienting and locating tombs; it was not conceived as a navigational aide.

Magnetism was known in Europe by 1180 and a compass created in 1269. Who sailed into uncharted waters guided by it? The great voyages of Zheng He in the early 1400s were predominantly to lands in trading contact with China. The voyages were terminated and the ships destroyed. At the same time, Prince Henry the Navigator founded his maritime research institute in Portugal. They were soon followed by Columbus and Magellan. The Polynesians and the Vikings managed long voyages in uncharted waters without a compass. But there was no practical substitute for paper or for gunpowder.

These inventions also illustrated the failure or delay in pursuing technological trajectories. It was an obsession with the specific and concrete, the absence of abstraction. What the Chinese saw as fire and noise, the Europeans conceived as power and energy. What the Chinese used mainly to locate and align tombs and other structures, they did not conceive at first as location or as a means of navigating uncharted waters or did not use for that purpose. Paper was very convenient for the state and the mandarins but not an open door for general literacy. Desire for stability and resistance to change and novelty may have been a factor as well.

All four allegedly greatest Chinese inventions were made after the end of civilization as an evolving, dynamic, advancing society, when it was already static and resistant to change and novelty. That may be one reason Europe developed and exploited these inventions much more rapidly and further than China itself. What appeared to be accelerated development in Europe, I would argue, was really retarded development in China. Europe was still in the early stages of the Scientific Revolution. Two great inventions were responses to the needs of the state: paper and movable type. They were bound to be made. Paper reduced documents from wooden venetian blinds to paper scrolls. Paper, or some equivalent, was a pressing need. Printing simply produced multiple copies and exact script. These major inventions were the outcome of prolonged efforts;

only the time and place were unpredictable. Compass and gunpowder were the eventual outcome of chance. Eventually, they might have been invented, but there was no immediate need or demand.

Why did it take more than a millennium from the invention of paper to printing with movable characters? It was not failure to conceive the uses to which it could be put as a writing surface. Perhaps failure to conceive of the potential for producing large numbers of identical copies or to appreciate their value? What we know is that the emperor deified the inventor and made him rich, but the next emperor had a different view, retrieving his predecessor's gifts and driving the inventor to suicide. That was in the Han dynasty. Later dynasties were prolific publishers.

The load-carrying wheelbarrow, invented in 400 CE, was a great invention for China, which lacked beasts of burden.

In around 400 CE, not for Europe, China had no draft animals, only humans. It lacked pasture. Horses, it imported from Mongolia. The Chinese wheelbarrow was designed for transporting large loads long distance. Its wheel was at the center of gravity.

There were other important inventions, such as the wheelbarrow in 231 CE and drilling wells for salt and natural gas, initiated in the first century BCE, almost contemporaneous with paper. The exhaustive survey by Joseph Needham and associates filled multiple volumes of *Science and Civilization in China*. A more accessible description is Temple's (1993) *China—Land of Discovery and Invention*. What was lacking was the theoretic foundation and understanding achieved by some Greek inventors.

TRAJECTORIES AND TRANSFERS

Significant inventions are not singular events but sequences or trajectories from digging stick to plough, from knitting to textile mill. The date of origin tells us something, but the rate of improvement tells us more. We cannot generalize from four examples, but their consequences were dramatic. It is not enough to explain the failure of scholars to develop modern science; we also need to consider the relative failure of craftsmen and technicians to develop their inventions. Part of the answer is lack of state interest in the inventions; many may have been stillborn. There was little motivation to discover, little to invent, little incentive for either. Users were reluctant to replace old technology with better new technology. For whatever reasons, inventors failed to utilize fully and to develop further many of their technological inventions. The long time lapses between inventions reported above suggest that much information is lost in the meantime; reinvention becomes necessary.

There was another issue—technology adaptation to new uses. They were slow in transferring the discovery of the explosive power of gunpowder from noise and fire to propulsion, impact, mining, and construction. They failed to adapt the technology designed to spin flax to the spinning of cotton. What was missing was the theoretical understanding facilitating the improvement of the original invention along a technological trajectory, to adapt it to different domains, and to transfer it to other persons and other uses. The absence of a scientific revolution may have been a factor. The beginnings of the Scientific Revolution, or the mentality that led to it, were already found in thirteenth-century Europe. By 1450, it was no longer possible for China to lead; it was already condemned to copy. The European ability to leapfrog was evident well before Galileo and Newton.

Many skills are field specific, such as playing a musical instrument, but analytical ability, the ability to synthesize—induction, deduction—and the ability to generate hypotheses are not. In fact, there was little transfer of general cognitive skills. If observation of an invention is a simple matter of fact, if it is not conceptualized, what is there to transfer? China suffers from both problems: failure to develop and use reasoning other than analogy in any field and limited transfer of what technology has been developed. The culture induces copying versus creation, commentary versus research.

DISCOVERY

One wonders about the astronomers whose learning was valued by the imperial court. The subject was important because the emperor was guided by the heavens and needed to know the meaning of its signs. The calendar was a monopoly of the government, and a new one had to be prepared each year, adjusting the lunar to the solar year. The knowledge of astronomy and its instruments were monopolized by the state after 653 CE. The bureaucracy's interest in astronomy was limited to observation of omens and their interpretation, not to mastering the celestial mechanics or even in conceiving of it.

For centuries, the court hired Arab, Persian, or Indian astronomers. They would be familiar with Ptolemy, some perhaps with Aristarchus and his heliocentric theory. Indian astronomers introduced Greek astronomy as early as the seventh century (Sivin 1990, 191). The chief astronomer was once an Indian. In later centuries, foreign astronomers would have known the Ptolemaic model as corrected and improved by Islamic astronomers, possibly with elliptical planetary orbits. But there was no Copernicus in China, another opportunity missed.

It is strange that such a reclusive culture would employ foreign astronomers instead of mastering their knowledge. China had the longest and most complete record of the movements of the heavens available anywhere.

The astronomers were not mandarins who had passed the civil service exams. It is difficult to believe that they did not wish to learn how to predict celestial phenomena. Some did learn. Chinese astronomer Fao Mun-Ji was on the staff of the Marāgheh observatory in Persia, the best of its time (Nasr 2001, 81). Shen Kuo had to know; he pressed the astronomical bureau to plot the orbits of the planets in the eleventh century. They refused (Qian 1984, 68–69). So why did those who did learn not pass on their knowledge; why was the knowledge not incorporated into the curriculum? There was a need to know; otherwise, how to account for the hiring of foreign astronomers who knew?

I have a hypothesis that I cannot prove but know of no other even faintly credible explanation. My hypothesis is that the astronomic bureau, the court, did not want to know. The ability to predict eclipses and planetary orbits would disemploy many court stargazers, who scanned the heavens for unusual events, and astrologers, soothsayers who interpreted the language of the heavens. Far more importantly, if the solar system were seen as a predictable mechanistic system, the emperor's religion and his prestige were threatened. Former omens were not heavenly agency communicating with the emperor but automatic clockwork. Such knowledge was heresy, risking capital punishment. Besides, there would be no need for any astrologers nor quite as many stargazers. Careers were at stake.

The Chinese wanted better predictions but not the knowledge that led to them. Foreign astronomers could think what they pleased. I believe that the Chinese did learn, over and over again, how to predict eclipses and other secrets of the heavens, but the knowledge did not imprint; it was not passed on (Huff 1993, 288). Five hundred years later, Matteo Ricci's accurate prediction of an eclipse opened palace doors for him and lent him status. This mentality may help explain why, on numerous occasions, individuals whose thinking was liberated from the standard doctrine left no intellectual progeny.

The system of imperial examinations diverted the best and brightest and most ambitious in the land from creative pursuits. Even before the examinations, the selection for government posts was based mainly on scholarship, and that meant erudition in the ancient classics. The study of mathematics was eliminated from the examinations in the Sung dynasty. Mandarins were unlikely to become discoverers or inventors or innovators. Nor were they inclined to contemplate the nature of the universe. The emperor's court, in turn, had little competence or interest in such abstractions.

Who were their discoverers, and what were their discoveries? They were the Taoists, who were interested in nature and sought to understand it. They investigated and made discoveries in biology, botany, and chemistry. In the process, they learned much about the medicinal potential of plants, generating a huge herbal pharmacopeia. Given the "organic" bias in Chinese worldview, it is not coincidental that the main sphere of discovery was medicinal. They studied the human body and how it worked, its ailments, and their causes and explored possible treatments. Their most notable achievement was the discovery/invention of acupuncture (Needham 1981, 85–106).

Physicians never understood how acupuncture worked or how many other treatments worked, settling for yin-yang and five-element "explanations" that explained nothing but sated their limited curiosity (Huisheng 1986, 219–24). Later alchemists did seek secular explanations of their therapies without, however, discarding the imaginary (Lloyd and Sivin 2002, 231).

Taoists learned by observation of natural experiments—differences in diet, environment of individuals with the same ailment. This was the only rational process employed. They also experimented by trial and error, but the choice of trial had no rational basis; it was almost random, not systematic experimentation. There were perpetual efforts to concoct an immortality drug for the emperors and to create precious elements from base materials. As we know, they failed. But at least the Taoists tried and had much to show for their efforts.

China lagged in astronomy, physics, optics, and mathematics. There was little systematic thought in the sciences (Sivin 1995, 169, 171). The issue of exaggerated achievement claimed by Needham refers almost exclusively to discovery, not invention (Qian 1985, 51–77). After all, most inventions are tangible products. The laws of nature are abstractions, about ideas. There were no Chinese equivalents of a Pythagoras or Democritus, never mind Aristotle or Archimedes. The ability to discover had limited value for subsistence or survival until recently; it did not meet Chinese demand for practicality. There was no concept of laws of nature, no search (Needham 1969, 36). Jin Guantao et al. (1986, 170–80) contrasted the bias toward technology in China versus stress on science in Greece and Europe.

We already noted that the Chinese refused to discover astronomical facts other cultures already knew, that they banned ownership of instruments and materials that might be used for discovery, and that they discouraged the study of nature, the very process of discovery. Science—physics, optics, astronomy, chemistry, medicine—was abstraction of general principles from particulars by systematic observation. Chinese contribution was mainly in medicine. Its great discoveries leading to gunpowder and the compass were accidental.

Invention is technology, engineering, applied science, problem-solving, analysis, much more concrete. Advance in technology can proceed only so far by chance, luck, or trial and error. At some point, it requires scientific understanding or instruments that magnify or supplement human senses. The absence of discovery precludes an industrial revolution. So there was reciprocal failure to develop the scientific foundation for invention and to invent the instrumentation that might have transformed the process of discovery.

MO-TZU AND THE MOHISTS

In China, there are exceptions to every finding, and the most important are the views and achievements of the Mohists more than two millennia ago. They were the followers of Mo-tzu, who was born on 479 BCE, the year of Confucius's death, and died in 400 BCE, sixteen years before Aristotle was born. Their concepts of time and space and of number, their work in physics and optics, and their interest in logic and evidence were far closer to those of modern science than anything in the subsequent two millennia. Not even the researchers in the Sung dynasty could approximate their degree of liberation from prevailing attitudes and beliefs. But they and their views vanished without a trace, without evolving into scientific thinking long before it arose in the West. Why nothing came of their concepts remained a mystery.

Mo-tzu's views on society were in sharp contrast with the prevailing culture. He was a universalist, believing in the equality of all people, barbarians included, and he opposed war, the main business of states. He advocated universal peace and love (Bodde 1991, 166–69). These views also conflicted with the teachings of Confucius. His opposition to devotion to rites suggested he was forward, not backward, oriented.

On attitude toward reality, he could not be further apart. Mo-tzu was a contemporary of Democritus and held atomistic views of the universe. He rejected the relativistic cosmology and ambiguity that would become the dominant yin-yang concept of reality, as well as its inherent contradiction.

The Mohists conceived of space and time as infinite, continuous, empty frames of reference (Yinzhi 1986, 206–21). They rejected the cyclical view of history. Their work on mathematics had the abstraction of Greek geometry. They viewed evidence and logic as the way to truth, approximating the scientific method, deductive and inductive logic, reasoning in terms of models. They rejected the yin-yang and five-element concepts of reality but did not develop an alternative (Needham 1956, 165, 170–71, 182–84).

As observers of nature, they made progress in physics, optics, kinetics, and geometry. We know very little about their accomplishments because the efforts to destroy all their work, the great book burning of the Qin dynasty, were very successful; very little was left. It might be memorialized as the funeral pyre of Chinese civilization. In the end, Mohism was a might-have-been.

EXPLANATIONS

Myths of Origin

A fundamental question is why Chinese culture was backward looking. One cannot blame Confucius; he merely canonized entrenched belief. I would suggest a hypothesis that cannot be tested—the myth of origin. Considering the creation myth of each civilization in its chapter would have seemed a stretch for explanation of its culture. But comparing the creation myths of all civilizations mentioned so far may help explain Chinese rear-vision bias and stagnation as well as the character of the other civilizations.

It's a hypothesis, not testable. There are too few founder civilizations. The implication of determinism I find difficult, if not impossible, to accept.

All founder civilizations were backward looking. Their creation myths started with primordial chaos. Supernatural beings brought order. Chinese civilization looked back on the early emperor-gods, the

Yellow Emperor, perhaps mythical sage-kings, who knew everything worth knowing. Hence, the quest for knowledge was a search for the meaning of ancient documents; it was, until recent times, a backward-looking civilization.

In Egypt, the gods Osiris and Isis taught the arts of civilization to the primitive people. Egypt remained backward looking, opposed to change and novelty.

Sumerian mythology tells us that Inanna, Queen of Heaven, brought the art of civilization to the Sumerian city of Erech (or Uruk). It tells us that humans had learned much on their own before receiving the gift from the goddess. One Sumerian story of human creation is the origin of the Hebrew Garden of Eden. Humans were created to relieve the gods of agricultural labor. The garden had a tree of farming, not knowledge. The characters of the Hebrew are all there in the Sumerian original. It may be more than coincidental that Sumer was less backward looking than the other founder civilizations. It was the progenitor of modern world; the others left no successors.

As to other founding civilizations, there is no direct evidence. But later cultures in India suggest that the Indus civilization also created humans endowed with language and other gifts. On the Olmec, we just don't know.

Later civilizations had historic origins; they borrowed from others, so any creation myth would be less significant. The Hebrew Eden had the tree of knowledge; Eve ate the forbidden fruit, and humans learned on their own. Thus, there was no going back; the myth had a forward-looking potential.

The founder civilizations were long established before the origin of the Greek people. Hence, humans had already been given knowledge or the ability to learn. The Greeks had several myths about the origin of humanity. The one most appropriate to the Greek people themselves was reported by Hesiod. Pandora's jar is analogous to the tree of knowledge. She opened the lid, although expressly forbidden, releasing plagues, diseases, and all other evils into the world but retaining hope. The myth warned the Greeks of the problems of civilization, if not the human condition, and the need to seek solutions. It was also about curiosity and initiative. Before Pandora, the Greeks had already made jars. It is analogous to both of Sumer's myths—curiosity and initiative.

The West adopted Christianity and with it the Hebraic myth of creation—the original humans who knew nothing. But it did not need an origin myth; it did not have one. Its origins were historical. Why the difference between the Garden of Eden and the sages and emperor-gods I do not know, but it mattered.

Many cultures have more than one creation myth. The typical common elements are superhuman agency that brings order out of chaos or that rules the diverse forces and features of the universe. Resistance to change is the prevalent attitude in nearly all cultures. Confidence in human ability to learn, to cope with change, is rare. Whether human knowledge is a gift from the gods or the product of the exercise of human abilities or agency predisposes a culture to a top-down concept of reality. A bottom-up concept, such as Darwin's, implies an agency-free concept. I am not aware of any primitive culture or any founder civilization with a bottom-up concept of reality. Even in Greece, not a founder civilization but heir to older cultures, the agency-free, bottom-up concept of reality was the perspective of a small minority.

On the persistence of backward looking or regression, Confucianism was a modern version of the sage-gods of antiquity. He was a sage. But sages had no power. Still, the Sung dynasty instituted neo-Confucianism, driving out Buddhist intrusions, which were a threat to acceptance of hierarchy. The god-kings were not perpetuated but recreated during the Han dynasty in the form of the emperor's religion, a single parishioner communicating with the heavens. This was a deliberate invention by the palace, not the old tradition. It was an insurance policy for the leadership.

Regression is backward looking, an aversion to change and novelty. I see it as perpetuation of the creation myth; god-kings and sage-gods gave the Chinese all that is worth knowing. Egypt had the same myth and also looked backward and rejected novelty. Sumer was slightly different. By contrast, Eve ate the fruit from the tree of learning, Pandora opened the box, and humans were on their own.

Script, Language, and Reasoning

The one significant factor that has not been discussed is the script and language. Their impact is on abstraction did not seem appropriate to discuss until after the section on cognition. Language is our main cognitive resource, script the principal means of preserving and transmitting knowledge.

Some 3,500 years ago, symbols were incised into "oracle bones," tortoiseshells. It is not clear whether the pictographs were already linguistic symbols or just simplified drawings. What is important is the content of their "vocabulary." They were not symbols for commodities or numbers such as merchants would have created. They were about events, locations, and phenomena such as rain, about which a magician might make predictions. They were the product of the temple or palace, the ancestors of the ideographs in use today.

Ideographic writing was abandoned in favor of more efficient and flexible phonetic syllabaries and alphabets more than 3,000 years ago in the Middle East, but in China, its ideographs were simply elaborated and improved. One must ask, why was the Chinese script retained into the twentieth century, although its burden on learning increased with the growth of vocabulary, and its burden on communication grew as contacts with the outside world expanded irreversibly? The Chinese were exposed to phonetic scripts early and often. An early exposure, not necessarily the first, was the result of Alexander's conquest of Bactria, where he founded a Greek city, where traders passed to and from China. The influential imperial envoy Zhang Qian in the early Han dynasty went to Bactria (Fitzgerald 1961, 178–82), which retained elements of Greek culture. During the Tang dynasty, they were in contact with the Muslim civilization and flooded with foreigners who knew several phonetic scripts.

The most common explanation for the lack of creativity in China is the Chinese script. There are actually several and complex explanations. In evaluating its significance, one must keep in mind that throughout the period of interest, literacy was rare. The first explanation is, in fact, illiteracy, given that learning to read and write was a difficult and very prolonged process by contrast with learning an alphabet. Illiterates are less knowledgeable and cognitively less capable than literates. The claim that the script deters invention and discovery by discouraging literacy has only become a strong argument in recent centuries since inventions in the more distant past were predominantly the achievement of illiterate individuals. Discovery, on the other hand, may always have been primarily the work of the literate minority. But the effect of the script on the language itself applies equally to literates and illiterates.

A second explanation is that learning to read and write diverts years of time and effort from other learning activities, particularly in the early decades of life, and the process is never over. Literacy is rote memory, character after character, year after year. It conditions the reader away from more advanced cognitive activities and inculcates a learning process ill suited for discovery or invention. It has little impact on cognitive ability, whereas learning a phonetic script changes neuron pattern organization (Hannas 2003, 140–41). Its demands on memory limit the written vocabulary of most. Chinese, at best, are semiliterate compared with users of phonetic script. Over the two millennia being considered, the vocabulary increased little; but once China was invaded by European culture and technology, needs for new vocabulary surged. Learning to read and write with Chinese script become ever more time consuming. Writing is the storehouse of the knowledge of a civilization. The script made the cost of learning exorbitant and increasing with time.

Their literacy level is low by comparison with the literate in phonetic scripts and always will be. The vocabulary that they can recognize in writing and that they are able to write is small. Precise comparisons are impossible because characters are not words; most of them are two or more words, which in turn may have more than one meaning. But a phonetic reader can read every word, even words he does not know; the logograph reader cannot.

Another hypothesis is that learning to read via an alphabet requires the exercise of an abstract cognitive process not needed in memorizing Chinese characters (Donald 1991, 163–65). This training in abstraction is transferable, applicable across a wide range of activities. Learning

Chinese characters is not training in abstract reasoning but in rote memory. Excellent rote memory has its uses, but promoting curiosity, creativity, discovery, and invention is not one of them.

The script complicates the storage and retrieval of knowledge. Search for information in a library, a book, an encyclopedia, or any text is difficult and uncertain without alphabetic classifications or indices. Numerous taxonomies of subject matter have been developed, but they are difficult to use, and none is efficient. This is a burden for research. The impact of script on the search for information is disproportionately on the ability to discover.

An additional difficulty in understanding and communicating is the lack of punctuation. Until recently, Chinese texts almost never had punctuation; there were few punctuation symbols and no paragraphs, no subtitles, and no pagination (Bodde 1991, 55–74). The last is particularly difficult to understand. Bodde noted these aids to reading, when used, were looked down on. Scholars' attitude toward writing was often self-expression more than clarity or ease of communication.

A third kind of explanation refers to the difference between a Chinese character and a word in phonetic scripts. What a Western language says in one hundred words, Chinese script may say in twenty-five or thirty characters. The original pictographs were discrete words, things in themselves. But the ideographs that have evolved from them, in most cases, are congregations of words or meanings (Hannas 2003, 109, 111). This is how Chinese is written and read. Is it the way literate people think? Aggregating several words or units of meaning into a single compound character sometimes is ambiguous about the interrelations of the parts. The character "henhouse" has a noun and an adjective, but we don't know which is which or which of several interconnections is intended. If there is a shortage of connective words— - prepositions, conjunctions, pronouns—zxthere is ambiguity or lack of precision in writing and reading and possibly also in thinking (Logan, 48–49; Nakamura, 177–78, 185–86). There is ambiguity in writing and possibly in thinking (Logan 48-49). Speech shares this ambiguity (Hockett 1974, 106–12). Western languages include a large number of compound words, but the relation between the components is almost always clear.

A fourth set of explanations refer to the effect of script on the structure and scope of language, which in turn impacts creativity. Although Chinese vocabulary in the fifteenth century has been a large multiple of cuneiform and Egyptian hieroglyphs, even today, it still suffers from the same problem—the shortage of abstract terms of every kind (Nisbett 2003, 48, 51, 53). Script constrains the development and evolution of language (Nakamura 1981, 177, 180). There is a shortage of abstract nouns, tenses, and the connecting, relating, qualifying terms that permit the precision required for communication in a scientific society.

Most thought is subvocal speech. But thought coame first and created language. It is not that the Chinese cannot or do not think in the same way as a Greek or European. It is simply less likely and much more difficult to convey some thoughts to others for lack of dedicated words and phrases. Thought creates language; language shapes thought. But script shapes language. It impedes the creation of words to express abstract ideas.

Understanding of abstraction, proliferation of abstract nouns, came late in linguistic evolution (Hattianagi 1990, 172–73, 181). It lags in China as does syntax that lends coherence and precision to speech and writing. Not just nouns but also articles, prepositions, conjunctions, pronouns, tenses, cases, number, gender, and punctuation add structure to language. The script prolongs and perpetuates an earlier stage of linguistic and cognitive evolution. It is possible to read today texts written two thousand years ago. Most modern languages not exist then.

It is writing and reading that expands a common vocabulary. The authors associating script with lack of creativity are not blaming the process of learning to read and write; illiterates have the same cognitive bias. Nakamura (1964, 171–84) and Hannas (2003, 6) stress the concreteness of East Asian languages, the poverty of abstraction. Logan (1986, 48–49) associates the concreteness of Chinese thought with the reliance on analogy and a preference for intuitive rather than rational apprehension.

The initial pictographs were stylized objects. Characters retain a remote association with their origins, which facilitates memorization, reading, and recall. Ideas that can be visualized are converted into pictographs and eventually simplified into logographs. But ideas that are abstract, or refer to other senses, have no pictorial equivalent. Characters for such ideas are very difficult to conceive, more difficult to adopt, learn, read, and recall. That is why Chinese thinking as well as vocabulary is about particulars, not generalities (Nakamura 1964, 185–87). So abstract ideas introduced in speech are unlikely to make their way into the written language. Even if it is possible to express any abstraction in Chinese script, if one must construct a complex linguistic structure to convey a precise meaning, one is unlikely to do it, and a listener is unlikely to understand it as intended by the speaker.

Speech is monosyllabic, an additional source of ambiguity in communication for literate and illiterate alike, whatever the script. Pinyin is included. The human ear can discriminate some three to four thousand sounds; thus, there is a large number of monosyllabic words with identical sounds but different meanings. Had the Chinese adopted a phonetic script, the language would have become more polysyllabic.

What needs explaining is the perpetuation of the script. Why do the Chinese resist change? The short answer is that the country was ruled by a scholarly elite that took great pride in its writing skills and seen no reason to share them with the common crowd. Writing was regarded as an instrument of power and prestige (Bodde 1991, 62). So authoritarianism and the bureaucracy were the effective causes of the perpetuation of the script, which in turn constrained the evolution of the language.

The problem is psychiatric, on a scale never before experienced. The Chinese are proud of their great civilization with its beautiful script. How to face the fact that it is very backward? For a people who regarded the rest of the world as barbarians, admission that its culture and civilization is backward is traumatic and tragic. That the teachings of Confucius are a facelift for oriental despotism and a cultural anchor around the nation's neck is equally hard to admit.

How important is the script as a contributor, or deterrent, to discovery and invention? When most people are illiterate, the effect of the script would be indirect, through its influence on the structure of the language and its linguistic resources. A logographic script impedes discovery and invention even among the illiterate because it is deficient in vocabulary of abstract nouns, relational words, and descriptive words. Script itself is not a fundamental explanation. It is the failure to replace it with phonetics that distinguishes China. It is the rejection of change that is fundamental.

An alphabetic script does not encourage; it is simply permissive. Rome and Islam have had alphabets and higher literacy rates than China. Other explanations must be sought for their failure.

Structure and Sequence

So far, we have suggested a very long list of possible deterrents to progress in discovery and invention. Most of the items in the list are mentioned by Bodde (1991, 356–68) as well as by Lloyd and Sivin (2002, 239–44). A list tells us little. What was trivial, what significant, what important? Which of these factors were causal, which merely effects of other factors? Our primary interest is China's failure to achieve a scientific revolution, a failure in discovery. But invention is also a concern since there were long delays and sometimes failures to develop the potential of major inventions. Invention almost ceased after the thirteenth century. This slowdown can be attributed to the Ming dynasty, but we will never know.

There cannot be a single explanation; different explanations explain different things. The passion for secrecy explains why some discoveries and inventions have been lost and forgotten but not why they were never made. There is no one explanation for the absence of a scientific revolution in China. Proving a negative is perhaps impossible. Some explanations themselves demand explaining. The most I hope to do is to convert a long list into something resembling a pattern.

I propose to group the items on the list in terms of requirements and deterrents: (1) the deterrents to the creation, dissemination, accumulation of scientific and technical knowledge; (2) the deterrents to reasoning and abstraction; (3) the deterrents to change and novelty; (4) the deterrents to the supply of talent; and (5) the limits of demand and market for invention and discovery. If one hunts for propitiating factors, all one finds is the Taoist interest in nature and its secrets.

First, as to knowledge, ideographic script was a major deterrent to its transmission, preservation, and accumulation because it meant illiteracy for the great majority. One must ask, however, why it was preserved to the present day. The answer is complicated—the backward-looking character of the civilization; Confucianism, which canonized it; and the bureaucracy that endorsed it. The script survived because it was the instrument of the state and because there was a reluctance to change that characterized the state.

The passion for secrecy also impeded the transmission and preservation of new knowledge, but I regard it as a by-product of authoritarianism. The despotic state assured secrecy, slowing accumulation and transmission of knowledge. It did not look kindly on opinions or knowledge in conflict with its ideology or policies and penalized unwelcome thoughts. The state and its bureaucracy, in turn, reflected Confucian thinking, reverence for the past, and opposition to change and novelty. So the ultimate source of impediment to knowledge was resistance to change and novelty, exercised through the authoritarian state. But the absence of trust extended beyond the jurisdiction of the state. It was a likely by-product of exclusive focus on the nuclear family and its ancestry.

Second, considering the inhibition of reasoning and abstraction, which are the ability to discover, script again was a major factor. On one hand, the struggle to master it consumed years of time and embedded habits of thought hostile to original thinking. On the other, illiteracy prevented the evolution of cognitive abilities that were enabled by learning and using a phonetic script. But the main effect of script was slowing the evolution of language, precluding the generation of abstract words and concepts.

Confucianism is often stressed as a deterrent to scientific progress. The stress is on the doctrine of authority and obedience. "Listen and learn, but ask no questions." Obedience to authority prevents inquisitiveness. Authority need not be regressive in mentality, but Confucius made it so. He condemned the use of logical methods of inquiry and promoted intuition. The training of bureaucrats perpetuated his curriculum and pedagogy.

It was the cosmology, particularly yin-yang and the five elements, that directly discouraged reasoning by pretending to provide explanations and by habituating people to think in correlative terms, about similarities, rather than in terms of evidence and logic. The origin of this pretend-organic way of thinking is unknown. It promoted top-down partitioning of reality rather than bottom-up generalization.

Third, there are two ways of thinking about deterrents to change and novelty. One is the preference for the known, fear of the unknown. This is universal, found in every culture, the reason why hunter-gatherer societies persist in all continents. The other is reverence for the past. Authoritarianism—the absence of individual autonomy, the credo of obedience to authority—assured fear of change. But it is the reverence for the past that distinguishes Chinese society. The ancients were demigods; all knowledge was ancient.

Regression is the perpetuation in the public mind of the creation myth, for which there is no explanation. What were the consequences? If your concept of the future is a rearview mirror, there is no such thing as novelty. The belief that there is nothing to discover and that humans lack the capability to discover is at the heart of Chinese stagnation.

It was regression that resulted in the preservation of the script, which delayed the evolution of language and of cognitive practices that could discover natural laws. It preempted the search for new knowledge, respectively the concept, the means, and the demand for knowledge. The cyclical view of history lent credence to regression and the quest to retrieve lost knowledge. Blind obedience or deference to one's elders is just one aspect of reverence for the past. What is reverence for the past for scholars is fear of change for all.

Fourth, the main deterrent to the supply of talent was the brainwashing of the most ambitious and the brightest via preparation for civil service exams and their employment in the bureaucracy. Long before the introduction of the meritocracy, it was the scholars in the Confucian mode who were at the top. A second deterrent was the hierarchical structure of occupational prestige. Manual work and manual workers, even the most skilled, were looked down on, and their earnings were a small fraction of those of lower-rank bureaucrats. Even engineers and architects were pretty low on the occupational prestige scale and were usually illiterate. Physicians were a little higher, and perhaps so were astronomers. High status was limited to those who used the ideographic script in their work, the mandarins. Both the position of the scholars and the occupational hierarchy were attributable to Confucianism, though implemented by the authoritarian state.

Finally, there was a problem of demand for discovery and invention. Demand for novelty by the mandarins was for luxury goods. The state's interest was largely limited to military technology and civil engineering inventions. Its interest in discovery was immortality drugs for the emperor. For health, there was demand independent of the state as well as practitioners, Taoists, and physicians, who were the discoverers. There was an absence of curiosity by the state and among the people, an absence of a need to know. The cosmology already provided the answers to many questions. The authoritarian state limited private incentives, resources, and organizations to such an extent that neither supply of novelty nor demand for novelty had much scope.

Most factors have multiple consequences and interact; one cannot allocate consequences precisely factor by factor. In the final analysis, there are just three explanations themselves unexplained, uncaused causes perhaps. The first is regression, the rearview vision of the culture; the second is the cosmology, the relational concept of reality. The third is the totalitarian state. Authoritarianism can be explained, but the explanation is external to the civilization. Totalitarianism is resistance to change and novelty. All other deterrent influences are related to despotism, regression, or cosmology.

The first fundamental factor is the cosmology, the concept of reality as "organic," as a whole, as one. There is no separate thing "in itself"; there are only bundles of interrelations. This concept of reality is incompatible with laws of nature and the cognitive processes required to arrive at such laws. I have no explanation for this cosmology, either its origin or its incredible persistence.

The basic difference between China and Greece is in terms of two principles. The first is the principle of noncontradiction. It is essential in the West, but China rejected it. Contradiction is at the center of the Chinese worldview and mind-set. The second principle I label tentatively as the principle of identity. In Greece, a thing or object is self-defined, self-limiting, discrete, and "atomistic." In China, there is no such thing as a thing in itself; reality is in the relationships. Reality like authority was top down in China, bottom up in Greece and the West.

The second fundamental factor is regression, the backward-looking viewpoint of the civilization. Everything worth knowing was known to the ancient sage-gods and kings, and learning was simply rediscovery of their wisdom. This viewpoint may be the default foundation of nearly all cultures for all I know; acceptance of change was the rare exception. It was one reason for replacing the hereditary power of nobility by the civil service, concentrating authority in the hands of the emperor. Perhaps it was a motive in creation of the emperor's religion. This resistance to change also accounted for the both/and aspect of Chinese culture. When something new was added, it did not replace the old; both were retained. Blind obedience or deference to one's elders was one aspect of reverence for the past. The civil service exams and the bureaucracy were created to implement and perpetuate this behavior. It was an insurance policy against change.

The third fundamental factor was totalitarianism. The state of a settled and productive population with seminomadic neighbors with predatory instincts required authoritarianism. Without it, there would be no China. I call it uncaused because the explanation is external. But it does not explain its indefinite perpetuation of a siege mentality. It was rule without dispute or constraint, without limits; call it for what it was—totalitarianism. For that, we must turn to resistance to change. Totalitarianism promoted secrecy, absence of trust, preservation of script, and illiteracy. More directly, it limited the demand for discovery and invention and the supply of talent through its training of civil servants.

CONCLUSION

The numerous possible influences on discovery and invention have been sorted into five categories: the supply of knowledge, methods of acquiring knowledge, the desire to learn, the supply of talent, and the demand for discovery and invention. Numerous interrelations between factors believed to discourage discovery and invention have been specified. Three original "causes" have been identified: regression or reverence for the past, the top-down relational concept of reality, and the totalitarian state. Regression and cosmology were under threat on two occasions: first by the Mohists, second during the Tang and Sung dynasties. But the threat was contained. The final question is the relative importance of these diverse factors for discovery and for invention. They are different.

Discovery was not a response to demand, nor did it require much elbow room—individual autonomy or resources. The indoctrination of the bureaucrats simply reduced the probability or the number of potential discoverers. So did the script by perpetuating illiteracy and slowing the evolution of language as a vehicle for abstract reasoning. The cosmology discouraged the cognitive processes likely to lead to discovery. The Confucian culture of authority and obedience was a wet blanket on curiosity and creativity, in particular discouraging the generation of hypotheses. But some discoveries would be made.

Regression mattered. Discovery of herbal medicines would be accepted, but of natural laws, it would not; such knowledge would be discarded in a well of secrecy and amnesia. That was the fate of astronomy and of the Mohists. Nor could a discovery be accepted if it conflicted with state doctrine. There was no demand for the discoveries that would constitute a scientific revolution.

Inventions were not precluded by regression, although they were discouraged by Confucius, if not of practical use. The state encouraged invention in certain areas, trained potential inventors, and financed their work. But its dominance minimized the role of the private sector as demand for inventions and as source of labor and financial resources for inventive effort.

The dominant constraint on discovery was cognition, the lack of abstract reasoning associated with the language and the script. It was also a by-product of the cosmology that obstructed generalization from particulars. Language and cosmology did not prevent initial inventions, but they reduced and delayed the technological trajectory of inventions and cognitive transfer—their application to diverse domains.

The sine qua non is abstraction. It is not an abstract, the quality opposed to the concrete, but abstraction, the process of derivation. Abstract can be the product of untrammeled imagination. Abstraction is derivation from reality—order from chaos or law, generalization from particulars, simplification of complexity. Abstraction is necessary for discovery and for the transfer or adaptation of inventions to different uses, perhaps to some technological trajectories. It is not necessary for most original inventions. Other factors reduce the probability of these achievements but do not preclude them. The Chinese were oversupplied with imagination but quite deficient in abstraction.

REFERENCES

Anderson, Mary M. 1990. *Hidden Power—The Palace Eunuchs of Imperial China.* Buffalo: Prometheus Books.

Angren, Hans. 1986. "Chinese Traditional Medicine." In *Time, Science and Society in China and the West,* edited by J. T. Fraser and F. C. Haber, 200–18. Amherst: University of Massachusetts.

Bittle, Celestine N. 1950. *The Science of Thinking.* Milwaukee: Bruce Publishing Company.

Bodde, Derek. 1991. *Chinese Thought, Society, and Science—The Intellectual and Social Background of Science and Technology in Pre-Modern China.* Honolulu: University of Hawaii Press.

Bodde, Derek. 1967. "Harmony and Conflict in Chinese Philosophy." In *Studies in Chinese Thought*, edited by Arthur F. Wright, 19–80. Chicago: University of Chicago Press.

Brook, E. Bruce. 1999. "Alexandrian Motifs in Chinese Texts." *Sino-Platonic Papers* 96 (June).

Carroll, John B. ed. 1956. *Language, Thought and Reality*. Cambridge: MIT Press

De Bary, Theodore. 1967. In *Studies in Chinese Thought*, edited by Arthur F. Wright, 81–111. Chicago: University of Chicago Press.

Desmond, Kevin A. 1986. *Timetable of Inventions and Discoveries*. New York: M. Evans & Company, Inc.

Donald. Merlin. 1991. *Origins of the Modern Mind—Three Stages in the Evolution of Culture and Cognition*. Cambridge: Harvard University Press.

Elvin, Mark. 1973. *The Pattern of the Chinese Past*. Stanford University Press.

Fallows, Deborah. 2010. *Dreaming in Chinese*. New York: Walker & Co.

Fitzgerald, C. P. 1961. *China—A Short Cultural History*, 3rd ed. New York: Praeger Publishers.

Fraser, J. T., N. Lawrence, and F. C. Haber. 1986. *Time, Science and Society in China and the West*. Amherst: University of Massachusetts.

Halpern, Diane F. 1998. "Teaching Critical Thinking for Transfer Across Domains." *American Psychologist* (April): 449–55.

Hannas, William C. 2003. *The Writing on the Wall—How Asian Orthography Curbs Creativity.* Philadelphia: University of Pennsylvania Press.

Harbsmeier, Christoph. 2001. "Rationalite dans l'histoire intellectuelle de la Chine." In *Rationality in Asia*, edited by Johannes Bronkhorst, 127–51. Brill Academic Publishers.

Hattianadi, J. N. 1990. *How Is Language Possible? Philosophical Reflections on the Evolution of Language and Knowledge.* La Salle: Ill Open Court Publishing Co.

Hockett, Charles. 1974. "Chinese versus English: An Explanation of the Whorfian Hypothesis." In *Language in Culture*, edited by Harry B. Hoijer, 106–12. Chicago: University of Chicago Press.

Hoijer, Harry B. ed. 1974. *Language in Culture.* Chicago: University of Chicago Press.

Hoshimo-Browne, E., A. S. Zanna, S. J. Spencer, M. P. Hanna, S. Kitayama, and S. Lackenbauer. 2005. "On the Cultural Guises of Cognitive Dissonance: The Case of Easterners and Westerners" *Journal of Personality and Social Psychology* 89 (3): 294–310.

Hsu, Francis L. K. 1981. *Americans and Chinese—Passage to Differences*, 3rd ed. Honolulu: University Press of Hawaii.

Huff, Toby. 1993. *The Rise of Early Modern Science—Islam, China & the West.* Cambridge, UK: Cambridge University Press.

Huisheng, Lo. 1986. "Zi Wu Flow Theory and Time." In *Time, Science and Society in China and the West*, edited by J. T. Fraser, N. Lawrence, and F. C. Haber, 219–24. Amherst: University of Massachusetts.

Jin, Guantao, Dainian Fan, Hongye Fan, and Qingfeng Liu. 1986. "The Evolution of Chinese Science and Technology." In *Time,*

Science and Society in China and the West, edited by J. T. Fraser, N. Lawrence, and F. C. Haber, 170–89. Amherst: University of Massachusetts.

Kwok, D. W. Y. 1971. *Scientism in Chinese Thought, 1900–1950*. New York: Biblo and Tannen.

Landes, David S. 2005. "Why Europe and the West, Why Not China?" *Journal of Economic Perspectives* 20 (2): 3–22.

Lawler, Andrew. 2007. "Beyond the Yellow River: How China Became China." *Science* 325 (August): 929–35.

Lewis, Wyndham. 1957. *Time and Western Man*. Boston: Beacon Press.

Lloyd, Geoffrey, and Nathan Sivin. 2002. *The Way and the Word—Science and Medicine in Early China and Greece*. New Haven: Yale University Press.

Logan, Robert K. 1986. *The Alphabet Effect—The Impact of the Phonetic Alphabet on the Development of Western Civilization*. New York: William Morrow and Company, Inc.

Muller, Herbert J. 1967. *The Uses of the Past—Profiles of Former Societies*. New York: Oxford University Press.

Nakamura, Hajime. 1981. *Ways of Thinking of Eastern Peoples: India, China, Tibet, Japan*. Honolulu: University Press of Hawaii.

Nasr, Seyyed Hossein. 2001. *Science and Civilization in Islam*. Chicago: ABC International Group, Inc.

Needham, Joseph. 1956. *Science and Civilization in China*, vol. 2. Cambridge University Press.

———. 1969. *The Grand Titration—Science and Society in East and West*. Toronto: University of Toronto Press.

———. 1981. *Science in Traditional China*. Harvard University Press; Chinese University of Hong Kong.

Nisbett, Richard E. 2003. *The Geography of Thought—How Asians and Westerners Think Differently . . . and Why*. New York: Free Press

Nivison, David F. 1967. "The Problem of 'Knowledge' and 'Action' in Chinese Thought." In *Studies in Chinese Thought*, edited by Arthur F. Wright, 112–45. Chicago: University of Chicago Press.

Qian, Wen-yuan. 1985. *The Great Inertia—Scientific Stagnation in Traditional China*. London: Groom Helm.

Renzong, Qiu. 1986. "Cultural and Intellectual Attitudes that Prevented the Spontaneous Emergence of Modern Science in China." In *Time, Science and Society in China and the West*, edited by J. T. Fraser, N. Lawrence, and F. C. Haber, 181–84. Amherst: University of Massachusetts.

Sivin, Nathan. 1986. "On the Limits of Empirical Knowledge in Traditional Chinese Science." In *Time, Science and Society in China and the West*, edited by J. T. Fraser, N. Lawrence, and F. C. Haber, 151–69. Amherst: University of Massachusetts.

———. 1990. "Science and Medicine in Chinese History." In *Science in Ancient China: Researches and Reflections*, edited by Sivin, 164–96. Aldershot, Great Britain: Variorum Reprints.

———. 1995. *Science in Ancient China: Researches and Reflections*. Aldershot, Great Britain: Variorum Reprints.

Spengler, Oswald. 1945. *The Decline of the West*. New York: Alfred A. Knopf.

Tathelm, T., Zhang X, Oishi S, Shimin C, Duan D, Lan X, Kitayama S, 2014. "Large-Scale Psychological Differences within China Explained by Rice versus Wheat Agriculture." *Science* 344 (May): 603–8.

Temple, Robert K. G. 1986. *China—Land of Discovery and Invention*. Wellingborough, UK: Patrick Stephens.

Toynbee, Arnold J. 1947. *A Study of History, Abridgement of Volumes I-VI by D. C. Somervell*. New York: Oxford University Press.

Usher, Abbot Payson. 1959. *A History of Mechanical Inventions*. Boston: Beacon Press.

Vogel, Hans Ulrich. 1993. "The Great Well of China." *Scientific American* (June): 116–21

Wittfogel, Karl A. 1957. *Oriental Despotism—A Comparative Study of Total Power*. New Haven: Yale University Press.

Wright, Arthur F. ed. 1967. *Studies in Chinese Thought*. Chicago: University of Chicago Press.

Yinzhi, Zhang. 1986. "Mohist Views of Time and Space." In *Time, Science and Society in China and the West*, edited by J. T. Fraser, N. Lawrence, and F. C. Haber, 206–10. Amherst: University of Massachusetts. Origins were historical.

Yutang, Lin. 1935. *My Country and My People*. Reynal & Hitchcock, Inc.

VII

Rome, Islam, and the Greek Legacy

Our purpose is to understand the environment conducive to discovery, invention, and innovation. Chapter 5 on Greece considered the conditions that appeared favorable for its achievements, whereas chapter 6 on China examined the factors that appeared to discourage progress throughout its very long history. But questions remain about which factors are essential, which are merely contributory, and what their significance is. Can we generalize from the experience of a single civilization to that of others? A brief survey of other civilizations that have failed may help sort out the important from trivial or irrelevant factors. Later, we shall consider our findings in explaining the European Scientific and Industrial Revolutions.

Why just these two civilizations? There were other cultures and civilizations. These were the ones most likely to advance to a scientific revolution. Rome and Islam were heirs of Greece, who squandered their legacy.

No other civilization or culture except Europe has succeeded. This is a study of success, not of failures. Rome we can dismiss in a few pages since it ended long ago, was short lived, and did not advance on Greek achievements or even master them. Islam has persisted to the present day, barely alive and in its death throes. Briefly, it mastered Greek knowledge and advanced beyond it. It will require a more extensive discussion. The Islamic civilization to which I refer is basically the Arab empire. Islamic peoples in East Asia India and much of Central Asia have different cultures and histories. All we can do is look for differences between China, Rome, Islam, and the Arab civilization on one hand and Europe since the fall of Rome on the other. The difference may not qualify as an explanation of their failure; that objective is limited to the success story of the West.

ROME

Rome is the most striking example because it was the heir of Greece but did not even master its legacy. Rome was contemporary with late Greek civilization and geographically contiguous, conquering it and incorporating Greek territory in the Roman Empire. The lingua franca of educated people in the Eastern Empire, in Constantinople, was Greek, not Latin. The Eastern Empire survived a millennium after the fall of Rome.

It had all the advantages of script and language available to Greece. Wealthy Romans employed Greeks as tutors. We still use Latin as the vocabulary of science worldwide (together with Greek). Romans valued education. Their school curriculum was adopted from the Greeks. The empire encompassed diverse peoples and engaged in extensive trade. Travel and trade exposed Romans to different ways and ideas.

The Romans had no interest in mastering Greek achievements, much less advancing on them. They gained from Greek achievements simply by employing Greeks. We do not know the names of the architects, engineers, and mathematicians of many of the complex Roman structures but suspect that the reason is that they were Greek. Romans prized orators rather than philosophers, soldiers rather than scientists. Career opportunities favored employment in government administration and the military and private trade, not scholarship and research. There were some Romans other than Plutarch, the great historian who were familiar with the writings of the Greek philosophers. But what they thought about them, or whether they thought about them at all, we do not know (Beard 2016, 471–73). For many centuries after the fall of Rome, Europe did not have any of Aristotle's works and only one of Plato's books. This fact implies that Greek classics were not standard items in Roman libraries, private or public. Few copies must have been available; how else could all have been lost or destroyed? Romans spent little time cogitating about such matters. They had a different agenda, an empire to run.

Authority and the State

Rome was founded long after the first civilizations had been established. Like Greece, it inherited their knowledge or the ability to learn. The origin or creation myth of Rome, Romulus and Remus, was not about learning and knowledge but of violence, war, and domination. Roman history is an endless series of often brutal wars. If they could not find an enemy to conquer, they fought one another, or so it seems. But in peace, it was another polity, particularly the option of citizenship for conquered peoples, which was egalitarian. There may have been much liberty in some Greek city-states as a matter of fact. In the Roman republic, it was an ideology, the limitation of authority (Beard 2016, 128–29).

The state was surprisingly secular. In the early years, it was a republic; some called it a democracy. There were elections, division of power, limits to terms, and limits to power established by law. But it was more a democracy for the aristocracy than for the common people. The republican period government had been described as a shifting balance of power among the senate, the consuls, and the people (Beard 2016, 188–92). In fact, only a minority had the right to vote. Only affluent citizens could compete for senate membership.

The greatest and longest-lasting achievement of the republic was the establishment of Roman law, initially the Twelve Tables. It limited the discretionary power of authority; it applied equally to all. It rendered predictable the legal consequences of personal conduct. The development of Roman law was initially a revolt of the common people against the privileges of the patricians; it was democratic (Beard 2016,

146–52). The Twelve Tables were mostly about domestic problems and focused on family life—private property, death and inheritance. Their significance to the people was shown by the fact that it became part of the school curriculum; schoolboys were memorizing them for centuries (Beard 2016, 141–42).

As the laws evolved over centuries, they came to encompass almost every issue and discord of relevance to society. Systematic procedures were developed for resolution. Roman law defined complaints and specified penalties. It created a system for evaluating complaints, reaching decisions and enforcing legal judgments. There were trials, presentation of evidence by the accuser, argument and counterevidence by the defender, and judgment and its enforcement. Late in Roman history, the loser had the option of appeal to a higher court. The law also came to consider age and other issues of the offender's responsibility as well as determining rights of ownership and contract.

In practice, the legal system fell short of its promise. Occasionally, the institutions were overburdened. There were too many complaints and long delays. The authorities were not interested in the problems of the poor. The process was complex and prolonged.

The Roman passion for order was focused on the human condition; hence, Roman law played the role in their culture analogous to that of hypotheses about the universe of Greek philosophers. Roman law was a taxonomy of human transactions.

Citizenship without regard to ethnicity, religion, or place of birth or residence was available from the very beginning of Roman civilization. The idea started with the mythical Romulus. It was almost automatic to those who rendered service to the state as soldiers or officials (Beard 2016, 60–69, 529–22). Defeated peoples became Roman soldiers and Roman citizens. Without this practice, there would not have been a historic Roman Empire, if empire at all. No other people in antiquity approached this level of openness. In fact, the policy, and the outcome, was not replicated until the nineteenth and twentieth centuries.

There were also changes in the structure of authority. The consuls of the republic that replaced the early monarchy were all patricians. Then plebeians were authorized to run for the office; finally, a plebeian consul was required. The class distinction persisted in the minds of the patricians, although differences in power and wealth were small. A revolt of plebeians against patricians resulted in the establishment of tribunes as their representatives, who acquired the power of legislation. Enslavement as punishment for debt was eliminated.

The republic was not a democracy, but citizenship and the rule of law were essential building blocks. A government of laws rather than of men provided a favorable environment for private enterprise by reducing uncertainty.

The empire, starting with Augustus in 27 BC, was autocracy with qualifications. Roman rule was not the unlimited autocracy and abject subjection of early civilizations such as Egypt and China nor the free spirit of inquiry of independent Greek city-states. In a huge empire of diverse peoples, monolithic, top-down authority was unworkable. Information flowed bottom up by hoof and sail. Much local, regional autonomy was inevitable. Furthermore, the tolerance of the state for different peoples and religions extended to local administrations and their practices. Authority was delegated. Its concern was practical—the flow of tax revenue, tribute, and trade. Rome was prepared to accept local institutions and practices that delivered the goods. This tolerance of diversity was present at the beginning but was institutionalized as public policy as the empire grew. The imperial structure of authority, both vertical and horizontal, scale and scope, varied widely. This practice bore some analogy to Greek city-states. But the default standard was Roman law.

What was the role of the state in encouraging or discouraging discovery, invention, and innovation? On the positive side, the scope of authority or its exercise was limited; it allowed the accumulation of private capital and relied on private organization of production and trade. The resources for invention were ample. The private sector dominated the economy and Roman law on property rights and inheritance a favorable climate for enterprise, although the concept of the corporation and limited liability did not exist (Malmendier 2009).

Authority of the state was not a deterrent for creativity. Severe penalties for debt—prison, enslavement—were deterrents and eventually eliminated. If there was a negative aspect to the state, it was the offer of bureaucratic careers to the best and brightest.

Culture

Rome did not lack the resources or opportunities for discovery and invention. It lacked the predisposition. The state had no interest in the search for the laws of nature, in discovery, in ideas, in the quest for knowledge beyond the practical. In invention, its interest was in the tools of war. The Romans had great respect for Archimedes. They certainly valued his war machines, the heavy artillery of the day. Rome was a builder of cities. It advanced civil engineering technology— invention—in urban and related infrastructure. And emperors built monuments.

Literate Romans were exposed to Greek culture. Their school curriculum was borrowed from the Greeks. They were exposed to the sophisticated lifestyle of the Greeks and adopted it in part, in the arts. There were reservations about the conflict with the perceived identity of the Roman citizen—stern, matter of fact, almost stoical. But adopt they did. However, Schlagel (2010, 445) tells us that Roman civilization produced not one distinguished scientist or mathematician. There were no counterparts of the Athenian philosophers or the mathematician-engineers of Alexandria.

If Rome can be said to have a cosmology, it was a panoply of humanoid deities in constant turmoil. It was a primitive, agency-riddled cosmos of the Greek people, not of the philosophers. Zeus was Jupiter. The gods of conquered peoples were readily admitted into this heavenly society. It was not that they rejected agency, as did the Greeks, but that they did not ponder about ultimate reality. The gods were irrelevant. Emperors themselves became objects of worship for the people.

The Roman cosmos was the Roman Empire. The search for order was the Roman legion, Roman law, and the incentive of Roman citizenship. Romans lived in a world of fact. They were individualists with a sense of autonomy, citizens irrespective of place, ethnicity, status, or religion.

The Romans did not lack the capacity for abstraction essential for discovery and contributory to invention. But they kept their eyes on the ground instead of gazing at the heavens. The Roman abstractive ability was reflected in their concepts of law—their greatest creation, a coherent taxonomy of human interaction—in the concept of citizenship. They were not just city builders but also planners with a model of multiple interacting parts and functions. Their propensity to debate and search for truth was directed to public policy. It did not extend to their clumsy number system. Their passion for order did not transfer to the domains of religion or cosmology. Their search for order was not for knowledge or understanding but for control and stability.

Their desire for novelty was not in the realm of ideas or inventions but for wealth and its display, games and spectacles to entertain the public; the complex performances in the Colosseum were the acme of their creativity. But Rome was not a backward-looking culture opposed to change.

Roman culture cannot be said to embody a particular cognitive process. But its thinking was historical and concrete, implying a tendency toward analogical thinking, similarity, and contrast. Thus, neither the cosmology nor the cognition was favorable for discovery. But neither were they highly inhibitive. However, the exercise of Roman law involved presentation of evidence, argument by both sides of a controversy, and judicial judgment. But judgment was in the hands of government officials, not a requirement of all citizens.

A new cultural factor entered Rome in its last three centuries, Christianity. Its impact will be discussed in the next chapter. Jehovah could not be integrated with the polytheistic Roman deities; it was Jehovah or Jupiter. There was persecution. But Constantine (306–337 CE) converted to Christianity and ended the persecution. As the population became Christian, it was the pagan's turn to be persecuted.

In 529, Justinian (527–565) closed what he regarded as the "pagan" schools and centers of knowledge and research in Athens, Alexandria, and elsewhere, including Plato's Academy and Aristotle's Lyceum. A century later, it was the followers of Muhammad who came to these places and many others in search of knowledge.

Invention

How were engineers, architects, and mathematicians trained? Education, until late in the empire, was private and mainly tutorial, which most citizens could not afford. Romans valued education, but it was a monopoly of the affluent. The curriculum was borrowed from Greece. There were schools, but they charged tuition. Schools were disciplinary, not forums for discussion. Training specifically designed for particular occupations, such as architecture, would be on-the-job tutorial training. After the conquest of Greek territories, there was a supply of educated Greeks for technical work, which probably reduced both need for or interest in training in mathematics and related skills or interests of Romans in pursuing such careers. "Let the Greeks do it."

We do not know the name of the engineers and, in most cases, of the architects. What of the great Roman structures—aqueducts, bridges, port facilities, roads? I suspect that most of the engineers and architects were not masters of Greek knowledge but highly skilled craftsmen who measured with precision. Their artifacts endured, in many cases, to the present day not because of their sophistication but because of the quality of the cement and overinvestment in materials. Columns were larger in diameter than needed, arches were small span and numerous, and more stone was used than necessary. But in monumental architecture, when arches, domes, and barrel vaults were involved, I suspect that Greek mathematicians were at work. The designer of the Pantheon was Apollodorus of Damascus, a Greek. Incidentally, writings of the Greek mathematicians and engineers did not survive the fall of Rome. Not many people read them.

The Eastern Empire was a different story. Alexandria was still training outstanding mathematician-engineers, if not scholars, after the fall of Rome. The architects of the Hagia Sophia were well-known Greek mathematicians/engineers in the tradition of Alexandria. They made a number of inventions in the design, structure, materials, and construction that reflected scientific understanding (Mark and Cakmak 1992).

Its major technological discovery/invention was cement of superb quality, whose composition and manufacturing processes were forgotten. Cement was widely used and on a large scale for centuries. It is strange that its manufacturing process should have been completely forgotten, to be rediscovered in the twentieth century. Romans, unlike Chinese, had no habit of secrecy. Could they have attached little value to their most important invention? I find this difficult to believe. More likely, the invention and the process were the work of illiterates.

A second significant invention was the use of waterpower to grind grain into flour. A third discovery/invention was crop rotation. In this case, the inventor is known, a Jewish woman.

What distinguished these inventions from most made in the past was that they were on an industrial scale, requiring land, capital, and a market for implementation. They were made early in the history of the civilization, during the days of the republic. How were they paid for? Cement was used mainly by the state and no doubt financed by the state. As to water mills, we just don't know.

There were minor improvements in catapults and other tools of war and in ships and minor discoveries in medicine, nothing of note. Most of the inventions listed by Ochoa and Corey (1995) and Desmond (1986) are infrastructure projects—the Appian Way, long-distance aqueduct and architectural structures such as the Pantheon, the Colosseum, the Arch of Titus, the mausoleum of Hadrian, and other imposing or complex structures. No doubt there were improvements in design, methods, or materials—small discoveries and inventions. But it is a stretch to list an aqueduct as an invention.

In fact, Rome was a great inventor, but its inventions were social, not technical, and institutional, not individual. The two great Roman inventions was Roman law, to which everyone was subject regardless of status. Even more radical was the right of citizenship, available without regard to place of birth, ethnicity, or religion. Roman citizenship was a concept far in advance of its time, in fact contemporary. It was the extension of citizenship and some, if not all, of its rights and obligations that enabled Rome to create and control such a vast empire. Also important were the Roman legion, a moving wall of steel that defeated enemy cavalry, and the complex and coherent city-building models, an improvement on Greek city building under Alexander and his followers. These cities ruled new territories conquered by the legions.

The problem with institutional invention is that they are culture rooted and may be culture bound. Each culture may learn from the inventor but may have to reinvent.

Rome had no potential for a scientific revolution, but it made that revolution possible, if not inevitable, a millennium after its fall. (That is a question for the next chapter.) Rome fell in 410, but the invaders who overran it became Christians and adopted Latin as the lingua franca for educated Europeans for the next 1,300 years. Today Latin and Greek provided the vocabulary, the former much of the script and for the universal languages of the sciences. Latin, Christianity, and the church provided the institutional framework for education and communication. Nearly all early contributors to the scientific evolution, including Copernicus, were members of the clergy. Without Latin and Christianity, we might still be waiting for the Scientific Revolution. Of course, there was more than just a bequest. It was the northern peoples who conquered Rome and who exercised the initiative, adopted Latin as their lingua franca and Christianity, and preserved its institutions.

The Eastern empire, Constantinople, lived on for another millennium, but its lingua franca was Greek. Its early centuries after the fall of Rome are best viewed as a requiem to the Greek civilization rather than to Rome. Its legacy was to the Islamic civilization.

ISLAM

Religion or Civilization?

The Muslim world and Islamic civilization are two different concepts and two quite different territories. Islam, the religion, is one from Gibraltar to Java. But there was more than one culture. The civilization to which I refer is one from Gibraltar to the Persian Gulf, associated with Arab dominium. The Persians, although not Arab, must be included in the civilization since they were major contributors to its achievements as well as to its foundation of knowledge. Other cultures from India to the east influenced the role of the religion itself. And there is a vast middle ground, influenced directly by Arabic culture but also preserving cultures of their own. These are the diverse Turkish peoples of Central Asia and the Mongols. They had their own cultures, languages, and histories; and some, such as today's Bangladesh, were part of quite different civilizations. Most of the world's Muslim population, in three of its four largest countries, lives in India and east of India and has little to do with the Middle East other than pilgrimage to Mecca.

At the time of Muhammad, most of the peoples in the area of the civilization did not speak Arabic. Most beyond this area still don't. The Arabs themselves were a tribal, seminomadic people, conquering cultures more advanced than their own. They had little to offer as an alternative to prevailing cultures other than their religion. Thus, Arab civilization initially was no more than that of the people it conquered.

Civilization and religion had different origins and trajectories. The core area of Islam included the detritus of several civilizations and culture, but the dominant culture was Greek, and the main religion was Christianity. The Greek culture was long past its prime, in remission. Its vigor was somewhat restored now that people and ideas could travel easily from Spain to Persia, and new knowledge could flow in from Persia and India. It was the Arab conquest that stimulated the revival, although religious leaders were supportive in the early centuries. The translation of Greek philosophical and scientific writings into Arabic and Persian greatly enlarged their readership.

Most of the people within the Arab empire were not Muslim. There were two centuries before mass conversion after military defeat Islamized the empire. In cultures with top-down authority, mass conversion would be possible and credible. As people learned Arabic, those who had called themselves Syrian or Egyptian called themselves Arabs. Language defined ethnicity. Persians retained their ethnic identity, but many adopted Arabic names. Thus, initially, there was quite limited overlap of membership in the civilization and the religion. Overlap increased over time but was never complete convergence. Civilization and religion remained far apart in culture, in conflict in some domains, one reason why the religion eventually had to suppress the civilization. The civilization was short lived; the religion endured.

Islam could be said to adopt a concept of citizenship analogous to that of Rome. But Roman citizenship open to conquered peoples referred to the state, to Roman law, whereas the Islamic concept of citizenship referred to the religion.

Islam initially adopted the Greek heritage and advanced it in some areas. The civilization ended in around the thirteenth century when Islam turned its back on much of it. The Greek heritage was then described as foreign sciences (Huff 1993, 52). That is one mystery; why did it choose to return to a more primitive stage of cultural and intellectual development? But that is the wrong question. What needs to be explained is not the regression of Islam after the thirteenth century but the progression of the civilization in earlier centuries and its eventual failure. Justinian's closing of the Academy and the Lyceum in AD 529 was the end of the protracted decline of Greek culture in the east. Alexandria survived and was conquered by the Muslims in 642. Constantinople did not fall until 1453. But the revival was not in Greek territory but in Córdoba, Baghdad, and other centers under Arab rule and Gundeshapur in Persia.

Perhaps Islam should be described as a religion that was imposed on a cauldron of past civilizations, particularly Greek. Only in later stages did it stress its own beliefs or discard the old. In Islam, the civilization came first and then stagnated into religion. In Europe, this sequence was reversed.

It was the Islamic civilization that was heir to the legacy of Greece, which I seek to understand since it was a culture of discovery and invention. The culture of the Koran was Arabic and had no interest in change or novelty, no prospect of a scientific revolution. Belonging in both required a high level of cognitive dissonance.

As in previous chapters, my concept of civilization is dynamic, a culture that develops, evolves, and progresses but retains its identity. Other cultures are static or backward looking or had too much culture change, and there is a loss of identity—a different culture.

I propose to consider civilization and religion separately. Religions can be created by a single individual at a particular point as was Islam. Civilizations are the product of many people over centuries. The civilization should be compared with Greece, from which it derived and with which it shared some attributes favorable for discovery and invention. The religion of Islam I will compare with China, with which it shared most of the attributes, discouraging discovery as well as invention.

There were attributes common to both civilization and religion. They shared the Arabic script and language, which were not deterrents, unlike Chinese script. Initially, the Arabic language was inadequate for the needs of science and technology, but the translators of Greek documents enriched the language with new word meanings and words adopted from the languages they were translating. By the end of the ninth century, nearly all Greek writings on philosophy and the natural sciences had been translated.

Civilization

The Islamic civilization does not refer to any one place, people, or ethnicity. China, India, and Europe have greater coherence.

China was isolated by deserts, mountains, and Siberia. There was no earlier civilization in its territory. Neighboring cultures, Indian Buddhism in particular, had some influence. But they were never superimposed on Chinese civilization. Conquerors—Mongols, Manchu—were easily absorbed.

The Greeks, Alexander in particular, opened the way to the East, defeating the Persian Empire and other barriers, extending Greek culture all the way to India. They Hellenized many peoples whose cultures were less advanced than their own. It was only the Arabs, motivated by religious fervor, who conquered and Arabized peoples with cultures more advanced than their own. Islam spread rapidly in the Mediterranean and far to the East along the path of Alexander but adopted Greek and imported Indian and Persian cultural achievements. What it exported was the religion.

The Islamic civilization was basically a second wind for the Greek civilization, minus the Greeks. It was enabled by the ease of travel of people and ideas between Spain and Persia and stimulated by the flow of new knowledge from Persia and India. The civilization was autonomous with regard to cognition and cosmology. Consequently, it had a near monopoly of discovery and invention. The civilization was tripolar at its peak; Córdoba in Spain and Baghdad in Mesopotamia were two thousand miles apart and Gundeshapur in Persia farther east.

The Western Empire in Spain lasted just seven centuries from conquest to final expulsion. Abd al-Raḥmān I (731–788), emir of Córdoba, founded it as a great center of culture, building schools, libraries, and the great mosque, attracting scholars from distant lands. The eminence of Córdoba as a cultural center faded early in the eleventh century as it lost power and declined in population, although the city was not captured until 1236. Religion gained the upper hand over philosophy. The gradual reconquest by the Christians, starting with the fall of Toledo in 1065, undoubtedly promoted this shift in the religion from tolerance to defensiveness. Córdoba's last great scholar, Averroës, who died in 1198, was condemned and pursued for his Aristotelian views, considered subversive of Islam. The civilization proper flourished for just three centuries.

Baghdad was the most important center from the inauguration of the House of Wisdom by Caliph Hārūn al-Rashīd (reigned 786–809) to its destruction by the Mongols in 1258. It contained multiple free schools, libraries, and laboratories. It was the main center for translation of Greek documents into Arabic. Here also, knowledge from India and Persia was brought and translated. Most of the leading achievers of the civilization spent time in Baghdad studying, working, or both. It was destroyed by the Mongols in 1258 but had already declined significantly and undergone a shift from primacy of scholarship to dominance of religion. As in the case of Córdoba, these changes were likely precipitated by the loss of confidence as Christian crusaders repeatedly invaded Islamic territory. The First Crusade was in 1096, the ninth and last in 1271. The civilization proper lasted some four centuries.

Gundeshapur in Persia was not originally a Muslim center of scholarship. It was created in the sixth century, before the birth of Islam. It owed its existence to Byzantine Christian hostility to Nestorian Christians and "pagan" scholars of Greek ethnicity or culture and their teachings. Nestorian Christians from Edessa first sought refuge there starting in 481. Greek scholars migrated there after the closure of the schools of Aristotle and Plato in Athens and other centers of Greek learning by Justinian in 529. Emperor Khosrow (531–579) created the academy, including a famous medical school, hospital, and other schools, libraries, and facilities for research. From here, emissaries sought knowledge from India and China and added it to the Greek storehouse.

The Greek documents and knowledge from India and China were translated into Persian centuries before their translation into Arabic. In fact, Gundeshapur was the model for the House of Wisdom in Baghdad, and some of its scholars went to Baghdad. The Persians had an early start in the study of philosophy and science. The Islamic civilization started before Islam. The academy of Gundeshapur declined in the tenth century as some of its scholars moved to Baghdad, by then a much bigger center of scholarship. The Mongols who destroyed Baghdad in 1258 also conquered the Persian Empire.

The fact that these centers of scholarship were founded by particular caliphs or other political leaders is incidental. In the early centuries, the religion itself sought knowledge as advocated by Muhammad. Arabs felt a need to master the superior knowledge of other ethnicities and religions in their own backyard. Only the state had the resources to build the Houses of Knowledge.

There were many other centers of education and research and depositories of knowledge largely modeled on Baghdad. Some—such as Damascus, Cairo, and Bukhara—occasionally rivaled the leading centers. Whether conquered by infidels or not, they underwent the same transition as Baghdad and Córdoba—a decline in scholarship, dominance of religion, and a sense of conflict between philosophy and faith.

One should not conclude that the civilization was ended by invasion and war. In Spain, it was the religion that overthrew the civilization before the fall of Córdoba, long before the final reconquest. The other major centers did not experience gradual encroachment of their domains but declined nevertheless well before their conquest.

The "golden age" of the Islamic civilization is said to have been from the inauguration of the House of Wisdom in Baghdad by Caliph Hārūn al-Rashīd to its destruction by the Mongols in 1258. If we define *civilization* as dynamic and evolving in terms of discovery and invention, it was even shorter. There was only one significant scholar before the ninth century, Geber, who died in 815. He was Persian. The last significant scholars, Averroës and Maimonides, died in 1198 and 1204 respectively.

Civilization and religion shared only an overlay of Mohammedanism and the Arabic language as a lingua franca. The overlap was small, one reason that when the religion gained dominance, it could suppress the civilization.

Who were the people of the civilization? It included many of other faiths, particularly Christianity and Judaism. There was discrimination by religion, and there was special taxation as well. No one knew how many of the Muslims were true believers, how many simply took advantage of the benefits of membership or avoided the penalties imposed on unbelievers. What was the ethnicity of the participants in the civilization? We know about the leading contributors, but all we know about less noted participants is that there was great diversity.

Some of the educated individuals with Arabic names were not Arab. It was a common practice before Islam for educated Syrians and others to adopt Greek names as Greek was the dominant culture. This practice also continued under Islamic rule. Al-Khazini, a prominent scholar, was Greek. Apart from affinity with the prevailing culture, they had practical reason to adopt Arabic names and claim Arab ethnicity as well as Muslim faith. Arabic names were also adopted out of religious fervor, a desire to belong. Naipaul (1998, 305, 330–31) reports that, even in the twentieth century, many Pakistani Muslims not only adopted Arab names but also pretended to be of Arabic ethnic descent. However, such individuals were unlikely to be participants in the civilization.

Islam succeeded the old civilizations of Mesopotamia, Egypt, Persia, and Greece without completely displacing their cultures. There was never a shortage of intertribal and interethnic conflict. It lacked the unity and coherence of other civilizations. Most of the population within the Islamic rule could not read Greek. Thus, the participants in the civilization were initially those who could. The writings of the Greek philosophers, mathematicians, and protoscientists had to be translated. Since initially most of the people did not know Arabic, they were translated into Persian and Syriac as well as into Arabic. But Persia was an exception, attributable to the earlier establishment of Gundeshapur.

The civilization did not have its own state. The caliphates, kingdoms, and other administrative jurisdictions provided for public services, education in particular. The state built and funded most of the facilities—schools, libraries, observatories—for the scholars. The civilization depended on its patronage. But the state was the agent of the religion. Secular and sacred authorities were inseparable. Civilization and religion had quite different attitudes toward authority. The civilization was open to debate and disagreement. Authority as the basis of belief was cognitive authority, evidence, and logic. There was a bottom-up option in the formation of belief. Religious authority was top down, self-justified. The religion evolved from tolerance and encouragement of search for knowledge to questioning the compatibility of knowledge with the teachings of the Prophet; so did state support for the civilization.

Creative Minority

Among the participants, who were the contributors to the civilization? Who were the discoverers and inventors? Most of them were highly educated individuals with diverse interests, great talent, and very wide knowledge. Many were physicians as well as philosophers. They were similar to their Greek counterparts since their education included exposure to the knowledge of their Greek predecessors, which had been translated in the ninth and tenth centuries. In the first two centuries, they had to be literate in Greek. Almost every scholar of distinction wrote on many diverse subjects as did the Greeks, whose works they studied. They should have been well prepared to transfer knowledge and cognitive approaches between domains. They differed from their Athenian predecessors in two ways: respect for the evidence of the senses and willingness to experiment. In these regards, they were closer to the Alexandrian Greeks.

Among the scholars, we know there was diversity, but a disproportionately large share was Persian. The irony of history was Persia, an advanced old civilization that fought against the Greeks for control of the Middle East. It lost. But the descendants of Darius and Xerxes were the ones who first mastered the Greek classics and adopted and advanced on them. The Persian dominance had two explanations. Most important was an early start. But they also had a late season stretch. Their institutions of higher learning retained in their curricula much of Greek philosophy and science that was expurgated in higher education from Baghdad to Córdoba. They continued to produce scholars capable of mastering past achievements and moving beyond them.

What did they know? In astronomy, their basic text was Ptolemy; in medicine, it was Galen. But other cultures contributed much to pharmacology. The main contribution of Arabia to knowledge was apothecary—knowledge of herbs and other medications and treatments for disease. India and Persia also made significant contributions. Pharmacology was perhaps the one area where Greek learning was not dominant. In mathematics, the dominance of Greek learning was less pronounced. Scholars started with Euclid and other Greek mathematicians but imported algebra from India and greatly advanced trigonometry initiated by the Greeks.

In cosmology, most were Aristotelians, but some were Neoplatonist, and there were Pythagoreans. Followers of Plato might conceive of Allah as the Demiurge. But how could followers of Pythagoras and other Greek advocates of agency-free, bottom-up cosmologies possibly accept the agency-ridden, top-down cosmology of Islam, with Allah the ultimate micromanager? Can authority or belief be based on the Koran and on logic and evidence?

As to the leading scholars, some were Jewish, some Christian. They did not appear to be troubled by differences between Aristotle and

Christian faith, although it was a controversy in the Catholic Church until settled by Aquinas. But what of the Muslims who adopted the teachings of Pythagoras, who commented on the works of Aristotle? The difference between Islamic civilization and Islamic religion in concept of authority and in cosmology are so large that the cognitive dissonance is beyond bridging.

Allah did not create a clockwork mechanism—wind it up and leave. One does not bow or kneel; one prostates oneself. It is not obedience but submission. No doubt some were unaware of contradiction, and some could live with it. Nasr (2001, 144) states that Islamic physicists such as Alhazen, an Arab, and Al-Bīrūnī, a Persian, saw natural phenomena such as light not abstractly, as did the Greeks, but as aspects of the spiritual emanations of divinity. "[E]ven a physicist like Al-Hazen lived in a spiritual and psychological milieu completely different. In the world in which he lived the phenomena of nature had not yet become completely divorced from their archetypes; light still reminded man of the divine intellect." Nature is subject to Islamic religion. Call it cognitive dualism.

Jewish and Christian scholars did not face so stark a conflict of religious and Greek cosmologies. Allah and the Jewish and Christian God were quite different divinities. Allah was the ultimate micromanager, leaving no scope for autonomy. Allah was the God of Abraham. The Jewish and Christian God was the God of Moses. In the Garden of Eden, Jehovah did not prevent Eve from eating the forbidden fruit from the tree of learning, and humans were on their own. In Europe in the thirteenth and subsequent centuries, Christians found the cosmology of Aristotle compatible with their beliefs.

In what domains was religion a deterrent? Not in mathematics, chemistry, or medicine. However, nearly all the scholars were knowledgeable in many domains, including cosmology and cognition, and had something to say about these subjects, even if their work was mainly in subjects that did not conflict with theology. The civilization cannot be said to have its own cosmology or cognitive style. But achieving individuals did. All we can do is infer their concept of reality and their cognitive practices from the evidence of their work.

In short, the religion was a deterrent to the agency-free, abstract thinking of the Greeks, which eventually would lead to the Scientific Revolution, but many of the scholars were not inhibited. Even believers might accept its ethical teachings and identity and sense of community while ignoring its cosmology. In cognition, the contrast was between logic and evidence on one hand and intuition and similarity or analogy on the other.

Nearly all the leading scholars of the Islamic civilization lived in just four centuries—the ninth through the twelfth. The religion started in the seventh century. Why so long a wait, so short a stay? During the first two centuries, emissaries sought the knowledge of India, Persia, and especially Greece. Translation to Arabic was required. The Arabic language was somewhat deficient; it had to be adapted, and disputes among translators had to be settled. The Arabic versions were copied and distributed. Places and institutions to house them were needed. But who was there who could read Aristotle, Euclid, and Plato and understand them? Governments founded or supported colleges, libraries, and astronomical laboratories, creating readership. Later, once governments restricted their educational mission to the words of the Prophet and little else, the supply of readers and scholars dwindled and almost disappeared.

Islamic scholars, unlike the Chinese, were interested in abstraction, in discovering the laws of nature. But the Chinese were interested in practical inventions; the Islamic civilization was not or did not direct its efforts toward invention. (Medical advances were mainly discoveries, not inventions.)

Accomplishments

Most of the leading scholars wrote on many different subjects, but that is biography. Our interest is in a contribution to knowledge, not just to education or debate. I rely heavily on Nasr's (2001) *Science and Civilization in Islam* in distinguishing contributions to discovery and invention from publication, commentary, or compendium.

Schools were free; hence, scholars lacked the earnings of the Athenian philosophers or the patronage of the Ptolemies. State support was for libraries and school buildings. It was the state that founded and funded the great centers of scholarship and most of the lesser centers as well. Thus, many of the scholars earned their living as physicians, biasing somewhat the direction of their creativity. Some discoveries were by-products of their work. Medicine was of interest to the state, which established medical schools and hospitals.

Ibn Ḥayyān (721–815), also known as Geber, was from Persia, although his ethnicity is disputed. He was the first of the outstanding Islamic scholars and arguably the best. There is a problem of attribution; what of the writings associated with his name were his, which commentaries by his disciples, and which written by others using his pen name? What is clear is that he worked before most of the Greek writings had been translated but referred knowledgeably to many of them, of which he may have read Persian translations. He wrote in many domains as did his Greek predecessors, including math, music, cosmology, logic, and law.

But his main contribution was in chemistry. He was a prodigious inventor. He invented many procedures for isolating compounds and elements from the matrices in which they were found, designed or invented instruments for performing his procedures, such as sublimation and discovered numerous compounds, notably acetic acid, nitric acid, white lead, and aluminum chlorides. Then he invented uses for some of these compounds. He employed precise experimental methods. There are disagreements over his use of the scientific method, whether he was testing hypotheses or following intuition, but there was no progress in developing a coherent general structure for ordering them. His concept of structure was the Greek four elements and their classification as wet or dry, hot or cold. Geber's concept of process was the transmutation of elements, the process envisaged as spiritual as well as material. He worked like a chemist but thought like an alchemist.

Al-Rāzī (854-932) advanced on experimental procedures of Geber and invented kerosene and kerosene lamps and soap antiseptics. He also created taxonomy of material substances and attempted to account for the differences between metals. Like Geber, he believed in transmutation, base metals into gold. But al-Kindī (801–873) rejected transmutation and the four elements, saying that there were many elements. What was missing was a conceptual structure providing some explanation and predictability for all of Geber's diverse chemical achievements. But chemistry was not the route to the Scientific Revolution, which was physics. It seemed inconceivable that any sequence other than the historic one of physics, followed by chemistry and then biology, could have resulted in the modern world.

In physics, Alhazen (964–1040)—an Arab—was perhaps the greatest of the Islamic scientists. He might have triggered a scientific revolution. Like his Athenian predecessors, he was deeply knowledgeable in many subjects. Unlike them, he saw experimentation as a source of knowledge and method of proof. In this respect, he was ahead of the Greek mathematician-engineers of Alexandria. His specialty was optics, which he advanced well beyond the achievements of the Greeks.

As a physicist, Alhazen organized the diverse Greek findings on optics into a coherent system, including his own findings, and proceeded to discover their mathematical structure. He made his own curved mirrors and ground lenses. Apparently, his interest was to derive and to test the mathematical theory of optics. He could have invented a telescope or a microscope, opening up new worlds for scholars to explore. But his interest was discovery. He argued that hypotheses must be proved by experiments based on confirmable procedures or mathematical evidence (Nasr 2001, 128–29). Among Islamic scholars, the practical applications of theoretical findings was rare. They did not appear to be of interest except in medicine.

Another area of physics in which Islamic civilization advanced beyond the achievements of the Greeks was the study of motion. Ibn Bājjah Avempace (1096–1138) analyzed the resistance of a medium to projection of an object as a function of the density of the medium and the consequent retardation or deceleration of the object. But most of his writing, including a book on physics, was lost. Alhazen discovered the principle of inertia. Al-Baghdādī (1080–1164) studied the acceleration of falling bodies. He and Avicenna (1201–1274) propounded conflicting theories of impetus (Nasr 2001, 314–15). Motion was the domain in which Islam was most original since the Greek foundation was limited and faulty.

A third area of physics was of great practical interest—hydrostatics. Water was the key resource of the society for agriculture, for cities, and for power. In this area, scholars may have been interested in practical results, not just theory. It was advanced by numerous scholars, in particular Al-Khazini (early twelfth century), who studied the role of gravity and centers of gravity in diverse applications, combining mechanics and hydraulics. His domain had a Greek foundation, including Archimedes.

Astronomical observatories were built and funded by the state. They also served as institutions of higher education and research in subjects related to astronomy. Knowledge of astronomy advanced in several ways. The astronomical data from China, India, and Persia were added to Greek and Babylonian data for a more complete and accurate map of the heavens. Also, very large and improved astronomical observatory instruments were built, reducing margins of error. The development of trigonometry and its employment in astronomy increased the accuracy of spatial location.

Islam adopted the Ptolemaic model of the heavens and clung to it for all its faults. Al-Battānī (858–929), an Arab astronomer, improved it through very precise observations. Greater accuracy led to discoveries of regularities in the motions of the sun, moon, earth, and planets (Nasr 2001, 170). Al-Bīrūnī (973–1048) went further, not only improving the accuracy of observations but also correcting errors in the Ptolemaic model, which assumed an immobile solar apogee, which led to discovering additional regularities. He was highly critical of Aristotle's (and Ptolemy's) cosmic model. He speculated that planetary orbits were elliptical and believed in the rotation of the earth. He was aware of the much simpler heliocentric model of Aristarchus and seriously considered adopting a heliocentric model but decided against it (Nasr 2001, 136–37). Other Islamic astronomers knew about Aristarchus and his heliocentric model. Many were aware of the shortcomings of Ptolemy and were highly critical. Later, Arzachel (1029–1087) discovered that planetary orbits were elliptical, not circular. Islamist astronomers still clung to Ptolemy. There were religious concerns about relegating Earth to a peripheral role in the cosmos. What was lacking was a Copernicus.

According to Huff (1993, 55–56), experimentation in medicine, optics, and astronomy failed to apply scientific experimental methods. But some scholars sought to prove hypotheses experimentally or mathematically, followed exacting experimental procedures, and validated their experimental findings by repetition—perhaps not textbook perfect but close enough. Chemistry, or alchemy, and biology were not ready for the systematic experimentation and discovery found in physics and astronomy.

The invention of trigonometry was initiated by the Greek Hipparchus of Nicaea (180–125 BC) but only for a single function. Islamic mathematicians developed the other five functions and developed them much further and are credited with the invention of trigonometry. Major contributors included Al-Khwārizmī (780–850), who produced accurate sine and cosine tables and the first table of tangents. He was also responsible for introducing Indian algebra and numerals to the Islamic world. Al-Battānī (Albatenius; 853–929) discovered the reciprocal functions of secant and cosecant and produced the first table of cosecants for each degree from 1° to 90°. Abū al-Wafā (946–998) invented spherical trigonometry and introduced negative numbers. In mathematics, Islamic creativity was invention, followed by discovery.

Trigonometry improved the accuracy of astronomic observations, contributing to discoveries in this domain. The religion valued it for its ability to locate the direction of Mecca for the purpose of prayer. Hence, trigonometry and math in general were spared controversy with religion.

Islamic contributions to medicine were a major part of their achievements. Biology did not contribute to the Scientific Revolution. But it was one of three revolutions that followed—mechanical, chemical, and biological or the so-called Industrial Revolution. Health and agriculture were its essential components.

The state had a strong interest in public health and supported hospitals and medical schools. Many of the scholars earned their living as physicians to the well-to-do, with discoveries and inventions as a by-product of their occupation. In this domain, it was not abstract knowledge but practical results that mattered; hence, achievements were in the diagnosis of ailments and their causes and therapies rather than in anatomy and physiology, which were but a frame of reference for physicians.

In biology, unlike physics, there is a fundamental residual nonreplicability. The subject of illness and its treatment may have no natural order. If there are natural laws, they are remote and remain hidden. Thus, discovery can proceed piecemeal without a conceptual framework.

The theoretical framework derived from the Greeks, the four humors of Hippocrates and Galen's correlation of humors and personality types, were of limited help and no hindrance to discovery and invention. Sickness and health were conceived holistically, referring to the organism rather than to particular components. But physicians focused on concrete causes and cures.

The best known physicians were renowned for comprehensive and detailed books, advanced textbooks for other physicians. They helped compensate for the inadequacy of medical education conducted in hospitals, which were instruments of the religion. It is sometimes difficult to distinguish their original contributions from the received knowledge of others. But two stood out as discoverers, al-Rāzī (854–932) and Avicenna (980–1037).

Al-Rāzī identified several diseases and discovered the antiseptic function of alcohol and the use of mercury as a purgative. He also mastered the diagnosis and treatment of smallpox. Avicenna introduced new drugs and identified new diseases and their diagnosis and treatment. He was experimental and methodical, but whether he was testing hypotheses or intuitions is debatable. He is best known for the medical textbook that prevailed in Europe for centuries, synthesis integration of Hippocrates and Galen, to which he added the pharmacology of the Arabs, Persia, and India and his own discoveries (Nasr 2000, 196–200).

The heritage of Greek medicine shared the fate of other Greek intellectual achievements and their Islamic additions, first frowned on and then no longer taught. Islam tended to view health and disease from a moral rather than a scientific, analytical perspective. There were accomplishments and discoveries in other areas peripheral to the sources of the Scientific Revolution, such as geography, natural history, geology, mineralogy, agriculture botany, and zoology (see Nasr 2000, 198–212). As in the case of medicine, they cannot be viewed as precursors to the Scientific Revolution or the Industrial Revolution. Their pursuit may contribute to practices useful in the search for knowledge in any domain. Their findings did contribute to the agricultural revolution of the past two centuries. The main contributors were scholars well versed in the scientific domains above mentioned.

The Islamic civilization was predominantly a Greek heritage; the religion was Arab. Conflict was unavoidable. The two scholars who best epitomized the conflict between civilization and religion were Ibn-Rushd also known as Averroës (1126–1198), a Spaniard, and al-Ghazālī (1058–1111), a Persian. Averroës was a defender of Aristotelian philosophy against theologians. But his main influence was on European clergy through translations of his commentaries on Aristotle into Latin. Averroës was a judge of Islamic law, fully conversant with the religion.

Al-Ghazālī reflected the conflict between the two worldviews in his personal life. He learned and taught the Greek version early in life and then turned against it. His influence at the end of the eleventh century might be described as the beginning of the end of Islamic civilization. He accepted Aristotle's uncaused cause and Plato's Demiurge as pre-Christian equivalents of deity. Mathematics and logic he saw as unrelated to religion, but training in these subjects predisposed scholars to question the religion, whose cognitive methods were revelation and intuition. It was Aristotle's natural sciences that al-Ghazālī rejected, their absence of agency and their self-determination. The issue was the scope of divine authority. The contrast between the Islamic and the Christian reactions to Aristotle's cosmology was that between Jehovah and Allah, implicitly about free will.

The scholars differed from the Athenian predecessors in two ways: they accepted the evidence of the senses, and they engaged in empirical research. They did not have the aversion to working with their hands of Chinese mandarins. There was no Archimedes among them, who applied his theoretical findings to practical use in diverse domains. Apart from medicine, there was little urge to validate their discoveries or put them to practical use.

Some of the scholars were inventors as well as discoverers. Geber invented equipment and tools for a chemistry lab; astronomer-mathematicians invented instruments for observing the heavens. But these were inventions for their own work, not responses to the needs of society. Was it knowledge for its own sake? The invention of trigonometry was for the benefit of the religion, as well as the astronomers. The Greek love of novelty was missing in the religion; could it be missing in a civilization that prized knowledge?

It is noteworthy that the majority of the leading scholars throughout these centuries were Persians or from Persian-ruled territories. The earliest noted scholar is Geber, and after the eleventh century, all the noted achievers with the exception of Averroes and Maimonides were from Persian areas. But for the Persians and others from Persian-ruled territories, the golden age would have been even shorter.

The greatest contributions of Islamic civilization were in domains in which Aristotle had little to contribute—protochemistry, optics, trigonometry, and medicine. Scholars engaged in too much recapitulation and commentary on Aristotle and other Greeks. Dispersal of attention to multiple domains may have discouraged intellectual breakthroughs.

Inventions

In addition to the advances of leading scholars mentioned above, most of which were discoveries, there were inventions and some discoveries by craftsmen and by inventors unknown.

Ochoa and Corey list one important mechanical invention, the windmill, in Persia, as well as bigger and better astronomical instruments, nearly all in Persia. In mathematics, they list decimals and trigonometry and, in medicine, casts for broken bones. I don't think the Islamic civilization invented the decimal system or that bigger versions of existing instruments qualify as inventions. The Great Mosque of Córdoba and other architectural masterpieces are not listed but may be more deserving of designation as inventions. Most of their listings are discoveries, already mentioned above, not inventions.

Hill (1993) describes some of the improvements in existing instruments and processes. They adapted water-lifting equipment, a chain of pots for lifting small amounts of water from deep wells, and improvements in mechanical operations and efficiency in other water-lifting devices invented by the Greeks. More inventive was a stream-driven water pump converting rotary into reciprocating motion and using suction pipes. There were improvements in waterwheels, grist milling, and windmills. Water clocks and astronomical observations were made more accurate. The Mūsā brothers, who were mathematicians, invented a large number of devices, most of which were trick devices but included useful tools such as self-timing hurricane, lamps, gas masks, and clamshell grab. The numerous automatons of performing humans and animals, fountains, and music are of interest only for the clever use of differences in water and air pressure as power sources.

The most prolific inventor was Al-Jazarī (1136–1206). He was not a scholar. Nor did he fit the mold of the Alexandrian mathematician-engineers; he was not a theoretician. But he knew of the Greek technological accomplishments, which were the basis for many of his contributions. Al-Jazarī built more accurate water clocks, with automatons to announce the hours. His contributions were not the final product but ingenious mechanics controlling the motion of parts and the flow of water and air. He contributed several processing inventions as well, including lamination of timber to minimize warping, static balancing of wheels, the use of wooden templates, paper models, grinding valves with emery powder to obtain a watertight fit, and casting of metals in closed mold boxes. Islamic inventions were little more than incrementalism.

There was no shortage of creativity reflecting the influence of Arabic language and culture, poetry, literature, calligraphy, and arts—magnificent buildings, intricate mosaics, carpets, metalwork, music, and architecture. There was superb craftsmanship in stone, clay, metal, ivory, wood, and paper in the arts. It was aesthetic rather than scientific. In terms of practical inventions, it was architecture, including landscaping more than anything else.

One should distinguish between inventions and discoveries that required funding by the state and those that could have been accomplished by individuals or privately enabled. Most of the discoveries were products of the civilization. The lack of major inventions or technological trajectories may be explained by the absence of resources or legal conditions rather than lack of motivation.

Islam was a transmission belt for Greek achievements to Europe, but it was also a transmission belt for major Chinese inventions and discoveries to Europe. Islam, like China, trailed Europe in technological trajectories and in cognitive transfer of new ideas to diverse domains. The great Chinese inventions came first to Islam, which then transferred them to Europe, which soon outdistanced both China and Islam in practical applications.

Paper was made in Baghdad in 793 but did not come to Italy until 1276, Cologne in 1320, and Nuremberg in 1391 (Usher 1959, 239). Printing with movable type evolved rapidly. Gutenberg got the credit by printing the Bible in 1454. Meanwhile, Muslim students spent too much time practicing calligraphy. The first books printed in Arabic were printed in Venice and Vienna. The early printing presses in the Islamic world were owned by Jews and Armenians, printing books in their own languages. Printing presses were forbidden in some parts of the Islamic world for many centuries (Huff 1993, 224–25).

The same lag was found in the use of gunpowder. Islamic states had only a small head start on the Europeans, who may have learned it from invading armies around mid-thirteenth century. But in 1509, there were sixteen Portuguese ships that destroyed the fleet of one hundred vessels from the Ottoman Empire, Egypt, and Gujarat—and Venice—in the Battle of Diu in the Indian Ocean. Their cannon and their ships were far superior to anything in Islam or Asia.

Whoever first used the lodestone or the compass, it was the Vikings, Portuguese, and Spanish who ventured into uncharted waters. The Arabs were on the Atlantic coast but did not venture far nor replicate the circumnavigation of Africa by the Phoenicians in the sixth century BC.

The use of gunpowder and the compass were primarily agenda for the state. So was paper and printing for the schools. Part of the difference was the capability of private organizations in Europe to undertake long-term and large-scale ventures, which in Islam and China were the near monopoly of the state.

The State

The civilization lacked the institutions and resources for training to advance and to perpetuate its own culture. It depended on the state for education and for economic resources—capital. There were many states—empire, monarchy, sultanate, caliphate, emirate—political entities large and small. All had much the same Koran-derived legal systems and scope of state authority and responsibility. Power was unlimited and often exercised in an arbitrary manner.

Education. The government did not provide some of the services and facilities normally regarded as public goods, including lower-level education. Instead, it induced their supply through the waqf system of pious foundations. The state allowed an estate to endow a foundation providing approved services. Since this was a means of conserving an estate rather than splitting it among many heirs, it attracted much of the private capital available and also misdirected enterprise. There was no limit on director self-payment or on patronage. Consequently, the waqf system was corrupt; it did a very poor job of providing public services.

The foundations of interest were the madrassas, lower-level schools. Their curriculum was the choice of the founder, but since the endowment was approved by the state, predominantly religious, it centered on the Koran and other prophetic writings, Arabic language, composition, calligraphy, and poetry. It was poor preparation in most cases for the work of scholars but also for the work of artisans. Perhaps it is not coincidental that the major Chinese inventions that came to Europe via Islam were much more rapidly adopted and advanced in Europe.

How did the Muslims with a comprehensive knowledge of Greek, plus Indian and Persian, achievements acquire their knowledge? The study of mathematics and the natural sciences was deferred to institutions of higher learning, comparable to universities, a few of which taught math, astronomy, physics, and other natural sciences. There were a number of astronomical observatories that were also centers of teaching and research in mathematics, astronomy and some natural sciences. Hospitals and medical schools were teaching centers for medicine and alchemy.

Higher education in the institutions funded by the state was mainly personal tutor-student relations, not the vigorous discussion and debate of Athenian schools. Accreditation was simply the assertion of the tutor that the student had mastered a particular subject or book at higher levels, that the student was qualified to teach it. The status of a scholar was based on lineage, a time series of endorsements of students by their teachers. The authority of knowledge was a top-down inheritance. Master-student relation of authority and respect allowed no room for questioning and debate. The curriculum and method of teaching remained much the same into the twentieth century as though the Scientific and Industrial Revolutions had not happened.

The state was subject to religion. It imposed major constraints on the creativity and resources of the civilization. Through its educational system, it limited the supply of talent. What the religion regarded as "foreign sciences" was excluded. This was true in Sunni institutions. The Shia, however, retained the Greek curriculum, especially in Persia. It is not surprising that Persians were disproportionately represented among leading scholars in later centuries.

Trade. The Arabs were great traders, within the empire and far beyond it, of spices from the Spice Islands to Europe via Venice. The trade was private but a source of revenue for Muslim rulers. Capital was required for such long-distance trade and much profit earned. The legal systems through which the traders navigated must have been favorable. Not so. Islamic law inhibited private enterprise. There was a shortage of capital for investment in invention and for the manufacture of new products. Inheritance law was egalitarian. Children of both sexes and other close relatives received two-thirds of the estate, fragmenting it, precluding accumulation of capital. Financing via joint ownership was discouraged by the absence of a law of corporations separating individual from corporate property. Financing by borrowing was limited by the absence of banks; lenders were forbidden to charge interest on loans. There were ways of circumventing the legal ban on interest, but they were precarious and uncertain.

Inheritance laws permitted the preservation of an estate diverted to foundations providing public services (the waqf system). The government's unsystematic intervention in trade added to uncertainty. The state could practice provisionism and fiscalism—assure supply by banning exports and encouraging imports; it could raise import taxes in search of revenue.

The absence of corporate law limiting the liability of individual investors precluded the aggregation of the resources of multiple individuals. It discouraged the formation of enterprises large enough and long lived enough to reap benefits of scale and specialization. Cooperative enterprise was limited to a single mission, debts were individual, and decisions needed unanimity.

What Islam did not inherit or chose to dump was Roman law, the concept of abstract law, applying equally to all. What the state adopted or retained was a hierarchical system of rights and responsibilities. The exercise of many laws was a marketplace procedure—bargaining between offender and victim rather than prescribed judicial decision, even in cases of murder and rape. The victim's right of retribution, if not compensation, was available. There was not just one legal code but also four major schools of Islamic law, plus separate legal systems available to Jews and Christians (Kuran 2004, 71–74, 77). The law was whatever a particular judge said it was; thus, legal practice was riddled with uncertainty and contradiction. Legal procedures were unpredictable. There were no rules of evidence, no reliance on precedents guiding the decisions of individual judges (Huff, 96–97).

Organization for production or trade was small scale and of short duration. The trading enterprise was a single caravan, a single shipload. At least there was trade. But much construction and manufacturing cannot be conducted in this manner. One would not build a windmill, a hospital, or a paper mill for a six-month life span. Thus, Islam lagged in exploiting the inventions it received from China. Inventions such as printing required scale—much capital, volume of output, market size. Who knew what inventions were never implemented?

What the legal system discouraged was not so much discovery and invention by individuals as the advancement of industry, the market for inventions.

Religion

Islam was founded by one man at a particular point. Religions are founded this way but not civilizations. Muhammad's beliefs and commandments should not be equated with Islam, which is an institution that evolved over time.

Islam is the only major civilization defined and dominated by religion. Faith took precedence over reason. What was surprising about it was not the regression from the twelfth century on but the progressive phase that preceded it. Europe, by contrast, although in its early centuries defined by Christianity, evolved into a secular civilization.

The dominance of the religion over the civilization was not a consequence of the decline in the civilization; it was the cause. The civilization was not created; it was acquired by conquest. The religion itself, as promoted and practiced by the state, turned inward and defensive and became less tolerant well before the centers of the civilization were invaded by Turks and Mongols. This withdrawal may have started in Spain with the loss of Toledo in 1085; it became pronounced with the loss of Córdoba in 1236 and repeated invasions of the heartland of the Islamic world by crusaders. There is another perspective. In the early centuries, it was a minority in its own realm; it sought converts. Once it became the majority, it attacked dissidents.

Palace and mosque shared the same roof. The religion required an institutional underpinning for worship, for propagation of the faith, for the sustenance and security of believers. As a union of church and state, it required labor and revenue—taxation. So it tolerated unbelievers as long as it needed them.

There is no questioning the Koran, the word of Muhammad. After the twelfth century, the cosmology of the Koran displaced that of the Greeks, authority and obedience ruled out creativity, and intuition prevailed over logic. All one needs to know is in the Koran and other prophetic writing. The search for knowledge is authorized and ordered but only for knowledge compatible with the sacred writings. The Prophet might not have approved the rejection of "foreign sciences." It became a counterculture to the Islamic civilization.

Islam, the religion, had a single authority, the caliph, but widespread Islamic society was organized in multiple administrative areas, or states, differing in location and also in ethnicity and policy. So the role of authority in limiting creativity was not so much the organization of society as the doctrine of authority and submission everywhere—Allah and believers, caliph and subjects, down the scale of authority to teacher and student, father and children. In the religion, authority was strictly top down. The Koran could not be questioned; its authority exceeded that of Confucius. Islam consisted of numerous states. Emigration was always an escape hatch from regimes with too restrictive interpretation or rigorous enforcement of its view of the Koran. It was the mind-set of submission, beyond mere obedience, to authority that dampened creativity. The humiliating posture in prayer, heads down, symbolized the mind-set.

Cosmology

Conflict between religion and civilization centered on cosmology. Arabs had more than one cosmology. There was first the concept of reality derived from the Koran and the sayings of Muhammad. But there were similar Arab cosmologies predating Islam. The alchemists' astrology focused on seven planets and seven metals. There were multiple levels as well as multiple concentric circles of reality, of states of being.

Whether considered religion or not, the common element is agency. They have to be top-down cosmologies, parallel to the structure of religious authority. Allah, or a divine intelligence, is responsible for everything that is, everything that happens. The structure of the universe is hierarchy that is subtractive and divisible. The whole is partitioned into five levels of reality, symbolized by five concentric circles. Allah is the highest reality; the lowest is the sensory world. At this mundane level of reality, the caliph is at the top.

Top down must be the cosmology prevalent in early cultures; otherwise, it is difficult to understand how Islam was adopted so quickly by many peoples with diverse cultures.

The Koran is poetry, highly condensed thought subject to multiple interpretations. It refers to the seven earths and seven heavens of earlier cosmologies, but there is no consensus on the hierarchy and partitioning of the universe. Scholars differ; sects differ. It is not a very well-ordered cosmos. Levels of reality stress vertical partitioning; concentric circles do not.

The universe is *one*, everything is derivative, and nothing is a thing in itself. There is no principle of identity other than one. Each is identified in the context of relations with all. Identity in Islamic cosmology, with its top-down perspective, is not personal and individualistic but belonging and communal.

There is no abstract space or time. Number is the denominator of reality, mathematics the network of interrelations. The One is Allah. Everything that is, everything that happens, is an expression of the will of Allah. With a top-down cosmology, there cannot be laws of nature, which are bottom-up generalizations. These two perspectives appear contradictory; Allah is the universal agent; *one* is organic.

The cosmic whole is in the mind of Allah. No stone falls unless Allah wills it. The Islam cosmos is agency ridden. Lower tiers of wholes were not prescribed as in China. The human whole was binary believers and nonbelievers.

The section on Islamic civilization discussed the conflict between the Aristotelian worldview and that of the Koran. The cosmos of the Koran had multiple levels of reality; Aristotle only had one, the sensory material reality corresponding to Islam's lowest level. The religion held a monopoly on all levels of reality except the last. To believe in Aristotelian and Islamic material reality required violation of the principle of noncontradiction. It was the religion that sought to impose its concept of reality on the civilization.

Cognition

During the first two centuries, the religion endorsed the search for knowledge in distant countries and promoted the translation of Greek documents into Arabic. The knowledge Muhammad advocated seeking was existing knowledge. The religion had no interest in discovery or invention, in creating new knowledge. Its search for knowledge was collection, not creation. Later, it turned against the search for knowledge as a thing in itself, accepting knowledge only if it contributed to the faith. All one needed to know was in the Koran. The achievements of other cultures were valued if they assisted the religion by accurately pointing the direction of Mecca for the alignment of bodies in prayer. This was an evolution of the religion from the faith of a backward people to that of an empire.

How did Islam know; how did it validate knowledge? By revelation, contemplation, and intuition, deciphering the mind of Allah. It was intolerant of reason, of logic and empirical evidence (Huff 1993, 55, 117). Muhammad advocated intuition as the highest reasoning process.

The absence of a principle of identity implies that there can be no logical cognitive process other than analogy and similarity. Inductive reasoning is a bottom-up process that requires things in themselves. Hypotheses are intuition, but testing them is not.

The religion discouraged all rational means of seeking new knowledge. With a top-down cognitive process, the commonality is known; examples are found. Inductive reason is the reverse, analysis of particulars in search of commonality. Islamic cosmology and cognition rely on similarity as the reasoning process. But "similarity" fails to distinguish between apparent and logical analogy, which requires structural or functional identity between the phenomena specified. Causality implies things in themselves instead of relational reality, different ways of learning different truths. Mathematical processes are tools for discovery and invention in the lowest level of reality, the material world of the senses. They are inventions. But mathematics is also pure pattern with no reference to any reality, a taxonomy for the higher levels of being.

Why Islam Failed

Had Islamic civilization persisted another two or three centuries with undiminished education of scholars in state institutions and tolerance of diversity, might there have been a scientific revolution? Perhaps, but I think unlikely. The civilization itself had its own limitations and constraints. It had the knowledge of the Greeks but not the culture. It lacked a passion for novelty. The culture of the civilization favored stability over change. It placed little value on discovery and invention. Its most respected scholar, philosopher-scientist Avicenna, was admired not for his discoveries in medicine but for his encyclopedic knowledge and his prodigious literary output. The range and diversity of knowledge of most of the scholars was itself a deterrent to discovery through its diffusion of attention. There was too much recapitulation and commentary on Aristotle and other Greeks, not enough effort to advance beyond them. The leading discoverers appeared to have had no interest in applying their knowledge, Geber excepted. They were not inventors in the mold of the Alexandrian mathematician-engineers.

Without an urge to apply, there could be no cognitive transfer between domains or accelerated technological trajectories. What was achieved in these regards was mostly the work of artisans, not scholars, who cannot be described as participants of the civilization. In astronomy, scholars had learned that planetary orbits were elliptical, an advance on the Copernican model. Some considered a heliocentric model of the cosmos but did not accept it. The religion was adamantly against it.

(So was the Catholic Church, to be discussed in the next chapter.) Had there been a Copernicus among them, he probably would have met the fate of Mo-tzu and his followers. There was substantial advance in the field of optics but no telescope or microscope. Scholars questioned the four humors taxonomy of medicine and the four elements of physics, but there was no advance. Geber's numerous discoveries in chemistry did not displace the alchemic belief in transmutation of metals.

These failures to advance, plus the slow pace of technological trajectories, suggested inability to abstract. The scholars certainly could think abstractly, but their practice of abstraction was passive, not the creative level of abstraction that would have propelled discovery and invention. Or there was just disinterest in novelty. "The Muslims have always considered the role of natural science to be the discovery of those aspects of Reality represented by physical existence rather than the creation of mental constructs to impose upon Nature, without their having a necessary correspondence to any aspects of Reality" (Nasr 2001, 196).

The community of scholars did not engage in the face-to-face debate of the Greeks. They wrote. Documents written in one century were disputed, corrected, or extended by another scholarly document a century later perhaps in another country. The synergy of Athens and Alexandria was largely missing except in institutions such as astronomical observatories. Study in the universities was a tutor-student tutorial relation; authority was the basis of belief. Status was based on lineage more than on accomplishment. Lineage was consistent with scholars' focus on ancient Greek philosophical writings. Absent was the principle of identity or individualism.

Earlier, we noted that Greek civilization achieved most of the ingredients of the Scientific Revolution but fell short, failing to combine them into systematic scientific method, failing to marry theory and practice. But it came close. The Arabs, heirs to much of the learning of Greece, with access to the learning of South and East Asia, should have been able to do better. But in fact, for all their own contributions in many fields of knowledge, they fell short of the Greeks in achieving a scientific revolution.

The culture that suppressed the civilization reminds one of China. In cognition, both relied on similarity or analogy, believed in intuition, and rejected logic and evidence as sources of truth. The search for knowledge was regressive; all worth knowing was in the Koran, in Confucius and the sage-kings of old. These were the core of their education, not to be questioned.

CIVILIZATION AND CULTURE—A REAR VIEW

Before addressing the remaining current civilization, whose end I do not wish to know, I need to consider the difference between culture and civilization. Throughout history, there are hundreds of cultures, but the number of civilizations is counted by some historians in single digits. Civilizations evolve; cultures persist. It is civilizations that advance and retreat.

A civilization is a work in progress, culture building, forward and outward looking, dynamic, an ethos of assimilation and evolution. Any civilization, if it lives long, tends to become a remembrance of things past, a dominance of memory and tradition. Prolonged continuity builds so much tradition that it tends to lapse into backward-looking culture. This is what happened to Egypt and China. But one cannot generalize from two examples. This is not a statement of determinism or inevitability, just of fact.

A culture is conservative and tradition bound. It looks backward, not forward, and resists change. It is inward looking, an ethos of exclusion. Cultures do adapt to environmental change, to population growth, and to new technology. Pressures from other cultures require responses. There is some seepage of novelty from outside. There are changes, of course, but they are episodic and disconnected rather than systematic and directional. Cultures are largely creatures of their environment; civilizations create their own environment.

Civilizations and cultures differ fundamentally in their attitude toward novelty, in their acceptance of change. They differ accordingly in their attitude toward knowledge; there is more to be learned, and the pursuit of knowledge is never over versus contentment with things as they are or longing for things as they had been. One would expect that acceptance of novelty would be a stimulus to invention and, in particular, to discovery. A backward-looking culture may be satisfied with the status quo but seeks the old, not the new—Eden versus utopia.

Civilizations change from within, channeled in limited directions self-imposed. There may be a logic in the cultural, societal patterns that lean to or dictate particular directions of change.

Cultures and civilizations alike are motivated to solve problems— to invent. But only civilizations are driven to discover—a quest for knowledge and for understanding, which often devalues or undermines established beliefs.

I realize that these definitions of *culture* and *civilization* are the reverse of those commonly used by some historians. I use them as they tend to be used in anthropology and understood in common discourse, which recognize many cultures as often static and resistant to change and which tend to view civilizations as dynamic. The basic fact is that there have been many cultures, and they are still numerous. But the total number of civilizations is small.

Cultures came first; a few developed into civilizations. When a civilization ended, it reverted to culture, never the same as the original. Toynbee called them the historic and the historic periods in a civilization. According to Toynbee (1947, 31), Egypt's history ended around sixteenth century BCE. Its static culture survived another two millennia, with only two events of historical significance, its expulsion of the Hyksos conquerors and the abortive revolution of Akhenaton. It left no progeny, just the pyramids and the tombs.

China was the other instance of a civilization that came to an end. Chinese civilization may be said to have ended early in the first dynasty of a united China, with the great book burning, but its culture survived for another two millennia. Sumer did not regress from civilization to culture. It was conquered and became a progenitor of other civilizations, Babylonia in particular, which adopted its achievements and continued to progress until they, in turn, were replaced. Greece's tapered off with the encroachment of the Roman Empire. But it had over time in Islam. Rome's ended with Julius Caesar; its great social inventions were the products of the republic. Islamic civilization ended in the thirteenth century at the hands of the religion.

MYTHS OF ORIGIN AND DESTINATION

This seems the best place to update a subject already discussed in the preceding chapter on China—the creation myths of the founder civilizations, Sumer, Egypt, and China, as well as Greece. They appear to predict the character of the civilization that ensued.

What of Rome and Islam? Rome's creation myth, Romulus and Remus, was all about war, and war was what Rome did. There was no allusion to knowledge or learning or to autonomy. Rome was not a discoverer, and most of its major inventions were social, not technological. As to Islam, all creation was the will of Allah, and Muhammad was his only messenger. Knowledge was the Koran. Islamic civilization was an extension of the Greek, apart from the religion, which destroyed it.

On the other side of the world, there was another civilization, the Maya, who advanced rapidly from writing to building the world's largest city to inventing zero and predicting eclipses. Their creation myth was a haunting version of the Garden of Eden. The gods wanted to be remembered and adored. The first creatures they created were failures; they could not speak. Finally, the gods succeeded, all too well. The humans were perfect in knowledge and ability, potentially divine. But the gods wanted worshippers, not competitors. So they reconfigured their creation with clouded vision who still had much to learn.

I do not believe in predestination. History is riddled with unpredictable, critical events, with what-ifs and but-fors. But in search for explanation, scrolling history backward to first causes, this is what I found.

REFERENCES

Beard, Mary. 2016. *SPQR: A History of Ancient Rome*. London: Profile Books Ltd.

Behrens, E. M. 1880. *The Myths and Legends of Ancient Greece and Rome.* New York: Maynard, Merrill & Co.

Desmond, Kevin. 1986. *A Timetable of Inventions and Discoveries.*

Hill. Donald R. 1991. "Mechanical Engineering in the Medieval Near East." *Scientific American* (May): 100–5.

Hourani, Albert. 1991. *A History of the Arab Peoples.* Cambridge: Harvard University Press.

Huff, Toby. 1993. *The Rise of Early Modern Science—Islam, China and the West.* Cambridge, UK: Cambridge University Press.

Kuran, Timur. 2004. "Why the Middle East Is Economically Underdeveloped: Historical Mechanisms of Institutional Stagnation." *Journal of Economic Perspectives* 18 (3): 71–90.

Lewis, Bernard. 2003. *The Crisis of Islam.* New York: Modern Library.

Lewis, David Levering. 2008. *God's Crucible—Islam and the Making of Europe, 570– 1215.* New York: W. W. Norton.

Malmendier, Ulrike. 2009. "Law and at the Origin." *Journal of Economic Literature*, 47 (4): 1076–110.

Mark, Robert, and A. S. Cakmak, eds. 1992. *Hagia Sophia from the Age of Justinian to the Present.* Cambridge University Press.

Mehin, Abdelkader. 2003. "The Arabic Language: Its Linguistics and Philology." In *The Different Aspects of Islamic Culture*, vol. 5, edited by Ekmelediun Tbanoglu, 33–48. Paris: UNESCO.

Naipaul, V. S. 1981. *Among the Believers.* New York: Alfred A. Knopf.

Nasr, Seyyed Hossein. 2001. *Science and Civilization in Islam*. Chicago: ABC International Group, Inc.

Needham, Joseph. 1969. "Human Law and the Laws of Nature." In *The Grand Titration Science and Society in East and West*, 200–331. London: Allen and Unwin.

Ochoa, George, and Melinda Corey. 1995. *The Timeline Book of Science*. New York: Galantine Books.

Schlagel, Richard H. 2010. *Seeking the Truth*. Amherst, NY: Humanity Books.

Usher, Abbot Payson. 1959. *A History of Mechanical Inventions*. Boston: Beacon Press.

VIII

The Europe That Could

INTRODUCTION: WHY EUROPE?

Why was there an explosion of theoretical reasoning and generation of new knowledge about the nature of reality in Greece and not elsewhere? Why were there Scientific and Industrial Revolutions in Europe and not elsewhere? For the future, there would be other issues—the changing nature of the process of discovery and invention—and questions about their direction and their limits that should be raised, even if they cannot be answered.

Was Europe singular or plural? The early Europe, the precursor to the Scientific Revolution, was singular. Its ruling institution was the Roman Catholic Church, its contributors the clergy, Latin the common language, and the domain of discourse religion. The church and the religion were progenitors of European civilization. But when the Scientific Revolution generated the Industrial Revolution, Europe was plural. The religion had been fragmented, and the domain of industry was secular. Different countries and regions advanced at somewhat different times and rates. Thus, it is possible to learn something about propitiating and deterrent conditions from these multiple trajectories.

The big question is why was it the barbarians to the north, in Europe, who forged ahead to the Scientific Revolution, not the more civilized peoples of Islam, who had access to the Greek achievements long before the Europeans? How were European minds prepared to move forward? The answer is implied by the fact that nearly all early contributors to the Scientific Revolution, and many later, were clerics, including Copernicus and Kepler. What did religion, a particular religion, have to do with the Scientific Revolution?

Long after the rise of Islam, Constantinople remained as a reservoir of Greek culture and Christianity. But it was a shrinking reservoir no longer a factor well before its final fall. It was Christianity in Europe, which had forgotten most of the Greek legacy, not in the Middle East, that forged ahead.

CHRISTIANITY

On the history of Christianity until the twelfth century, I rely predominantly on Gonzales's *The History of Christianity* and Hughes's *The Church in Crisis*.

The Religion

Religion is the ultimate authority. All religions, theologies by definition, are top-down authority. But there are major differences between religions in authority structure and scope. Jehovah, the Christian God, has limited authority. Christians believe in free will (although there were dissenters); the individual is responsible for his/her behavior and has a conscience, a sense of guilt. Free will is an implicit assertion that the scope of authority is limited. As to the institution of authority, Christianity has arrived at a separation between church and state, the sacred and the secular. Islam recognizes no such division; the sacred rules over all.

There was a similar contrast with China, whose mythical early emperors were gods. Human emperors remained godlike with unlimited authority. The religions of most, but not all, other early cultures and civilizations were polytheistic and disorderly, including Greece, whose great thinkers, however, were not believers.

All historical religions ask the important questions about origins and destinations, even if they have no answers. They provide ethics, and they promote community. The big difference in consequences is in their origins. The God of Abraham is the ancestor of Allah, a micromanager demanding unthinking obedience. Islam was created by Muhammad, sole communicator with Allah. Islamic scripture is the Koran and the sayings of Muhammad; not one word must be questioned. The creed is the same in the twentieth century as it was in the seventh. The main division of Islam between Sunnis and Shiites is not about creed but authority. Christians, on the other hand, could be of many minds and usually have been.

The God of Moses was the ancestor of the Christian God. Jehovah's tablets requested allegiance of the Jews—that they worship no other gods—and provided a brief ethical code, exclusively negative: "Thou shall not kill." It was later prophets who developed the positive side of ethics, one of whom was Jesus Christ. Judaism was not the creation of Moses but of many people over an extended period.

The God of the Jews, and of the Christians, was quite different from other top gods. The Jupiters were authority figures whose rule was about power. Yahweh or Jehovah may have created the universe but did not run it or rule it. His domain was ethics and morality.

The scope of divine authority in religions such as Islam has no limit; a stone does not fall unless Allah wills it. There is no individual autonomy; reality is deterministic. Individuals with this frame of mind are unlikely to seek new knowledge and new ways, but Jehovah, the Christian God, allows human autonomy and a quest for knowledge. In the Jewish creation myth, Eve disobeys God and eats the fruit of the tree of learning. This attitude toward knowledge is the key difference between Christianity and Islam and Chinese culture. It is a forward rather than a backward perspective.

Christianity and Judaism are the historical religions not created exclusively or predominantly by a single person at a particular point. Christianity has been in continuous evolution. Jesus did not invent it; he promoted the reform of Judaism from a tribal to an ecumenical morality and faith. Christianity was the work of his disciples, their followers, and many others over the next two millennia, and the work is never over. There were debates over the nature of divinity, the nature of reality, the appropriate rites of worship, and the structure of the institution. The Bible is a committee product, what to include or exclude. Different branches of Christianity have slightly different Bibles, but all are equally holy. The original manuscripts were written in several languages; there is no one holy language. One can argue over the original meaning of a word when first written, the interpretation of the gospels.

Religion was universal. I claim that it still is; the preponderance of the so-called irreligious is simply members of secular sects with most of the characteristics of sacred faiths. They may have given up hope of an afterlife but replaced it with some form of salvation in this one. They extend the morality of traditional faiths to new spheres and retain a sense of belonging. The cosmological role of religion, by now, has been largely relegated to science by sacred and secular believers alike.

Christianity and the State

Christians were loyal Roman citizens, but they did not worship emperors or any Roman gods or participate in any activities that implied such worship. Romans, in turn, could not add Jehovah to their pantheon of pagan gods. It was Jehovah or Jupiter. Christians came in conflict with the state. The religion was declared illegal. In subsequent centuries, sometimes they were persecuted; sometimes there was accommodation, no initiative to prosecute. Martyrdom became a badge of honor. The difficulty many had in readmitting members of the faith who had compromised or strayed to save their lives spoke of the intense sense of community that characterized Christianity in its early centuries.

Their interaction with the state was not debate but a clash of cultures. Roman gods came from some place; the Christian God was rootless and universal. Christianity proselytized and admitted converts by a formal ritual of conversion. The religion preached the virtue of poverty. Its concepts of the nature of the world and of the origin of humans were contrary to those of Romans and Greeks. The willingness of some believers to be tortured and executed rather than pretend to recant their faith confounded magistrates who sought to spare them (Beard 2016, 516, 519).

Then Constantine converted to Christianity, which became the state religion. Tables were turned; it was the Christians who occasionally persecuted or tolerated pagans. Justinian closed Plato's Academy and Aristotle's Lyceum and other centers of "pagan" learning, but Hellenism survived mainly in the Eastern Empire and was adopted by Islamic scholars.

The fall of Rome was a protracted process ending in 476. Most of its conquerors were Christians and Arians who believed in the unity of God. But the Roman state was gone; the church stood alone.

Slowly, over time, the Arians came to accept the Nicene Creed of the church. In the Eastern Empire, however, the state survived another millennium. The church remained subordinate, and both were encircled by Islam from the seventh century on.

Christianity's Early History

Christians during their first four centuries were engaged in constant argument and debate, first with others and then among themselves. During the first century, followers of Jesus Christ were accused of heresy by their fellow Jews. They retorted that they were the ones who recognized that Jesus Christ was the fulfillment of Jewish prophecy. This debate was carried out in Palestine. But there were Jewish communities in all the major cities of the Roman Empire. Facing persecution at home, some Palestinian followers immigrated to these communities. Among them were missionaries, of whom Paul is the best known.

The early Christians who emigrated from Palestine to other parts of the Roman Empire were mostly of Greek culture, described as Aristotelian. What did this mean? Aristotle's cosmos was material, ordered from the bottom up, whereas Christianity was spiritual, ordered top down. It was more compatible with Plato's view of reality than with Aristotle's. What the émigrés shared with Aristotle was reason. They employed reason and logic in defense of their faith and in its propagation.

Although the missionaries from Palestine initially addressed Jewish communities, some Gentiles heard their message and became believers. The issue now was whether Gentiles could be members of the community of believers. Paul himself answered that question by converting an Ethiopian. Since Gentiles were not Jews, at this point, Christianity was born as a religion separate from Judaism. This partition is reflected in the Bible to this day.

As their numbers grew, in the second century, Christians were on the defensive. Christianity faced attack from educated pagans on the credibility of its core beliefs. How could an all-powerful God allow himself to be crucified? How could he die? The resurrection was not credible. Some defenders of the faith sought to reconcile it with Greek philosophy, in particular Plato's view of reality as ideational rather than material.

Disputes in the second and third centuries were mainly within the religion and were theological in nature. They were of particular interest because the topics were much the same as those debated in Athens in earlier centuries. Many of the protagonists were Hellenistic in culture and cognitive style. But their issues were in theology, not in physics. One was the conflict between the belief in Creation, or beginning, and the belief in eternity, no Creation or ending. Another was the conflict between the idea of unity and plurality; how could one become many? For the Christians, it was the Trinity. More specifically, was Jesus Christ divine, one with God, or was he human and mortal? Was human destiny causal and predetermined, or was there uncertainty and choice? But the domains of physics and theology did not collide until a millennium later. They were alternative and analogous quests for order by a process of abstraction. Religion went further; it imposed the order we called morality.

In the second century and for many centuries thereafter, there were movements or sects so different in beliefs from those that became the church that they barely qualified as Christian if the church was regarded as the standard. Gnosticism was found among Jews as well as Christians. It was a cult of pessimism. It questioned the divinity of Creation. Not God but spiritual beings created the world, which Gnostics regarded as evil. Humans sought salvation by escaping the prison of the body. The Christian Gnostics saw Jesus as the messenger from the spiritual world who reminded humans of their spiritual origins. They rejected the Trinity and transubstantiation. Gnostics formed reclusive communities rather than churches.

Marcion also regarded the world as evil. He sought to divest Christianity of all reference to Judaism. He rejected the Old Testament and most of the New. He distinguished between Yahweh, who made the world as it is, including humans, and God who fathered Jesus Christ. The sect he founded persisted for several centuries. Unlike the diverse views within the church, which were vigorously debated, Gnosticism and Marcionism were defections. Against the assertions of the Gnostics and the Marcionites that the world is evil, Augustine of Hippo argued that evil is not a thing or an attribute but the consequence of bad human choices.

The great controversy within the church was Arianism. Arius believed that Jesus was human and mortal, not divine. He also believed that the Word, or Holy Spirit, was a creation, not a divine being, and that God was one, not two or three. His numerous followers, the Arians, at first considered heretics, came to be viewed as Christians mistaken in their beliefs. The Arian controversy preoccupied the church in the third and early fourth centuries. In 325, they adopted the Trinitarian view of deity or Nicaeane Creed, settling that issue for centuries to come. It condemned the Arian beliefs, but the Arians persisted. There was much disturbance until a second council in Constantinople, in 451, declared all Arianisms heretic. But the Arian view would remain a permanent argument with mainstream Christians. It was similar to the conflict of views of reality of Aristotle and Plato.

The protracted dispute was not just about theology; it was also political. Nearly all the emperors after Constantine were Christians, but many of them were Arian supporters as was Constantine. Christianity was de facto the state religion, and emperors were the ones who appointed bishops and sometimes replaced and exiled them. The Arians were mainly the Hellenized elite, whereas supporters of the Nicene Creed were the common people.

The Nicene Council discussed many other matters, such as penance for those who had strayed under persecution, readmission of heretics, ordination of clergy, the date of Easter, and issues of the church as an institution. But it was the perennial arguments about abstruse concepts of theology that prepared minds for the future. The agendas and accomplishments of the general councils, the first being Nicaea, are the best guides to the preoccupations in the minds of the clergy, if not also the laity in ensuing centuries. The councils were called by popes, sometimes by emperors, when they thought that issues important for the entire institution needed resolution.

The Arian controversy preoccupied the church for the third and fourth centuries. Then other sects and cults grew to challenge the Nicene Creed. The principal ones were the Nestorians and the Monophysites. They differed primarily in their concepts of the nature of Jesus Christ, his humanity and his divinity. The Nestorians regarded Mary as the mother of Christ, not of God. Jesus was both human and divine—two natures, two persons. Two general councils in the fifth century were devoted primarily to the issue of the Nestorian sect. They condemned it, tried reconciliation, and finally declared it a heresy. There was some persecution. Some Nestorians fled from Alexandria to Antioch and then as far east as Persia, introducing the Greek classics, which later became the foundation of Islamic civilization.

The Monophysites' belief that Christ had only one nature was so different from the prevailing theology that there was no prospect of conciliation, but it was not condemned by the church. The emperor Justinian condemned the Monophysites and persecuted them.

In the sixth century, the issue was the Monothelitic cult, very similar to the Monophysites, that Christ had only one will, but did still have two natures, human and God. This sect was ultimately condemned.

The seventh general council in 787, the second in Nicaea, was about images and idolatry. It ruled that images were acceptable and should be honored but must not be worshipped as though they possessed divinity.

The general council of 869–870 was the exception; the issue was personalities and power struggles, not ideas and theology. From this council to 1179, there were councils but no discussion of ideas, just condemnations of immorality in the church and power struggles between clerical and secular authority and domain.

A dispute among the orthodox not settled by the Nicene Council was the issue of transubstantiation, about the possibility and reality of converting at Mass wafer and wine into the flesh and blood of Christ. The ritual of bread and wine at Mass and the belief in transubstantiation went back to the first century. But the belief was still being debated a millennium later. The practice became official church policy in 1215 at the fourth Lateran Council convened by Pope Innocent I.

There is an analogy between the theological belief in transubstantiation and the alchemical belief in the transmutation of base metals into gold and glass into gems. In both cases, spirituality is immanent in the material world. In alchemy, innumerable experiments have resulted in the discovery of many compounds and new elements and eventual development of chemistry. But there was no cognitive transfer between alchemical and theological domains; transubstantiation was an article of faith.

Acceptance of the Nicene Creed did not bring an end to disputes. It was about articles of faith. Other issues remained that might be described as a search for understanding, an explanation of faith itself. A major issue engaging Christian theologians in the fourth century was about the freedom of the will and individual responsibility for their choices and their consequences versus predestination. This dispute was not about God but about humans. Nevertheless, some theologians regarded free will as heresy. The Manichaeans believed in predestination. Augustine of Hippo was the principal proponent and defender of freedom of the will, including the freedom to do evil.

Human will and human decisions are not simple. Choices are complex; there is will against will in the mind of an individual. It may be difficult to make up one's mind. Sometimes all choices are bad. Mistakes are made. Thus, humans do not always have the ability to overcome their sins, contrary to the belief of the Pelagians, whose concept of will was simplistic (Gonzales 2010, 247–49). Irrespective of the reasoning, Christians persisted in assuming responsibility for their behavior and in seeking indulgence for their sins.

This is a difference of opinion that extends far beyond the domain of theology and religion. The issue persists today in legal systems that consider motives and intentions, in dispute about meritocracy and two kinds of secular predestination—genetics and environment. What was theology in the early centuries is secular morality and psychology today.

Theologians also debated a closely related issue—the existence of evil. How is it that God allows evil to exist, and what is its origin? To the Gnostics, evil is characteristic of reality. For the church, evil is human behavior, not a divine creation. How can one account for the evil that humans do by choice? To Alexander of Hippo, it is an accident of choice. To others, it is human intention.

Most of the Christian in the early centuries were culturally Greek. Some thinkers among them sought to relate classical Greek achievements to Christianity and to assimilate them, notably Justin, Clement of Alexandria, and Origen of Alexandria, the leading center of Greek philosophy at that time. They saw the Greek concept of the origin of the universe from a single creator, its orderliness, as comparable to the Christian view of Creation. Plato's Demiurge, ultimate reality as spiritual, was more in keeping with Christian concepts of reality and creation than Aristotle's materialism and causality.

After the fall of Rome, the church in Rome and the Eastern Church in Constantinople grew apart. In Rome, it stood alone; in the east, it remained subject to the emperor. The Greek legacy was preserved in Constantinople but lost in Europe as the two grew apart.

Since Boethius (480–525) planned to translate all of Aristotle into Latin, Aristotle's works in Greek must have been available in Europe at that time. He only succeeded in translating the logic and some commentaries. By this time, the Aristotelian legacy had been lost. The only Hellenic influence was Plato, whose book *Timaeus* was the main survivor. Christian theologians found the concept of Demiurge as creator of the universe, reality as idea, and the material world mere derivation, a shadow of reality, compatible with their own beliefs. Plato's world is one, an organic whole. His world had a soul. If Plato's cosmogony can be described as aesthetic, then the Christian cosmology at a lower level of reality, the human level, was moral, not material. There was heaven and hell, reward and punishment, salvation, and sainthood.

What went on in the minds of the clergy between 787 and 1179 is a matter for speculation. I suspect that thinking remained much the same until the eleventh century, shortly before European scholars began to gain access to Aristotle's writings and to other Greek classics from the Arabs. They continued to think about all the controversial issues of the early centuries, but open argument raised the threat of accusations of heresy since the church had made up its mind. Transubstantiation was still to be judged. The brilliant achievements of the councils of 1179 and 1215 (to be discussed later) suggest that many of the clergy had remained alert and accomplished during the last of those centuries, if not throughout.

The centuries of intellectual struggle to explain articles of faith, to identify contradictions, and to resolve differences of belief were exercises in discovery. But the subjects were products of the imagination, beyond evidence, proof, or disproof. The product was faith, not knowledge. It was discovery in search of domain.

The signal event between 787 and 1179 was the creation of a European state with Charlemagne as its emperor in 801. But this was a challenge to the church's secular role, not to religion. The main issues were no longer those of the faith but those of the church as a dominant institution. To this subject, we now turn.

THE CHURCH

The Institution

Well before the final fall of Rome, the church evolved from a collection of churches largely autonomous into an institution with shared creed, cult, and leadership. The first step was the selection of leadership to succeed the apostles. Who could represent the religion and speak for it? In the second century, the successors of the apostles and their disciples were the bishops. Some of them were direct heirs of apostolic authority. New bishops sought and received the approval of their colleagues. The bishops were collegial. They met frequently, usually at the funeral of one of their own. In the absence of any other authority, they sought consensus. Once Christianity became the state religion, emperors acquired the power to appoint bishops and sometimes to replace them.

But what was Christianity? The equally essential step was to agree on the teachings of the church and compile a text, the Bible, for all Christians. There was no disagreement on the Hebrew religious book, the Old Testament, which was quickly adopted. But there were many gospels, epistles, and other writings by the apostles and other Christians. The search for consensus on the basic books for inclusion in the New Testament was a protracted one, in sharp contrast to Constantine's Nicene Council. Complete, final consensus was not reached until the last half of the fourth century. It was the Bible that separated the Catholic Church from competing cults such as the Gnostics and Marcionites. The holy book did not have answers to every question raised. It was not a textbook or a compilation of prescriptions and proscriptions. It was a compendium of mythology, much history, many memoirs, biographies, sermons, short stories, parables, puzzles, and poems. It was open to diverse interpretations, always open to discussion and debate.

The third step in the institutionalization of the church was a procedure of admission to membership. Who was a Christian? Christians were not born; they must be converted. The procedure was baptism. Agreement was also needed on how Christians should worship Jesus in their congregations—on liturgy and on a church calendar.

Authority

While the religion changed little for many centuries after the Nicene Council, the church evolved. It grew affluent and influential. Not all matters could wait on a prolonged dialogue for decision. It was the bishop of Rome who gradually became first among equals and later the pope. It survived the fall of Rome and replaced the autocratic empire of the Caesars with the theocratic empire of the popes. The church became the guardian of order and justice. Pope Gregory the Great (590–604) acted as head of state as well as church.

Until the election of Charlemagne in 801, the church was the ruling European institution. For centuries thereafter, it remained much of the time the dominant institution. There were no nation-states. Secular political entities were small, often short lived, subject to wars and territorial change. Secular organization was more ethnic than national or territorial. It was the only European institution, de facto the state. It shared a common language, common culture, and a sense of identity subordinating ethnicities. Most importantly, it exercised the power to raise revenue, to tax. It had schools as well as churches and created its own legal system, the canon laws.

How did it differ from the authority structures of other civilizations/religions? The protracted process of decision-making in the creation of the Bible reflected a structure and scope of authority quite different from that of the state or of most other religions. Earlier, we noted the difference between the God of Moses and the God of Abraham. It was echoed in the contrast between the Christian God, the libertarian, and Allah, the totalitarian. Christian freedom of the will is a limitation on divine authority.

The discussions, debates, and decisions of the church in its councils in the first eight centuries had been mainly about faith. There was no authority structure. The councils were free for all. Collegiality was promoted by long journeys, long waits, and long councils. Interchange was often a search for truth or justice, sometimes a debate between devoted adversaries, rarely a flurry of mutual excommunications. Participation was not limited to bishops; there were many lower-level clergy and occasionally an emperor.

The leading proponents of the diverse sects and cults being investigated by the councils were given the opportunity to explain and defend themselves. The search for harmony did not prevail over the search for truth. The desire for unanimity did not prevail over majority rule. This was the character of authority in the church as a religion on questions of faith and principle.

The contribution of the church to the Scientific Revolution yet to come was not the content of the faith. It was the character of the decision-making process employed. Authority was needed for unity of belief. The search for truth was collaboration, dialogue between equals, not debate between opponents or dictates. The apostles and their disciples and successors were the repositories of the faith and the teachers of the laity. The ultimate authority that Catholics accepted was not an agent but a book. The method of resolving differences concerning the faith and its practice was a council of the bishops and other clergy. There were fourteen general councils between the fourth and thirteenth centuries and innumerable smaller councils whose participants were not limited to the higher-ranking clerics.

Authority in the church as an institution required hierarchy and obedience. What was the motivation? Service is the test of performance. The pope is the servant of the servants of the Christians. Not all popes have understood this. Authority in the church is the revealed authority of the scriptures exercised in a society of the faithful. Authority is service, nothing else. Every relation involving subordination should be transformed into agape, beyond love, which is reciprocal, an organic sense of community (Mara 1965, 161–70). We see this reflected in the honor of martyrs and the disgrace of those who have bowed to Caesar to save their lives, the penance required to readmit them. The abuse of authority has been the leading issue of the church through much of its history. But clergy who have disagreed with official articles of faith have usually remained on the payroll.

Law and Morality

As long as the church was the dominant organization in Europe, it was the habitat of men who sought power and wealth. Some prelates were such chronic sinners that I questioned their faith. Their behavior cannot be explained as cognitive dissonance. At times, they dominated the upper echelons of the church, including the papacy. This was inevitable, and much of canon law and the agenda of general councils were devoted to the problem of morality of the clergy. Historically, the main threat to the church in the first four centuries was competing creeds and cults. After it became the state religion, especially after the fall of Rome, it was the corruption within the church Itself. The problem had been recognized since the church first became influential and affluent. All previous general councils had condemned corruption, to little avail. The main purpose of the general councils of 1179 and 1215 was not to condemn corruption but to eliminate it once and for all.

The great intellectual achievement of the general councils of 1179 and 1215 was canon law. The motivation was recognition of the corruption and other forms of immorality rampant among the clergy and fear for their consequences for the respect, if not survival, of the church itself. The need for a moral order for its own sake was certainly part of the motivation.

Canon law built on Roman law, retaining the principle of equality under the law, but its structure was quite different. Whereas the Romans dealt with particular activities and their punishment, the church dealt with motives and the diverse ways in which they could be expressed and how to prevent these expressions. Roman law was about crime—prohibition, prosecution, penalty. Canon law was about sin—prohibition, confession, remorse for sins of behavior—punishment, yes, and penance or self-inflicted punishment but prevention preferably.

For sins of belief, heresy, there is excommunication, redemption, reconversion, and the prospects of salvation and damnation. Forbidden behavior is not limited to acts that may be harmful to others and to society. They include acts and beliefs that may be harmful only to themselves. As to virtues, their reward is beyond the reach of canon law; it is in the hands of the deity. It is a consideration in appointments to clerical positions.

A central issue was corruption in the power of appointment; there was patronage, sale of positions. Canon law specified that no vacancy should remain vacant; no appointments or promises should be made before a position became vacant. Candidates must be qualified. Positions must be filled by election. There should be opportunity for influential sinners.

A second issue was the extravagant lifestyle of some clerics. This abuse was attacked on several fronts. Upper limits on expenses were set for each clerical rank. The number of persons in a cleric's retinue in travel was limited according to rank. Compensation for indulgences and other services of the clergy helped finance the extravagance. It was condemned; these services were free. It was not enough to say, "No payment for indulgences." One must think of all the subterfuges and circumventions a would-be sinner might employ. Clergy were limited in income and in expenditures in other ways. Enjoyments such as hunting, fowling, taverns, and games of chance were proscribed, simplicity of dress and accouterments prescribed. As further insurance against corruption, bishops of each province must meet once a year to discipline one another. A common evasion of limits on income and spending was multiple job holding. This was self-patronage.

As to the laity, it has the obligation to pay the tithe before any other tax. It should confess its sins at least once a year. Holy lives are often not rewarded in this world; evil is not punished. But believers were assured that there is justice in the end. If not in this world, then there is salvation and damnation in the hereafter. God is the divine accountant who makes the books balance in eternity. This was the expectation of martyrs and payers of penance. Heaven and hell is the idea of justice—compensation for the inequities and injustices of the current world. On education, cathedrals, churches, and monasteries were required to have schools, teaching gratis—open to the poor. Cathedrals also provided training for parochial clergy. This is justice in the herein.

Heresies were condemned. Heretics who persisted in false beliefs were subject to appropriate penalties and would lose most of their legal rights. The principal heretics at that time were the Albigenses, who believed the universe was dual, a struggle between forces of good and evil, spiritual and material. They were descendants of the Manichaeans. The condemnation by the council had been preceded by military victory. (Manichaeism or equivalent cults are found throughout the first millennium. They are analogous to the Chinese yin-yang cosmology, both binary—good and evil in Europe, male and female in China.) But some accusations of heresy were false, and there was excessive resort to and abuse of excommunication. Individuals charged had the right of appeal. Judgment of cults and creeds apart from individual participants embodied the concept of a group, a corporation, as a legal person.

Canon law was an ongoing process, always under revision and expansion after the council of 1215. The fight against corruption and other immoral behavior could never end because enforcement often was the responsibility of some of the worst sinners. It was the problem of immorality among the clergy that motivated monks, monasteries, and later the great monastic orders that took pride in poverty, in contrast to the bishops who were guilty of greed and overindulgence. The issue contributed to the eventual breakup of the church by Martin Luther. But what is relevant for discovery and invention is the cognitive process involved in the conceiving of and creating canon law.

The reasoning of canon law started not with particular and concrete sins but with generic abstract motives such as greed, avarice, vanity, envy, hate, and passion for power and control. The highest level of reality was truth, love, justice—the virtues. Motives were not products of mind but of soul. Canon law was a great invention, a solution to a problem. But the approach to problem-solving was one of discovery—of the fundamental causes of corruption, of sin. The virtues and vices, the motivation, were a moral taxonomy. The vices were conceived to condemn them, preclude them if possible, or punish the deeds or beliefs otherwise. Punishment was appropriate to the offense. Canon law extended the range of behavior control beyond the social—into the purely solitary behavior and belief that had no victims other than the perpetrator.

It was a Platonic cosmos—abstract motives, virtues and vices, from which are subtended a vast number of possible acts and beliefs. A particular sin may have diverse motives, so it is not possible to construct this legal universe from the bottom up. It is also a cause-and-effect relationship. This is the implication of freedom of the will. The search for means to prevent such behavior is synthetic; what is the motivation of the sinners? Spending, absence, delay, and inaction are not per se corruption or incompetence

Reasoning was about abstract concepts, some of which, such as the virtues and vices, were abstracted from reality. But others, such as transubstantiation, were imaginary. Their existence and their interrelations were not subject to evidence, to proof or disproof. The product of reasoning was faith and meaning rather than knowledge. They were attempts at discovery of explanation and then search for solution.

Cognitive development beyond simple judgments of similarity is awareness of contradictions and effort toward their resolution. But this is contradiction within a single domain—the drinker who preaches abstinence. The higher level demonstrated in canon law is awareness of contradictions in different domains. This requires abstraction and cognitive transfer, a step beyond mere wide-angle vision. It is exemplified by the difficult reconciliation of love and punishment for sins, of justice and war, which is a conflict of wills.

It was not new in the church. The early clerics who decided that free will conflicted with the perception of the omnipotence of God were transferring cognition between domains, the psychological and cosmological or theological domains. But the canons represented these abilities on a large scale, so many clerics were involved. It must have become widespread earlier.

Unfortunately, there is no record of the proceedings of the two councils. All we know is the outcome. We do not know which proposals were controversial or how they were resolved. On the basis of past councils and the prolonged duration, there was extensive discussion, much debate, and full exposure to conflicting views, a search for truth with precedence to the desire for harmony.

Canon law epitomizes cognitive change from the specific to the general, from the concrete to the abstract. Comprehensive and coherent, it was the product of a collective mind. All we know about individuals involved is that Gratian did much work collecting and consolidating canon laws in preparation for the councils. It reveals popes, and many lesser clergy, long capable of abstraction in theology, now exercising this ability in the domain of law and human behavior. The result was synthesis beyond the particularistic thinking of the past.

We do know something about scholars at the time, in particular some whose working life preceded the general councils. Five who died before the council of 1179 were Anselm, Abelard, Bernard and Thierry of Chartres, and William of Conches. We turn to them, seeking evidence of a cognitive revolution preceding the work of the councils.

EARLY SCIENTIFIC REVOLUTION

Nearly all contributors to the early Scientific Revolution were members of the clergy. What they had in common other than the ability to communicate in Latin was the practice of abstract reasoning. They were the ones who thought about the creation of the universe, the origins and destination of the human race. It was their job to interpret the gospel in terms of human behavior and to judge behavior in terms of the gospel.

A century before the first canon-writing general council, there was intellectual stirring in Europe. We knew this from the writings and letters of St. Anselm of Canterbury (1033–1109). He argued that religious beliefs could be proven by reason alone, without reference to the authority of scripture. His writings were logical proofs of the existence of God, and his letters were replies to critics who questioned his reasoning. His stress on reason rather than authority prevailed among scholars who followed him. But he was a Platonist who distrusted the senses and believed that truth was in the realm of ideas.

Peter Abelard (1079–1142) went further. He argued that all belief must be explained by reason alone (Norman 2007) and made it his main business to identify contradictions in religious texts and to resolve them if possible. He then practiced and promoted a dialectical method of resolving contradictions. Apart from writing his dialogues (or debates), he had numerous face-to-face dialogues or debates with others. He was not alone in his thinking nearly a century before the councils. Incidentally, he credited Augustine of Hippo for similar thinking six centuries earlier.

The term *dialectics* is used by so many, from Greek scholars to medieval clerics and modern philosophers. What did Abelard and other scholastic of his time meant by the term? What is relevant to our subject is objectivity and rationality. But the domain within which scholastics preached, if not practiced, objectivity was theological, and their cosmology was Platonic. Dialectics today is called conflict resolution. It is a search for truth that could be conducted by two or more individuals in a cooperative effort. It is not debate. A single individual might try, but impartial objectivity is very difficult. The resolution of differences or contradictions could take several forms, including proof that one or both are wrong. It is the objectivity of the search for truth that characterizes dialectic. (Abelard himself was more competitive than cooperative.)

The difference between Abelard and the Greeks was attributable to his subject matter, which was the scriptures, sacred beyond question. Pointing out discrepancies was a hazardous undertaking. This assumption limited the possible outcomes of dialectics. Ideally, apparent contradictions were simply different aspects of a common concept, an exercise in abstraction. Or they were different positions in a continuum. These were cognitive, not theological, issues—a search for order applicable to secular issues uninhibited by any presuppositions.

In his book *Sic et non*, there were many questions on the nature, knowledge, and power of God. They would be inconceivable with reference to Allah. Abelard himself was charged with heresy. Several questions concerned the freedom of will of humans. Most of the questions were about theology, but some were philosophical: Is reality accidental or determined? If humans have free will, are they responsible for evil? The same reasoning applied to secular and to sacred domains. What is notable about his work is that he did not reason from assumptions; he asked questions and sought answers. I described *discovery* as seeking order out of chaos. Whether or not a contradiction is chaotic, it is disorder.

The dialectic approach prevailed, and soon many questions were in the domains of philosophy, cosmology, and natural law. Minds were ready, and so were questions before the first writing by Aristotle on the natural sciences became available to Europeans. Their subject was physics.

The scholars who followed Abelard, almost without exception, were advocates of reason and logic as explanation of faith. Their primary concern was cosmology, the relation between Plato's concept of the cosmos and the Christian beliefs. The cosmology of the scriptures was limited to the creation story and the Garden of Eden. Attempts over centuries to reconcile it with Plato's view in the *Timaeus* can be seen as efforts to create a coherent and complete Christian cosmology.

Both were two-tier universes; the higher was spiritual (Plato's Demiurge and his realm of ideas), the lower tier material. In each, the lower tier was the creation of the higher tier. Plato's material world had structure. It was the interrelation of its elements that was predictable on the basis of mathematical laws. There was a creator and a beginning; time started with the moment of creation. Since the mathematical structure was based on the triangle, no doubt some scholars associated it with the Trinity. But Plato also had an organic view of the cosmos— phenomena were not self-defined, things in themselves; they were identified by interrelations. In such a world, there were no natural laws. Plato's worldview was imaginary. The material world was just a derivative of unobservable ideas. Yet the material world we know is causal.

Bernard of Chartres (died in 1124), a contemporary of Abelard, discussed the problem of universals (distinguishing between the abstract, the process, and the concrete—its exemplification). According to Bernard, there are three categories of reality: God, matter, and idea. God is supreme reality. Matter was brought out of nothingness by God's creative act; in union with ideas, it constitutes the world of sensible things. Ideas are the prototypes by means of which the world was formed. All eternity is present to the divine mind. Forms—copies of the ideas created with matter—are united with matter. Although matter is created by God, it existed in eternity. Before its union with the forms, it was in a chaotic condition. Forms have been abstract but not abstractions; it was the concrete materials that were derivative. Bernard's cosmology amounted to a Christian adaptation of Plato—the intellect as ideas becomes the world-soul; matter is the source of imperfection.

Thierry of Chartres, who died circa 1150, saw the world as rational. The universe is lawful, orderly, and hierarchical, sequence is predictable. He criticized the Bible as contrary to the nature of things; it should not to be taken literally. Teaching the nature of reality is a task for the philosophers. The scriptures teach about God's existence. Thierry's explanation of the creation of the world is based on a theological interpretation of Aristotle's four causes as the Trinity, plus matter. The Creator is the Trinity, equated to Aristotle's efficient, normal, and final causes. The Greek's four elements are the material cause. God created the four elements in the very beginning of time. The four elements then evolved by themselves, mixing according to mathematical proportions to make up the physical world. God has or exercises limited authority. The material world is self-determined, agency-free.

William of Conches (1090–1154) was different. His concerns, his writings, were not about theology but about the material world. He distinguished between the forces of nature and the miraculous. Nature, orderly or hierarchy, was lawful. The Bible was not literally true. He advocated the study of Greek writings and encouraged empirical work. He died when Averroës, the initial source of Aristotle's writings to European scholars, was twenty-eight. His source was the translations from the Arabic by Constantine the African, who died near the end of the eleventh century. Constantine was a North African Muslim who migrated to Italy and was converted to Christianity. What he translated were the works of Islamic scholars, much of which were commentaries or supplements to the Greek writings on physics, astronomy, geography, meteorology, and especially medicine. He was a forerunner, but his interest in the material world was not integrated with his theology, which was Platonic.

We do not know the year of birth of some of these scholastics, but the difference in age of death was only forty-five years. They knew one another and interacted in diverse ways and places. To understand how new knowledge and new perspectives were so rapidly propagated and adopted, one must look at the educational institutions in which these scholars worked.

Theological education began early in the history of Christianity. The laity had to be prepared for baptism and the clergy trained to perform its duties. But the clergy also had to dissuade heresies and defend itself from critics. Aristotelian reasoning was part of its repertoire almost from the beginning. Disputes with heresies and disagreements within the faith were always on the agenda.

The first cathedral schools were opened in the sixth century. Their role was training of clergy. In 789, before becoming emperor, Charlemagne decreed that cathedrals and monasteries in the kingdom of the Franks provide education for the clergy. But he also was interested in the education of the laity. Children should be taught reading, music, computation, and grammar. In the eleventh century, some such schools throughout Europe evolved into institutes of higher learning, which became universities, autonomous and self-ruled. Paris and Oxford were the most important ones. But what was their curriculum?

Those who sought a career in the clergy studied philosophy and humanities before theology. These included logic, arithmetic, geometry, astronomy, and music. Universities were very prompt in adding new knowledge to their curricula, including Greek and Arab learning, Aristotle prominent among them, even if they were a challenge to the faith. They were also the sites where novel perspectives were developed and propagated. Such standardization of curriculum across Europe allowed many of the scholastics to move from one university to another. The scholars mentioned above were also teachers. They propagated their views among many students as well as among those who read their writings.

Universities also initiated professional standards and certification for occupations, assuring minimum quality of practitioners. Medicine was the first, followed by law. They standardized the course of study, evaluated competence, and restricted practice (Huff 1993, 197–201).

Pope Innocent III required that all cathedrals, churches, and monasteries must have schools. Well before the printing press, there were quite a few persons fluent in Latin and highly educated who were not clergy. Nevertheless, essentially all the contributions noted above were by clergy.

Huff (1993, 201–3) stressed the fact that universities had the de facto rights and obligations of a legal person (i.e., autonomy). Legitimacy of such judicial personalities required evidence of representation of the interests of the members, which required majority rule. What this did was to impose bottom-up authority. Universities, guilds, cities, and other juridical persons, in turn, developed their own internal legal system. Authority now was plural and representative.

The scholastics who followed the five mentioned above had access to much of Aristotle's work and a growing share of the Greek legacy. The authority of reason in the search for truth was accepted by scholars. So was a secular cosmos well ordered, thanks to Plato. What followed considered only the achievements that appeared relevant to the forthcoming Scientific Revolution.

Grosseteste (1175–1253) was the first of the scholastics to fully understand Aristotle's description of the dual path of scientific reasoning—generalizing from particular observations to a universal law and from universal laws to prediction of particulars. Grosseteste called this "resolution and composition." He added experimental verification to Aristotle's induction and deduction. He also disproved generalizations by reduction ad absurdum. On cosmology, he agreed with Aristotle's materialist universe. He held that prime matter was created first, which then penetrated matter, creating three spatial dimensions and motion. Schlagel suggested that he foreshadowed the big bang theory. He was a big advance on Abelard by focusing on secular domains and by relying on experiment both to arrive at generalizations and to test hypotheses (Schlagel 214–15, 218).

Albertus Magnus (1200–1280) was another cleric who knew almost everything and wrote on most of them in the Athenian model. His major work was the presentation of Aristotle's writings, together with commentaries and corrections, his own and those of Arab scholars. He saw no conflict between Aristotle's worldview and Christian theology, making a clear distinction between philosophy and theology. Philosophy is autonomous; it seeks truth apart from revelation by rational methods. But the church and most of its members did not agree; most were still Platonists. It was his student Thomas Aquinas who changed their minds.

Thomas Aquinas (1225–1274) argued that some truths are within reach of reason and are in the domain of philosophy. Others cannot be known by reason, only by revelation. They are in the domain of theology. But this domain extends to some truths proved by reason. All truths needed for salvation have been revealed; hence, they pertain to both philosophy and theology. They seek the truth on the same subjects by different means; they cannot conflict. Knowing the truth in philosophy means understanding why; in theology, trust in someone else's understanding. Scientific reasoning is based on first principles derived from sensory experience.

The search for knowledge as enablement of the faith was the beginning of the Scientific Revolution. Thomas Aquinas turned philosophy, regarded as a threat, into an instrument of faith. His arguments for God were all empirical; they started with the senses. This was rejection of the Platonic worldview at a time when the clergy was predominantly Platonic. But the Platonic world of ideas was, like the Christian, a matter of faith. It lacked an autonomous material reality. There was much resistance; Aristotle was often condemned and forbidden. But Aquinas prevailed in his lifetime and thereafter. The search for truth was now based on a foundation of observable reality. The study of the laws of nature became a search for explanation of faith. The study of human reasoning became explanation of the knowledge needed to explain faith.

The change from a top-down to a bottom-up concept of reality was one of perspective. Bottom up would lead to the science and technology of our time. Top down did not. The explanation is simple: one does not build a house from the roof down to the foundation. Such a structure cannot stand; it cannot exist.

A century before Thomas Aquinas persuaded the church to reconcile Aristotelian cosmology and physics with Christian theology, al-Ghazālī had accomplished the reverse. He condemned Aristotelian thinking as a contradiction of Islamic theology.

What was the significance of the works of Aristotle and other Greek scholars acquired from the Arabs? The main consequence was domain shift in scholarship, from the sacred to the secular, from ideological to the material and empirical. It changed the agenda. Aristotle's physics and astronomy propelled research, critique, and discovery. But the process was already in place. Domain shift and research objective were not enough for a scientific revolution. The third component was the replacement of Plato's two-level top-down cosmology with Aristotle's single-stage materialist, bottom-up causal cosmos. This was the accomplishment of Aquinas. Aristotle opened up many secular domains for investigation by the clergy but especially physics, cosmology, and astronomy that provided views of reality alternative to those of theology. They were also an alternative to the vision of Plato.

The universities, if not always the church, were tolerant of divergent views among their own theologians. The writings of Aristotle and other Greek philosophers came to minds prepared to understand them, to learn them, and to improve on them. It was the practice of rigorous argumentation with reason as the test of truth that prepared the minds of clergy to unlock the secrets of the universe. The very subjects they had debated could be found in the writings of the Greeks, divorced from their theological context—cause and effect rather than predestination, free will and uncertainty, the structure of the universe, beginning and end, the nature of evil. There was cognitive transfer. Theologians became astronomers and physicists.

Roger Bacon (1219–1292) followed up on Grosseteste's stress on experiment to acquire new knowledge. He was a prominent promoter of math and the opening of new fields of inquiry. His *Opus majus* surveyed the range of human knowledge at the time. He contributed to the reform of university curriculum. Like Aquinas, he sought to reconcile Aristotle with a modernized theology. His own research was on optics— the rainbow, human eyes. John Peckham (1230–1292) followed up on Bacon's research on optics and astronomy and wrote a text on optics.

Duns Scotus (1266–1308) was interested in the nature of reality. He argued that it is possible to know reality without divinity. He asserted the principle of the uniformity of nature. Many repetitions amount to certainty. Whatever occurs many times from some cause is the effect of that cause. All phenomena are individuated and self-identified, contrary to Plato. There is no distinction between essence and existence contrary to Aquinas. Scotus argued for the existence of prime matter without form. Not all created substances are composites of form and matter; there is spirituality. Some substances can have more than one form.

William of Ockham (1285–1347) is perhaps the most profound and certainly the most advanced thinker of his time. Like Scotus, he was interested in the nature of reality. He has believed that only individual phenomena exist. There is no distinction between essence and existence. Universals are mental concepts, abstractions from individuals by humans, which exist but only in their minds. He sought to view reality directly, unencumbered by classifications, which are constructions rather than observations of reality. Concepts such as number and species are not real. Theological beliefs are not provable, just a matter of faith. He refuted Aquinas's arguments for the existence of God. His evidence that there is influence at a distance, such as light and magnetism, refuted Aristotle. Discarding the intellectual armory of Aristotle and the scholastics proved unpopular. He also sought to understand knowledge, distinguishing between intuitive and abstract cognition, describing the process of inductive reasoning.

In the fourteenth century, Thomas Bradwardine (1290–1349) and a number of mathematicians in Merton College, Oxford, worked on the mathematics of motion. They corrected Aristotle and extended their work to motions not considered by Aristotle—velocity, acceleration, and deceleration. Bradwardine discovered the mean speed theorem, anticipating Galileo.

Jean Buridan (1295–1363) condemned the theory of multiple worlds and eternity of the world. God could have created many possible worlds but didn't. Once created, it cannot be changed. But he was known for his work on impetus theory, advancing on the work of Avicenna. Impetus was a function of the speed and weight of the projectile. The trajectory could be changed and terminated only by resistance of the medium in which the projectile moved or by a counterforce. He described that the acceleration of a falling body was accumulation of impetus. But the mathematics required to model trajectories, the calculus, had not been invented. Buridan believed that explanatory models useful in one domain could also prove useful in other domains and applied his impetus concept widely.

Nicole Oresme (1320–1382) proposed action at a distance. He also rejected Aristotle's four-cause explanation of change; all causes were immediate. What followed were efforts to correct Aristotle's theory of motion and create a more complete explanation. Astronomic observation improved the accuracy of the astronomic models of Aristotle and of Ptolemy. Nicholas of Cusa (1401–1464) claimed that stars were suns with planets, that the earth was not the center of the universe nor motionless, and that orbits were not circular. But his views were speculation, not based on observation or analysis. Then Copernicus published his solar-centric model of the planetary system, which was the central controversy of the next century.

COPERNICUS, KEPLER, GALILEO, AND NEWTON

The geocentric astronomy of Ptolemy was compatible with Christianity. Differences between Aristotelian cosmology and the Bible were avoided by separation of secular and sacred domains. But the idea that the earth was not the center of the cosmos and that there were other planets was such a threat to Christian cosmology that Copernicus (1473–1543) did not dare publish his model until near death. He rejected the geocentric astronomy of Aristotle and Ptolemy but retained many features of their models, such as circular orbits and constant motion. It was Kepler (1571–1630) who corrected these errors and discovered elliptical orbits and the three laws of planetary motion. Although mathematics was accepted as a means of describing and measuring phenomena, it was not widely accepted as a method of proof. Kepler hypothesized a force analogous to magnetism issuing from the sun, acting at a distance, to explain the orbits of the planets.

It was Galileo (1564–1642) who terminally confirmed the Copernicus-Kepler model with his telescope. Discovery of the moons of Jupiter made it impossible to maintain that the earth was stationary.

Visual evidence of other planets and moons could not be refuted, but it could be ignored and forbidden. Confirmation of a heliocentric model advanced a secular worldview and ended the dominance of the clergy in the natural sciences. What it changed was religion. They paved the way for Newton. It was Newton who called Kepler's force gravity.

Galileo contributed significantly to the physics of motion through his experiments with inclined planes and falling bodies. He proved Aristotle wrong and incomplete, undermining the authority of Aristotle as Aquinas had done to that of Plato. Experimental evidence could only be challenged by contrary evidence. There was no going back to Aristotle or Ptolemy. His discovery of the moons of Jupiter ended any pretense that the earth was the center of the solar system. His experiments with falling bodies refuted Aristotle and contributed to the theory of gravity. But he did not reject Aristotle so much as correct and extend his physics of motion. Aristotle had some things right. His cosmos was materialist, constructed bottom up, causal, and agency-free, compatible with scientific thinking in the future.

Newton's accomplishments cannot be overstated. He extended Galileo's reasoning from the sun to the solar system and the entire cosmos, defining gravity as a function of mass. He also revolutionized our knowledge of light. What a dramatic change in one lifetime from the persecution of Galileo to the acclamation of Newton (1642–1727), whose *Principia* was published in 1686, a mere 44 years after Galileo's death, in both Protestant and Catholic countries. Culture and civilization had changed in the 143 years since Copernicus published in 1543 and Newton in 1686. To this subject, we shall turn. But first, some perspective on Galileo and Newton.

They were great discoverers, but they were also inventors. Newton's great invention was the calculus, but he also invented the reflecting telescope and a cat door. Galileo invented a hydrostatic balance, a thermometer, and a trigonometric military compass and made major improvements in a number of mechanisms, including the water pump, pendulum clock, and the telescope. Incidentally, both of them made their own telescopes. Galileo was in the tradition of Archimedes, the greatest of the Greek mathematician/engineers. Newton was different, perhaps unique, or the remote descendant of a Pythagoras who sought the mathematical structure of reality and set it to music.

There was also a dramatic change in the church. The general Council of Trent ended the year of Copernicus's death. It was the final recognition of Protestantism as a Christian alternative to the Catholic Church. Somehow minds changed as horizons widened. The cognitive change among scholastics was accompanied by cultural change in the society.

The Scientific Revolution was the product of a creative minority—a very small minority. What of the great society in which it was embedded? We have noted that the opposition faced by Copernicus, Kepler, and Galileo had largely vanished by the time of Newton. What else was going on in Europe?

There was another creative minority—the inventors. The scholastics were discoverers, but there was accelerated invention in their time. In the twelfth century, when scholastics began to stress reason as the means to truth, others were initiating an early industrial revolution. Roger Bacon scanned the stars with a spyglass, which evolved into a key scientific instrument in the hands of Galileo, an early example of collaboration of science and technology.

The age of geographic discovery opened people's eyes and minds to novelty. It might have been propitiated by the Crusades, but initiated by the Portuguese, Henry the Navigator. The discovery of America by Columbus was followed by Vasco da Gama's voyage around Africa to India in 1498 and Cabral's discovery of Brazil in 1500. In just eight years, Europe began its world dominion. Spanish and Portuguese were followed soon enough by the Dutch, British, and French.

EARLY INDUSTRIAL REVOLUTION

The early scientific evolution that started perhaps with Anselm and led to the discoveries of Copernicus, Kepler, Galileo, and Newton had its counterpart in the realm of problem-solving invention.

From the fall of the Roman Empire to the twelfth century, very little was invented in Europe. Only the horse collar, in use around

800, was of some significance. The early Industrial Revolution started symbolically with the flying buttress, invented in 1137, leading to a Gothic cathedral-building competition across Europe. The other signal invention in the early 1200s was in optics—spyglasses and spectacles. These were not simple inventions; they implied understanding of mechanics and of optics. Early revolutions in invention and in reasoning and discovery started almost simultaneously. By the fourteenth century, European inventions outnumbered the rest of the world and retained this dominance centuries to the twentieth century.

There were early outside influences. Chinese inventions of paper and gunpowder came to Europe via Islam. The Crusades may have hastened their transmission to Europe in around 1200, but they did not explain their accelerated development. In little more than two centuries, the Europeans were in advance of both Islam and China. Europeans used cannon in battle in 1346. Soon they developed the harquebus in 1450 and then the rifle in 1520. The Chinese never developed small arms but built the biggest cannon in history in terms of bore and powder change. It had no range, accuracy, or mobility, but it was loud. How? Why did this happen? Gunpowder was concentrated power. Part of the answer is that scholastics studied the physics of impetus and missile trajectories. Others, some of whom were graduates of the same universities, produced weapons of increasing range and accuracy. They were also prompt in transferring the concept of concentrated power to the domains of construction, mining, and quarrying.

The printing press was one of the greatest inventions. Gutenberg got the credit; he was first but in a crowded field. It was the third step in the revolution of information, the first being language and the second being script. It dominated for six hundred years until the inventions of the personal computer and the Internet. Revolutions in information take much time to achieve their potential, and their achievement is intangible; hence, they are underrated compared with a steam engine, whose consequences are immediate and tangible.

One reason why there were several individuals in more than one country working on the invention of the printing press was that the Catholic Church required that cathedrals and many other religious organizations have schools and that these schools be open to the poor. Many universities were also open well before Gutenberg. So there was a large and growing demand for written material. Spare the sheep. Soon enough, improved printing machines were churning out diverse reading material in several languages. Would there have been an industrial revolution three centuries later without the printing press? I think not.

The Gutenberg printing press was a cognitive evolution. Printing on paper has made knowledge far more accessible than had it been written on papyrus and parchment. It greatly increased literacy. As noted earlier, reading and writing are exercises in abstraction. They change minds and promote logical thinking, if not the ability to understand and persuade.

Another significant technological trajectory was optics. It was studied in antiquity by the Greeks and later by Islamic scholars. The magnifying property of glass (and water) was known, but little use was made of it. Glass in those days was not clear but amber or green. Suddenly, in the early thirteenth century, there were spyglasses and eyeglasses. Colorless glass was invented in 1291. Roger Bacon and others advanced the study of optics, but the technological trajectory was slow compared with gunpowder or paper. There was less urgency, less public demand. Spyglasses were military inventions for everyday use for information. Galileo's telescope was in 1609, the compound microscope in 1590; they were inventions serving as instruments of discovery. The telescope terminated any pretense that the earth was the center of the solar system. The microscope opened up vast new worlds to explore. These two inventions made a scientific revolution unavoidable.

The measurement of time was important for cooperative endeavor, for organized society. Mechanical town clocks were invented in the 1300s, pocket watches in 1504. The mainspring in 1470 and the pendulum in 1641 were improvements in accuracy. Town clocks and pocket watches measured time in hours and minutes. But the scientific study of motion the law of falling bodies, acceleration, and deceleration required much greater precision.

The measurement of space was essential for navigation. The compass and the astrolabe were important instruments. So was the compilation of detailed star charts. Discovery of ocean currents and winds were important for navigation in particular regions. So were improvements in the design and structure of seagoing ships. Other measuring instruments invented included the thermometer and the barometer.

The inventions mentioned are not fully representative of the whole range of inventive activity up to Galileo and the Scientific Revolution. The Industrial Revolution was really a mechanical revolution, about physics. During the early period, there were numerous discoveries and inventions in chemistry, biology, and medicine and other subjects. Some contributed to the public health revolution that followed the industrial or mechanical evolution. But a scientific revolution would not have been generated by biology or chemistry; it had to be physics.

Mechanical inventions were numerous and in every field of endeavor in the centuries immediately preceding the official dawn of the Industrial Revolution. Technology trajectories were speedy, and there were instances of technology transfer between domains. Another characteristic of early inventions was a growing linkage of discovery and invention. The influence of inventions on discovery, of technology on science, is clear; that of discoveries on inventions is more speculative. The telescope and microscope illustrate both relations. In later stages, it is science or discovery that tends to lead, with technology or inventions as consequence.

What the rapid technological trajectories and the ability to transfer technology to different domains had in common with the advances in discovery was abstraction and generalization. Optical instruments were about magnification, gunpowder was concentrated energy, the compass was about location, and the printing press was about publication. The falling apple exemplified gravity. This ability seemed analogous to Plato's world of ideas and their representation but viewed backwards. The form generated the idea.

Who were the inventors of mechanical devices? Discovery may have been the province of clergy until Galileo, but invention was always dominated by laymen. They were the work of educated laymen, whose education in the early centuries was largely in church schools. Their names are known in many cases. As in the case of scholastics, often several artisans, engineers were working on the same problems, sometimes together. Inventions were not isolated achievements but steps in a trajectory; the inventive process was never over.

Going back to change in attitudes from the prosecution of Galileo to the acclamation of Newton, some inventions had opened minds, especially printing. It greatly reduced the cost of learning for the literate and, by promoting literacy, increased the number of people who were knowledgeable in any subject. But probably much more important was the impact of what is called the Age of Discovery (not the laws of nature but new lands, peoples, products, and practices). Another indicator of attitude change was the beginning of patent law in fifteenth-century Venice, granting temporary monopolies to inventors.

Finally, the most important trajectory of them all—steam as a source of power—was revived. Steam had been used by the Greeks to open heavy temple doors and by the Chinese to blow whistles. The Greeks understood steam as power; the Chinese did not. The Savery pump of 1698 was soon displaced by the Newcomen engine of 1712, forerunner of the Watt steam engine, centerpiece of the Industrial (mechanical) Revolution.

AGE OF DISCOVERY

The Vikings discovered an uninhabited Iceland in 870 and settled it, a sparsely populated Greenland, and North America, where settlement failed. They were settlers, and their discoveries had no impact on Europe. They were also raiders who destroyed large libraries of monasteries in Ireland.

The Crusades were not discoveries but learning experiences. The intellectual achievements of the Greeks, Islamic scholars, and India were for the clergy. Spices, sugar, and luxury goods from China and other countries were for those who could afford them.

The conventional beginning date of the Age of Discovery was the founding in 1418 by Prince Henry of Portugal of a navigation and exploration center at Sagres. Discovery at that time meant geographic exploration and the knowledge gained of new peoples, products, and cultures. Initially, the mission was the exploration of the west coast of

Africa. It found products it could export to Europe, and in 1441, Portugal initiated the slave trade. Exploration continued, combined with trade. But events in Asia—the Arabian dominance of sea routes from India and other sources of spices and the Ottoman conquest of Byzantium— turned minds to another purpose, an alternative trade route around Africa. Bartolomeu Dias rounded the Cape of Good Hope in 1488. Four years later, Columbus sought to reach India by sailing west. In 1498, Vasco da Gama sailed on to India. Exploration continued, now of the east coast of Africa, but trade became the dominant consideration. Then Cabral landed in Brazil in 1500. Those were eight spectacular years. European voyages of discovery were motivated by the desire for direct trade with Asia and by curiosity. Overseas empire came later with the discovery of the New World.

Sagres was not just a seaport. It was also a school, a workshop, and a research and development center, the first of its kind. Prince Henry employed cartographers, shipbuilders, and instrument makers. Sagres trained sailors and navigators, studied winds and ocean currents, and built ships, furthering knowledge of geography, mapmaking, and navigation. There was continuing change in the design of the caravel. Once the caravels began returning to Portugal with valuable cargo, it became necessary to redesign them to incorporate heavy cannon to protect them from pirates. Gunners were trained. Portuguese caravels were very fast, stable, maneuverable, and able to sail against the wind. Cannon were also improved in accuracy and range, although this was no doubt a by-product of inter-European warfare. Ships and firearms were the tools that converted small European nations into world empires overnight.

In 1509, Francisco de Almeida destroyed a huge combined Arab, Ottoman, Indian, and Venetian fleet at Diu. There were other decisive victories against much larger forces in the Arabian Sea, opening the way to India and China without the intermediation of Venice and the Arabs.

It is remarkable how swiftly the Spaniards were followed by the Portuguese and then the Dutch, English, and French in the Americas. The Portuguese in Asia were promptly followed by the Dutch, the English, the Spaniards, and the French. It was about trade and empire, with settlement a means, not an end. But the priests and monks who traveled to Asia and the Americas to convert the pagans were avid explorers of the lands and their peoples. The great European voyages of exploration and exploitation had multiple sponsors, not just the five nations. Columbus was an entrepreneur who first sought support from the Portuguese. Many of the explorers whose names survived in historical memory were entrepreneurs and private adventurers.

The early beginnings of the Industrial and Scientific Revolutions coincided with what would be known as the Age of Discovery and made it possible. The compass and the astrolabe informed on direction and location. Without superior ships and much better cannon, plus small arms, Europe would have failed in Asia. In America, without small arms, the Spanish would have met the fate of Vikings. They would have been overcome by far superior numbers. European traders and Jesuits would have had minimal impact. The key invention was gunpowder, invented in China and acquired from the Arabs.

The fundamental question, whether we think of technological advance or geographic exploration, was motivation. It was not the discoveries that mattered but who did the discovering, when, and why. The discovery of America and the exploitation of its resources gave Western Europe world dominance in almost every field of endeavor for the next four centuries. The five languages spoken on every continent in the twentieth century were all European. Linguistic dominance and its implications will increase in the twenty-first century as local languages and monosyllabic languages decline. Four centuries of dominance by two small and three middle-sized European countries over most of the world's population is not explainable by guns alone. Only one non-European nation managed to make it to the Industrial Revolution on its own in the second half of the nineteenth century, Japan, which was never colonized.

What the Age of Discovery contributed to the Industrial Revolution was resources. The sixteenth was a great century for Europe in some respects. There were spices, silks, and much else from Asia; slaves from Africa for its American colonies; and gold from America. Exploitation of the resources of the Americas and Africa, including its manpower, gave Europeans the disposable income to build empires. Most of the shipping and trade now became the work of private enterprises.

CULTURE CHANGE

The sixteenth century was a turning point in the civilization. The exploration of Africa started early, in 1418, but the big impact of discoveries on the minds of Europeans was the discovery of America. It was the concentration of discoveries of the Americas and of the passage to India in just a few years that kick-started a change in culture, a global perspective. What the discoveries generated was awareness of change, the expectation of change as the new normal.

All civilizations experienced change in particulars, but none had a sense of change in general, an abstract concept of change. They had no sense of the future as different from the present, of the present as different from the past. The future, like change, was about particulars.

Expectation

LePan (1989, 173–249) describes the birth of expectations of change—a sense of the future as different from the past or present. He surveyed the plots of leading literary works from the twelfth century onward. At first, stories and dramas were blood and thunder, a series of episodes or particulars whose sequence bordered on the arbitrary. They offered little scope for reasoning. The plots lacked complex chains of causation and did not recognize the difference between belief and experience, between words and objects (22).

The reasoning was very much like China's. The prevalent interrelation was based on similarity; there was no causal connection. Nor was there awareness of contradiction. Gradually, a string of episodes evolved into a story with beginning and end and complex interrelations between events. Plots evolved into Shakespeare's plays, which were not isolated events but intricate, complex interrelations of motives, behavior, and consequences. They reflected the extension of the range of reasoning from the here and now to an extended range of time and space. A collection of discrete events was timeless. But a connection, an interrelationship, was historical; it can only exist in time. History was not a single-lane road. Plots had become analogous to the great voyages of discovery and exploration. By the late sixteenth century, the cognitive evolution was complete. The future had been invented. People were still jiving in the present, aware that past and future were different from present, accepting change as part of life.

The evolution of story plots is just one aspect of change in the concept of history. In the twelfth century, the Greek views of history prevailed. In the span of human memory, humans had advanced to a golden age, followed by regression. In the longer term, history was repetitive and static. The concept of history, like the story plots, evolved from static repetitiveness to a complex expectation of change. This evolution was initiated well before the discovery of America, which accelerated it. Initial impetus must have been the early Industrial Revolution. What had been a particular history of a city-state, a people, became the history of humanity. Jean Bodin (1530–1596), who rejected the golden age and regression view of history, proposed three successive stages of progression, characterized respectively by religion, sagacity, and war and invention (Bury 1957, 212–13, 37–41). This view of universal history went beyond expectation of change to expectation of progress. It was the idea that humans can be makers of history, not merely its subjects; they had choice, not destiny.

Time

The historical future must be measured in universal time. Sundials measure the daily cycle of the sun. Water clocks measure time day and night, rain or shine. Calendar time is based on the annual and daily cycles of the sun. It is concrete, providing specific information—holy days, festivals, planting time. It structures memory and recollection. But it is static and repetitive. Calendar time is for reporting and representation, not for the imagination.

As Europeans have adopted a view of history as continuous change, they have developed a corresponding sense of time. Its instrument was the mechanical clock. Clock time is abstract time, empty time, time to be filled. It promotes future orientation and is required by those who are future oriented. In the West, it is to be filled by choice. In some other cultures, by destiny, there is no choice. Everywhere, it brings order to urban society. The town clock was the symbol of change: it measured the future. Europeans were obsessed with precise time measurement. Living and working together requires time-sharing. Punctuality was cement for progress in work, transportation, and communication.

Timekeeping had to be standardized. The twelve-month year and double-twelve day were adopted from Babylonia and Egypt, the seven-day week from the Bible. Daybreak varies by season and location. Midnight varies only East and West. But when does the year begin? It is not the shortest day, January 21, but the day of baptism.

And there was need to synchronize. A benchmark year had to be adopted so that dates across the globe could be matched. Thus, the BC-AD system was adopted. The year zero is missing. Now historians have adopted a different label, same benchmark, BCE and CE. For Muslims, the benchmark year is 621. All this has taken many years.

Awareness of history as universal and comprising multiple complex interconnections invites explanation. It opens the door for causal reasoning. Precise timing of events creates opportunities to observe and search for patterns and learn from experience. We may be able to identify and distinguish between coincidence, correlations, and causal relations of historic times.

Progress

The culture of expectations required future orientation, but it had no content or direction. Expectation of change was not prediction. It implied uncertainty. Soon it evolved into directional change, the expectation of progress, limiting the range of uncertainty. It was experience; the early Industrial Revolution and the discovery of America in particular gave the expectation of change an upward bent.

Progress is a process with many meanings. For scholars, it is knowledge, which means discovery. For craftsmen, progress means improvement in production process or product, invention. Each achievement is regarded not as complete, a thing in itself, but a step in an interminate series of advances in knowledge and utility or further discovery and invention.

Roger Bacon was perhaps the first scholar with an understanding of progress. He was motivated by the translations of the Greek classics, plus Islamic contributions, at the time, but his writings had little influence. It was Francis Bacon (1561–1626) who propagated the idea of progress at a time when Europe itself had forged ahead of other civilizations. He was a contemporary of Galileo. He stressed experiment in the search for knowledge and assumed that discovery was of benefit to humanity. But he did not extend the idea of progress to history. The present age was regressive, and ideal societies were in remote lands, not a distant future. This perspective was not implausible at a time when many new lands and peoples, some advanced and affluent, had been discovered. But he also clung to the geocentric model of the cosmos. It was not until 1770 that Louis-Sébastien Mercier placed the ideal society in the distant future (Bury 1955, 193–95).

It was René Descartes (1596–1680) who exemplified the idea of scientific progress, with the qualification that the advance of knowledge should be to the benefit of humanity (Bury 1955, 50–51, 64–65). He stressed the invariability of the laws of nature and the need for rigor in scientific research. His idea of progress was widely accepted. Later writers differed primarily in priorities of their research agenda and in their visions of the future.

Utilitarianism was about invention rather than discovery. The abbé de Saint-Pierre went so far as to belittle the accomplishments of Newton and the cathedral of Notre-Dame (Bury 1955, 129).

Much of J. B. Bury's description refers to a wide range of concepts of progress, not all of which are consistent with the ideal of scientific and technical progress. Institutional progress is expected to attain perfection, no more change. Perfectibility of human nature or behavior also has limits. Progress in discovery and invention has a different motivation and no end point to our knowledge. Behavior and institutions, rather than beliefs about them, are relevant as climate for discovery and invention.

Bury's analysis of the idea of scientific progress is about discovery. Scientific progress is a search for knowledge that never ends. Each advance is but a step in the long journey. And the search is undertaken for its own sake. Most inventors do not meet these standards. They do not invent for the sake of knowledge but for practical uses and personal profit. There is a subconscious assumption that knowledge is of benefit to mankind, a motivation not found among the Greek philosophers.

Bury's analysis of the development of the idea of progress can be viewed as the idea of history, initially from the particular to the universal and then adding stages such as Vico and structure, Malthus and subsistence, Darwin and evolution. His own concept of historical progress is, first, the Copernican revolution that dethroned the belief in predestination and, second, the Darwinian theory of evolution that dethroned the human species. But his epilogue warns us that the idea of progress may not be the final word on historical thinking. What comes after?

Zilsel (1957, 265–76) argues that the idea of progress in invention originated with craftsmen and artisans, not with scholars. The accelerated trajectories of invention already noted are evidence of a sense of sequential development rather than isolated particular inventions. This leadership is debatable. Scholars were more discoverers than inventors; progress to them meant knowledge, not artifacts or processes. Discovery was for scholars; invention was for craftsmen and artisans, many of whom would be called architects and engineers today. Motivations and achievements were different. The early Industrial Revolution slightly anteceded the early Scientific Revolution. Gutenberg was ninety-nine years ahead of Copernicus.

Zilsel's (259–62) main evidence of the idea of progress is the treatises written by master artisans describing their methods and detailing their knowledge for the benefit of the next generation of artisans who might, in turn, further advance their work. An early treatise, on painting, was published by a painter circa 1400. Others in the sixteenth century were on architecture, gun making, gunnery, and measuring instruments.

This behavior represented a major change in status and attitudes of artisans. Traditionally, status was based on lineage, backward-looking master-apprentice relation. Now it became achievement, performance, and present and future orientation. The master-apprentice model was secretive; the achievement model was the reverse. Zilsel (1957, 257) credits the rise of capitalism for the change. Artisans now labored in workshops together with other artisans rather than in isolation. They collaborated and competed with one another. Status had to be on the basis of performance. He also credited the antiauthoritarianism of the Reformation.

The expectation of change, which evolved into the belief in progress, accommodated the Scientific and Industrial Revolutions, but they did not provide the impetus. That came not from belief but from demand—demand for novelty. The Greeks were reported by Plato to have a passion for novelty by contrast with the Egyptians. But they had no concept of change. The future was repetition of the past. There was acceptance of novelties, not demand for novelty. Some of the Athenian philosophers sought novel ideas not for their own sake but in their quest for order, not for novelty. There was demand or appreciation of particular novelties—mechanical toys, self-opening temple doors, not for novelty. They had no concept of change or progress. The difference between novelties and novelty was between the new and the different, between particulars and universals.

China illustrated the difference between novelties and novelty. The mandarins were adamantly opposed to change and would have been horrified by the perpetual change implied in the idea of progress. But they had a strong demand for novelties—luxury goods—to exhibit their wealth and distinguish themselves from others. Novelties were incidental.

Demand for novelty is demand for change, without specifying direction or content. It implies high tolerance for risk and uncertainty. It does not require belief in progress, although it is associated with it. The relation between novelty and progress is not analogy but ambivalence. The experience of novelty is not a sequential process. Change is the process; novelty is the product. It is qualitative change.

Thorndike (1957, 443–57) attributed the recognition of novelty in the seventeenth century to the great geographic discoveries and the Scientific Revolution. "New" was no longer contrasted to "old," a time sequence, but to "customary," a qualitative difference.

The evolution of cognition and culture—could it have been autonomous? What can be said about explanation? The Age of Discovery, the fifteenth and sixteenth centuries, overlapped the early Industrial Revolution, notably the Gutenberg press, 1454; Copernicus and the beginning of the Scientific Revolution, 1543; and the Reformation, 1517. Simply ordering the initial dates for each of the major events tell us little about their impact over generations and centuries.

As to the idea of progress, it was the discoveries, both scientific and geographical, that gave the sense of the future an upward trend, predisposing the people to adopt the findings of Newton and steam power still two centuries away. The geographic discoveries of Columbus and others were a panorama of novelty; they must be held accountable for the demand for novelty in the sixteenth century. But the earliest step in the evolution of culture was the expectation of change. It was well on its way to completion before the major events of the sixteenth century. Shakespeare was already writing late in the century.

The search for explanation, whether the dominance of reason or the belief in change, has to stop somewhere. There were progenitors of the expectation of change, including Epicurus. Individuals are born in every civilization who are ahead of their times. Most of them are ignored or condemned. But in twelfth century, Europe minds were prepared to listen and learn.

It was the expectation of change, the idea of progress, the desire for novelty shared by the educated population that provided the demand for discovery and invention. The supply side was already in place. It was the evolution of Christianity. The reliance on reasoning rather than revelation as the search for truth started with St. Anselm, preceded by a millennium of argument of theological subjects analogous to the secular subjects that preoccupied Athenian philosophers. The European clergy advanced to separation of the spheres of reason and faith. Aquinas persuaded most clergy to adopt the secular cosmology of Aristotle. The shift from a top-down to a bottom-up concept of creation encouraged observation and experimentation, culminating in the work of Galileo and Newton.

The church did not discourage discussion, even though it disagreed with some of the views. It accepted the right to reason. The universities were independent and open to diverse opinions, Copernicus aside. Clergy with dissident views were allowed to teach and remained on the payroll.

There was also an early mechanical revolution, whose creators were not clergy but were educated in church schools. The rise of science and of technology had common roots—invention. Technological trajectories were rapid, and so was transfer of technology from its original domain to others.

The current civilization is one of a kind. It differs from all others in two key respects. First, it achieved a scientific revolution; there is no marching in place or return to the past. Second, it developed an expectation of change, a culture of progress, and a demand for novelty. There is no precedent, no basis for comparison. It is a new stage in the history of humanity. But is civilization almost over? Is progress self-limiting?

Why England?

Margaret Jacob's (1997) *Scientific Culture and the Making of the Industrial West* provides a detailed explanation of why, initially, the Industrial Revolution was British. England had lagged behind the continent in the seventeenth century but now forged ahead. It can be summarized in terms of the mind-set of the scientists, the education and training of the craftsmen who did the inventing, the society in which they worked, and its structure and culture that encouraged enterprise.

British scientists and scholars followed the cosmology of Newton, which was mechanical. Most of the continent followed the cosmology of Descartes, which was mathematical. Descartes believed that all the cosmos was matter, that motion was relative (Schlagel 1996, 192–98). But in the absence of space, motion was impossible. His cosmos was material and inert. The idea of relative motion was a semiorganic concept of the cosmos. The difference between the two was that of abstraction versus subtraction. Newton abstracted the core essence of the cosmos. It was the cosmic constitution that all mechanical inventions must follow. Descartes subtracted this essence. No consequences followed from the remainder.

Thus, in much of the continent (the Netherlands was an exception), there was a disconnect between scientists and mechanical workers. The Cartesians devoted little attention to devices intended for industrial applications despite Descartes's utilitarianism. Descartes insisted on certainty in scientific research, by which he meant deductive reasoning. He doubted the evidence of the senses and rejected Galileo's experiments of motion (Schlagel 1995, 174) and the empirical methods prevailing among artisans.

In England, science was not a quest for knowledge for its own sake but for the benefit of mankind. Francis Bacon (1561–1626) propagated science as practical benefit and foresaw indefinite progress in scientific achievement (Jacob 1997, 50–52).

The Protestant idea of progress focused on material gains. There was another version of progress that was utopian—millenarians. Puritans, in particular, viewed progress more in religious than secular terms. Progress was toward perfection of man and society. It had an end.

There was another difference between the British and much of the continent. The British scientists were empirical. They did believe in the scientific method but also in the less rigorous experimentation of creative engineers and artisans that generated discoveries and much of the invention. On the continent, concern for scientific rigor rejected or ignored the trial-and-error creativity of the craftsmen. During the French Revolution of 1789, the craftsmen reciprocated the disregard. The court that ordered the decapitation of the great chemist Lavoisier declared, "La republique n'a pas besoin de savants, ni de chimistes."

In England, there was a bridge between scientist and craftsman; on the continent, there was a gulf. Scientists in England, in turn, were not averse to hands-on work themselves. Newton made his own telescope. Scholars in Catholic jurisdictions were constrained in their speech, if not in their thinking, by memories of the condemnation of Galileo and reluctance to antagonize the Catholic Church. In Protestant countries, there were no inhibitions.

The engineers, mechanics, and other craftsmen in England were better educated and more knowledgeable than those on the continent. Their practical experience was combined with theoretical understanding. (James Watt was admitted to the Royal Society.) They were largely self-taught by reading textbooks available on mechanics and on other areas of technology (Jacob 1997, 106, 109–10). These texts linked theory and practice. The best mechanics and engineers understood the scientists. They were the ones who gave England a head start. But it was the environment that gave England a lasting advantage. Authority, faith, and economy were all propitious.

The society in which the scientists and artisans worked experienced dramatic change in the sixteenth and seventeenth centuries. In the sixteenth, it was the Protestant Reformation, especially in Scotland. Starting in 1642, there was civil war between the monarchy and the Parliament. The monarchy was overthrown. An antiauthoritarian Parliament ruled, followed by Cromwell's Protectorate. The monarchy was reinstated in 1660.

The struggle for power was also a contest of religions. The Stuart dynasty favored the Catholic Church; Parliament favored Protestantism. Finally, in 1688, the so-called Glorious Revolution enthroned a new dynasty, William and Mary, under the condition that it must seek the consent of Parliament. That same year, a bill of rights was approved. It was light monarchy. Protestantism and democracy gained the upper hand. Meanwhile, the Anglican Church—which had deep early roots distinguishing it from Rome—evolved slowly, approximating a balance or compromise between Protestantism and Rome. In 1776, Parliament formally separated the Anglican Church from Rome. Authority was secular and democratic.

England was a single nation. In the seventeenth and eighteenth centuries, it had a large market at home, a worldwide empire, and trade with much of the world. With democracy, the private sector of the economy was dominant and autonomous. The law recognized legal persons apart from the individuals involved in partnerships and corporations, encouraging accumulation of capital. There was a patent law to promote and reward invention. Stress on economic progress elevated the status of business.

On one hand, there was a large market for new products and on the other the resources—capital, enterprise, and organization—to create and produce such products. Craft shops became industrial firms. James Watt did not simply patent an engine. His firm manufactured engines, installed them at the site of the buyer, continued improving its performance, and restructured it for new uses and new industries.

Mechanical inventions are laborsaving devices. In England, the steam engine replaced artisans with machine tenders. But the lower cost of production allowed England to replace imports with its own products and export items it had not exported before. It exported unemployment. But great inventions can create jobs. Gutenberg's press displaced innumerable scribes and saved many sheep. But literacy and book printing more than compensated for this loss. The same was true of the steam engine.

The Reformation was credited by R. H. Tawney and others with the growth of capitalism and acceleration of the Scientific and Industrial Revolutions. There was no implication that, otherwise, there would not have been such progress. When Luther started his rebellion in 1517, Copernicus had already written his book, which was not published until 1542, just before the final separation of Lutheranism from the Catholic Church in 1543, the end of the general Council of Trent. The Catholic Church was on the defensive, no longer the only Christian church in Europe, and facing demotion from a cosmic to a planetary faith. What Protestantism helped explain was the technological leadership of the countries that adopted it. The effect of Protestantism on attitude changes was the elimination of the power of the Catholic Church to impose its views and discourage the dissemination of contrary views. It was also the democratization of society that reduced the power of the state over the e economy, liberating capital and enterprise. This process also occurred in Europe but later.

In terms of impact on discovery and invention, the Reformation was not about doctrine but about authority. It was the corruption of the leadership that motivated Luther. He eliminated the hierarchy of the church. Authority became bottom up and democratic. The domain of the Lutheran Church was strictly spiritual. Limits on authority favored growth of competitive capitalism and private investment in new technology. Minds were ready. The belief in change and progress was in place.

In most of Europe, the Catholic Church remained dominant. Memories of the condemnation of Galileo intimidated scientific thinking. An authoritarian state was a counterforce to the Catholic Church, limiting the scope and autonomy of the private sector. Most of the continent was fragmented into numerous small jurisdictions, monarchies, principalities, and cities. Only France was a large nation under a single government. It also had an empire.

In France, scientific education and knowledge were monopolized by the academies, which had no interest in the work or methods of the artisan inventors. Nor were French entrepreneurs collaborators with mechanics and engineers and new technologies. Introduction of the Watt steam engine was delayed at least ten years, and then it was copied illegally (Jacob 1997, 173–74). During the revolution of 1789, the Jacobins destroyed the scientific academies and executed many of their leaders. After the revolution, the French sought to copy the British approach, but the artisans and mechanics needed had to be trained first. Chaptal, minister of the interior under Napoleon, was a scientist who promoted applied science and mechanical knowledge. He reformed education and advocated private enterprise. However, the state controlled engineering. Scientists served the state. So it was more bureaucracy than enterprise. But foreign competition stimulated education reform (Jacob 1977, 178–84).

INDUSTRIAL REVOLUTION

Steam power had been developed by the Greeks to open heavy temple doors and by the Chinese to blow whistles, but nothing came of them. The Archimedes screw powered by draft animals pumped water from mines into the seventeenth century. It could be turned on and off at will. A steam pump required continuity to perform efficiently; it required scale. England in the eighteenth century had developed scale in mining, textiles, and other industries. The use of steam for pumping water from mines was initiated in the early eighteenth century. By 1730, more than one hundred steam engines were in operation in England (Jacob 1997, 95).

The Industrial Revolution was dated 1775 because this was the steam engine far superior to the Newcomen engine it replaced. It was the big invention that generated cheap energy available anywhere. But rapid technical progress began much earlier. Printing, firearms, and optics involved few industries and had limited transferability, however important they may have been for the society. The difference between these very important inventions and the steam engine was domain. There was no limit to the domains in which it was applicable. It initiated many technological trajectories.

The Industrial Revolution really was a mechanical one, specifically the energy revolution. The steam engine did not encounter the opposition that bedeviled the Copernican theory. There were the Luddites, craftsmen who occasionally destroyed the machines that were depriving them of jobs and occupation. There were unintended consequences, such as the smokestack problem, which few welcomed.

Watt's achievement was not a single invention but a technological trajectory. His first patent was in 1969; he received another in 1782 and a patent for a locomotive in 1784. He adapted what was originally a pump to diverse industries and uses. Watt was an exemplar of the English (or Scottish) mechanic-engineer—self-taught—who worked with his hands and understood the scientific knowledge of his time.

Watt was both inventor and entrepreneur (Jacob 1997, 99–103). The earnings from sale of engines provided resources for partnership with Boulton, which not only invented but also manufactured steam engines and installed them. It was a predecessor of Edison's research enterprise focusing on uses of electricity. Patent rights in intellectual property were incentives to invent and, in Watt's case, helped finance additional inventions.

The effects were immediate. In less than half a century, it revolutionized transportation on land and at sea, never mind the textile industry. The first commercial steamboat was in 1787, the first commercial railroad in 1812. The nineteenth century was about production in place and transportation by rail and steamship.

The second great invention was on the same technological trajectory—electricity or the ability to transport energy by wire on any scale to any location or use. This, like the steam engine, created the possibility of numerous other inventions, using power far removed from its place of production, including another major technological trajectory—communication. Electricity was first used for the telegraph early in the nineteenth century. The Morse code telegraph was in 1838. The first central electric power station was in 1882. It had been made possible by Edison's invention of a workable light bulb in 1879. Then there was light twenty-four hours a day.

It was the twentieth century when delivery of energy by wire became ubiquitous. The electric light was the most important use throughout the economy, but it revolutionized communication and entertainment—telephone, radio, TV. It mechanized the household, releasing labor from home to workforce.

Energy storage eliminates wires, leading to the flashlight, the laptop, and the portable phone. In the past, storage was only hydropower in a few places, the power of gravity. Batteries provided portable storage. The final stage in this trajectory, now in progress, is the ability to store large amounts of energy for long periods at a low cost. It is a requirement for the replacement of steam power as the main source of energy by wind turbines and solar panels.

In the early nineteenth century, there were numerous attempts to develop an internal combustion engine vehicle, a locomotive that could ride on existing roads operated by a single individual. It could be a source of power on a small scale. In 1885, an engine developed by Benz powered the first motor vehicle. Twenty years later, the Wright brothers took flight. The internal combustion engine did not displace steam power. Initially, it supplemented the railroad but eventually largely displaced it and created air transportation. Nuclear energy was not part of the energy trajectory described above but an unintended by-product of an unrelated technology.

The revolution in energy had other consequences. It created great economies of scale that would eventually restructure the economy and society.

The Computer

The last half of the twentieth century belongs to the computer and the Internet. The computer itself was developed as a calculator. The earlier stages were all about processing of information. Its role in communication came later. More recent developments are also about storage and processing of information. The personal computer started as a personal printing machine, an advanced typewriter. It is the Internet that made it a post office, library, and café. The computer and the Internet provide information access anywhere, anytime. We are approaching end points in all these functions of the mechanical revolution.

The personal computer and the Internet have changed our lives. But the household economy is not counted in our national economic statistics. Productivity trends in the economy tell a different story. Productivity growth rates declined in the 1970s and 1980s. This is not surprising. The post-WWII decades were catch-up of new investment after fifteen years of the Great Depression and war. But growth rate has not recovered and has declined further in the past fifteen years (Baily and Montalbano 2017). A partial explanation is timing. It came late. We already had telephones, radio, and TV—multiple technologies for transmission and storage of information. Electricity is the common prerequisite. But evidence of gains in efficiency is all around us—in offices, shops, factory floors, and savings in labor, time, and costs. Why was there no surge in productivity?

I believe that this is a temporary adjustment problem. The workers in place had much to learn and much to forget. There are no national programs for training and certification in new computer-related skills. And there is overreach, premature or counterproductive computerization. It is early to draw conclusions on the long-run contribution to productivity or employment and occupational structure.

The virtue of the original computers was the ability to perform a very large number of simple calculations in a very short time, such as tracing the trajectory of a ballistic missile. Now this capability has a new mission. With the accumulation of massive amounts of data, it can search for sequence, repetitiveness, potential correlations, and patterns in the data and perhaps identify key variables.

AI (artificial intelligence) preceded the computer. Primitive AI has been with us for a century. It supplemented or replaced the need for persistent attention. The fire alarm is alert twenty-four hours a day. In hospitals, a more complicated AI keeps track of vital signs of patients and alerts medical personnel of any major deviation. Self-driving cars are a more complicated means of replacing human attention and stimulus response.

Spell-check on my computer is AI. It substitutes for human attention but also for human memory. Perpetual attention and perfect memory are useful for learning. They are cognitive inputs, but they are not reasoning or cognitive outputs. Spell-check does not replace my ability to write. It is a poor grammarian. It cannot tell which preposition is correct and the meaning of a manuscript; for that, it must identify and understand the sentence. If I misspell "buy" with "by," will it know? Can it correct it? Should I fail to punctuate, can it determine which series of words is a sentence? That requires a deep understanding of language. Most thought is subvocal speech.

AI is mechanism, bound by the laws of physics. Its "reasoning" is a statistical approximation of human reasoning. Words and ideas are not things in themselves, mathematically expressible and manipulable. They are relational. Speech is biologic and organic. AI's translation ability depends on the structure of the language. If it is indicative or analytic, it is possible because the relation of each noun and verb to the rest of the sentence is specified by prepositions, conjunctions, and so on. But for agglutinative languages, either there are no relational clues or, like Latin cases, they have multiple potential meanings. Monosyllabic languages are near impossible to computerize.

What else or more? How much can a binary sequential machine do cognitively? In mechanics, it should be able to do many, if not most, analytical tasks. But what outside mechanics? Induction perhaps? Synthesis, no. Current propaganda is part of the culture of futurism, the demand for novelty, the desire to live in the future. This book is not the place for fortune-telling. Consider the possibility that the AI domain is limited, that much of what is achievable has already been achieved.

It should be noted that all these major inventions were inevitable. A particular individual may be first to invent or to patent, but in every case, there were several, often many others, in several countries working on the same problem and close behind.

Inventions have life spans. Many early inventions lasted for millennia. Is seven centuries the span of the printing press? Since the Industrial Revolution, the life expectancy of inventions has been greatly compressed. Within a century, they are barely recognizable, if not replaced altogether. It was only sixty-four years from the first manned flight to landing a man on the moon.

The Three Revolutions

The Industrial Revolution was, strictly speaking, a mechanical revolution. It was one of three nearly simultaneous revolutions, the others being public health, which led to a near doubling of life expectancy and rapid population growth, and an agricultural revolution, which fed and clothed this growing population. The sequence was critical.

The mechanical revolution reduced cost of energy. Costs of production plunged, a cumulative effect throughout the economy. It transformed the service and household economies as well as industry. Potential per capita income soared. By itself, the mechanical revolution would have resulted in a modest decline in infant mortality, a modest increase in population growth. Had the public health revolution come first, there would have been a large decline in infant and child mortality, rapid population growth, and a drop in per capita income and starvation.

Had the agricultural revolution come first, there would have been some increase in per capita income, but transportation of farm products and their processing would remain slow and costly. The economy would have stagnated at a somewhat higher level of income.

The agricultural revolution required inputs from the mechanical revolution, cheap transportation; a public health revolution required biological and chemical knowledge rather than mechanisms.

With all three revolutions, the course of history depended on which came first, the decline in mortality or the increase in agricultural productivity. The sequence varied from country to country, but international trade minimized the effect of differences in sequence. The industrial and agricultural revolutions should precede public health, indirectly promoting it. Foreign aid had often failed because it ignored this sequence.

Agriculture

Estimates of agricultural output per agricultural worker showed little trend between 1300 and 1600 but soared thereafter in England and the Netherlands but trended down to 1800 for France, Belgium, and Spain (Allen 1988, 20–21).

Productivity of farmland globally had been rising slowly. Draft animals had been adopted for plowing. Selective breeding converted wild plants into better sources of food and fiber and wild animals into food and sources of power. But chemical and biological knowledge lagged. Another gain in productivity was the spread of maize, potatoes, and cassava—three of the highest-calorie yield crops in the world—from the Americas. European settlers brought large tracts of wild land under cultivation. The African slave trade converted subsistence farming into large plantations, producing for export.

But it was the sharp decline in transport costs of rail and steamship that most lowered costs to the consumer. Only in the twentieth century did farm costs decline as internal combustion machinery was adapted to farm use. It is not possible to quantify the agricultural output of food, fiber, and pastures and feed of all the animals we would eat. But output can be related to population.

World population was around one billion for centuries before the Industrial Revolution. It increased to 1.6 billion in the nineteenth century and more than quadrupled to 7.0 billion in the twentieth. Meanwhile, per capita income increased. So supply of food and fiber must have grown even more rapidly. In the nineteenth century, most of the increase in agricultural output was attributable to growth of land under cultivation and pasture, especially in North America. In the twentieth century, most of the huge increase in agricultural output was in productivity, yield per acre attributable to growth of knowledge of plant genetics, soil chemistry, and use of pesticides and of fertilizers. Humans were better fed at the end than in the beginning of the century.

Health

Large gains in public health could be independent of the Industrial Revolution. Existing knowledge of safe drinking water, sewage disposal, and pest control only needed implementation. World population remained one billion people for centuries until the nineteenth century. Europe did not do much better, although it experienced the Black Death, wars, and emigration. Since fertility rates remained very high throughout this period, clearly, infant, child, and maternal mortality remained very high. In the nineteenth century, world population grew to 1.6 billion and quadrupled in the twentieth. The large declines in infant mortality were from 1870, well after the mechanical revolution had transformed the economy. Data did not exist that would permit allocation of this decline to particular causes. This was a time of rapid urbanization, and that alone may have been the major explanation. It was public health, not private medicine.

It was urbanization that created a social need for disease prevention, notably Rome. There were aqueducts to deliver clean water, sewers for disposal, and public baths for hygiene. But cities were also subject to the spread of infectious diseases. The causes of such disease, their methods of transmission, were unknown. The only policy devised, quarantine, was initiated in the fourteenth century and persisted to the twentieth.

Galen's remained the principal medical text into the sixteenth century, plus apothecary resources collected by Islam and some diagnostic findings. Paracelsus (1494–1541) advanced from Galen's taxonomy of four humors to a chemical taxonomy of elements and compounds that were causes of illness and cures for illness. But it was Vesalius (1514–1564) whose careful dissection of human corpses advanced on the Greeks, who based anatomy mainly on animal dissections. He also corrected several errors Galen had made. Harvey (1578–1657) provided a complete description of the circulation of blood to the brain and heart and its properties. The microscope was the key invention leading to the germ theory of disease. Antoni van Leeuwenhoek (1632–1723), with a microscope of his own design, was able to identify blood cells, muscle fibers, and other components of anatomy. He discovered bacteria and other microorganisms in 1674. These findings were advances in understanding, advances in health care; prevention and treatment would come later. James Lind, by careful observation, learned in 1754 that scurvy could be cured or prevented by citrus juice; now we know it was a vitamin C deficiency of sailors long at sea.

The first vaccine, Jenner's for smallpox in 1796, was the beginning of a major progress in prevention. Pasteur invented vaccines for cholera in 1897, followed by anthrax and tetanus. Then came the Salk vaccine for polio. One man, Maurice Hilleman, starting in the early 1940s, developed more than forty vaccines, some of which were for animals, including measles, mumps, chicken pox, pneumonia, meningitis, and hepatitis. But his greatest achievement in terms of lives saved was the development of an influenza vaccine during the influenza pandemic of 1957. These most recent vaccines led to an abrupt decline in infant mortality in the second half of the twentieth century. Other important preventive inventions were industrial rather than individual—the pasteurization of milk in 1864, chlorination of water supply in 1893.

The most important medical discovery/invention of the twentieth century was penicillin by Fleming as treatment of infectious diseases and the subsequent antibiotic revolution. It boosted longevity for the population of retirement age.

The public health and agricultural revolutions, described above, are mainly applications of biology. Progress in biology has been episodic rather than systematic. The discovery of the chemical structure of DNA by James Watson and Francis Crick in 1953 may be said to correspond in biology to the Copernican revolution in physics. Now there is structure in the search for knowledge. There will be great gains in human health, but the future is speculation, not prediction.

The alchemist goal of the twenty-first and subsequent centuries is not conversion of base metal into gold but the inheritance of acquired traits and of mind as well as brain. It will also be a form of immortality. The religious-minded would see this as vindication of divine justice, if not in this life, then in the lives of our descendants. It will, however, disintegrate the human species.

Increases in life expectancy were via lower infant mortality until WWII. Infant mortality had been over 200 per thousand in the early nineteenth century and was still over 100 at the end. By 1950, it had fallen to 29.2. Vaccination for childhood diseases helped drive it down to less than 7 today.

The great reduction of infant mortality mattered for population growth in the nineteenth and early twentieth centuries. It was public health, which is prevention more than medical care, both correlated with urbanization. Demographic data for the nineteenth century would not be good enough to tell us how much progress was attributable to new discoveries and inventions. The increase in longevity of the retirement-age population was a recent development post-WWII, mainly attributable to penicillin and other antibiotics.

The Americas were a safety valve for several European nations. Immigration to underpopulated lands precluded rapid population growth, and the agricultural output of many of the migrants increased food supply.

DISCOVERY AND INVENTION: THE SINE QUA NON

The conditions for discovery and invention discussed in previous chapters referred only to progress up to the Scientific and Industrial Revolutions. Europe alone went further, requiring additional explanation.

The ability for abstract reasoning—thinking in generalizations, beyond particulars—is required for discovery and for the rapid improvement and broad application of inventions. It is not needed for many particular, isolated inventions. Abstraction is a derivation of reality, not a figment of the imagination. The practice of abstraction is not genetic but acquired; it is mind, not brain. How this practice becomes widespread in some cultures but absent in others is the fundamental question. I do not believe in uncaused causes. A culture of argument and debate is propitiating; one of harmony and tranquility is discouraging. Cultures that engage in such practices have promise. Those that stress harmony and peace have pause. Alphabetic writing enables while logographic script precludes abstraction.

An atomistic concept of reality promotes abstract reasoning. The reverse, top-down or organic concept of reality, deters. It is the difference between a thing-in-itself concept of reality and a purely relational concept. One is relation as causal interaction; the other is relation as organic coherence—correlation.

Limitation of the scope of authority is also required for most discoveries and inventions. Democracy, or bottom-up authority, is not necessary and not always propitiating. Authority must be limited in scope, whatever the form of government. It is freedom that is essential. The state has been interested in invention only in a few domains. These are the supply-side conditions for discovery and invention.

Preoccupation with the past, its glorification, greatly discouraged both discovery and invention, which are departures from that past. What was missing in all past civilizations was the future, the belief that it would be different from the past. There was no expectation of change.

Since the Scientific and Industrial Revolutions, there are additional conditions for continued discovery and invention. First, the role of government has changed. Its support is now essential for much discovery. Second, demand has become essential for most inventions. In both cases, the requirement is the result of rapidly rising costs and complexity of discovery and invention, to be discussed in the section on limits.

The demand side is acceptance of change, the expectation of progress. Thinking in terms of the future prepares minds to expect change and demand novelty. Now it is demand for change for its own sake.

Contrast the West with China. Chinese inventors were illiterate (the inventor of paper was an exception) government employees. Search for truth was based on authority and intuition. An organic concept of reality discouraged discovery. So did Chinese aversion to change.

FUTURISM

Already noted was the rise of the idea of novelty in the seventeenth century. In earlier centuries, the new was the opposite of the old, and then it became the opposite of the customary—a simultaneous, not a sequential, relation. The recognition of novelty in the seventeenth century was a result of great geographic discoveries and the Scientific Revolution.

Today the expectation of novelty is the consequence of two centuries of the Industrial Revolution. What was recognition has become expectation and now demand for novelty. It can survive the end of progress. The perspective of the past has shrunk; it is quickly forgotten. Fifty years is long ago, "gone with the wind." An object made seventy-five years ago is already an antique. The historic national holiday in the United States in its first two centuries is the Fourth of July. Washington's and Lincoln's birthdays are now generic Presidents' Day. The only historic date since July 4, 1776, still celebrated now is Martin Luther King Day. Forgotten are November 11, end of WWI, and Pearl Harbor. Mother's, Labor, and Memorial Days are timeless and ahistorical.

The present is but a moment. We live in the future. Science fiction is our historical novel.

Jules Verne (1828–1905) was the grandfather of science fiction. His plot was in his own day and was a plausible projection of current technology. Buck Rogers comics started in 1929. Buck was a man of his time, transported nearly five centuries into the future by an accidental suspended animation. His travels were limited to this planet. The society he described was a product of imagination, the technology a reasonable projection. But the emblematic futurism of the twentieth century was *Star Trek*, a product of the 1960s. Like Buck Rogers, it was in the twenty-fifth century, much more fiction than forecast.

Some technologies of the future cannot be conceived as projections of the present. What all these visions share is a future interminable; there is no end in sight. None offers any prospects of utopia. Progress is in science and technology, nothing else but stress and struggle, perhaps because they were both post-world-war products.

Initially, they were on this planet. But now Zamboanga has an airport and Ultima Thule is melting. We have been to the ends of the earth and must seek novelty beyond our planet. By the century, it was in the future. But the future never arrives. *Far* and *future* are interchangeable, the same in our science fiction.

The search for novelty is not just fiction. We seek intelligent life in other worlds. We do not want to be alone in an insentient universe? The other worlds of our imagination are not so friendly. Since humans exist, one can imagine the possibility that others exist. A possibility is elevated to a probability, multiplied by infinity, and confirmed to a certainty. Should scientists generalize from single examples? It is not a hope or fear, just a thirst for novelty. We analyze the clutter of interstellar radiation for ordered patterns that suggest agency. We send interstellar messages to putative intelligent organisms capable of interspecies communication. Our message riding gravitational waves may arrive at some destination long after we have ceased to exist. We want the universe to know that we once existed and thought we mattered.

Billions of dollars are being spent, eventually trillions, seeking evidence that once there has been life on Mars. What for? There are no undiscovered continents, a loss of the unknown. In the words of Arthur C. Clarke (1958, 83), "The road to the stars has been discovered none too soon. Civilization cannot exist without new frontiers."

The early civilizations conceived of particular futures. But the future as an abstraction, a mental space to be filled, subject to human decisions, is recent. Time is a function of change, of event density. The future is our creation. It is far from utopian. It is escape from the present, change for the sake of change.

THE AGE OF UNINTENDED CONSEQUENCES

History is being driven largely by the unintended consequences of the Industrial Revolution at a rate without precedent. The towering achievements of discovery and invention in the last two centuries are a quadrupling of world population in the past century and at least a sextupling of gross world output. Their unintended consequences include environment degradation, resource depletion, and climate change. Now research is being diverted to prevent or to adapt to its own consequences, reducing its autonomy. But the Industrial Revolution has also meant urbanization, education, and lower fertility of women. Discovery and invention in recent centuries has reduced the need and desire to work. It has been a driverless journey.

Work and Leisure

Homo faber may have to adapt to a half-life of leisure. In 1938, the United States adapted to the effects of invention on leisure, rising working age from fourteen to sixteen, establishing a retirement age, and limiting the workweek to forty hours. Since then, legal working age had risen to eighteen and effectively closer to twenty with the increase in college attendance. Recently, the labor force participation of the working-age population had dropped abruptly.

Before 1938, working years have been fifty out of a life expectancy of sixty-five. Now they are forty-five out of a life expectancy of seventy-nine. Meanwhile, working weeks in manufacturing have declined from sixty hours in 1890 to forty hours. Today they are slightly lower as leave time and sick days have risen. What has declined dramatically is working hours in the household economy. By the end of the century, individuals will work only half their lifetimes and work perhaps thirty-hour weeks.

The computer has done little to increase affluence, more to eliminate jobs. AI is intended to eliminate jobs. What does it offer in return other than leisure? What is leisure for? Were it not for the intrusive industry of advertising, whose output is demand, we would be facing this issue today. It is time to reconsider human identity.

The issue of the future is the distribution of the opportunity to work and income from labor. Egalitarianism and meritocracy conflict and always will, but compromises are in order. If we eliminate jobs for the illiterate and semiliterate (which I doubt), what will they do, and how will they live? Not everyone can be above average. Further gains in longevity will redistribute time from labor to leisure, requiring more redistribution of income from workers to nonworkers.

Japan's life expectancy is now eighty-four, that of Western European nations circa 82, so it is reasonable to expect life expectancy of eighty-five late this century. But what is the value of longevity? Today children are long grown before parental death; grandchildren do not need working grandparents. Longevity is a burden on the next generation.

Growth in life expectancy adds a third stage to life—retirement—and a third purpose to work, provision for a comfortable retirement. But what use is to be made of all this surplus time?

Population

The public health revolution resulted in rapid population growth to potentially unsustainable levels. The Industrial Revolution had the opposite effect, reducing fertility below replacement rates, presaging population decline in advanced nations with no end in sight.

For advanced nations, the fundamental problem of the century is longevity; for the globe, it is population. The Industrial Revolution is almost over. As to agriculture, the prospect of the future is not further reduction in costs but limits inputs—water, farmland. Much depends on the future of population, past mid-twenty-first century. It is population that depletes resources and degrades the environment.

Nearly all advanced nations have fertility rates below replacement; some have very low rates. Most of the other nations outside Africa have rates at or not much above replacement. Rates are falling in nearly all nations with high rates. Sometime this century, migration aside, the population of the Americas should begin declining. Fertility rates in the United States and Brazil are already persistently below replacement, and Mexico's is at bare replacement. Population in Eurasia should also start declining. Only one of the seven largest nations, Pakistan, has a rate significantly above replacement. China, Russia, and Japan are far below replacement. The only growth area in Eurasia is Pakistan and four contiguous Central Asian 'stans and Afghanistan (plus several small Middle Eastern nations in constant turmoil).

By contrast, all nations in Africa have fertility rates above replacement, most of them far above. When world population will peak, and at what level, depends almost exclusively on the pace of decline in fertility in Africa. Increased longevity is a minor factor. Malthusian conditions—disease, occasional famine, and much warfare—motivate millions to emigrate. It is public health—greatly reducing infant, child, and maternal mortality—that has accelerated population growth. Discovery and invention are contributing to future population decline in Eurasia and the Americas and to current population explosion in Africa.

Urbanization, education, affluence, and liberation of women are all associated with low fertility rates; they raise the cost of bearing children. None of the causes of decline in fertility is going to be reversed. How fertility will be increased and at what level of world population, we have no idea. Large-scale immigration is not an acceptable solution for countries whose national identity is ethnic historical. Europe and Asia are riddled with examples of the long-term failure of assimilation, integration of large immigrant minorities. Nor can it be maintained indefinitely. Africa will eventually face the same problem. The United States remains an exceptional nation. Always the creation of immigrants, it remains dependent. If growth continues at the pace so far this century, it should number 700 million by century;'s end

Smaller world population will reduce pressure on resources and impact on climate, but depopulation could be brutal. Cities are capital-intensive, complex machines. Cut their population, and the price of housing declines, but all other costs will increase. Beyond some point, decline becomes a downward spiral. Subsidies for child-rearing have not worked.

THE END OF THE INDUSTRIAL REVOLUTION

Limits

The previous section was on the limits to growth of population and income enabled by the three revolutions. The limits to be considered here are to discovery and invention themselves. Historians of civilization note that civilizations have life spans; they flourish and then stagnate and decline.

In China, the turning point was the burning of the books; in Islam, al-Ghazālī, who prevailed over Averroës; and in Greece, nothing so dramatic. All failed to adopt an agency-free heliocentric model of the solar system. In Europe, Copernicus and Galileo prevailed. Discovery and invention dominated the civilization thereafter as they had never done in other civilizations.

The limits that concern me here are to discovery and invention, not to civilization. Are there limits to what there is to discover or invent or to human ability? Such hypothetical questions are beyond the scope of this book. They are considered by John D. Barrow (1998). My concern is about the self-limiting consequences of the achievements of the past two centuries. The advances in technology, the gains in income, and the changes in lifestyle are without precedent and without sequel. Diminishing returns, increasing costs, and ceilings on demand presage a new stage in human civilization.

The limit of cost of production is zero. Energy is so much cheaper than it was two centuries ago, never mind before steam, that historically its cost is approaching zero. A decline to zero would be tiny by comparison, and so would the decline in costs of production of energy-using activities. Travel time from stagecoach to subsonic plane has shrunk so much that any further shortening would be minute. The cost of farm food and fiber has declined not as fast but more than halfway to zero from its level in 1870, when half the U.S. population lived on farms. Forget the percentage gains in productivity; the amounts keep shrinking.

What remains to cut are the staggering costs of health and education, the two major industries whose costs of production are rising. However, the Watt steam engine is a museum display, whereas humans today are the same as they were in 1776. On health, infant mortality is down from double digits to less than 1 percent. If life expectancy were to rise as much as it did in the last century, it would be in triple digits. Few consider this attainable; it may be near its limits already. Much can be done to improve health and quality of life simply by implementing what we already know. Nor is it clear that prolongation of life much beyond our current potential is a desideratum for society. Since most advanced nations spend half as much as a share of the GDP on health as the United States with superior results, costs could be cut as much as 9 percent of GDP by policy changes, no research required. For a partial explanation, see Stewart (2014, 41–46).

As to education, there is much more schooling than before, more learning, but I am not aware of evidence of any gains in productivity since the little red schoolhouse. At first, libraries—more recently computers and the Internet—have made it much easier to access information, but is there a gain in knowledge? The learning machine, the student, is no better than earlier versions. The teaching machine, the teacher, can deploy some advances in technology. But test scores are stagnant.

The issue is not cost, which will remain high, but quality and relevance. In the United States, there is a disconnect between educational requirements for the economy and the occupational supply (Stewart 2008). The nation depends on immigrants not only for scientists and technicians but also for skilled artisans and craftsmen. Meanwhile, millions are educated in fields that have few jobs.

Can there be a third century with comparable rate of change? Not in energy, transportation, communication, information, or life expectancy. The Industrial Revolution is coming to an end, and so are five centuries of rising expectations. The struggle in the future is distribution of the work that still needs doing and of the income derived therefrom. As J. B. Bury anticipated, the idea of progress is not forever. The train must come to a stop. Or the destination is redefined.

There is another perspective on the end of the Industrial Revolution—not cost but scale. The production of things, including agricultural products, has been shrinking rapidly as a share of total output and employment. It is the production of services that, by now, is the main economic activity (Bell 1976, 123–32). This change in structure involves geographical relocation of economic activity, occupational distribution, and educational requirements.

Demand

The desire and ability to consume are limited. Consumption is funded by income. Most income is the product of labor. Some love their work; it is an end in itself. But most work, because they need the income and because it is socially expected, is a means, not an end. There are limits to the willingness to work. Hours worked per year, per week, per day have all tended downward and are headed for additional declines. Simultaneously, the household economy has shrunk almost to the vanishing point, saving labor and raising incomes by shifting work from the household to the labor market. This shift is over, and labor force participation rates are down. People seem to be choosing more leisure rather than more goods and services. The current level of demand could be increased by reducing the great inequality of incomes prevailing today, raising the floor on income closer to median earnings.

Much consumption is time intensive. Our days are short, our years too few. Travel is very time intensive. So are spectator activities and participant activities—sports, arts, entertainment, education. The rich have no more time than the poor. As incomes rise, consumption does not keep track.

Saturation of demand is another limit on consumer demand. Few of us are like Imelda Marcos with three thousand pairs of shoes. More is better up to a point. Two TV sets in the average household are better than one. But are five better than two? As households have shrunk from four people to two and a half, the indoor space of new housing has doubled. They are warehouses. In the last half of the last century, consumption expanded from sustenance to sufficiency to saturation. Then for some, it graduated to collection. But large warehouses are costly.

Meanwhile, the intrusive industry of advertising buoys demand by inventing new needs, by creating demand not for subsistence or collection, just for self-esteem and identity. Commodities and services are the company we keep. They help us belong but also stand out. Advertising promotes novelties, trinkets, and toys, not novelty as a lifestyle but trivia that differentiate us from others or allow us to participate with our peers.

The longevity of durable goods dampens demand. Manufacturers promote and accelerate psychological obsolescence by frequent changes in style, appearance, and trivial function. It is deliberate reduction of productivity. Durables are not consumed; they are accumulated, collected, and discarded.

The willingness to work limits spending and does not affect inventions reducing cost of living, just additional new goods and services. What can we invent that will increase demand for work and income? There is always the demand for change and novelty in particular. It is so deeply entrenched that it is divorced from the expectation of progress. What new commodity or service can be invented that will induce millions to work to buy it? As to discovery, most of the funding is government; hence, it is not market but political demand that is needed.

A market for new goods or services requires a demand for novelty. Productivity growth has been slow for several decades. Inequality, the cost of being a full participating member of society, has been increasing. The expectation of change may no longer have an upward slant.

Evolution of Research

Two centuries of achievement have created a scientific community, a culture of discovery that is now global. Kenneth Boulding (1970, 13) describes modern science as a cult or subculture whose high values are veracity and curiosity. It has a positive distaste for obedience. "The very success of the scientific community is a result of the fact that it succeeded in legitimizing failure and thus removing the main obstacle to the growth of human knowledge." Meanwhile, discovery has become increasingly dependent on invention of instruments dedicated to that purpose. Research has grown in complexity and escalated in costs. Discovery is now mainly the responsibility of government.

Interdependence

For most of human history, discovery and invention had been only remotely related. Discovery depended on observation limited to human senses. The telescope and microscope were only the beginning of a multitude of instruments that provided information on natural objects and phenomena beyond the reach of human senses. Technique and equipment for multiple manipulations of materials led to ever closer interdependence of discovery and invention. Until the nineteenth century, discovery was largely autonomous. In the twentieth century, discovery became the stepchild of invention.

Ever more sophisticated instruments opens up possibilities for additional discoveries. An important component of invention is not directed toward practical application but for advancing basic research. The Hubble telescope orbiting in space or atom smashers on the earth offer no prospect at this time of affecting our lives, whatever they may contribute toward understanding. However, the nuclear industry illustrates the reverse direction of influence.

Complexity and Scale

Aristotle has been described as the last man who knew everything. In the twentieth century, Enrico Fermi has been described as the last physicist who knew all physics. The accumulation of knowledge has been so great that ever narrower specialization is mandatory. Meanwhile, the process of discovery has grown ever more complex. Scientists cannot read most of the articles outside their specialization. The pace of advance renders much knowledge short lived. The days of the lone Newtons and Galileos are over.

Invention and discovery are now the near monopoly of scientists and engineers, for many of them is a full-time endeavor, not an incidental or casual activity. And most discovery and invention is a collective effort. The cost and scale of R&D activities has converted much of the discovery from autonomous, private enterprise to public and international commitments.

How can one quantify complexity? For discovery, I have noted the great increase in the number of coauthors of research articles in *Science*, leading journal, over the last seventy years. The solitary author is an extinct species. The typical article now has eight to ten coauthors; many have a dozen or two. Coauthors often differ in specialization. Typically, the authors are from and work in several nations. Discovery has become a global enterprise. The articles also acknowledge their sources of research funding, telling us that discovery is now funded largely by government and international philanthropies.

Inventions have followed the same path. Discoveries are published; inventions are patented. Before the twentieth century, patents were awarded predominantly to individuals. Now they are mainly applied for and awarded to corporations.

There is an unbundling of the cognitive requirements for creativity and a need for cooperation and management among individuals and organizations with different functions and different skills. Thus, the social component of invention and discovery has become paramount. R&D is now institutionalized.

Scale and complexity pervade the economy, not just research. Their unintended consequence is a decline in the work ethic that threatens the integrity of the research process.

Before the Industrial Revolution, identity except for unskilled labor was occupation as shown by common family names—Smith, Baker, Carter, Farmer, Hunter. A change in identity started as artisans and craftsmen were replaced by machine tenders, whose contribution was a minor part of the final product. This fragmentation of occupations deprived workers of a sense of personal achievement or occupational status or sense of community in the enterprise (Wiener 1993, 47–48; Gehlen 1980, 50–51). In the twentieth century, the fragmentation of occupations extended to technical and professional work, including research laboratories, threatening the work identification of many.

The occupations whose workers are most likely to work long hours and delay retirement are not of those who need more income to satisfy their wants and needs but of those who retain a strong occupational identity, such as the artisans, artists, doctors, lawyers, and professors. The loss of occupational identity has led to the commodification of identity abetted by advertisers and manufacturers. They have created wants and need but not the income required, just more dissatisfaction. The balance of pressures is toward commodity identification and demand for more leisure time. The facts are clear—limits on hours of work, introduction of a retirement age, rise in labor force entry age. But the large increase in leisure in this century is not about a change in self-identification but an increase in longevity.

Cost and Funding

Multiple coauthors of discovery and corporate patents of invention both imply the scale of R&D. In many fields, the tools required for research cost millions, in a few cases billions of dollars. A Hubble telescope or giant earthbound ones, CERN, are not only extremely costly to create but also costly to operate and maintain. Experiments in biology may take many years to complete. Most science requires expensive laboratories, powerful computers, and highly trained staff.

Costs rise because most of the simple discoveries and inventions have been made. What remains is increasingly difficult.

The amount spent on R&D as a share of GNP rose from 0.3 percent in 1930 and 0.7 percent in 1940 to 1.7 percent in 1950 and 2.7 percent in 1960 (Rescher 1978, 67). In the next fifty years, it remained stable at just under 3.0 percent. This estimate should include most basic research, discovery, which is performed or funded predominantly by government. But some inventive activity research by private firms is not categorized as R&D. With rapidly increasing costs, stability of expenditures implies decreasing returns.

There is no way of estimating the trend in cost of R&D resulting in a patent. But Rescher (1978, 88) notes a steep decline in productivity—the ratio of the number of scientist and engineers to number of patents granted. As to patents, many inventions are not patented, but significant ones are. Frankly, their number tells us little. U.S. patents reflect global, not national, inventive activity.

Rescher (1978, 188, 195–97, 201) gives examples of the exponentially increasing costs of capacity gains in the instruments of discovery. These trends in costs and productivity are extremely compressed in time—decades, not centuries. Many instruments have short effective life spans.

Given the high cost of R&D, demand for invention is essential. Private inventors have something to sell, but innovation must be prompt and extensive for profitability. The costs of inventing are a multiple of the costs of copying, so the imitator can undersell the inventor. Patent violation is a big industry in some countries.

The state in advanced nations has assumed a dominant role in basic research or search for knowledge for its own sake. This is not a response to escalating private costs but to the change in culture, the demand for novelty. The protection of intellectual property is another response to belief in progress and desire for change. It is the democratization of society that has converted the state from the instrument of the ruler, providing law and order and defense, to the agent of the people, their subject.

This leadership of government has been a dramatic change. In past civilizations and in early Europe, the main source of support for scholars engaged in discovery and invention was patronage, and that was scarce. Athenian philosophers supported themselves with student fees; Islamic scholars practiced medicine for a living. There was a brief period in Alexandria when the Greek rulers of Egypt patronized scholars and built research institutions.

Research by governments had an early beginning with Prince Henry the Navigator in 1418. But governments focused on navigation and weaponry. Before the twentieth century, the only other major area of government research was agriculture.

All government departments and many agencies conduct research in their areas of interest (Sargent 2018). Many of them also fund research conducted by others. However, most of the "research" in-house does not qualify as scientific efforts to discover and invent. It is only search for information. Practices vary. The Department of Energy funds much research by private contractors; the Department of Agriculture conducts its own via the Agricultural Research Service. It is the institutes—such as NASA, National Institute of Standards and Technology, and National Oceanic and Atmospheric Administration—that engage in discovery and some invention. They conduct research and fund research by others primarily in universities. The National Science Foundation funds a much wider range of research projects.

Research is a high-risk investment. Government now provides or secures the institutional framework for discovery and invention. These include the legal system that assures property rights and that creates the corporation and nonprofit organization, the financial system that funds private R&D and investment, and the educational system that provides the skills required.

Private sector funding has mutated from patronage to nonprofit foundations for research. Some have large endowments; others raise money for research. Much of the research they fund is conducted in universities.

The Ford and Gates Foundations focus on the social sciences. Sloan, Welch, Leakey, and Keck are some of many funding science and engineering research. In addition to private foundations, most occupations have their own organizations that fund research or education in their area.

Hughes, Wellcome, and Robert Wood Johnson fund research in biology and medicine across the board. Almost every human ailment has a foundation raising funds for research on its causes, prevention, and treatments.

Quite a few colleges and universities have similar origins—Vanderbilt, Rockefeller, Carnegie Mellon, Stanford—some of whose founders have stressed their research function. It reflects a passion not just for knowledge but for new knowledge. These and other universities also help compensate for the shortage of Americans majoring in the sciences and mathematics by attracting foreign students, many of whom remain as working scientists and faculty.

In chapter 3 on prehistory, I asked whether there was pattern in discovery and invention. Different means of making fire were invented independently in several locations; so were its uses. Ceramics and agriculture were invented independently and almost simultaneously in several locations. So was metallurgy, writing, and the discovery of the solar system. More recently, had Gutenberg delayed, the inventor of the printing press would have been a mechanic from the Netherlands. Since the sixteenth century, Europe was the only civilization standing.

For almost every important invention or discovery, there were multiple scientists and technicians at work. Newton was not the only inventor of calculus. Watt was not the first or only one harnessing the power of steam. Today the research project is artificial intelligence. The Greeks had the idea, but the time was not right. It had to wait for the computer. The computer, in turn, had to wait for the Industrial Revolution and electric power.

The pattern of discovery and invention is the sequence. Needs for instruments of observation and manipulation dictate physics as the first domain of discovery and invention. Simultaneity may have been initiated with the invention of agriculture and then promoted by writing. What is next, or are there limits, an end to discovery or to invention?

END OF PROGRESS IN SCIENCE AND TECHNOLOGY?

The human quest for certainty requires both an origin and a destination. The end of the world or of humanity has been an aspect of religions in the past. Now it is a secular expectation—the end of science. Hope for salvation by science is a modern version of cargo cults and primitive religions. End and salvation are contradictory. There is a factual basis for decline. As to salvation, that is an act of faith.

Today the heartland of discovery and invention is a culture of immigrants from many lands, whose core belief is perpetual change and progress. As the earth's population reaches limits of affluence and size, others with different ideology and culture will lead the way. A culture of constraints and limits calls for communal sharing instead of individual enterprise and risk-taking. This is far from the frame of mind of the physicists puzzling the secrets of the universe and pursuing elusive particles and of the biologists deciphering the genetic code.

One reason science and technology have been so productive in the past one hundred years is that the number of very able and highly trained scientists, engineers, and technicians has multiplied. The big increase has been in the United States, which has quadrupled in population, largely through emigration from Europe and Central America. This rate of multiplication is impossible to maintain because population growth has slowed down, and increase in educational attainment has nearly ended. Other industrial nations are in the same ballpark. The proportion of American college students majoring in the sciences and mathematics has declined. A large proportion of graduate students in these subjects in American universities are themselves foreigners from developing nations.

I do not think that numbers matter much; culture is more important. And great discoveries and inventions are not statistically predictable. In the twenty-first century, it is India and China that will supply the numbers. The cost of discovery and invention continues to rise. But China, India, and other nations will increase their R&D. They could delay but not prevent decline. Each has four times the population of the United States.

China concentrates on engineers, the inventors, and India on the scientists and mathematicians, the discoverers (Stewart 2008, 115–76). As stated in chapter 6, Chinese culture has been hostile to discovery and slow to invent. China's script is doomed; its language requires intensive therapy to persist. The basic question is whether Chinese scientists and engineers will embrace the scientific subculture's values of veracity, curiosity, and openness and discard their belief in yin-yang and feng shui. Major culture change is rare and usually the consequence of disaster. Traditional culture cannot prevail or survive an industrial revolution. Adaptation takes generations. Neither the scientific culture nor the civilization it now dominates faces any external threat. The only threat is internal.

India is not a nation but a federation of multiple nations with diverse cultures. In economic development, it lags China by half a century. But it already has technological institutions and universities of high quality. And the Indian, according to Amartya Sen, is argumentative.

This century, an increase in the supply of scientific manpower may counteract the increase in cost difficulty of discovery and invention. Biology will open up new opportunities. DNA—the genetic code—may be the greatest recent discovery, the incipient revolution in biology. It opens up new opportunities for discovery and invention.

What can be said at this time is not scientific but social. The human species is diversifying. The combination of higher education, the liberation of women, and delayed marriage age means assortive mating—college graduates marry each other; so do high school dropouts. Law students marry each other, medical students likewise. Inheritance, once near random, will be systematized.

What about the demand for discovery and invention? Two centuries of Industrial Revolution have promoted interest in science and technology. The population of the Western world has been educated. The information technologies of the twentieth century—radio, television, the Internet, in addition to the press—widen horizons. Science and technology have become spectacles. The scientific subculture is so large in numbers and so pervasive, old enough to have its own traditions and to gain autonomy. It will survive.

Historians have long sought to systematize history and to search for patterns in the past. Spengler and Toynbee assume that civilizations are the basic units of history. Spengler fits the facts of history into his structure. Toynbee does not, regarding his pattern as adaptable, civilizations as interactive, subject to some modification.

Carroll Quigley's *The Evolution of Civilizations* goes further. He believes that there are unique aspects of Western civilization, and of the United States, that offer better prospects for survival. First, it has been called the technological civilization. Its technological accomplishments have extended its reach throughout the globe; no other civilization can develop in isolation or survive in autonomy. Second, the Western worldview is that truth is discovered, not revealed, not invented; that learning is an endless process; and that man has the capacity to understand the world through unending investigation and analysis. This worldview accommodates change and is incompatible with any lasting dogma. Ideas do not become institutions, particularly those of the United States. Its constitution provides for its own amendment. The law evolves on the basis of precedent and learning. The political system limits and divides power so that institutions cannot persist indefinitely as ends in themselves and provides for the mobility of elites. Mass migration has institutionalized revolution and perpetuated diversity and change.

What is the end of science? Everything there is to know, everything we want to know, or everything possible for us to know? Proliferation of the concepts of *the end of science, impossibility, limits* and *boundaries* are modern versions of *millenarianism, apocalypse, end-of-the-world* mentality, but with a technological rather than a theocratic dimension. Some writers view limits as end points, goals rather than constraints on further change: we have arrived at our destination; this is where we want to stay. But there is no end point. The thread of uncertainly runs through the fabric of reality. Our search for knowledge can never end.

The trajectories of increasing cost and complexity and of declining gains in productivity and performance may appear to meet eventually and cross over but never do. Gains in knowledge and costs of achieving it do not have a common denominator. Utilitarianism is about means, not ends. Its domain is limited, but the quest for knowledge as an end in itself is not part of it. It will never end.

Change observed and experienced is so prevalent that it is impossible to conceive an end to expectation. The quest for knowledge in this civilization is future oriented. It has no end, which makes it a quest for novelty. Invention knows no limit of which we are aware. It is the key to discovery now and for the foreseeable future.

Let me close with a final comment on destination. The correlation between myths of origins and the destinies of civilizations makes no sense to me, but it exists. If European civilization can be said to have a creation myth, it is not the Garden of Eden nor Pandora's jar; they are given. It is the Crucifixion and resurrection.

REFERENCES

Allen, Robert C. 1988. "Economic Structure and Agricultural Productivity in Europe, 1300–1800," 1–21. Vancouver, BC: Department of Economics, University of British Columbia.

Baily, Neil, and Nicholas Montalbano. 2016. "Why Is U.S. Productivity Growth So Slow? Possible Explanations and Policy Responses." The Brookings Institution Hutchins Center Working Paper no. 22.

Barber, Bernard, and Walter Hirsch, eds. 1962. *The Sociology of Science*. Free Press.

Barrow, John D. 1998. *Impossibility—The Limits of Science and the Science of Limits*. Oxford: Oxford University Press.

Beard, Mary. 2016. *SPQR*. London: Profile Books.

Bell, Daniel. 1976. *The Coming of Postindustrial Society*. New York: Basic Books.

————. 1976. *The Cultural Contradictions of Capitalism.*

Bury, J. B. 1955. *The Idea of Progress.* New York: Dover Publications Inc.

Gonzales, Justo L. 2010. *The Story of Christianity*, vol. I, rev. ed. New York: Harper Collins.

Huff, Toby E. 1993. *The Rise of Early Modern Science.* Cambridge University Press.

Hughes, Phillip. 1960. *The Church in Crisis—A History of the General Councils, 325–1870.* Garden City, New York: Hanover House.

Jacob, Margaret. 1997. *Scientific Culture and the Making of the Industrial West.* New York; London: Oxford University Press.

LePan, Don. 1989. *The Cognitive Evolution in Western Culture—The Birth of Expectations.* MacMillan Company Ltd.

Mara, James A. 1965. "Authority in the Church." In *Current Trends in Theology*, edited by Donald J. Wolf and James V. Schall, 161–70.

Norman, Ralph. 2007. "Abelard's Legacy: Why Theology Is Not Faith Seeking." *Australian Journal of Theology* (May).

Quigley, Carroll. 1979. *The Evolution of Civilizations.* Liberty Fund.

Rescher, Nicholas. 1978. *Scientific Progress.* Pittsburgh: University of Pittsburgh Press.

————. 1982. *Empirical Inquiry.* Totowa, New Jersey: Rowman and Littlefield.

————. 1984. *The Limits of Science.* Berkeley: University of California Press.

Sargent, John F. Jr., coordinator. 2018. *Federal Research and Development Funding: FY2018*. Congressional Research Service.

Schlagel, Richard H. 1996. *From Myth to Modern Mind*, vol. 2. New York: Peter Lang.

———. 2010. *To Seek the Truth*. Amherst, New York: Humanities Books.

Stewart, Charles T. Jr. 2014. "Medical Education and Health Care Costs" In *The Malthusian Century*, 41–46. New York: Nova Science Publishers.

———. 2008. *Decline of Learning in America*. New York: Nova Science Publishers.

Thorndike, Lynn. 1957. "Newness and Novelty in Seventeenth Century Science and Medicine." In *Roots of Scientific Thought—A Cultural Perspective*, edited by Philip E. Wiener and Aaron Noland, 443–57. New York: Basic Books.

Whaples, Robert. "Hours of Work in U.S. History." Wake Forest University.

Wiener, Philip E., and Aaron Noland, eds. 1957. *Roots of Scientific Thought—A Cultural Perspective*. New York: Basic Books.

Zilsel, Edgar. 1957. "The Genesis of the Concept of Scientific Progress." In *Roots of Scientific Thought—A Cultural Perspective*, edited by Philip E. Wiener and Aaron Noland, 251–75. New York: Basic Books.